Finding Families

Finding Ourselves

English Canada Encounters
Adoption from the
Nineteenth Century to the 1990s

Deb
All the best!

Veronica Strong-Boag

[signature]

OXFORD
UNIVERSITY PRESS

OXFORD
UNIVERSITY PRESS

70 Wynford Drive, Don Mills, Ontario M3C 1J9
www.oup.com/ca

Oxford University Press is a department of the University of Oxford.
It furthers the University's objective of excellence in research, scholarship,
and education by publishing worldwide in

Oxford New York

Auckland Cape Town Dar es Salaam Hong Kong Karachi
Kuala Lumpur Madrid Melbourne Mexico City Nairobi
New Delhi Shanghai Taipei Toronto

With offices in

Argentina Austria Brazil Chile Czech Republic France Greece
Guatemala Hungary Italy Japan Poland Portugal Singapore
South Korea Switzerland Thailand Turkey Ukraine Vietnam

Oxford is a trade mark of Oxford University Press
in the UK and in certain other countries

Published in Canada
by Oxford University Press

Copyright © Oxford University Press Canada 2006

The moral rights of the author have been asserted

Database right Oxford University Press (maker)

First published 2006

Library and Archives Canada Cataloguing in Publication

Strong-Boag, Veronica Jane, 1947–

Finding families, finding ourselves: English Canada encounters adoption
from the nineteenth century to the 1990s/Veronica Strong-Boag

Includes bibliographical references and index.

ISBN-13: 978-0-19-542492-8
ISBN-10: 0-19-542492-1

1. Adoption—Canada—History—19th century. 2. Adoption—Canada—
History—20th century I. Title

HV875.58.C3S77 2006   362.7340971'09034   C2006-901345-4

1 2 3 4 – 09 08 07 06

Cover and text design: Brett J. Miller
Cover Image: © Foodpix/First Light

This book is printed on permanent (acid-free) paper ∞
Printed in Canada

Contents

Acknowledgements   iv

Abbreviations   vi

Introduction   vii

1   Beyond the Nuclear Family: Childrearing in English Canada   1

2   Setting the Rules: Adoption and the Law   25

3   Class Matters   52

4   Gendered Lives   80

5   Religion, Ethnicity, and Race   107

6   Native–Newcomer Contact   135

7   Foreign Affairs   174

8   Origins and Destinations: Connecting Individuals and Communities   211

9   Conclusion   242

Notes   246

Index   310

Acknowledgements

Finding Families, Finding Ourselves was written with a great deal of support. I am extremely grateful for funding from the Canada Council's Killam Program, the Social Sciences and Humanities Research Council of Canada, and the University of British Columbia's Hampton Program, which allowed both precious time to research and write and the employment of talented research assistants. The latter included Nicholas Clarke, Stephanie Higginson, Heather Latham, Lorie Macintosh, Mark Rautenhauser, Michelle Lynn Rosa, Christopher Ross, Dominic Ross, Bianca Rus, Amy Salmon, Melanie Scheuer, Anna Treadwell, Susy Webb, Jenn Wilcox, and Almas Zakiunddin. I have also been fortunate to have two supportive departments at UBC: both Women's Studies and Educational Studies have provided lively progressive environments. At various times, staff members Wynn Archibald and Sharon Hu offered invaluable assistance. Under its directors, Valerie Raoul and Sneja Gunew, UBC's Centre for Research in Women's Studies and Gender Relations supplied continuing reminders of the value of engaged interdisciplinary scholarship, not to mention much laughter and chocolate. Good friends such as Donna Andrew, Denyse Baillargeon, Jean Barman, Bettina Bradbury, Cynthia Comacchio, Karen Dubinsky, Carole Gerson, Mona Gleason, Craig Heron, Jan Hare, Melody Hessing, Franca Iacovetta, Andrée Levesque, Kate Macpherson, Kathy Mezei, Suzanne Morton, Marilyn Porter, Ian Radford, Nancy Roberts, Leslie Roman, Judy Russell, Mary Lynn Stewart, Jennifer Stoddart, Cheryl Krasnick Warsh, and Joan Wolverton have variously sustained me over the course of this work. Angus McLaren, Rob Rutherdale, and Chris Shelley helped me understand better the male part of the adoption tale. I am especially grateful to Gillian Creese, Jo-Anne Fiske, Arlene Tigar McLaren, Joan Sangster, and Neil Sutherland who commented on the penultimate version of the entire manuscript. They, like the anonymous readers for Oxford University Press, made this a better book. At a critical juncture, Laura Macleod, the acquisitions editor at Oxford, supplied invaluable encouragement. I am also fortunate that the incomparable Barbara Tessman has been my editor through several books. My mother, Daphne Bridges Strong-Boag (1924–2005) improved everything I wrote and me. Judy Dogao has helped keep my household going for many years. Without her reassuring presence, much less would have been accomplished. My sons, Chris, Dominic, and Gabe, and my niece, Miranda, have always reminded me how families are daily constructed. Finally, in the course of preparing *Finding Families, Finding Ourselves*, grief became my constant companion. This volume is dedicated in particular to Michelle Lynn Rosa (1980–2004), cherished daughter of Sharon and Jack and granddaughter of Myrtle, dear sister of Matthew, beloved fiancée of Chris, close friend of Leanne, and my wonderful graduate research assistant and about-to-be daughter-in-law. In life and in death, she has taught me how much we depend on those who become family.

Abbreviations

AFN	Assembly of First Nations
AIM	Adopt Indian Métis
ARENA	Adoption Resouce Exchange of North America
AWARE	Awareness to World Adoption and Responsibility to Everyone
CACY	Committee for the Adoption of Coloured Youngsters
CAS	Children's Aid Society
CCF	Co-operative Commonwealth Federation
CCNM	Canadian Council of Natural Mothers
CJC	Canadian Jewish Congress
CNCR	Canadian National Committee on Refugees
CSC	Children's Service Centre
DIA	Department of Indian Affairs
DIAND	Department of Indian Affairs and Northern Development
DOCFS	Dakota Ojibway Child and Family Services
FASD	fetal alcohol syndrome disorders
FFC	Families for Children
HCIA	The Hague Convention on Protection of Children and Co-operation in Respect of Intercountry Adoptions
IAP	Indian Adoption Project (US)
ICA	intercountry adoption
IODE	Imperial Order Daughters of the Empire
IOF	Independent Order of Forresters
ISS	International Social Services
NAD	National Adoption Desk
NGOs	non-governmental organizations
NSHCC	Nova Scotia Home for Colored Children
ODS	Open Door Society
RCAP	Royal Commission on Aboriginal Peoples
UBCIC	Union of BC Indian Chiefs
UN	United Nations
UNICEF	United Nations International Emergency Children's Fund

Introduction

Renée Rosnes, Buffy Sainte-Marie, Mitch Hepburn, Cynthia Kereluk, Eric Schweig, Sarah de Vries, Joni Mitchell, Cameron Kerley, Carole Laure, Garnet Raven, Marie-Josée Lord, Michel Chrétien, Barbara Frum, Anne of Green Gables, Eric Clapton, Bif Naked, Mazo de la Roche, Pierre Berton, Florence LaBadie, Grey Owl, Stan Mikita, Luke Baldwin, Frank Drea, Sarah McLachlan, Penny Priddy, James Michener, Denys Arcand, Wayson Choy, Sonja Smits, Ed Broadbent, Michaëlle Jean . . .

The list of girls and boys, men and women, in Canada's real and fictional adoption circles is long. Its membership is not select. Such adults and children have been found in all walks of life and in all time periods. Some names are known; many more are hidden by design or lost by accident. By the beginning of the twenty-first century, most Canadians, if they knew the history of their kin over several generations, would discover both official and far-from-official exchanges of youngsters. An Ipsos-Reid poll in summer 2004, which found that three in five Canadians knew someone who was adopted, two in nine had a personal adoption experience, and one in seven knew someone who had placed a child for adoption, could only hint at the actual numbers involved.[1] No one has ever traced the unfolding of this commonplace story. *Finding Families, Finding Ourselves* begins that telling.

This book has evolved through many titles. Alternatives such as *Belonging, Making Families, Searching for Self,* and *Adoptive Nation* sum up my conviction that adoption, despite being regularly ignored by historians until relatively recently, is a far from marginal phenomenon in Canadian history. In fact, it stands close to the heart of who we are as individuals and as a national community. Obligations and rights in both surrendering and receiving households supply only the more intimate expression of what happens or is expected on larger stages. As American feminist scholar Patricia Hill Collins has reminded us, the nation-state very often operates as an 'extended family marked by citizenship and alien status.'[2] The reverse is also true: families sometimes operate much like nations. They too have borders, criteria for acceptance, insiders and outsiders.

Like immigration in the national context, adoption in the domestic sphere critically informs and shapes relations and legitimacy. To surrender, to adopt, and to be adopted, with or without the benefit of legal sanction, are facts that have distinguished girls and boys, men and women, in both negative and positive ways. Too frequently, adoptive relationships have been regarded as somehow less valid, normal, or natural than those conferred by biology or birth. And, just as within the country as a whole, not everyone is equal in the adoption circle itself. Inequalities of various kinds flourish. Children have been shifted from one site to another in response to the relative disadvantage of those left behind and the resources of the adults they are to join. Birth parents have been handicapped in comparison with adopters, but the latter in turn have frequently been frustrated in their desires for offspring. At the same time, second chances for everyone involved, again much like immigration, may offer extraordinary benefits. Adoption can mean a promising future, even life itself, to those it directly touches.

In the course of working out possibilities, adopters and adoptees most obviously 'find' kin, but birth parents, especially mothers, have also had to come to terms with what family means for them. Many have struggled to make sense of who they might be in relation to lost offspring and their subsequent households. They and adoptees have frequently sought out one another to renegotiate once more the meaning of family. Such quandaries are not, of course, unique to households touched by adoption. Whatever the myths to the contrary, kin have always had diverse responses to the supposed rights and duties of members. All live by fictions as well as by facts. Uncertainties about who may be properly claimed as intimates dog everyone. This book's final title, *Finding Families, Finding Ourselves*, in the end best seemed to capture the wide range of predicaments and associated opportunities facing all adults and children in their encounter with adoption in English Canada.

H. David Kirk's *Shared Fate*, the study of adoptive families that one contemporary hailed as 'complacency-shattering', first alerted me to adoption's connection to the bigger social picture.[3] Kirk, a professor of sociology first at McGill and later at the University of Waterloo and himself an adopter, observed that an adoptee was very much like 'a first-generation "immigrant"' into another family. The new arrival's 'acceptance by them would be no greater or less than any other immigrant who has to find her way.'[4] Adoptive parents in their turn were distinguished by a 'role handicap': like their new offspring, they were deprived of commonly taken-for-granted biological ties.[5] In new households, as in new homelands, both children and adults had to construct composite identities that recognized difference even as they forged common bonds. An early refugee from Nazi Germany, Kirk understood that surrendering individuals—or nations, for that matter—possessed stories far more complicated and sometimes more tragic than recipients of youngsters readily acknowledged. Although he did not pay birth parents the same attention as adopters, both have frequently been handicapped when it came to making sense of themselves as competent and normal individuals in a society that routinely made successful childbearing and rearing the test of maturity, especially for women. Both have had to forge identities without much help from conventional social scripts that regularly celebrate biological connections within families.

Anthropologist Eva Mackey's thoughtful assessment of Canada's management of the politics of pluralism in *The House of Difference: Cultural Politics and National Identity in Canada* offers a valuable way to think further about adoption as more than an expression of personal relations, a supposedly natural realm that functions largely independent of greater political concerns. Like the popular culture to which she turns her attention, the supposedly private lives of families tell a good deal about the nature of nation itself. Drawing on Benedict Anderson's influential *Imagined Communities: Reflections on the Origin and Spread of Nationalism*, she notes that the construction of Canadian identity has relied on both the creation and the deletion of history. So too has adoption. Whatever may have occurred in reality, the transfer of girls and boys has promised both beginnings and endings to various life narratives. It is the tension between what has gone before and what is to come that legislation, policy, and practice have tried, as we shall see, to organize and control. Like immigrants and other suspect members of the national community, individuals within adoption circles have regularly been forced to negotiate what part of their pasts is to be remembered and told in the making of the future.

In a country of diverse Natives and newcomers, Canadian authorities have been compelled to govern carefully. The product of nineteenth-century nationalist dreams, the Canadian state has attempted to construct homogeneity in order to guarantee survival. Mackey also reminds us, drawing on Michel Foucault, that this modern project is simultaneously 'endlessly recuperative and mobile, flexible and ambiguous, "hybrid" as well as totalizing.'[6] Elites in Canada as elsewhere have not had free rein. On the one hand, they have endeavoured to guarantee the authority of the unmarked centre, which Mackey describes as embodied in the privileged discourse of 'ordinary citizenship' and which *Finding Families, Finding Ourselves* generally locates in the 'mainstream', with its supposedly 'normal' or 'ordinary' households. On the other, they seek to win general loyalty; some degree of difference or hybridity must be tolerated in the course of nation- or family-building. Both coercion and concession have been employed to draw together all constituents. So too in adoption.

So much of Canadians' public identity as the 'peaceable kingdom' and the 'mosaic', vertical or otherwise, has been dependent upon faith in generosity and inclusiveness superior to those in the United States. Such an identity requires both 'insiders' and 'outsiders'. Within adoptive families and the state, insiders have been called upon to demonstrate, at least perfunctorily, the required virtues, and outsiders to accept largesse or exclusion with gratitude or resignation.[7] The script they act out has commonly positioned the nation and mainstream English Canadians, in particular, as the stars of the modern West's classic rescue story. White and middle-class households save the world, especially its more savage bits, one child at a time, and their complicity in the creation of the conditions of war, unemployment, poverty, and general tragedy that commonly propel youngsters into the arms of others is nicely sidestepped.[8]

'Difference' is to be 'allowed', even encouraged, 'in defined and carefully limited ways—as long as the *project* of Canadian nation-building', or that of the adoptive family, 'comes *first*'.[9] Other loyalties, to what is imagined as marginal and often inferior in other countries or in other families and communities, must defer to new identities and allegiances. Entry into new relations has regularly demanded surrender of the past, or at least critical elements of that past, on terms largely agreeable to the host. Not all potential recruits have met the conditions for inclusion. Some migrants have always remained unacceptable, deemed too foreign, too damaged, or too dangerous (which may be one and same) to adapt. When the difference of some outsiders appears non-negotiable, other sources of supply may be sought or doors closed entirely. Criteria for inclusion by the mainstream may also be revised to encompass formerly repudiated diversity. All this has occurred in the course of adoption, as in nation-building. It is no coincidence that the history of adoption legislation and that of Canada as a largely independent state after 1867 are largely conterminous: both represent modern efforts to establish rules for the forging and control of diverse communities. Recognition of this connection between the personal and the political, between the domestic and the national, informs all the arguments here.

Although Canadian legislators and other authorities have attempted to define the conditions for inclusion and acceptance, they have never been all powerful or in total agreement. Adoption in modern English Canada has similarly evolved in a series of frequently discontinuous conversations and confrontations. Demands to assimilate, to act just like the imagined 'everyman' (or -woman), have always provoked resistance. Transfer into new families produces citizens, who, like transnational migrants, 'have multiple connections and attachments' that they may wish to retain and reflect upon, sometimes to nurture.[10] The nature and extent of this retention—and its merits—provide many of the grounds for controversy. A kilt may be very well and fine, but what about the Sikh kirpan? The 'chosen baby' story constructs one past; reminders of illegitimacy, abuse, and exploitation offer another. Even when it concentrates on 'official' policies and practices, *Finding Families, Finding Ourselves* pays close attention to how individuals in the adoption circle, both insiders and outsiders, have tried to negotiate what was to be known and what was to be told.

Like the evolution of Canada more generally, the transfer of children among adults and communities has also never been either monolithic or static. Welcome by would-be parents and vulnerability to loss have ebbed and flowed over the more than 130 years since New Brunswick enacted Canada's first formal adoption law in 1873. As the ideal of a tightly bounded and privatized nuclear family grew, to reach its apotheosis in the 1950s, adoption, under the custodianship of adopters, was more commonly hidden not only from a curious public, as was the practice, but also from offspring and other family members. As an institution, it metamorphosed in response to the power of various groups to determine the fate of youngsters and to the faith in the power of the environment or that of heredity in childrearing. *Finding Families, Finding Ourselves* charts that slow, often uncertain, evolution of ideas and implementation and the varying involvement of different communities in English Canada from the nineteenth century to the 1990s.

My attention to this 'big picture' in adoption means that not every debate and experience receives equivalent, or indeed any, attention. I have not conducted interviews, either with members of the adoption circle or child welfare practitioners and policy-makers. That choice was deliberate. In part, it was driven by my awareness that other social scientists, many of whom I cite, are doing this important work and that unprecedented platforms, such as the listserv managed by the

Adoption Council of Canada, now exist for various voices. In exploring the many decades of adoption history, I also discovered an extraordinary wealth of data in public records of every kind. That evidence, in sources as diverse as legislation, the popular media, royal commissions, biographies and autobiographies, fiction and poetry, provides an unexplored vantage point from which to assess the overall development of adoption as a central and too often under-appreciated institution in English Canada. This motherload of information reveals the shifting contours of a critical phenomenon and the efforts of a modernizing nation to address fundamental issues of diversity and inequality and the responses this provoked. Quebec, especially French Quebec, is not treated here. Its story, while similar in many respects, is also distinguished by different legislative traditions and the dominant role of the Catholic Church until late in the twentieth century.[11]

In the course of reading and listening to accounts featured here, I have been regularly reminded that not all family-based solutions serve girls and boys well. Kin and adult guardians of every description have all too frequently abused and tormented those in their care. Some girls and boys fared far better when they could escape parents and communities, and sometimes the latter did as well. Traditional domestic ideologies to the contrary, not all women or men can or should act as custodians of offspring. Heredity offers few guarantees, whether of 'good' or 'bad' blood, as many past adopters expected, or of 'natural' affinities, as some modern searchers hoped.[12] New beginnings have sometimes been very good. When mainstream Canadians opened their homes and hearts to more diverse communities of children, they frequently extended opportunities and broadened perspectives for themselves, children, and their country. That greater receptivity, even in the context of state efforts to manage diverse communities in the service of elites, as described so usefully by Eva Mackey, is worthwhile. Adoption can sometimes be best for all concerned. So, too, may foster or group homes, but that is another story.

As the continuing appeal of *Anne of Green Gables* to Canadians and many others around the globe reminds us, fictions have often overshadowed what has actually happened in adoption. We have only to open a newspaper, watch a television program, or attend elementary school classes where children are routinely asked to construct family genealogies, to see the strength of 'the classical family of western nostalgia', the common refuge of the historically illiterate. That credo goes something like this: loving families, supported by a wider kin group, produce and support offspring with little or no outside interference or assistance. Stability and order prevail as children link families' pasts to common futures.[13] A second, related myth also relevant to adoption takes for granted Canadians' love for children. Girls and boys, we fondly believe, have as a group received generally sympathetic treatment.[14] While not without elements of truth, these visions of children and families supply yet another version of 'invented tradition'[15] and obscure the fact that many youngsters and households have had very different experiences. *Finding Families, Finding Ourselves* offers one antidote to the sugar-coated domestic lies we tell each other. Reality, for all its complications and horrors, is ultimately a far better guide than mythologies to finding loving families and getting life right in general.

In telling the various stories in *Finding Families,* there have been many shoals to avoid. Most particularly, in adoption's commonly highly partisan landscape, where emotions flow often at their most raw, it is always dangerously easy to demonize and essentialize. Birth parents readily become irresponsible and vicious or innocent and permanently wounded. Adopters loom as abusive and selfish or figure as altruistic and noble. Adoptees emerge as thoughtless and demanding or harbingers of a better day. Social workers, legislators, and authorities in general are likely to come off especially badly: unfeeling handmaidens of an essentially brutal system and society. Much popular commentary on the continuing sad state of child welfare in Canada has chastised adoption workers and child-rescue professionals. Their record has never been perfect. Ultimately, however, many appear much like northern British Columbia's fabled post-Second World War social worker Bridget Moran. Equipped with pitiful resources, they fought the good fight on behalf of youngsters and families. Too frequently they had to do this largely alone, shortchanged by governments and by Canadians in general. In charting state involvement in the care of youngsters, these pages are often especially critical of those in power. Too often, it has appeared easy for them to forget the advantages of their supporters and the humanity of those with fewer resources. Too often, pennypinching reigns supreme, at the cost of human dignity and fair play. In dealing with all groups, however, I have tried to be even-handed and to avoid stereotypes. Inevitably, however, some caricatures loom close to the surface in what follows, and some contain more than a grain of truth.

Two other caveats are worth emphasizing. The first concerns the choice of language; the second, the role of the First Nations. Words can be weapons, as those formerly, and sometimes currently, designated 'bastards' know well. This is never the intention here. I have employed terms such as 'birth parent' and 'first parent' and 'adoptive parent' and 'second parent' and avoided others that include the adjectives 'natural' or 'real'. Some potentially hurtful usages, by authorities I cite or in my own writing, remain, but they convey a diversity of viewpoints that is useful to remember. I hope trespasses against some sensibilities will be forgiven, for I have not intended pain. Language has also been important in considering the role of indigenous or Aboriginal communities, commonly, by the end of the twentieth century, referred to in Canada as First Nations. I employ the names of particular tribal groups when they are known. I use 'Métis' to signify a mix of the dominion's European and Native populations. I have tried to preserve distinctions when they are apparent or known to be preferred, but in general I use indigenous, Aboriginal, and First Nations interchangeably. 'Indian' appears only where it turned up in my sources. In Canada, as in other settler colonies such as Australia, Aboriginal populations have stood close to the heart of much child transfer in the twentieth century. While African-origin youngsters have suffered substantial disadvantage in Canada, their actual and symbolic presence does not match that in the United States. In the dominion, the fate of the First Nations, as representatives such as the writer and performer E. Pauline Johnson have reminded audiences, has frequently been inextricably linked to the survival of a northern nation.[16] Certainly fair dealing with the land's original inhabitants has tested both the nation and individual families. Their symbolic significance, plus the sheer number of Native children in care, explains why the First Nations appear in every chapter and preoccupy one in particular.

Ultimately, *Finding Families, Finding Ourselves* offers many particular tales of ordinary women and men. Canada's renowned red-haired heroine well summed up adoption's broad embrace: 'There's such a lot of different Annes in me. I sometimes think that is why I'm such a troublesome person. If I was just one Anne it would be ever so much more comfortable but then it wouldn't be half so interesting.'[17] 'Interesting' and frequently 'uncomfortable' aptly sum up diverse accounts. In order to make clearest sense of what they may mean, the telling here is simultaneously thematic and chronological. Each chapter directs readers to a particular set of individual stories—childrearing, legislation, class relations, gender, religion, ethnicity and race, Aboriginal–settler contact, international exchanges, and (re)connection—that shaped and informed the thinking and practices of adoption as they emerged over the years. Separate treatment is intended to clarify the special significance of various themes. It is not to suggest that individuals embodied solely class, gender, race, or some other characteristic. Everyone in adoption, as in much else, is multiply positioned as the increasingly abundant literature on intersectionality rewardingly reminds us.[18] Read collectively, the chapters emphasize complicated associations and plural identities embedded alike in both custom and innovation. Like Anne, members of Canada's adoption circles found many ways of being in the world.

Chapter 1, 'Beyond the Nuclear Family: Childrearing in English Canada', spotlights the often forgotten reality of variously shared responsibility for youngsters. Although domestic mythologies and the limitations of data collection have often obscured the fact, households consisting of heterosexual couples and biological offspring have never been all-pervasive. While some communities among the First Nations or immigrant groups have been routinely singled out as employing a variety of caregivers, this chapter reminds readers that children have been reared in diverse domestic and institutional settings. Biological parents, many of whom, especially single mothers, have had little choice but to concentrate hard on breadwinning, have frequently been limited in their involvement in day-to-day nurture. Shifting progeny among both kin and strangers has persisted, especially in disadvantaged groups haunted by death, disease, and disability. Little fanfare or public acknowledgement has accompanied many private exchanges. Transfers among adults might endure until children's maturity or be quickly terminated at the wish of youngsters, birth families, or foster households. Many mothers, fathers, and other kin have not readily relinquished ties. The casualness with which young Anne passed from hand to hand has been commonplace and frequently threatening. The irrepressible redhead ultimately found caring adults, but not all her counterparts have been so lucky. Beginning in the late nineteenth century, frequently tragic histories, plus the needs of a modernizing state to manage its human resources more effectively, led provincial governments to regulate more closely the rights and obligations of youngsters and guardians. That impulse, simultaneously both humanitarian and bureaucratizing, always operated in the context of long-

recurring trade in children desired for labour love

standing custom that took for granted not only the private right to dispose of girls and boys but also a recurring trade in children desired for both labour and love.

Chapter 2, 'Setting the Rules: Adoption and the Law', explores how provinces, beginning with New Brunswick soon after Confederation and Nova Scotia in 1896, endeavoured to set the legal terms by which youngsters could be permanently transferred to new parents. Early legislation nevertheless largely took for granted persisting connection to birth families. Inheritance from the past remained relatively uncompromised, while that from the adopters' kin was initially restricted. Newcomers to better-positioned households arrived together with, rather than stripped of, critical parts of their individual histories. In the early years of legislation, suspicion of hereditary taint as well as desires to protect property meant that the precedents of adoptees were not, officially at least, to be entirely erased or forgotten. Yet, they were not to be subject to casual public gaze, as varying provisions for confidentiality made clear. Over the course of the twentieth century, as the doctrine 'like our very own' increasingly justified the complete repudiation of the past, connections to origins received less legislative protection, and members of the adoption circle were encouraged in collective amnesia. By the 1970s, the tide turned once again. Slowly, with great trepidation and in face of substantial lobbying both for and against, legislators moved to recognize the continuing interests of relinquishing and relinquished kin and communities. Open adoption, disclosure registries, mandated consultations with First Nations communities, and international conventions marked new hopes and concerns as adoption drew more headlines than ever before and as the Royal Commissions on New Reproductive Technologies and on Aboriginal Peoples suggested new constraints on surrendering and acquiring offspring. Like Canada itself at the close of the twentieth century, the politics of adoption had to attend to historical grievance and calls for redress.

Chapter 3, 'Class Matters', sets forth the fundamental material and structural disadvantages that prompted the majority of youngsters' shift from families of origin. While regularly uncommented upon, the injuries of class remain central to almost every tale of adoption and of fostering, its often unheralded twin. Neither adults nor children escaped. The poor, whether they lived in Canada or abroad, and whether Aboriginal or newcomer, have always had fewer opportunities to nourish and protect their progeny. Youngsters have been taken away, sometimes effectively abducted, because impoverished parents within communities have been regularly unable to match the material and other standards by which the mainstream has set out to judge them as adequate and respectable and because adult disadvantage readily imperilled children, sometimes in terrible ways. When times have been bad—and they have always been bad somewhere—groups with fewer resources, whether for housing, health care, opportunities for respite, or expert assistance, have been especially, although never uniquely, vulnerable to disruption and tragedy. As Rickie Solinger in *Beggars and Choosers* has noted for the United States, options for some women and men have always been predicated on others' lack of choice. Troubles have ebbed and flowed with the state of national and global economies and the fate of social security systems.[19] Good employments, pensions, and allowances helped keep families intact, or at least offered the prospect of regaining guardianship, once surrendered. At no time has class disappeared as a major contributing factor in the apprehension and transfer of youngsters.

Chapter 4, 'Gendered Lives', sets out the variety of ways in which gender has regularly made a difference to adults and to children within Canada's adoption circles. Girls and women have always been especially visible, sometimes as particularly vulnerable and sometimes as relatively lucky. Birth mothers, especially the unwed, start the story off. Their struggles to survive and to produce good outcomes for their offspring have occurred in the midst of much material deprivation and recurring calumny. Elsewhere within the adoption circle, would-be adoptive mothers were most often the ones to initiate discussion about including youngsters in households. Because successful membership in the modern female community has often been held to coincide with mothering, many women, both single and married, could not readily confront with any equanimity the prospect of permanently empty nests. Among adoptive children themselves, Canadians have regularly demonstrated a preference for girls. Boys appeared more likely to face rejection and to encounter harsher outcomes. Men, too, played different roles. As searchers, they were always less numerous and less active. Birth fathers were often conspicuously absent as well, at least until the late twentieth century. Adoptive dads commonly appeared less involved than prospective mums. These different trajectories reveal how gender regularly structured much individual engagement in private and public life.

Chapter 5 examines the trilogy of religion, ethnicity, and race that has bedevilled so many exchanges of girls and boys. Long-time requirements for matching Protestant and Catholic adults and youngsters invoked a deep rift that divided Canadian politics and society. Their near disappearance in the years after the Second World War testified to growing secularism, the reduction of old hostilities, and, less positively, the triumph of Protestantism masquerading as ecumenicalism. Sectarianism has also been regularly associated with the racialization of various communities. In particular, non-British but European ethnicity initially curbed the mainstream's acceptance of potential progeny. By the 1960s, however, such background was of relatively little import. Yet, youngsters standing at greater distance from the norm, notably Blacks and Asians, continued to meet far more reserved reception. Racism in the selection of offspring has been endemic. Only slowly did the 'colour-blind' liberalism that flourished in the context of Canada's consideration of the 'just society' erode familiar prejudices and offer new groups of children some purchase on the hearts of officially multicultural Canada.

Chapter 6, on Native–newcomer contact, turns to the group that captures much of the varied world of disadvantage that has resided close to the heart of adoption in Canada. First Nations peoples have their own substantial history of exchanging children. Mythology to the contrary, their youngsters, like those in other communities, have also faced a variety of fates. Native girls and boys have not been equally vulnerable in interactions with settler populations. Those standing on the margins of Aboriginal societies have had still fewer resources to deal with domestic disasters of every kind. Residential schools proved the first bleak test of mainstream Canada's pervasive indifference, much like its attitude to the young of the work-

ing class, to the well-being of First Nations youngsters. Experiments with fostering and adoption, the well-termed 'scoop' of the 1960s and 1970s, saw English
Canada shipping indigenous youngsters across provincial and national boundaries
and uncertainly reconsidering its own long-standing rejection of these children.
Tragic outcomes and rising protest from First Nations quickly tarnished naive
optimism about seamless inclusion and assimilation. By the end of the twentieth
century, the plight of Native children in care testified to the bankruptcy of much
adoption politics and of Aboriginal–mainstream relations in general.

Chapter 7 takes up the question of foreign affairs. International candidates for
adoption have existed since Europeans colonized Canada. Irish famine orphans,
immortalized in a well-known 'Heritage Minute' were succeeded by Britain's
'home children', who were brought in the thousands to toil in overseas homes.
Some arrivals were welcomed as members of new families; many more were rel-
egated, like so many of the domestic poor, to the sidelines, there to serve, without
much hope of nurture or just reward, the best interests of others. Their class, conveyed by accents and forced migration, made youthful newcomers often suspect
intruders on dominion hearths. Waves of children swept from domestic moorings
by global poverty, wars, and recurring disasters of every kind succeeded early
recruits. The Second World War produced both British evacuees and Holocaust
survivors. They might be cultural kin to some Canadians, but they frequently
found acceptance uncertain. As the most desired domestic candidates for mainstream households fell in numbers in the last decades of the twentieth century,
would-be parents broadened their horizons to include youngsters from previously
scorned areas of Europe, Asia, and Latin America. While rescue claims were pervasive, as with the initial outpouring of enthusiasm following the great Asian
tsunami of December 2004, they rarely extended to Africa, a continent where
children were in the greatest need. Hearts, like Canadian development funds and
trade, harboured certain preferences.

Chapter 8, 'Origins and Destinations: Connecting Individuals and Communities', highlights three complicated stories. The first explores the contemporary
searching movement, which has built on long-standing desires for knowledge of
the past on the part of adoptees and of outcomes on the part of birth relatives.
Modern advocates of reunion, who have for the most part been white and middle class, have employed both essentialist and social justice arguments in making
their case for recovery. They have been a powerful lobby, frequently forcing legislatures and the public to recognize the extent of historic injury and establishing
the case for redress. The second section outlines the demand for the repatriation
of Native youngsters and its close ties to Aboriginal campaigns for recognition
more generally. Recovery of lost girls and boys often stumbled over the depths of
the tragedies involved and debates about what resources were to be employed and
what entitlements were to be shared. The third section turns to end-of-the-twen-
tieth century experiments in open adoption, which signal a return in part to some
customary practices. At their best, they hold some promise for dismantling the
prejudices, ignorance, and secrecy that have regularly crippled Canada's ability to
nurture all its children.

The conclusion reminds readers how the stories told in *Finding Families, Finding Selves* contribute to our understanding of the flexibility and evolution of families and of the nature of Canada itself. Kinship may be regularly typecast as primordial and unshifting, but its players have regularly deserted conventional scripts to set their own mark upon both biological and social households. Adoption has been one way that families and communities have consciously and not so consciously remade themselves in the course of fashioning a variety of futures out of shared and diverse pasts. Canada, with its history of interchanges among different peoples, has supplied a critical stage for the unfolding of adoption's many tales. Shifting narratives have sometimes corresponded to shifts in the national imaginary. In the course of more than a century and a quarter after New Brunswick first legislated the permanent transfer of youngsters, official or mainstream Canada began to present itself differently. Adoption reflected that change.

Finally let me make my own position very clear, although I am in no way claiming to be disinterested or objective. I am not adopted nor have I formally adopted offspring, as has been the experience of many authors in this contentious field. I did, however, foster my sister's child from the time she was four until she was eight. That experience was wonderful but, even as it honoured biology, it was also often painful for all concerned. That personal history has regularly informed *Finding Families, Finding Ourselves* in ways that are not always calculable, at least by me. I trust that my long training in history and women's studies, my extensive research and writing on Canada's women and children, both Native and newcomer, and my heartfelt desire to help Canadians better reflect on the meaning of their past in the interests of a more equitable future have helped me avoid the worst of errors. Readers will decide whether adoption's complicated tales emerge fairly here.

Beyond the Nuclear Family: Childrearing in English Canada

Adoption can best be understood as part of recurring efforts to match families and resources. Some parents have always been hard pressed to offer children care, affection, or a roof over their heads; other adults have needs, whether economic or emotional, that youngsters are believed to satisfy. Supply and demand have ebbed and flowed in response to community standards of care, material conditions, and prejudice. Although adoption received legislative support beginning in the last decades of the nineteenth century, Canadian children had been, and would continue to be, exchanged among adults under a variety of conditions and for varying periods of time. This chapter explores that enduring fluidity over the course of the nineteenth and twentieth centuries and provides the backdrop for the subsequent thematic discussion of modern English Canada's encounter with adoption. It begins by drawing attention to the persistent power of family ideologies and then turns to problems of data, the vulnerability of birth parents, the prevalence of private arrangements, the role of institutions in facilitating substitute care, and the emergence of support for formal adoption. The adoption legislation that we examine in the next chapter was intimately connected to long-standing ideas and practices about the proper provision for children.

Family Tales

'Fictions, more or less curious', was the pithy summary provided by one early-twentieth-century judicial commentator on Canadian families.[1] As this judge recognized, families were unpredictable and were ultimately social creations. Fluidity has been a basic fact of kin and community relations. Membership might be inclusive or exclusive, could acknowledge blood ties and/or recognize social relations, might stretch over decades or continents or be restricted to a single individual or one generation, could involve remuneration, might represent affection and support or embody violence and indifference. As Neil Sutherland so profitably reminded readers in *Growing Up: Childhood in English Canada from the Great War to the Age of Television*, youngsters have been embedded in a 'wider environment of care', well beyond the nuclear family, that took more or less responsibility for their well-being.[2] In individual family histories, the possible permutations by which responsibilities for children and childcare have been allocated have been legion.

Diversity in both the past and present has frequently been obscured by persisting tendencies to romanticize or homogenize 'normal' family life. Powerful domestic ideologies have largely ignored the flexibility required for survival and the differences in power, and thus parenting options, conferred by gender, class, status, race, age, and a host of other distinctions. Despite ample proof that poverty and inequality have been widespread right up to the present in the northern half of North America and that life for many mothers and children in particular has often been brutal,[3] 'the classical family of western nostalgia,'[4] whether it surfaced to invoke 'an idealized, rural, pre-industrial society'[5] or the hetero-normative family in urban or suburban settings,[6] has regularly camouflaged reality. Canadian champions of imagined mainstream households, whether extended or nuclear, promised social peace and economic stability to their loyalists. By contrast, families that did not embrace Eurocentric and middle-class models have been frequently suspect and marked for remaking by external experts, from missionaries to schoolteachers, social workers, and doctors.[7]

Targets of such efforts frequently offered, in turn, their own version of what was natural and proper for kin. In defending their integrity, First Nations commentators, including many testifying before the Royal Commission on Aboriginal Peoples (1991–6), have frequently articulated kin-based utopias: in pre-contact Edens, the Aboriginal story often goes, respect, mutuality, responsibility, and equality knit together whole communities in the care of all their members, young and old alike. Abuse and neglect were unknown in the past, and should control of child welfare be returned to indigenous peoples that state of grace would return.[8] Modern adoption practices represented an attack on an older and preferable social order.

Central to the domestic visions treasured by Canadian communities have been assumptions that children are treated fairly and appropriately. Not surprisingly there have been many versions of what this might mean. Natives and newcomers often disagreed right from the beginning about how girls and boys should be reared, treasuring various degrees and kinds of discipline. By the mid-nineteenth century, mainstream attitudes to youngsters were shifting markedly and becoming increasingly influential in the assessment of all girls and boys. Patricia Rooke and Rudy Schnell have summed up the resulting ideal in which children emerged as a special category of human beings with considerable potential for good and to whom the community had special obligations.[9] While honoured more in theory than in practice, belief in dependence, protection, segregation, and delayed responsibilities for children has often encouraged those in power—whether private philanthropists, professional social workers, or reform-minded citizens in general—to ignore the merits of other approaches to childrearing. Those children who were closest in character and potential to Canadian elites have regularly received the fullest benefits of shifting sensibilities. Less privileged youngsters were left to compare their lives with those of Anne of Green Gables or her equally atypical successors, increasingly mass-marketed in magazines, books, and on television and movie screens. Native and disabled youngsters typify the large numbers who have frequently found it unwise to depend on mainstream adults. Whatever domestic ideology has promised, many children have experienced want and abuse on the road to adulthood.

Wherever they flourish, familial ideologies regularly obscure the range of reality. More dangerous still, as one American historian observing disadvantaged youngsters has pointed out, 'ideology easily obscured the fact that family preservation was a risky venture for many children.'[10] Margrit Eichler's *Families in Canada Today* effectively sums up the commonplace biases of this disabling discourse as 'monolithic', 'conservative', 'sexist', and 'microstructural.' In short, the classical family, whatever its provenance, understates diversity, change, male dominance, and external influences.[11] A temptation for both conservative and radical critics of contemporary social arrangements, nostalgic memory of supposedly better times has routinely rallied opponents of modernization in all its forms, whether the target is the welfare state, feminism, new reproductive technologies, or European incursions. It lurks behind most accounts of the transfer of children, both Aboriginal and non-Aboriginal, to institutions and new homes. As a result, matters have often had to become very bad before dominant assumptions would be questioned. Only when two orphaned nieces 'had been reduced to the position of drudges, their clothing was ragged, and they were fed from a big-tub' and at least one was 'stripped and beaten' were an Anglican vicar and his wife in a small town near London, Ontario, hauled before authorities in 1898.[12] Similarly, at the beginning of the twenty-first century, a Native community saved its public condemnation until a Vancouver Island aunt and uncle had murdered one nephew and abused another.[13] Like many others, observers in both cases may have been initially blinded to reality by idealized visions of kith and kin.

Facts: Missing, Fabricated, and Revealing

Even as modern life demanded increasingly that citizens keep track of personal records of every description, adoption—legal or otherwise—has been regularly viewed as an aberration or sometimes an embarrassment to be shunted aside. As the influential Canadian scholar H. David Kirk recognized, twentieth-century adoption often brought efforts 'to cancel the child's past'.[14] Not surprisingly, the numbers involved have been notoriously difficult to track. In Britain it has been estimated that perhaps one-third of the population is affected as birth or natural families or as adoptees; in the United States proportions are similarly high.[15] In Canada, both Aboriginal and non-Aboriginal populations contribute to large numbers, but data offer only guesses at how many have been touched. From one part of the country to another, records vary enormously—some were never created and others remain incomplete, have been lost or falsified—and are regularly not comparable among various jurisdictions, governments, and agencies.

While birth statistics have been reckoned fairly reliable in Ontario by 1930,[16] child transfers of every sort regularly escaped bureaucracy's net. In 1928, Montreal social worker Jane B. Wisdom typically complained that, 'though adoption establishes a permanent relationship, it is very often the most hastily and casually arranged. . . . Because of its strong emotional appeal, the method certainly has become widespread and is largely a social custom which has little regulation. . . . It is indeed a vital statistic of which there are practically no figures.'[17] A year later the

New Brunswick Child Welfare Survey confessed that it was 'obviously impossible to obtain any statistical data [on adoption], applicable to the whole Province.'[18] In 1931, Newfoundland's Child Welfare Association urged 'compulsory registration' of the 'illegitimate child,' admitting that, 'of the 250 known to us to have been born during the last five years, a big number are completely lost trace of.'[19] As late as 1954, the federal Department of National Health and Welfare was paying family allowances for 'a substantial number' of unregistered Nova Scotia children.[20] And in 1956, a social worker from Ontario's Temiskaming District had to report that 'we have had the Vital Statistics Act for a long time and yet in our area we still find a number of children whose births have not yet been registered.'[21] Adoptions within kin groups further complicated matters. Kerry Daly and Michael Sobol noted in the early 1990s that the some 10 per cent of domestic adoptions by relatives rarely came 'to the attention of adoption service providers.'[22] No wonder H. Philip Hepworth found 'extremely shaky statistical data and a dearth of good research findings' in his major study of Canadian fostering and adoption.[23]

Yet if story-telling can sometimes mislead and data prove unreliable, they can also be rich, incorporating to various degrees both reality and romance. In particular, sources regularly illuminate how care for children has been variously distributed. Family histories are particularly revealing. Just as they often do in life, grandmothers loom large in many tales of kin. Katie, my mother's mother, born in Somerset, England, in 1894, received little formal education or family money but was expected to be a lady. As a teenager, she married a recent widower and was soon, too soon by some accounts, mother to the daughter of the first wife, who had died shortly after childbirth, and to the first of five more children, four daughters and one son. She also fostered her brother's offspring when he sought his fortune in London. Her husband found cricket more absorbing than his family, and in her thirties Katie found herself running a pub. During the Second World War, the Cavendish Arms and subsequently her own home provided a respite for young Canadians and Americans. The youngest of the family, two teenage daughters, were carried away, one to British Columbia and another to California. Katie's merchant seaman son married a Dutch girl and her three eldest girls found boys from home. Her home sheltered paying guests, both individuals and families, and welcomed daughters and grandchildren when husbands left for war, wages, or other women. She rarely moved from her small Somerset town, presiding over several generations of kin as well as neighbours and friends who became courtesy cousins, aunts, and uncles. Geographic adventures occurred only twice, once to confirm respectability for her American daughter facing fault-finding Armenian in-laws and, much later, to confer her blessing on her daughter in Canada, who had survived loneliness and poverty to complete university, enter a profession, and nurture three children. That British war bride in turn went on to inspire more grandchildren, fostering one, incorporating the prior offspring of a new daughter-in-law, and loving all.

As her daughter, I knew my British and American relatives first through my mother's eyes and then through my own. For many years I saw little distinction between blood and social kin. In contrast, I knew little of my father's family, descendants of Scottish settlers from the 1820s. The Second World War, which saw him desert a wife and an adopted son to court British women, left him an alcoholic. No wonder one respectable British aunt wanted to incorporate me in a household that included only a son. As it was, my grandmother and aunts tried to nurture children both nearby and at a distance. Grandchildren and nieces and nephews knew they were under a scrutiny that went well beyond birth parents. Weekly letters filled with gossip and advice, cash when matters were especially difficult on one side or another of the Atlantic, and visits fostered ties for over half a century. Only in the 1990s, more than twenty years after Katie's death, were there time and money enough to assemble in the spacious British house of one of her grandsons. We still told stories about Katie, but my mother, now a senior family member, had become the matriarch. The family's only professional historian, I was assigned a wall-length genealogy, where I contributed to family lies. A 'half-aunt' and her offspring became full kin; an adoptee was seamlessly integrated. No mention was made of suicides, kin with disabilities, children born out of wedlock, including my eldest son and myself, sisters raising nieces, or disappearing or unknown fathers. And there was undoubtedly much else that the colonial branch did not know. My generation nevertheless conspired with the departed Katie to preserve respectability and assert common cause.

While its details are specific, this account is not unusual. As Carol Smart has pointed out, families regularly gloss 'over little (and large) "irregularities" in order to present themselves to the outside world as respectable. . . . Generations of kin disguised the fact that families are fluid things which spill over into irregular shapes with irregular bondings and unions, with improper relationships, with too many or too few children, with children of different parentage, with "aunts" who are not really aunts, "cousins" who are not really cousins, and "fathers" who are not really fathers.'[24] The 'disappearance' by death, institutionalization, or other means from family memory of many disabled adults and children frequently provided yet another instance of contrived fiction.[25] Adoption, both formal and informal, has similarly been part of a recurring pattern of variously imagined households.

The irregularities of family life have supplied the stock-in-trade of much Canadian fiction. In *Anne of Green Gables* (1908), Lucy Maud Montgomery famously depicted a spirited red-haired girl who gave an elderly brother and sister a chance to parent.[26] Farley Mowat's classic teenage novel *Lost in the Barrens* (1956) made the white orphan Jamie kin to the Cree protagonist, Awasin, and allowed both to find a home with the Inuit, traditional foes of the Cree. In *The Diviners* (1974), Margaret Laurence paired the orphaned Morag with the disinherited Métis in the struggle for survival. Lee Maracle incorporated a sister-in-law, a 'sixties scoop' survivor who had been adopted out to a white family, in *Sundogs* (1992), the story of a loving and conflict-ridden Aboriginal household. Best-selling children's author Jean Little created a host of displaced heroines and heroes. Her *The Belonging Place* (1997), with its Scottish orphans and reconstituted families in nineteenth-century Canada, was dedicated to 'adopted children everywhere.' Alistair MacLeod set out still another narrative of grandparents, orphans, adoption, and kin with vastly different fates in his *No Great Mischief* (1999). Whether self-consciously genealogical or fabricated, such accounts have offered ample reminders of domestic breakdown and the transfer of youngsters among different settings.

Vulnerable Families

The vulnerability of many Canadian families to the dispersal of their members, especially in the years before social security made a dint in widespread poverty, was vividly captured in one late-nineteenth-century novel's casual reference to a woman preparing to 'go orphan-hunting in the country'.[27] Death, ill health, and economic disaster have always threatened material and psychological well-being. A substantial number of youngsters, whether orphaned, half-orphaned, or not orphaned at all, have always been in need. The loss of a parent has been especially likely to change arrangements for their care. Such was the case in 1826, when a destitute Montreal widow, Elizabeth Pitre, placed her infant son in the 'service' of Lisey Mcdonald until he was age twenty-one. She could not retrieve him unless she paid the full cost of his keep.[28] Bettina Bradbury has charted the desperate situation of many such women searching for childcare in Montreal, and there is no reason to believe that they survived better elsewhere.[29]

Male opportunities for employment and property ownership gave widowers somewhat better prospects, but they too were likely to lose children. In 1869, a Montreal day labourer and widower handed his two-year-old over, supposedly until adulthood, to a merchant and his wife. Four years later, with a new wife at home, he demanded his daughter's return.[30] Vulnerability persisted even after Canadians began to experiment with social security. In the 1960s, a CBC program supervisor struggled to cope with his wife's death. When his older daughter, who had become his housekeeper, married and his older son left home, he had to turn over his younger daughter to 'live full time with my sister-in-law.' At much the same time, a part-time student and bartender from Lethbridge, Alberta, surrendered his three-year-old to friends during the week. A Prince Rupert hospital orderly found much the same remedy:

> When my wife died, I advertised for someone to look after my 7-year-old daughter. I got replies, but quite a few people were more interested in the money than helping out in a difficult situation. Finally I found some neighbours who took her right into their own family. She stays with me on the weekend and I take her out at every opportunity. She has adjusted well to her new life and is having a ball. When my wife died, I had the choice of leaving her with relatives or bringing her up on my own. My family doctor recommended the latter and I've never regretted it.[31]

As such examples demonstrate, single parenthood presented enormous challenges even in better times.

Unwed mothers have always been especially vulnerable to the ill match of revenue and expenses. Their plight made it clear why abortion and infanticide were facts of life in many quarters. Harsh reality lay behind the choice in 1925 of one

Saskatchewan spinster. 'Obliged to earn her living by her own exertions' and find-ing 'it impossible to do so and at the same time to care for, nurse, bring up and educate the said child in a proper and suitable manner,' she signed away her new-born. Although the province had an adoption law on its books, she and the adopt-ing couple used a form much like older indenture agreements. The latter con-tracted to treat the boy 'in a proper and suitable manner' and the surrendering mother agreed not to disturb their 'possession' or management. As with many older arrangements, she did not lose him entirely. The contract permitted her 'access to the said child occasionally and visit[s] for the purpose of seeing him.'[32]

The options of the unwed were always highly contingent. Families and neigh-bours might well be understanding, especially if they knew both the mother and father, and sympathized with the circumstances.[33] New babies could be incorpor-ated, their arrival signalled by expressions of solidarity or by carping criticism. The existence of common-law unions, many of considerable duration, has also meant that not all mothers of illegitimate offspring were in fact single parents. A woman might not marry her partner for a variety of reasons, including other legal spouses or limited funds, but she might have his support.[34] Throughout the nineteenth and twentieth centuries many, even the majority of, single mothers, driven by circum-stances or sentiment, appeared to have kept their babies, though how many and for what length of time is impossible to determine.[35]

Although the degree of opprobrium might vary, illegitimacy or bastardry was a social liability.[36] The challenge was summed up by the Newfoundland Division of Child Welfare in 1948: 'There are people in the country who still regard the unmarried mother as a social outcast and her child as untouchable. . . . There are still many people who feel that they cannot stand the "disgrace" which their daughters have brought on the family and they cannot even think of permitting them to ever "darken their doors" again. . . . The very suggestion that the children should be given care by the grandparents is nauseating.'[37] Offspring did not nec-essarily escape ignominy even when surrendered. One girl, whom loving parents informally adopted from Nova Scotia's Ideal Maternity Home, found herself, far from atypically, labelled a 'bastard' when she attended school.[38] Such humiliation fuelled long-standing efforts to eliminate the legal concept of bastardry and the distinction between children born in and out of wedlock, but not before it was a factor in many mothers' decisions to surrender their babies.

By the late nineteenth century growing numbers of institutions for unmarried mothers demonstrated the limits of public and private tolerance. Until the 1960s and occasionally beyond, 'homes' such as the Salvation Army's Anchorage in St John's, Newfoundland, and the Catholic Our Lady of Mercy Home in Vancouver were jammed. Many inmates, escaping from family scrutiny elsewhere, were expected to atone for perceived moral or psychological lapses.[39] For years, suspi-cions about inheritance of maternal moral and other shortcomings, not to men-tion both the desire to punish and the recognition of the strength of maternal affections, meant that mothers were encouraged to keep their offspring. By the 1940s, the enthusiasm for Freudian explanations for women's slip from grace— they were now more likely to be cast as psychologically maladjusted rather than im- or amoral—helped justify relinquishment to increasingly eager adopters, who assumed that new environments would check unwanted tendencies.

Unwed mothers themselves were increasingly interpreted as 'good' when they surrendered offspring. Such a commonplace opinion was shared by one worker in the Unmarried Parent Department of the Metropolitan Toronto Children's Aid Society in 1959: 'In our experience in the Children's Aid Society of Metropolitan Toronto over the past few years, we have found that the more emotionally healthy unmarried mothers are the ones likely to relinquish their children: not because they do not love them, but because they care enough to want this child to have the love and protection of two parents, who will cherish and nurture him in a normal home setting.'[40] Self-sacrifice demonstrated both a finer kind of maternalism and a better heritage.

Not all women faced equal pressure to surrender. 'Blue-ribbon babies'—white and preferably female—appear to have topped demand in all periods. Other children, whether boys, older, Aboriginal, black, in sibling groups, or with physical or mental disabilities—in modern parlance, often 'special needs'—always faced a more uncertain welcome from English Canada's Anglo-Celtic mainstream. As the executive director for Nova Scotia's Pictou County Children's Aid noted in 1946:

> We are able to work with the unwanted normal child of good background, placing him for adoption by the unsatisfactory method of private arrangement. In nearly all these cases the mother must maintain the child until a suitable adoption home can be selected. We are in the anomalous position of being able to make no immediate provision for the inferior or abnormal unwanted child of an unmarried mother. We can only persuade or coerce the inferior or abnormal mother to take her child, and when neglect develops, bring the case before the Juvenile Court.[41]

The birth mothers of offspring little in demand faced an especially difficult dilemma. Left behind, such children might well never find alternate parents.

Even when single mothers found encouragement to parent, women's low wages ensured that many could not afford to support themselves, let alone an additional mouth to feed. Although the inauguration of mothers' allowances or pensions after the First World War subsidized the respectable poor, provinces always limited eligibility. Widows were preferred, and only British Columbia initially included a handful of unwed mothers. Nova Scotia was the provincial laggard, withholding equality in welfare between married and unmarried mothers until 1968.[42] Nor did state assistance anywhere mean comfort. Finances left little room for anything beyond the minimum, and sometimes not that. One study of eighty-seven unwed adolescents in Ontario in 1983 painted a typical portrait. About 85 per cent relied on social assistance in the first eighteen months after childbirth and were hard put to make ends meet. Such young mothers also frequently endured a lonely existence, with 'one-fifth of the grandmothers and three-fifths of the fathers' spending 'no time at all with the child in the past four weeks.'[43]

The predicament of Canada's unwed mothers has not been uniform. The well-

founded awareness of some minorities that their daughters would receive little welcome in mainstream institutions such as church refuges could foster on-going community support. Single black mothers in Nova Scotia were much more likely than
their white counterparts to take home babies whom they knew mainstream experts
might well classify as 'inferior' or 'abnormal'. In 1966, Halifax's Grace Maternity
Hospital credited black patients as the least likely to surrender infants; they were
followed by poorer white and then middle-class patients.[44] The same city's child
welfare institutions concluded that 'more negro than white children were placed
with relatives, which conforms to the recognized trend in the negro community to
place children in need of care with relatives,' rather than to turn them over to
strangers.[45] Aboriginal women also sought aid from religious or lay institutions
more rarely than did white women. They hoped for support from family and
friends, who might well regard pregnancies out of wedlock as conferring little or
no shame. The frequent lack of welcome for Native, black, and other racialized
groups by homes for the unwed was echoed by the rejection of many orphanages
and prospective adopters. Throughout much of the nineteenth and twentieth centuries, black and Native mothers must often have understood that they and their
offspring would not readily find families or shelter outside their own communities.
Their predicament persisted as a leitmotif of adoption in this nation.

Private Arrangements

Adult authority over children has regularly justified the movement of the young
from one site to another. Parents and those who stood *in loco parentis* have taken
for granted their right to determine appropriate arrangements. John Gillis's *A
World of Their Own Making: Myth, Ritual, and the Quest for Family Values* has usefully
summed up the commonplace habit of shifting girls and boys around. Even among
the wealthy, three-generation families have always been relatively rare.[46] There
were always 'spare' children and adults who moved in with others. The shifting
boundaries of households and the regular inclusion of non-kin meant that 'for
most of its history, therefore, the Western family system has functioned with an
imagin[e] that has enabled individuals to form familial relations with strangers and
to feel at home away from home.'[47] Distinctions between kin and non-kin have
frequently been far from firm: 'Families past were not especially familiar with their
relatives, especially those who lived at a distance, and they did not distinguish
clearly between their various in-laws. . . . The term "friend" was used for relatives,
neighbors, and members of the same religious faith. In turn, the familial idiom was
extended to guilds, confraternities, monasteries, and the military.'[48] Readers of a
1882 novel set in Ottawa would not have been surprised to see the request from
one man to another 'to open his heart and home, to the only child of an old
friend, to father an orphan girl for the sake of "old times," and the happy "long
ago."'[49] When life was uncertain, it behooved all concerned to extend obligations
to as many potential guardians as possible.

In nineteenth-century Canada, many parents, including the relatively well-to-
do, assumed it was appropriate to transfer even their youngest children to other

families as visitors, students, or apprentices or into boarding schools. Elites considered the offspring of others—notably workers and marginalized ethnic and racialized groups—appropriate servants and apprentices in better-off households and suitable candidates for reformatories, orphanages, and industrial schools. While Protestants preferred to place children within other families, believing family instruction was an inspiration for faith, Catholics were more likely to consider residential institutions staffed by nuns and priests as equal or better guarantees of spiritual benefits and ultimately better guardians of youngsters than placing out.[50] Whoever did the choosing and whatever the choice, non-kin residence and congregate living have never been the preserve of any single class. The appearance of commonality contributed to insensitivity and injustice, as children from disadvantaged groups were directed to institutions that their families, unlike those with more power, could not hope to control.

The uncertainties of migration, resettlement, urbanization, and industrialization encouraged the sharing of space, albeit not necessarily equitably, among different constellations of kin and friends in rural and urban areas such as Peel County and the city of Hamilton in nineteenth-century Ontario.[51] These categories often overlapped as relations shifted with time and need.[52] The results could be very positive. As the genteel settler Susanna Moodie observed:

> The system of adopting children in Canada is one of great benevolence, which cannot be too highly eulogized. Many an orphan child, who would be cast utterly friendless upon the world, finds a comfortable home with some good neighbour, and is treated with more consideration, and enjoys greater privileges, than if his own parents had lived. No difference is made between the adopted children and the young ones of the family; it is clothed, boarded, and educated with the same care, and a stranger would find it difficult to determine which was the real, which the transplanted scion of the house.[53]

Early in the twenty-first century, one 'adopted' daughter recalled how noted Canadian poet Ethelwyn Wetherald had given her everything but blood. In 1911, the fifty four year old Wetherald hired a deserted wife with a five-month-old infant to work on her farm. Both soon became part of the spinster's family, and, when the mother returned to the city, the baby remained 'where she will be healthier and you may come back at any time.' The daughter settled in happily with her 'Nan', visiting 'Mama' on holidays, until the latter's premature death. Ethelwyn's sense of what had occurred was revealed when she renamed the toddler Dorothy, meaning 'gift of God'.[54]

The persistent desire for young children, especially by the infertile, whom the Royal Commission on New Reproductive Technologies in the 1990s reckoned to constitute about 7 per cent of all couples at any one time, insured demand for adoptable children in all periods.[55] As Canadians told commissioners, 'infertility is not something that is easy to deal with and move on from, because having children is so firmly embedded in the everyday social and family interactions in which most of us take part.'[56] The celebration of motherhood that flourished in both the nineteenth and twentieth centuries made it especially difficult for women to forego parenting. Sharing children offered one means of affirming femininity. Ironically, the same dogma made it all the more difficult for birth mothers to accept the loss of offspring.[57]

The fact that even relatively young girls and boys might be useful in a frontier economy, whether in Upper Canada, Ontario, or the Prairie West later on, contributed significantly to their welcome. An essentially material calculation fanned the hopes of Anglican John Strachan in York, later Toronto, in 1832, when dealing with cholera orphans: 'We have between two or three hundred children of both sexes and of all ages. . . . Children above 5 may be made immediately useful.' He was relieved to find the colony's residents coming 'forward for the purpose of selecting from among the orphans and fatherless such as might suit them as servants and apprentices.'[58] In contrast, changing sensibilities sharpened by Charles Dickens and other nineteenth-century child-savers, who questioned child labour, were revealed by a late-nineteenth-century English visitor, Catherine Johnstone, who, while also extolling Canadian generosity, acknowledged mistreatment of immigrant boys. In Canada, they might well find not homes but hells.[59] Even the native-born did not escape domestic brutality, as an investigation of Alberta's child welfare practices in 1947 revealed: 'The practice, so popular in Alberta, of placing young boys and girls at farm labour or domestic service under the guise of providing them with family homes, may have the merit of cheap labour in the eyes of the employers, and of cheap care in the eyes of the supporting community but, in the eyes of those whose interest is in the boys and girls, it is child labour and poor child care.'[60]

The immigration of British children, as young as four or five, arranged by Dr Barnardo's, Miss Rye's, and the Quarrier Homes, as well as many other evangelical and imperial groups, beginning in the mid-nineteenth century and concluding in British Columbia with the Fairbridge Farm experiment after the Second World War, testified to a mixture of motives in receiving households. It also recognized the desperate situation of many British families, notably those led by widows. Repeated cases of abuse, suicide, and violence, and changing views about child labour—not to mention Canadian suspicion of imperial authorities ridding themselves of social problems, British anger at exploitation by Canadians, and the Great Depression of the 1930s—eventually ended subsidized child emigration. Its practice, over close to a century, however, reflected commonplace commitment to the idea that youngsters could profitably, at least to others, be moved from natal families.[61]

Although Canadian First Nations and African Canadians have been especially identified with kinship care of girls and boys, relatives and neighbours have regularly served as substitutes for birth parents of all backgrounds when times were tough.[62] In the years before social security, and even later, the addition of youngsters to a family offered the prospect that care-giving and other benefits might be returned to adults in old age. In such relations, fostering, both paid and unpaid, has frequently been little different from adoption. The introduction of subsidized adoptions in the 1970s, like foster placements that might well last throughout childhood, confirmed the common blurring of distinctions. Social workers' advocacy of paid kinship foster care, and child welfare acts that endorsed placement in communities, testified to the wider network of care in which children might well be embedded.[63] Unknown numbers of youngsters have also lived in unofficial foster care arrangements that relied on families known to birth mothers. In 1999, between 1.3 million and 4.3 million American children resided with relatives, most often older women.[64] Such kin care represented 20 to 30 per cent of all fostering in many countries and was on the rise.[65] In Ontario, some 2.5 to 8 per cent of recipients under the provincial mothers' allowances program between 1922 and 1963 resided with other kin.[66] Such responsibility has not been shared equally. In Britain, for example, some 70 per cent of caregivers have been reckoned to be grandmothers and another 20 per cent aunts, and responsibility has been twice as likely to be assumed by maternal, as opposed to paternal relatives.[67]

When authorities struggled to create alternate families, they frequently recognized long-standing preferences of mothers, kin, and communities. In 1982–3, social workers responsible for child welfare in and around Charlottetown were typically relieved to note that offspring of 'long-term multi-problem families have been placed in stable homes of relatives.'[68] In March 1986, Newfoundland and Labrador reimbursed relatives for the care of 846 children, reckoned 'at least . . . an equal number' were unpaid, and counted about 55 'neighbors and friends' as sheltering youngsters.[69] Although the emotional and financial advantages of kin care have been obvious, the possible exploitation of or by caregivers and their possible shortcomings as substitute parents need also to be remembered, especially in conservative cost-cutting times.[70] As in other situations, the idealization of kin ties can offer a handy opportunity for abuse.

Canadians have frequently recalled how kin and community offered respite or permanent care of children. In the 1890s, Ethel Wilson left her South African birthplace to take up residence with a maternal grandmother and aunts in Vancouver, a story that inspired her novel *The Innocent Traveler* (1949). In the 1920s, English girls Sheila and Mary Walker, who lost their father in the First World War and their mother in 1923, were similarly packed off to that Pacific city to live with aunts.[71] The 1976 confession of a Canadian member of Parliament emphasized the value of such solutions. To the applause of his colleagues, he paid tribute to his great aunt for taking him in: 'She did this knowing I was a premature child. . . . I, as an adopted child, owe my adoptive parents a debt of gratitude which I can never pay back, verbally or otherwise, in my lifetime or in all the lifetimes of all the adopted children in the world.'[72]

Despite the invocation of the bonds of kinship and friendship, the costs of such private exchanges could sometimes be considerable in terms of personal humiliation and obligation. Nancy Christie's observation of nineteenth-century Canadian families is true more generally: 'no family member had an intrinsic right to material assistance without some form of reciprocal act.'[73] Misunderstanding and conflict have been common. In October 1902, one Ontario widower brought his toddler to his wife's aunt. When he tried to retrieve his son more than a decade later, the Ontario Supreme Court ordered him to pay $500 for the child's care and education.[74] In 1916, another bereaved husband first surrendered his daughter to a maternal aunt and then, after that relative demanded permanent custody, left the child with friends. In 1923, when he was in better shape and his daughter more self-sufficient, he sought her return but again met opposition from the recipients of his offspring. In 1925, the Saskatchewan Court of Appeal ordered the birth father to pay $1,200 for past support.[75] In 1952, the same court heard a compli-cated story in which a widowed farm labourer tried to get his wealthier sister and brother-in-law to accept his son. For a long time, they were so indifferent that they demanded payment and kept threatening to place their nephew in the local Orange Order orphanage. Sentiment finally triumphed, but not before the father struggled to recover his son from a non-related family who wished to adopt him.[76] In 1959, the court heard an appeal by a woman who wished to revoke her con-sent to adoption. She had given her child to her sister and brother-in-law when they otherwise refused to pay medical and health costs incurred when the daugh-ter fell ill. The mother later married the birth father and desperately wanted to reclaim her four-year-old, but her sister resisted, ultimately unsuccessfully.[77] In 1993, another sister and her husband, this time in Ontario, succeeded in winning judicial support for their adoption of two siblings, and the biological mother was refused access.[78] As these cases demonstrate, transfers within families offered ample opportunity for disagreement.

If kin were usually the first private option to be considered, wider networks were also regularly drawn upon in times of desperation. Montreal journalist Victor Malarek remembered that his parents' violent marriage led to his father giving him away to a friend, a father of four daughters in Lachine, Quebec: 'I had the vague impression he thought I was his to keep.'[79] In 1957, two fathers, one the parent of a murdered daughter and the other of five youngsters he could not support when his marriage broke up, made their own arrangements. The latter agreed to let his young daughter, Christina, take the place of the dead youngster. That seemingly irrepressible birth father was also heard to say of a son: 'Now I must find a home for five-year-old David.'[80]

The variety of private arrangements emerged clearly in the pages of the *Globe and Mail,* when it began to publish its 'Lives Lived' column in 1996. These stories, for the most part of Canadians who had rarely made headlines during their own lifetimes, often movingly communicated the diverse practices that created com-munities of adults and children. In the 1920s, the death of parents within days of each other left four orphans in Blairmore, Alberta. The granddaughter of one cred-ited a 'very strong Masonic Lodge,' 'whose members took on the task of making sure the siblings were cared for and remained together . . . in their own home and hired a housekeeper to care for them.' As she explained, it was 'no wonder' her grandfather became a mason and was 'keenly aware of the importance of com-munity service.' In 1933, Harriet Ethel (Fry) Killins, an Ontario farmwoman, had just seen her own children fly the nest when she and her husband took on a sec-ond family with 'the parenting of a treasured niece and nephew who had been orphaned.' After the Second World War, another beneficiary of kindness designated Reta Ellen Woodward a 'Cabbagetown angel'. This hard-working spinster rose above her own deprived childhood to nurture nine nieces and nephews and pro-

vide 'stability and hope'. One contributor to 'Lives Lived' shared a similar memory of Isabel Strickland, resident of another working-class Toronto district in the
1950s and 1960s. This young widow supplied food and clothing to a growing family next door and, when it collapsed, raised a young girl 'just as though' she 'were
her very own daughter'.[81]

Many families have provided moments of such social parenting. People whose
work, whether paid or unpaid, put them in touch with young people have
appeared particularly likely to provide shelter. My mother regularly gave space on
our living room floor, sometimes for months at a time, to my brother's friends who
had run afoul of birth families. As a teacher, she matter-of-factly cited colleagues,
often spinsters, who took in charges when times were rough. Years later, I knew
social workers who did much the same. In some cases, as with the examples written up in the *Globe and Mail*, close links continued for years. Sometimes, all that
was needed was temporary respite, and youngsters moved on to tackle lives on
their own.

Private initiatives also produced their own horror stories. In 1938, British
Columbia's superintendent of neglected children complained:

> If an unmarried mother does not know where to turn for help, she is apt to
> hand her baby over to the first person who offers and the result is often
> deplorable. The home is not generally bad enough so that the child can be
> removed because of neglect, but is a home which could not be recommended
> for adoption. This year, under the Infants' Act, we managed to remove a beau-
> tiful little girl who three years ago was handed out to a woman who answered
> an advertisement inserted by the mother. The woman was said to be an alco-
> holic and a drug addict, but it was a case upon which it was difficult to get
> evidence. However, with the help of the natural mother, who came from out-
> side the province at our request, we were able to have the child removed, and
> hope to place her in a good adoption home.

In 1941, he once again lamented the efforts of unwed mothers:

> Many of these placements are the most difficult we have to deal with, both
> because of the child's background and the history of the adopting parents, and
> because the mother knows where the child is and is apt to interfere. One case,
> in which we are still trying to find a solution, is one where an unstable mother
> placed her child with the people for whom she worked. Every few weeks she
> changes her mind as to whether she wants the child adopted.... Even should
> the adoption be completed legally, the adopting parents' home can never offer
> the child complete security because of the fact that the natural mother knows
> where the child is and is just unstable enough to keep upsetting the child's
> loyalties from time to time.[82]

Poor outcomes regularly caught the attention of the press and judiciary. In 1943,
Maclean's told the story of thirteen-year-old Ned, who was facing court charges.

'An orphan, he would stay first with one set of relatives and then with another—none of them interested in his welfare.' Eventually he was sent to a reformatory but upon release re-offended.[83] In October and December 1960, the *Vancouver Sun* profiled other perils of private transactions. A North Surrey couple facing hard times had, in writing, given their daughter away a year earlier. Although admitting the merits of the new mother and father, they demanded her relinquishment. Other biological parents who had similarly surrendered '3 year old Tammy' to a building contractor and his wife proved unable to retrieve her, even when the recipients planned a move to Nova Scotia.[84] Such arguments might well end up in the courts. In 1973, Ontario's High Court heard a sad case that involved charges and counter-charges of immorality, including alcoholism, abortions, infidelity, and adultery. Ultimately a mother who had surrendered her daughter, as she claimed, on the understanding that it was only temporary, retrieved her from would-be parents who moved some seven times in two to three years to avoid detection.[85]

The long history of such conflicts encouraged modern states to regulate the traffic in children and many modern adopters to desire secrecy and confidentiality. The Division of Child Welfare in Newfoundland understood commonplace fears when it noted, 'We have found reluctance on the part of prospective adopters because they think that if they take a child for possible adoption the child may later know who the parents were, or the natural parents will know who the adopters were. We can give absolute assurance that there is no grounds for alarm on that score.'[86] The resurfacing of past families supplied a recurring nightmare to those who wished fresh starts.

With the passage of adoption laws, authorities soon discovered that birth parents, especially mothers, persisted in efforts to control offspring's future. They regularly aspired to turn the legislation to their advantage. Many women tried to incorporate previous offspring legally into new marriages. In Saskatchewan in 1947–8, the director of child welfare noted that 257 of 720 children were privately placed for adoption, many to the natural parent, commonly the mother.[87] Step-parent applications by new husbands and birth mothers quickly constituted a significant and rising proportion of adoptions across the country after 1945. Court records are filled with birth mothers who went on to wed and then attempted to recover children from agencies and foster families.[88] As the nineteenth-century records recovered by Peter Gossage remind us, however, blended families had their own full share and more of domestic conflict. Later observers have come to similar conclusions about step-families resulting after divorce. One adoption expert condemned the proclivity not to investigate agreements involving step-parents. In fact, in his mind, they required particularly careful scrutiny, as they 'pose subtle problems of the social dynamics within a family. . . . The welfare of the child does not necessarily coincide with the wishes of the adult members to assert ties with him.'[89] In particular, mothers' frequent wish to cement relations with new male partners was not always best for youngsters, who thereby might lose important connections to paternal blood kin.

The assumption of rights to allocate children as they saw fit and without resort to authorities was not limited to birth kin. Children chosen by others might also be reassigned. Such was the case, for example, with a girl born in 1942 who, with her older brother, was adopted from Nova Scotia's Ideal Maternity Home by an older couple whom they would address as grandparents. When that couple died, their daughter took the boy and their grandson and his wife took the girl. In neither case was there legal sanction.[90] Newfoundland welfare authorities were typical of those across the country in reporting in 1946 that, despite adoption legislation, 'there is ample evidence that the prevailing idea in many places is that no legal procedure is necessary for children to be adopted, and we frequently hear of boys and girls having been "given" to others without any ceremony or on the authority of mere slips of paper.'[91]

Custom Adoption

The persisting informality of many arrangements to shift children from one household to another in all parts of the country in all periods sometimes appears much like the customary adoption that has been especially identified with Aboriginal communities. That practice has been commonly described, in benign terms, as widespread, voluntary, reciprocal, public, and open-ended in the sense that relations may well evolve over time. As the numerous tales of white captives and coureurs-de-bois living with bands early in Canada's history suggest, the first stages of European–Native contact often involved forms of adoption. The twentieth-century cases of the inclusion of a Jewish black youngster in a Quebec Mohawk community, another boy of European descent at Ontario's Six Nations territory, and a white female toddler in a BC Native family evoked long-standing connections that have shaped many Aboriginal populations.[92] In the last decades of the twentieth century, customary adoptions usually involved at least one birth parent who was Aboriginal. When their bands were functioning well, First Nations mothers could often anticipate that a relative or neighbour would welcome progeny they could not rear.

Transfers among Aboriginal households could well be significant. In 1921–2, in the tiny eastern Arctic community of Repulse Bay, 44 per cent of children were adopted, and close kin were 'preferred as adoptive parents in part because the Inuit believe that they will treat adopted children better.'[93] In 1939, Blood Reserve households in southern Alberta 'always' seemed to include 'a relative or his family'. Adopted children were singled out as 'exceptionally well-treated', as such Sioux adopters hoped 'he will be especially grateful to those who gave him a good home.'[94] On Baffin Island, during the years 1965–9, the rate of adoption in Pangnirtun was 12 per cent for male infants and 8 per cent for female; at Frobisher Bay it was 20 per cent and 22 per cent respectively.[95]

As in non-Aboriginal communities, poverty frequently forced relinquishment. Typically, in 1968, most of the eleven residents of Old Crow in Yukon who had been added to other families from the 1880s to the 1950s had lost parents or experienced extreme deprivation.[96] Cultural forces were also at work. One study from the Northwest Coast pointed to community values that held it 'terrible for people to be without children. They wouldn't think of leaving grandparents without some young children around.'[97] Relations could be affectionate but practical: additional youngsters might provide key support in old age. The ties could be intense. One Aboriginal lawyer described how, at the end of the twentieth century, friends had given his grandparents their infant son when the mother was very ill. When his birth parents tried to retrieve him at age four, 'he threw a prolonged tantrum' and won the right to stay. Such behaviour was counted 'not unusual as it is a cultural norm for children to have great influence in the decision making process.'[98]

Only in 1961 did Canadian courts begin to recognize the legitimacy of Aboriginal custom adoption, with the Inuit case *Re Katie's Adoption Petition*. In Yukon and the Northwest Territories, modern adoption practices that required official investigation, formal records, and confidentiality had proved especially unworkable. Territorial judges found themselves dealing with a backlog of hundreds of customary Inuit adoptions for which they issued 'declaratory judgments on circuit'.[99] The 1969 decision *Re Indian Custom Adoptions, Re Beaulieu's Petition for Dogrib* extended the same recognition to long-standing Indian practices. Strategies to accommodate different approaches to custody were not, however, always self-evident. In 1972, the courts had to deal with the case *Re Deborah 14-789*, where Inuit birth parents attempted to recover a daughter traditionally adopted. The judges ruled against them, arguing that 'revocation was not part of custom'.[100] Other decisions extended old principles, as with *Re Wah-Shee* (1975), which allowed a white woman and her treaty status husband to employ custom adoption. After 1982, the new Constitution with its declared protection of existing Aboriginal rights increasingly made customary adoption the equivalent of state procedures.

Exchanges made by Aboriginal families often seem quite similar to those found in many other communities. Anna Davin's *Growing Up Poor: Home, School, and Street in London, 1870–1914* (1996) provides a good comparison. Households encountering hardship in Britain's capital welcomed babies even when they were economic liabilities. While English authorities, much like critics of Native practices, condemned 'indulgent' childrearing, 'infants were petted, cuddled and indulged.' And since households, even when they pooled resources, might lack beds and baby carriages, children 'were continually held', slept communally, and had little privacy, precisely the shortcomings believed to damage Native communities. Also similar was the observation that spoiling was soon enough superseded by the stress on 'self-sufficiency and co-operation', as 'hard-working mothers could not give their children constant attention and care.' In much the same way too, deaths, illness, and hard times sent girls and boys elsewhere. When the 'crisis was chronic', kin and neighbours might well prove insufficient, and the workhouse loomed for those in the metropolis on the Thames.[101]

The situation for Scotland's urban and rural working class invokes much the same story, although the cold prospect of Poor Law institutions in England was replaced by an elaborate system of placing out or fostering that saw apprehended youngsters shipped off to households often only slightly better off than their own and many miles away in remote areas. Straitened resources, personal histories, and individual temperament might well limit generosity. In this context, as Lynn

Abrams notes, the 'image of the caring, close-knit community where children were treated as everyone's responsibility can be taken too literally.'[102] Fostered children in Scotland, as in Canada, were likely to be especially vulnerable when work was heavy and alternatives limited. They, and those around them, knew the difference between their situation and that of blood kin.

As the long history of informal assistance and private exchanges suggests, there were often 'deep wells of support for self-help within the working class itself.' The poor in Canada, like their counterparts across the seas, had frequently to make a virtue of necessity. As one Newfoundland observer has concluded, 'there was also a populist anti-statism which emphasized the importance of self-help as a means by which working people could maintain their independence both from the state, and from the fickle and degrading charity of others.'[103]

Institutional Options

The often limited capacity and willingness of kin and neighbours to take on additional duties has meant that institutions regularly played a role in allocating youngsters. The early days of newcomer settlement brought the establishment of orphanages for 'deserving' youngsters, which overwhelmingly meant those of European origin. Where the Poor Law reigned, as in the Maritimes, girls and boys might well be consigned to omnibus institutions alongside the poor and ill of all ages and conditions. If they survived, they might face auctioning off to the lowest bidder who would remove them from the books of the municipality for labour in fields or residences. Between 1832 and 1847, Halifax's Poor Law Asylum bound out, or apprenticed, some three hundred youngsters.[104] In Upper Canada, later Canada West, apprenticeships were the only legislative provision for poor and orphaned children from 1799 to 1851. 'In general, then, child servants in the late eighteenth and the early nineteenth centuries were orphaned, abandoned, or poor children who were apprenticed by parents, guardians, or magistrates in order to provide for the maintenance of the child.'[105] Essentially a business deal, apprenticeships offered limited protection. Rights might be transferred yet again to others without further permission of original guardians. By the mid-nineteenth century, obvious shortcomings, together with a shift in sensibilities that increasingly justified the segregation of children from adults, at least in their early years, encouraged institutional experiments.

Middle-class and often deeply religious founders of early childcare institutions were driven generally by two sets of impulses regarding needy children and their birth families. On the one hand, they assumed that some adults were simply unsuitable parents, unable to raise healthy, moral, and industrious offspring. Such reprobates deserved to be deprived of daughters and sons. On the other, they recognized that whatever the merits of mothers and fathers, children sometimes simply could not be supported for shorter or longer periods of time. Respite care might well be justified. These perspectives required that distinctions be made between the deserving and the undeserving poor, but frequently this proved impossible. When Ontario legislation provided for 'neglected, dependent, and delinquent children' in 1893, the categories were far from clear-cut. Recurring ill health, unemployment, and poverty regularly made such subtleties difficult to determine in any time period.

Institutional initiatives were far from monolithic. They ranged from impressive edifices that dominated rural and urban landscapes to 'a home for little boys' run 'by the family of a deceased physician—the Misses Cole of Clinton.'[106] Historians Patricia Rooke and Rudy Schnell have set out the variety of Canadian institutions that began with the Halifax Orphans' Home in 1752 and extended to most cities and towns in the emerging nation as it struggled to address adversities that frequently shattered families. While these scholars saw much to praise in the initiatives of early founders and particularly in small residences, they were generally critical of their evolution: 'Orphan asylums were frequently overcrowded institutions operating on limited funds and . . . were selective in their admission policies. Bastard children were frequently prohibited from them just as were infants, epileptics, defectives, and delinquents.'[107]

High mortality rates, which sometimes shot up well above 50 per cent for babies, casual and deliberate brutality, and unrelenting demands for conformity were typical charges against institutions. Many early child-savers, such as J.J. Kelso, Ontario's first superintendent of neglected, dependent, and delinquent children,[108] and the social workers who succeeded them identified such problems as they turned to fostering and adoption for remedies. Investigations by child welfare professionals, as with studies of Toronto's last remaining orphanage, the Neil McNeil Home, were overwhelmingly negative.[109] Still later studies of the institutional abuse of children at Mount Cashel in St John's, the elite Upper Canada College in Toronto, Coombe Orphanage in Hespeler, Ontario, and Vancouver's Jericho School for the Deaf, not to mention horrific stories emerging from Native residential schools, merely confirmed a bad reputation.[110]

Child welfare experts have, however, also regularly pointed out that institutions may be preferable for some children, notably teenagers or those whose needs, physical or psychological, could not be readily accommodated in household settings. Residential treatment programs and group homes may well meet both short- and long-term exigencies. Historians are also revisiting the past to re-examine institutions. In Canada, Bettina Bradbury began the reassessment with her revelation of the flexibility of Montreal orphanages that offered the poor one way of dealing with disaster and preserving parent–child relations.[111] The story she told has been extended to other sites. One of the earliest congregate experiments was the Protestant Asylum of Montreal, established by the Montreal Ladies' Benevolent Society in 1822. Although founders tried to impose their will on clients, refusing those they considered intemperate or dishonest and retaining inmates longer than parents wanted, many city-dwellers, with limited kin and neighbourhood ties, used the asylum to tide them over hard times. They demanded access to and retrieval of offspring when they deemed it fit. While the female directors may have 'never developed a real affinity with the women of the poor', they slowly reconsidered policies, including apprenticeship and adoption that entailed sharper breaks with blood kin. Themselves mothers of offspring who were regularly sent to elite residential schools, the directors assumed institutional care had real merits. Eventually, shocked by the abuse of those they fostered out, they preferred to train boys and girls themselves and thus guarantee a minimum standard of care. They came to conclude that even 'undeserving' parents sometimes merited support and that children should be returned unless they faced a substantial threat.[112]

Across the country, similar institutions negotiated a range of services, with some permitting adoption and apprenticeship and others determined to keep children until they left to work on their own or rejoin families. The Toronto Boys' Home, founded in 1859, saw its female managers endeavouring to affirm parental responsibilities and families to assert claims.[113] So did Vancouver's Alexandra Orphanage, established in 1892, which Diane Purvey has concluded 'was an adequate, temporary familial substitute'.[114] The Charlottetown orphanage, run by the Sisters of St Martha, was also typical: in the latter half of the 1930s, the majority of its children had at least one living parent, and some 19.5 per cent of inmates were returned to relatives.[115] In 1965, Mount St Mary's Orphanage in Halifax operated for ten months a year, and was 'generally regarded as a boarding school more than as a child welfare institution.'[116]

Residential institutions that emerged to meet the needs of particular communities may have identified especially closely with those they admitted. Nova Scotia's Home for Coloured Children represented the long-standing tradition of self-help in the face of endemic racism. When the Halifax Explosion shattered many black families in the city's North End in 1917, founders responded with a farm-based residence that resembled many others. It was unusual only in that it addressed the needs of black children not only from Halifax but all across Canada.[117] Defying external denigration and prejudice, Jewish orphanages in Winnipeg, Montreal, and Toronto have also been credited with creating supportive environments for inmates.[118] Special provision was also arranged for orphans and half-orphans of men serving overseas during the First World War, but a rare account notes that the general community's sense of obligation to these children did not last very long.[119]

Churches have often played a key role in caring for girls and boys. This was most obviously demonstrated in their administration of orphanages and residential schools, but they also had a long history in placing individual children in new families. In 1832, a Methodist periodical, the *Christian Guardian*, matter of factly requested donations to the Society for the Relief of Widows and Orphans in order, among other matters, to 'procure places for the children, either binding them to trades or as domestics in families.'[120] Such periodicals also discretely advertised for homes for respectable children. In 1896, the same magazine set before its readers 'a good opportunity' for an 'orphan female child in a respectable agricultural family, the heads being members of the Methodist Church.'[121] Later on, in 1913, 1914, and 1917, respectively, high hopes for good parents were held out, in turn, for a six-year-old 'ruddy-faced, bright English lad, of good parentage,' for a seven-year-old 'clever, healthy, well-born and well-bred little boy,' and for an 'exceptionally bright boy of four years old, temporarily with friends but otherwise quite destitute.'[122] Whether their situations proved as happy as those promised by one ad from the Anglican *Canadian Churchman* reading, 'Wanted to Adopt or raise, in a clergyman's home in Southern Ontario, child, aged from one to four years, as companion to his own boy. Parentage of child must be vouched for by clergy or other responsible party, as to moral character and health,' or another ad searching for baby girl to age two, with 'good parentage, and healthy' for a 'clergyman's home, no other children' is, of course, unknown.[123]

Parents' membership in fraternal societies sometimes also promised to improve children's options.[124] The Independent Order of Foresters (IOF) operated a number of orphanages for members, including Forester's Island, founded by the Mohawk doctor and IOF president Peter Martin (Oronhyatakhe) in Deseronto, Ontario.[125] It also ran a residence in Oakville, outside of Toronto. Set in farm acreage, it offered dorms to both sexes and required both to work, outside for boys and inside for girls. In 1920, conscious of the rising condemnation of institutions, it claimed 'to preserve the children's self-respect, to make them feel that they are natural, normal citizens.' Unlike many of their predecessors and some of their contemporaries, the Oakville residence dispensed with uniforms and enrolled children in public schools. Like Montreal's Protestant orphanage, the IOF resisted adoption and fostering. Instead it offered sponsorship by a 'court of Foresters, who write to him regularly, send him presents at Christmas time and on his birthday and sometimes take a little monthly collection for him.' The Foresters also initiated pensions for fatherless families so they might not have to be broken up.[126]

The internationalism of many fraternal societies sometimes required children to leave Canada. Mooseheart, the orphan city founded by the Loyal Order of the Moose took in Canadian and American children as well as their mothers, who were expected to provide cheap labour as housemothers, secretaries, nurses, and laundresses. In 1958, the widow and eight children of a Sudbury plumber joined an estimated fifty-six mothers and children from Canada at the institution in Illinois.[127] Like other dependants of the fraternal body, they were promised shelter, food, clothing, and educational scholarships. In 1930, it was estimated that more 34 per cent of male and female graduates of Mooseheart high schools went to college, compared with 7.6 per cent of US males and 4.8 per cent of females.[128] Special as Mooseheart and its counterparts might have been, they shared a singular virtue with other institutions. As one American historian has concluded, the great appeal was that parents did not fear them 'as rivals for their children's affections'.[129]

Whatever their shortcomings, orphanages may have been among the least pernicious of institutions sheltering children. Canadian parents have sometimes consigned offspring to reformatories and industrial and residential schools of varying quality. When children proved incorrigible, they might well find mothers and fathers, or other guardians, approaching the judiciary, especially after juvenile and family courts began to appear early in the twentieth century. This avenue promised at least some hope of respite, especially from the strain of dealing with adolescents. The judicial system might force respectability and obedience on unruly youngsters.[130] Children were also hauled before the bench without their parents' consent, and youthful behaviours that might once have escaped notice were likely to become increasingly criminalized in the twentieth century. In any case, many boys and girls tagged as delinquent frequently differed little from those identified as neglected and dependent in orphanages. They too might well have families in trouble, unable to muster the economic and emotional resources to cope.

The experience of Indian residential schools is both the same and different. They began as industrial schools, which, like those of the same name dealing with settler children, were part of a continuum of disciplinary institutions to enforce habits of labour, sobriety, and obedience on suspect populations. Native children might be regarded as savages, but so too were the Irish and many immigrants who came to Canada. The rising tide of scientific racism, however, increasingly targeted Aboriginal children. The missionary ambitions of Protestant denominations and the Catholic Church coincided with the dreams of Ottawa bureaucrats such as Duncan Campbell Scott and the interests of newcomers eager for Native land to create an unmatched host of 'total' institutions. By the 1880s, residential schools became European Canada's instrument of choice to remake Aboriginal children and to erase their distinctive cultures. Native languages, spirituality, and dress were to disappear in the creation of new beings, suitable candidates, as were their working-class counterparts in orphanages and reformatories, for domestic service in the case of girls and for agricultural labour in the case of boys. The fervour of the assault on Native children was all the greater because empathy was less likely, and the threat of the increasingly racialized other was viewed as more egregious. Perhaps guilt at a massive land grab had something to do with it as well.[131]

Like other parents, Native mothers and fathers tried to influence institutional behaviours. They complained loudly to Indian Affairs, principals, and teachers about poor instruction and brutal treatment. They withdrew and hid children. Because Native communities and parents might well live at a considerable distance from the schools and lack resources, such efforts could not deal with the scope of abuse. Also damaging was the fact that children who were already neglected and abused, as least as defined by Indian agents, were specially targeted for residential schools.[132] A 1953 survey designated 4,313 of 10,112 inmates as welfare cases.[133] Another assessment in the next decade concluded that 'many neglected children of school age are still sent to residential schools owing to the absence of proper child care services in the provinces.'[134] One head teacher of a Yukon residential school remembered that

> the staff knows that many children are welfare cases and has heard lurid tales of drunkenness, sexual promiscuity, and family neglect about various parents. No records are available to show which parents are in such categories and which have children in the school simply because the family home is remote. The staff therefore tends to assume that the visitor is of the dissolute category and is not expected to accord the visitor the same respect that a non-Indian parent might expect during a visit to a regular public school.[135]

Yet even as prejudice exacerbated the distress of Aboriginal boys and girls, their plight was ultimately perfectly consistent with, if an exaggeration of, the patterns employed with other 'suspect' populations.

Residential schools, like orphanages, survived well into the twentieth century but belatedly succumbed to changing sensibilities about the appropriate care for marginalized children. Slowly and uncertainly, especially in the case of First Nations and other racialized women, the state stepped in, first with mothers' pensions and allowances and then with a limited range of provincial and federal initiatives to support poor parents to raise their children at home. This funding kept many children out of institutions, even if rarely offered real comfort. Many Canadian orphanages, such as the Victoria's Cridge Centre for the Family,[136] like those in the United States, re-emerged as agencies dealing with short-term placements or specializing in children with special psychological and physical needs.

The Move to Fostering and Adoption

While at the end of the twentieth century there was some effort, at least in the United States, to revive orphanages as solutions to a widely recognized crisis in child welfare, not to mention the supposed excess fertility of African Americans,[137] advocates of placement in substitute families had largely won the day. The fostering initiatives celebrated by children's aid societies, which began to appear first in the 1890s in Ontario and then in Nova Scotia, Manitoba, and British Columbia, and their state and private counterparts in various jurisdictions, drew on traditions that had long placed children, immigrant and otherwise, in individual households. They were strengthened by the concurrent growing romanticization of the nuclear family.

While early fostering and adoption practices took child labour for granted, its growing unacceptability to modern sensibilities meant other inducements were required to secure responsible adults. Frugal and optimistic child welfare authorities more and more emphasized the emotional and psychological benefits of adding girls and boys to households. Children were to cross the thresholds of non-kin not so much to toil as to be loved and to love. In his opening report as Ontario's superintendent of neglected, dependent, and delinquent children in 1893, J.J. Kelso, an outspoken champion of the move to family placements, conveyed shifting motives:

> There must, in this Province, be numerous cases where children, having grown up, have married and secured homes of their own, or have gone into the world to do for themselves, leaving the old homestead childless and lonely, and where well selected children would be welcomed for their bright and gladdening presence and influence in the depleted family circle. Many homes have been blessed with children who have been removed by premature death, and others have never been brightened by their presence. . . . [In new homes, children would] progress towards independent, useful and honourable citizenship. . . . The system contemplates the gradual absorption by the community of the neglected and dependent children of the State.

Newcomers would provide companionship and pleasure and, it was understood, perform tasks that might otherwise be taken on by blood kin. Kelso always preferred free homes: children as sources of labour—albeit less so than in the past—and as objects of affection paid their own way.[138]

Kelso's efforts and those of his successors soon confronted the harsh reality that many families had difficulty enough feeding and housing their own offspring and that more prosperous householders were not easily convinced to extend hospitality to those they often considered inferior and potentially dangerous. Only when the respectable working class was able to keep wives and mothers at home in the male-breadwinner family and to afford larger premises did more potential foster parents emerge.[139] Even then, social workers, desperate throughout the twentieth century to extend recruitment, soon recognized that payment for these children was almost always essential. Working-class women learned to incorporate duties for paid fostering into the cluster of remunerated and non-remunerated tasks necessary to maintain households. When the male-breadwinner ideal faltered in the last decades of the twentieth century—it had never embraced the majority of workers—and more and more wives took waged employments, candidates for foster parenting became still harder to find. Stay-at-home women willing to accept especially troubled or disabled children were especially rare, underscoring the continuing need for child welfare institutions.

Yet, for all the potential of orphanages and other group homes for kin reunification and specialized treatment, they have not matched the appeal of substitute kin. Not only have institutions had obvious shortcomings, especially for young children, but fostering and adoption promised solutions that were both attractively frugal and culturally consistent with long-standing practices and the modern romanticization of the nuclear family. To advocates, legal adoption's promise of permanent solutions also appeared better than the uncertainties of fostering, while at the same time saving the scant funds allocated to child welfare.

As this chapter has demonstrated, Canadians have always explored a wide range of solutions to the problems of childrearing. Traditions of informal arrivals and departures in families, as in the nation itself, have never disappeared. Yet modern-minded Canadians have been increasingly concerned about the fate of children in unsupervised exchanges. Those fears combined with persisting faith in the nuclear family to generate support for legal adoption. As they made their way into strange homes, children surrendered by less fortunate families and countries faced increasing regulation over the course of the late nineteenth and twentieth centuries. Just as they increasingly marshalled bureaucracies to more tightly supervise migration and citizenship rights and obligations in the same years, modern-minded Canadian authorities set out to govern the exchange of children. New rules and supervisors promised to guarantee social security, stability, and well-being as they set the terms of admission to new households. What such hopes meant for all members of the adoptive circle was, however, far from certain. The next chapters consider just how adoption evolved in the context of the long history of negotiation about provision for children who could not remain with birth parents.

Setting the Rules: Adoption and the Law

In 1873, New Brunswick inaugurated the long, slow, and conflicted process by which provinces, territories, and the colony, later province, of Newfoundland tried to regulate the permanent transfer of children. Although practice might well differ, legislation was one way Canadians, and the Newfoundlanders who entered Confederation in 1949, struggled to negotiate the maze that one late-twentieth-century judge of Alberta's Court of Appeal called the 'multitude of circumstances that give rise to the desire and need to adopt children: the ravages of war, the need of intergenerational support, the need to provide security and nurture for abused, abandoned and neglected children, and the strong desire for children in those who are childless.'[1] Even as Canadians continued to assert private rights to determine the fate of girls and boys, legislatures and assemblies attempted to put their stamp on domestic relations. Over more than a century and a quarter, the legislative record of provinces and territories—which constitutionally have responsibility for child welfare and family law—reveals key trends in official thinking about the appropriate relations of youngsters, birth parents, prospective adopters, and the communities they represented.

This chapter considers that history in four parts. The first takes up the early concerns that preoccupied political decision-makers from 1873 to the passage of Ontario's Adoption Act of 1927, which has generally been considered the single most influential piece of early legislation. The second section considers provinces' and the colony of Newfoundland's expanding efforts to regulate the behaviour of birth and adoptive parents from 1927 to 1945 and the gradual convergence of much legislation. The end of the Second World War encouraged a renewed familialism. That spirit, essentially optimistic in its assessment of the possibilities of integrating racial and other strangers into mainstream families, informed much legislation from 1945 to 1970, the year that provided the twentieth century's highpoint in domestic adoptions. The last section reviews the years from 1970 to the mid-1990s, when the reports of the Royal Commission on New Reproductive Technologies (1992) and the Royal Commission on Aboriginal Peoples (1996) signalled key issues in end-of-the-century adoption debates.

Pioneering, 1873–1927

Six years after Confederation and twenty-two years after Massachusetts passed the first modern adoption legislation in North America, New Brunswick quietly pioneered adoption law in Canada. Hardly anyone noticed at the time, and its initiative has often been forgotten. In 1929, the *Report of the New Brunswick Child Welfare Survey* erroneously concluded that the province was 'entirely without adoption legislation similar to what is in force in Great Britain and other Canadian Provinces' and claimed that 'scores of so-called "adopted children" are scattered throughout the Province today, with no stronger legal claim or position than that established by these legal contracts of adoption.' It strongly recommended a 'simple and workable' adoption act.[2]

That is probably what legislators believed they had supplied decades earlier in their Act Relating to the Adoption of Children (1873). Like the majority of later enactments, this law allowed application from unmarried persons or married couples, required the consent of children at age twelve and of birth parents, if not 'hopelessly insane' or divorced and without custody, and provided for change of surname. Judges were required to satisfy themselves that petitioners could 'bring up and educate the child properly, and of the fitness and propriety of such adoption.' The custody and obedience of children was transferred to the adopters, 'as if they had been the natural parents.' Rights of inheritance recognized a dual orientation. Adoptees could inherit from adopters but not from other new kin. They continued to inherit from 'natural' parents and relatives. If adoptees died under age or intestate, property received from the adopters would return to that family and goods from the 'natural' kin would return to them as if no such adoption had 'taken place'.[3] In 1903, New Brunswick amended its legislation to eliminate the need for consent if guardians or parents had deserted or neglected the child and emphasized that no consent was required from 'the putative father of an illegitimate child'.[4]

In 1896, the Nova Scotia legislature responded with an Act Respecting the Adoption of Children. Local newspapers, preoccupied with the ongoing crisis of the Conservative succession to deceased prime minister John A. Macdonald in Ottawa, paid little attention. The sponsor, twenty-eight-year-old barrister Henry Wickwire, explained that the measure was sparked by his clients' frequent request for legal adoptions and the need for a 'simple and inexpensive procedure'.[5] The bill quickly passed in a session that the *Halifax Chronicle* reckoned as possessing 'no disturbing questions'.[6] Time had, however, not stood still since 1873. The 1896 legislation was considerably more elaborate. While both single persons and couples could adopt, they had to be at least twenty-one years old. Adoptees had to be younger and not a wife, husband, brother, sister, uncle, or aunt, of the whole or half blood, of the prospective parent. At age fourteen, children had to give consent, as did their spouses, if any. So too did 'natural' parents or, should children be illegitimate, mothers. No consent was necessary by persons deemed insane, facing more than three years of imprisonment, having allowed offspring to be supported by charities for more than two years 'or as a pauper', or having 'been convicted of being a common night walker, or a lewd, wanton and lascivious person.' The court had to find that petitioners had 'sufficient ability to bring up the child and to furnish suitable nurture and education, and that it is proper that such adoption should take place.' As in New Brunswick, children could inherit from adopters and their descendants but from no collateral kin. More particularly, in 1896, adoptees could not inherit as if 'born in lawful wedlock to the adopting parent unless it plainly appears to have been the intention of those making legal provision and settlement.' The right to inherit from the 'natural' family affirmed old ties, as did continuing prohibitions regarding incest and marriage. These early provisions in New Brunswick and Nova Scotia also invoked pervasive notions of respectable parenting. Whatever their relations with youngsters, the poorest Canadians would have greatest difficulty measuring up either as birth or adoptive parents.

Their disadvantage did not go entirely unrecognized. Unlike the New Brunswick model, Nova Scotia provided for appeals within one year of the court decision.[7] In 1901, an amendment also specified that 'natural' parents had twelve months to revoke consent if it had been 'obtained by fraud, duress or oppressive or unfair means of any kind, or that the person signing such consent did not do so of his own free will, or did not, at the time of signing the same, clearly understand the full effect and purport thereof.'[8] This amendment was far from insignificant, as it introduced the issue that would bedevil twentieth-century courts and legislatures: what constitutes 'free will' and 'understanding' when children are surrendered? Birth parents and adopters might well have very different opinions.

This early legislation also stood out in several other respects. First, it apparently attracted relatively little attention. Residents of both provinces, particularly one suspects the less well-to-do, continued to exchange girls and boys much as before. Second, the capacity to parent was not restricted to married couples. Spinsters and bachelors, widows and widowers, could make claims here, just as they often did in unmediated family exchanges and would continue to do in the vast majority of legislation to follow. Third, children were only imperfectly separated from former allegiances that, as the references to neglect, imprisonment, insanity, and other forms of aberrancy implied, were commonly associated with surrendering adults. While individuals and couples might take suspect newcomers to the family bosom, they could not burden blood kindred with additional legal heirs. Fears of a different sort also sustained blood ties. Children could not be stripped of rights to inheritance, and others thereby gain, through their surrender to other families.

Despite the legislative initiatives of New Brunswick and Nova Scotia, provisions for the transfer of Canadian children before the First World War were more likely to be in line with the provision for 'indenture or other instrument in writing', whereby parents consigned responsibilities for their children to others, that Manitoba enacted in 1877.[9] Economic concerns typically infused the same province's Infants' Act of 1897 and Alberta's 'Infants' Act of 1913. Manitoba authorized youngsters to be transferred by indenture to 'any respectable, trustworthy person' who 'in writing doth assume the duty of a parent towards the child.' Boys were to consent at age fourteen and girls at age twelve.[10] Alberta's act affirmed the commonplace permission to both single persons and couples to adopt and adoptees' inheritance from blood kin but not from the kindred of adopters. At age ten, that province's children were deemed able to give consent. Fathers' authority was spelled out as superior to mothers' in decisions about custody and education. Women alone lost parental rights when convicted of adultery.

In 1913, and for some time, Alberta legislators made specific provision for 'Dividends of Infant's Stock or Proceeds Thereof,' a concern forever unique to wild rose country.

If stock or capital preoccupied some westerners, Prince Edward Island's passage of an Act Regarding the Adoption of Children in 1916 hearkened back to long-standing concerns with labour. Parents or next of kin could assign all rights to a child to a third party. A written agreement could bind boys until age twenty-one and unmarried girls to the same age. Charitable institutions holding guardianship could contract out youngsters, 'notwithstanding any defect in form or substance' of such transfers. Anyone harbouring or encouraging a child to leave 'the employ of any such guardian' could be fined.[11] The resemblance to indenture agreements was clear: in the minds of largely rural legislators, disadvantaged youngsters remained first and foremost labourers.

Recourse to old assumptions was, however, increasingly uncertain. The Great War altered many lives, generating both orphans and mothers and fathers who mourned casualties. As Suzanne Morton has aptly demonstrated in her discussion of appeals by would-be parents for young survivors of the 1917 Halifax Explosion, adoption offered one solution to family and national losses.[12] Just as significantly, the war helped trigger a succession of suffrage victories that promised women of European origin in particular new authority in public politics. Their early agendas included more child-centred laws. Ultimately, youngsters were to become the heirs of the brave new world promised by the sacrifices of Flanders Fields.

Postwar legislators, including the first elected women, hurried to usher in better times. Provincial mothers' pensions or allowances, initiated during the war, expanded in the 1920s and 1930s. Embodying in many ways the more progressive postwar spirit, they promised respectable single mothers, for the most part widows, unprecedented support. Their offspring need not so often face the cold prospect of orphanages, Poor Law institutions, and premature labour.[13] Occasionally, as with Saskatchewan in 1926, legislators also provided for spinsters or widows, who, as relatives or other 'suitable' persons, were supporting orphans.[14] But if pioneer social workers, many legislators, and much of the electorate favoured, at least in principle, preserving original families, there was also considerable enthusiasm for fresh starts, not to mention punishing the poor. As the interwar decades' recurring interest in eugenics legislation suggested,[15] some parents were simply viewed as unfit. At the same time, a surging faith in the influence of environment, expressed in the behaviouralism of much childrearing literature and the steady fascination with the Dionne quintuplets, who were removed from their own poor, rural family in the 1930s, kept hopes high for transplanted offspring.[16] Adoption exemplified the fresh start that many Canadians hoped for after 1918.

New or amended adoption and child welfare legislation appeared across the nation. British Columbia's Act Respecting the Adoption of Children (1920), Ontario's 1921 and Saskatchewan's 1922 acts of the same name, Manitoba's Act Respecting the Welfare of Children (1922), and Newfoundland's Act for the Protection of Neglected, Dependent, and Delinquent Children (1922), together with amendments in Nova Scotia and Alberta, revealed the dominant views about the

proper deposition of youngsters whose birth parents were unable to care for them.

Certain provisions remained, notably the eligibility of single persons and couples, restrictions on inheritance from adoptive kindred, continuing inheritance from birth families, provision for change of name, and the elimination of otherwise required consents from birth parents or guardians deemed unworthy. Some shifts in these years reflected women's new power at the polls. Alberta, home of the suffragists who would become the 'Famous Five', conferred equal parental rights on women in 1920. Yet, an equally long-standing convention went unquestioned; that province's revised Infants' Act legally required religious matching of adopter and adoptee, a condition that was commonplace across the country into the 1960s and beyond. In contrast, other aspects of personal histories might disappear. In 1921, British Columbia provided for a 'certificate of adoption,' that 'retroactively legalized former agreements to transfer children, and prohibited mention of illegitimacy.' The concealment of bastardy was a progressive step in a period when such status regularly conferred shame and humiliation.[17] The continuing plight of such youngsters' mothers was further suggested in British Columbia's 1922 amendment that set aside the need for consent from unwed mothers who could not be located.

Birth parents who had surrendered children to charities or the state were, for the most part, in the same position as disappearing birth mothers. Nova Scotia's 1921 provision typically allowed for dispensing with their consent to the adoption of offspring committed to the superintendent of neglected and delinquent children.[18] Across the strait, the colony of Newfoundland's legislators also emphasized the need to control and maintain youngsters against the claims of birth kin who were deemed unsuitable. The persistence of old patterns was further signalled when judges were at the same time enjoined not to send children to 'prison' but to homes 'for destitute and neglected children or Industrial School or Society for the Protection of Children.' These institutions could arrange 'adoption by a suitable person, or may apprentice it to a suitable trade, calling or service, and the transfer shall be as valid as if the Director or managers were the parents of such child.'[19] In a further testament to long-standing assumptions of what was important, religious matching continued to be required.

While demanding sectarian matching and recognizing connections to former kin, Manitoba legislators also paid homage to the new age. They required records and certificates to confirm the transfer 'as fully as by natural birth', the sealing of records in a separate file to be opened only by provincial authorization, and a one-year probationary period during which adopters had, for the first time, to report to provincial child welfare authorities. The Prairie province was also unusually explicit in forbidding the practice of adoptive parents' transferring 'the control or custody' of new offspring to others. In 1926 Manitoba tried to tidy up the type of 'loose ends' that worried all jurisdictions: amendments provided that all adoption agreements between the Children's Home of Winnipeg and any persons or societies with 'legal guardianship of a child' were retroactively approved by application to a country court judge and further directed employees of the Child Welfare Board and others to secrecy.[20]

Saskatchewan followed suit in many ways. It provided for applications to be heard in judges' chambers, which, as with the requirement that illegitimacy go unmentioned, screened past from future. Amendments in 1925–6 provided that if girls and boys had resided since they were very young with adopters, their consent, and presumably knowledge of their situation, was unnecessary. In 1927, Alberta's Domestic Relations Act typified western inclinations with its provision for the child's agreement, concealment of illegitimacy, limitations on the need for birth parents' consent, a year's probation before finalization, dual inheritance, and closed records. The result was intended, as the legislation specified, to make the child as if he or she had 'been legitimate from the time of birth.'[21]

Although it embraced many of the same conclusions as other jurisdictions, Ontario, as the most powerful of the English-speaking provinces, was often the most visible in its adoption initiatives. In 1921, it followed British Columbia in eliminating reference to the stigma of illegitimacy, continued Nova Scotia's cancellation of the need for consent from guardians who were insane, in prison, neglectful, or deemed otherwise inadequate by a judge, and continued the dual approach to inheritance. In 1925, amendments provided for judges to dispense with children's consent if they had lived with adopters since infancy. More innovative was the influential 1926 amendment that left adoption unaffected by the subsequent marriage of birth parents. The 1927 Act Respecting the Adoption of Children affirmed the nationwide shift to greater confidentiality, with provisions for in camera hearings and sealed records. It also offered some novelties: for the first time, unless they were blood kin, adopters had to be at least twenty-five years old and twenty-one years older than prospective offspring, and bachelors could adopt girls only in 'special circumstances'.

At the same time Ontario explicitly prioritized the 'welfare of the infant' and provided that courts could insist that adoption orders 'may impose such terms and conditions . . . and in particular may require the adopting parent by bond or otherwise to make for the adopted child such provision (if any) as in the opinion of the court is just and expedient.' Such statements suggested the increasing emphasis on what would become 'the best interests of the child' doctrine in adoption legislation.[22] This trend was already visible in Canadian court decisions. In 1916, an Ontario housemaid in the case of *Re Grafasso* lost an appeal to recover her illegitimate daughter from a couple because the judge held her circumstances to threaten the child's well-being. Judicial decisions about the meaning of best interest were never, however, predictable. An unwed mother might well encounter harder scrutiny than a widower. While Saskatchewan judges were not without reservations in the 1925 case of *Brown v. Partridge et al.,* for example, they ultimately favoured a widower's appeal for the return of his daughter from a couple to whom he had given her.[23] Yet if courts were never unanimous in upholding new or old rights, as one Canadian legal authority has concluded, 'the main failure of the best interest test is that in its preoccupation with the child it fails to recognize these rights of the parents. . . . The second major fault of the best interest test is that it is indeterminate and arbitrary.'[24] Canadians would confront such problems throughout the twentieth century.

Child's Personal history

Sealed Records

By late 1920s, adoption legislation, like the judiciary, was clearly wrestling with the appropriate relationship between children and adults, past and present. Just how much of children's personal histories should move with them into new lives? When exchanges were conducted within communities by relatives or friends, members of the adoption circle commonly knew one another. In contrast, assumptions increasingly informing modern legislation assumed connections might well be dangerous. Birth parents were clearly regarded as, at best, unfortunate and all too likely to be criminal or incompetent. In hard times, they had to rely on authorities' deference to blood ties and sympathy for the parental feeling of birth mothers in particular. But such sentiments were an uncertain refuge in an age that increasingly stressed the influence of environment. Like much other child welfare legislation, however well-intentioned, adoption laws put the poor on notice that parental rights were not sacrosanct.

Adopters, like Canada itself, seemed ready after the First World War to embrace the promise of new beginnings. In camera proceedings, sealed records, concealed illegitimacy, and restricted power of consent promised a clean slate. Although members of the birth circle might still know each other's identities, the public would no longer be privy to private matters, and respectable nuclear families would thus more readily claim normalcy.[25] To be sure, prospective parents did not escape regulation. While in the past they might have had to measure up to informal community examination, they now had to begin to confront direct state efforts at child protection. Their motives and eligibility could well be at issue. And yet adopters always possessed overwhelming advantages. For much of the century, they would be in demand. They were the volunteers who assumed financial and other obligations that otherwise might well fall to governments and certainly did fall to hard-put children's charities. They could count on secular and religious authorities to affirm their rights by reference, affidavit, or insider action. They were much more likely than those who surrendered offspring to preside over legislatures and other powerful institutions. Not surprisingly, the prioritizing of children's welfare highlighted in the 1927 Ontario legislation was frequently presumed to coincide with the material and other advantages promised by respectable adopters.

Confirming the Rules, 1927–1945

In the Balfour Report (1926) and the Statute of Westminster (1931), Canada was freed, some patriots hoped, from the dead hand of the past to reject older dependent or childlike statuses within the British Empire and to move ahead as an autonomous dominion or mature state. When the Supreme Court of Canada in 1938 confirmed that adoption, as well as issues of 'legitimacy, custody, guardianship, child protection, affiliation, and child maintenance' were all properly provincial responsibilities, the way became all the more clear for legislation remaking families and altering the public record to recognize social relations, not biology, as key determinants of modern life.[26]

Adoption legislation continued to develop in fits and starts from one part of the country to another as the economic, demographic, and bureaucratic character of the various provinces spurred and restrained initiatives. Some jurisdictions, like Newfoundland and New Brunswick, shifted more slowly than richer provinces like British Columbia and Ontario, where social workers and other child welfare experts were more available to press for professionalizing the transfer of children. The Yukon introduced its first legislation, playing catch up with provisions for single or couple applicants, dual inheritance, unmentioned illegitimacy, and prohibition of disclosure. While differences in legislation never entirely disappeared—nor did they in practice—influential trends encompassed all Canadians to some degree as they strove to move children from settings regarded as unsuitable into the arms of those who would support and educate them into the responsible modern citizenship that was especially associated with the middle class.

If, in these years, the state became more dedicated to intervention in previously private matters, some Canadians remained unconvinced and uninterested. The still uncertain recognition of the need for legislation was revealed in Prince Edward Island's published acts in 1930. As the compilers explained, the 1916 adoption act had been 'inadvertently' included in a taxation act and repealed. While the loss had hardly been noticed, the Transfer of Guardianship Act of 1930 was made retroactive to cover all assignments of children that might have been affected.[27] Other legislation also indicated that some long-standing practices continued to present problems. In 1927, for example, Saskatchewan's Child Welfare Act found it necessary to explicitly forbid children's assignment to 'penal or pauper institution', unless 'absolute necessary'.[28] In 1931, in a similar acknowledgement of presumably detectable, albeit now discredited, behaviours, Newfoundland mandated that 'No child who is held for examination as a neglected or delinquent child shall be confined in a gaol, lock-up or a police station, except for such period as under the circumstances is unavoidable' and prohibited 'the placing of children with the lowest bidder.' Not surprisingly, indentures that treated youngsters as workers remained a vital concern for elected representatives in St John's.[29]

Change was nevertheless accelerating. In 1929, Nova Scotia confirmed modern legislative preferences with an amendment that made the consent of the director of child welfare sufficient if the child had been committed to a children's aid society or the department; the province emphasized the point by making the provision retroactive to May 1921. In 1931, Newfoundland authorized the director of child welfare to approve all adoption agreements and to issue certificates. Also indicative of shifting opinion regarding the value of legal documentation was its 1944 recognition of 'de facto' adoption, whereby a child who resided for two or more years with a person or spouses could be adopted without otherwise required consents. In Manitoba, the de facto adoption of a child maintained for seven years similarly eliminated the need for such agreement.

The same inclination to ease the process of transfer, at least for potential parents, was evident in greater attention to the safeguarding of documentation and in shorter probationary periods before adoption became absolute. In 1935, British Columbia prohibited unauthorized access to adoption documents and reduced the probationary period from two years to one. By 1936, Manitoba permitted those who had parented 'under an adoption contract' and, in a section unique to this

Nature · Nurture

jurisdiction, foster parents who had operated 'under an agreement with the Director of Child Welfare or a Children's Aid Society' to secure absolute adoption in a closed court.[30] While Prince Edward Island continued to hearken back to the past with its provision for 'Adoption by Deed'—essentially youngsters' transfer by guardians or parents to a third party—and the familiar inheritance from birth parents, 1940 saw it for the first time set out necessary consents, closed hearings, and concealment of illegitimacy.[31]

In 1941, Alberta, like other jurisdictions in these years, amended its regulations to confirm that 'natural' parents could not by their subsequent marriage challenge earlier consent to the loss of offspring. It also established a 'special register', which was not subject to search, except with judicial authorization, to record adoptions.[32] By 1944, Newfoundland was in a similar position, with illegitimacy going unmentioned, confidential records, the irrelevance of birth parents' later marriage, curbed consents, and new birth certificates. Nova Scotia's greater insistence on the confidentiality of all records in 1945, like a provision that permitted dispensing with the probationary period before finalization, similarly acted to curb the options of first parents. Manitoba likewise moved to reinforce secrecy, even as it acknowledged in 1943 the dilemma of many birth kin when it permitted the withdrawal of consents by writing to the director of child welfare 'at any time prior to the placement of the child for adoption.'[33]

Adopters also came under closer scrutiny as the Second World War put a greater premium on state planning. In 1940, the judge of the court of chancery in Prince Edward Island was 'in every case' to 'make a thorough inquiry into the moral qualities' of the adopters.[34] Four years later, in Nova Scotia, George F. Davidson, the executive director of the Canadian Welfare Council reported on public welfare services for the province's Royal Commission on Provincial Development and Rehabilitation. He dismissed early initiatives regarding adoption as 'purely legalistic' and 'concerning only the adoptive parents themselves, acting through legal counsel, and the Courts of the Province'. In 1943, a series of amendments updated the legislation so that local children's aid societies were properly mandated to investigate and supervise adoptions.[35] A year later, Alberta authorized judges to obtain any information 'affecting the adoption and may direct investigation as to the physical, mental or moral fitness of the child or the adopting parents.'[36] In 1945, Newfoundland required applicants to meet additional conditions: unless specifically permitted, they had to be older than twenty-five and more than twenty-five years older than the child. Like Ontario, but unlike all the other Atlantic provinces, the British colony also invoked particular fears in prohibiting single men from adopting girls except in 'special circumstances'.[37]

Nor were specific adoption laws and special sections within child protection legislation the only ways modernizing governments tried to address the traffic in children. In the 1920s, Saskatchewan's legislature identified maternity homes as major culprits. Large or small, their frequent lack of licensing and their customary practices were regularly associated with irresponsible or exploited birth mothers and the gullible or unprincipled in search of progeny. The owners and employees of such institutions in Saskatchewan were expressly forbidden to transfer children under seven years of age to anyone's custody from parents without the consent of the province.[38] The dangers were embodied in Nova Scotia's struggles with the Ideal Maternity Home, which from the 1920s to the 1940s ran a profitable business by supplying Canadians and Americans with 'surplus' youngsters. In 1940, that province responded to mounting scandals by requiring comprehensive institutional records that had to be completely open to child welfare authorities.[39]

Other provinces moved similarly to control an informal but frequently highly effective system for transferring illegitimate children to new parents without too much public attention. Licensed enterprises, run notably by Protestant, Catholic, and Jewish authorities, continued nevertheless to receive favourable mention by over-stretched provincial departments that in fact relied on such voluntary initiatives to shift the burden of disadvantaged youngsters to waiting families. Jurisdictions before the Second World War were increasingly codifying procedures under which girls and boys could be transferred, but their efforts were in the context of older, continuing traditions by which birth and adoptive families made their arrangements both individually and through intermediaries.

'Like Our Very Own', 1945–1970

In the post-1945 period, adoption increasingly evolved to become a declaration of faith in a new world and in the shedding of problematic pasts. While a small group of child immigrants committed to Vancouver Island's Fairbridge Farm continued to endure ignominy and expectations for toil, domestic adoptions increasingly steered a different course. Adoptees were more and more likely to be viewed, whatever their realities, as rescued innocents whose best hopes lay in their remaking in the image of their benefactors. White, largely middle-class Canadians' desire for children increasingly overwhelmed long-standing suspicion of other classes, ethnicities, races, and religions. The lessons of the Second World War and the national liberation movements that followed inspired some Canadians to deny that differences made any difference. The offspring of 'Others' increasingly offered the prospect of becoming, as one American scholar has explained regarding her nation, 'like our very own'.[40] The desire for child labour that had marked so many early exchanges of children became nearly invisible.

Growing acceptance of adoption nevertheless had to confront the common-law and society's persisting deference to the rights of the 'natural' family. These years brought no end to the struggle over what exactly constituted sufficient justification for removing girls and boys from blood relations. Some authorities always recognized that the poor, often through little fault of their own, were especially vulnerable to state intervention. In the face of disagreements about the proper way to handle family poverty, legislators moved carefully as they sought to provide more certainty in the surrender of youngsters and, not so incidentally, to spare the public purse.

In 1946, New Brunswick's much expanded Adoption Act brought the province largely in line with other jurisdictions. A child welfare officer was authorized to investigate all parties involved. Children who had lived with applicants since their 'earliest years' and had 'known no other parents' need not give consent, and consents generally could be dispensed with if the court deemed 'it necessary or desirable.' The confidentiality and secrecy that had become commonplace were likewise affirmed. Yet, integration into new communities remained uncertain. Adoptees here as elsewhere could inherit from 'natural' kin but not from new parents' kindred.[41] A little more than a decade later, in a move that reflected growing interest in obscuring problematic pasts, the province allowed 'such statements and evidence as may be detrimental to the welfare of the child or the interests of the applicant' to be omitted from the adoption application.[42]

Notwithstanding efforts to update legislation in these years, some transfers of youngsters continued to occur with little state supervision. In 1948, for example, the New Brunswick legislature passed a private act 'to authorize and make legal the Adoption and Change of Name' of two Moncton girls, long in the custody of their paternal aunt and her husband, an inspector of transportation for the Canadian National Railway.[43] Five years later, An Act to Validate Certain Adoptions of Children Formerly under the Care and Control of What Is Now 'New Brunswick Protestant Orphans' Home' legalized surrenders 'made by indenture prior to March 1, 1941'.[44] In 1956, Manitoba similarly amended its Child Welfare Act to legitimatize adoptions made from 1924, ordering that they be 'validated and confirmed, whether or not the consent of either of the natural parents of any such child to the adoption was given; and no such decree of adoption shall be quashed by an order of any court.'[45]

Canadians never relinquished long-established private arrangements regarding children. Applying for state sanction or accepting regulation was not part of everyone's plans. Jurisdictions' recognition of de facto adoptions responded at least in part to just such reluctance or indifference. In 1956, in silent acknowledgement of the survival of informal exchanges, Manitoba reduced the time required for de facto adoptions to five years, from the previous seven. Modern regulation appeared especially unwelcome in Yukon and the Northwest Territories, where isolation, itinerant employments, and Aboriginal traditions stood in the way of any easy accommodation. In his memoirs, *Judge of the Far North*, Jack Sissons titled chapter 28 'Fight over Eskimo Customs'. Moving north from Alberta, he encountered an enormous backlog of applications and cut through the logjam with his judgment in *Re Katie* (1961), which ruled that 'adoptions in accordance with Indian or Eskimo custom were as good before the law of the Territories as those under the new ordinance.'[46] Not until 1994, however, did the Northwest Territories set out in its Aboriginal Custom Adoption Recognition Act a 'simple procedure' to respect custom adoption and arrange for a 'custom adoption commissioner'. Revealingly, the resulting certificate was not to 'be put in a sealed packet', like other adoption documents, although the original birth registration was to be withdrawn.[47]

The recognition by Canadian courts of the legitimacy of Aboriginal adoption practices in cases such as *Re Tagornak Adoption Petition* (1984), *Michelle v. Dennis and Dennis* (1984) and *Casimel v. Insurance Corporation of British Columbia* (1993) assisted in the retention of children within communities and offered overdue respect. It was not, however, without its problems, as anthropologists Jo-Anne Fiske and

Claudien Herlihey have pointed out. Practice by its very nature can evolve and change in response to shifting circumstances. Once enshrined in legal codes, customs that represented moral injunctions designed to meet past needs may become onerous and discriminatory, most especially for women, who as mothers and grandmothers are most likely to bear the weight of childrearing.[48]

If Canadians sometimes operated independently of the law, legislatures offered inducements to adopters to come on board. Orders for greater secrecy and specified conditions for eliminating otherwise necessary consents typified all jurisdictions. In 1966–7, Newfoundland provided that new birth certificates could inscribe not only altered names but birthplaces requested by adopters. In 1968 and 1969, respectively, BC and PEI mandated that adoption orders identify youngsters solely by given names and birth registration numbers and leave unnamed the natural parents. Some consequences of more stringent requirements for secrecy were not always intended. Alberta was, however, the only province to take the logical step, between 1958 and 1966, of permitting the clergy or marriage commissioners, when one of the parties to a marriage was adopted, to refer to the adoption registration in order to ascertain whether the couple fell 'within the forbidden degrees of consanguinity'.[49]

The issue of consents and their revocation emerged as a major concern in these years. In particular, legislators recognized that special provision had to be made for the agreement of new mothers, commonly but not always unwed and often underage. In 1957, British Columbia prohibited consents from birth mothers within ten days of childbirth while at the same time ordering that 'no person who has given his consent to adoption, other than the child to be adopted, may revoke his consent unless it is shown to the Court's satisfaction that such revocation is in the best interests of the child.'[50] Amendments in 1961 requiring the witnessing of 'free' and 'voluntary' consents, within the ten-day period of grace, offered some protection to the birth mother, even as they further guaranteed finality.[51]

In 1958, Ontario provided that maternal consent could not occur before babies were seven days old. Birth mothers could repudiate their agreement within twenty-one days. A later clause in that legislation mandated that consents could be withdrawn only 'if, having regard to all the circumstances of the case, the court is satisfied that it is in the best interests of the child.'[52] In 1961, the Northwest Territories forbade consents before fourteen days (reduced to four days in 1966) after delivery and gave birth mothers sixty days to cancel (in 1969 this was restricted to the date when the child had been placed for adoption). Conflicts of interests were to be avoided by the requirement that maternal acquiescence be confirmed by an 'affidavit' from someone who was 'not an officer, servant or agent of any society or other agency that is concerned with the placement of the child for adoption', and no such person was allowed to be present when the consent was signed. At the same time the affidavit had to certify that the mother signed 'in knowledge of the consequences'.[53]

As they clarified conditions of consent, jurisdictions attempted to insist on its finality. In 1946, Saskatchewan stated that 'the order or decision of the judge' in case of appeals 'shall not be subject to further appeal'.[54] In 1950, Anne of Green

Gables country provided that adoption orders were 'final and without appeal' unless 'new facts are alleged'.[55] The desire to block lengthy disputes helped inspire Halifax's 1954 provisions that no adoption could 'in any direct, or collateral proceeding, be subject to attack or to be set aside' after one year and that judges could determine who was 'entitled' to be present at hearings.[56] The intent was all the clearer in a 1959 Nova Scotian amendment that ordered that 'No person who has given his consent to the adoption of a child, other than a child to be adopted, may revoke his consent unless it is shown to the court that the revocation is in the best interest of the child'; eight years later, another provision made the consent of 'a person whose consent in all circumstances of the case ought to be dispensed with' officially unnecessary.[57] The relative power of adults in the adoption circle was suggested by a BC provision stating that adoptions between 1957 and 1961 remained valid, even if no witness confirmed that someone surrendering a child understood the consequences. In 1964, Newfoundland specified that consent could be cancelled with twenty-one days in writing but was 'irrevocable' later on and that no proceeding against the order could occur after one year unless this was deemed 'in the best interests of the child'.[58] In 1966, Alberta provided that 'no action or proceeding' could 'set aside an order of adoption' after one year unless it had been secured by 'fraud' and if 'it is in the interests of the adopted child to do so.'[59]

Canadian courts had to interpret what all the legislation relating to consent actually meant in practical terms. Opinion was far from unanimous. As one leading Canadian legal commentator on adoption law has concluded, 'it is obvious that up until the 1950's there was no real agreement' as to how to interpret 'best interest'. On the one hand there were judgments, as in the case of *Price v. Cargin and Cargin* (1956) that affirmed the rights of respectable adopters.[60] The British Columbia case of *Re Wells* (1962) treated adoptive and natural parents as equal claimants and the provincial 'Court of Appeal upheld the trial judge's refusal to allow the mother to revoke her consent, "having regard only to the welfare of the child and none to maternal rights."'[61] In contrast, other influential decisions supported natural parents. In the Ontario case *Re Duffell* (1950), an unwed mother retained the right to custody. The justices argued that she could lose her rights only 'by abandoning the child or by misconducting herself . . . or [if] her character is such as to make it imprudent that the child should remain with her.' In another decision, involving the infant twins of two young Dutch immigrant parents in Ontario, the ultimate ruling supported birth parental rights and revoked consent. The 1966 case of *Re Roebuck Adoption* upheld the birth mother, a sometime waitress from Prince George, British Columbia, who had surrendered four children. Despite evidence of a 'promiscuous life', leaving a child in the home of another without direction or funds, and giving custody to the Children's Aid Society (CAS), she did not automatically sacrifice her rights.[62]

Legislators sometimes challenged judicial decisions favouring natural parents. In 1969, when the Supreme Court of Canada ordered a son returned to an unmarried mother who had agreed to the CAS's placing him for adoption, the Ontario government amended the Child Welfare Act to place 'beyond the reach of his natural parent a Crown ward who has been placed for adoption.'[63] While Lynn Penrod has argued that lower courts overall 'insisted on applying the best interest standard in all types of disputes', effectively emasculating the rights of birth parents,[64] this proclivity thrived still more frequently in legislatures. As she also acknowledged, this preference continued not only because of the relative power of adopters and natural parents but also because parental rights theories were associated with the idea of property in general.[65] Whatever their feelings about contestants for children, few legislators or litigators have been prepared, at least explicitly, to regard offspring as no more than chattel. As a result, birth parents were increasingly treated as possessing conditional, rather than absolute, rights over offspring.

In these years, as infant adoptions became increasingly common, the frequent reduction of probationary periods to one year or even six months also threatened original guardians. It meant less time to consider options and sort out affairs. Legislation that permitted exceptions to otherwise required investigations of suitability could well have the similar effect of handicapping 'natural' parents. Like many other provinces, Manitoba sent some children—often, but not only, racial minorities, and most notably Aboriginal—beyond its borders. In 1967, it empowered the director of child welfare to dispense with investigations in such circumstances.[66] Once youngsters were sent to other provinces, to the United States, or to Europe, supervision for the most part disappeared, and reunions were made all the more unlikely.

Changes to provisions for inheritance reinforced the message that a new life had begun. Property rights were, however, never readily altered. As Lynn Penrod has observed, 'quite probably the most litigious issue historically arising in the post adoption phase is the question of inheritance and succession to property by and from the adopted child.'[67] In 1946, Saskatchewan extended inheritance rights to adopters' kin while retaining those to the original family.[68] In 1953, an amendment to BC's act did much the same, as did Ontario a year later.[69] In 1956, the Pacific province eliminated all reference to inheritance from and to the birth family. Responding to concerns about lost opportunities, University of British Columbia law professor Gilbert D. Kennedy wrote to the *Canadian Bar Review* to point out that the amendments did not 'prevent gifts from the natural family to the child . . . in the same way that a member of any family can make a gift to any stranger.' Blood relatives could place gifts with the superintendent of child welfare 'in trust for the child, under its original name'. Kennedy's enthusiasm for eliminating all original ties was made obvious by his subsequent comment that 'anonymity can then be preserved in those cases where it is desirable, as it is in many cases.'[70] By 1958, when amendments in Ontario and Alberta mandated that 'for all purposes', except incest and marital prohibitions, the adopted child became the child of new parents and ceased to be of his birth parents,[71] the bugbear of dual inheritance was fast disappearing.

Other relics of the past were also under assault, most notably the requirement for religious matching. In years when Catholic youngsters outnumbered prospective parents of the same faith and when Protestant and Jewish would-be parents were crying out for offspring, old bars were vulnerable. Such issues were not new. In 1933, in the case of *Bland v. Agnew*, involving the placement of a Catholic child with a Protestant family, a BC court concluded that 'a difference in religion is no bar to an adoption.'[72] Some thirty years later, the long-simmering debate came to a boil in most jurisdictions, as we shall see in chapter 5. In the case of *Re Lamb* (1961) an Ontario District Court ruled, 'It is not a condition precedent to the adoption of children in Ontario that the applicants for adoption must be of the same religious faith as the child. The presence or absence of a spiritual or religious influence in the lives of those seeking to adopt may be a factor in determining the child's best interests. However, the particular denomination to which an adoptive applicant belongs should not be a bar to adoption.'[73] In 1966, Alberta lawmakers affirmed that statements of religious preference remained effective for only a year, during which time 'reasonable efforts' at such accommodation were to be undertaken.[74] In 1968, Saskatchewan amended its Child Welfare Act to provide that if all 'reasonable efforts' had been made to match youngsters, they could be placed with parents of another faith.[75] In 1970, Manitoba updated its Child Welfare Act to allow natural and adoptive parents the choice whether to specify religion. If a faith was preferred and no match was found within three months, authorities could place children in any 'suitable adoption home'.[76] By 1985, the Charter of Rights and Freedoms raised concerns among denominational agencies such as Toronto's Jewish Family and Child Service and Ontario's Catholic Children's Aid Societies that they would be compelled 'to accept adoption and foster-care applicants from other faiths or from non-practising members of their own religions.'[77]

If the adoption market was somewhat deregulated with respect to religion before 1970, it was tightening up with regard to the character of prospective parents. As adoption grew more popular, legislators could afford to indulge their preferences about suitable families, which they overwhelmingly interpreted as headed by respectable heterosexual couples. Between 1946 and 1958, Saskatchewan required husbands and wives to be twenty-five or older. Widowed and single adults could apply only if the child they wished to adopt was 'of the same sex' and had 'been maintained for at least two years in his or her home as a member thereof and has attained the age of at least eight years.' Only a blood relationship or other special circumstance permitted any escape from what was often effective exclusion from candidacy as a parent. Saskatchewan, like some other jurisdictions, also began to require proof of marriage.[78] From 1948 to 1961, the Northwest Territories also demanded both marriage certificates and that applicants be at least twenty-five years of age. It restricted the widowed and the unmarried to children who were already resident in their homes for two years and who were at least eight years of age. All candidates for parenthood had to submit documentation of their average yearly income for five years and a health certificate specifying they were not mentally defective or carrying a communicable disease. In 1954, Yukon made much the same demands. In 1950, Prince Edward Island mandated that adopters be twenty-one years old and eligible to adopt only those younger than themselves. Island judges could exempt relatives or others in 'special circumstances' if 'the best interests' of the unmarried minor were served. In 1958, Newfoundland amended its Child Welfare Act to prohibit the reception of a child 'with a view to adopting' without prior written approval from authorities. Exceptions in the new province included prospective adopters related to the mother of an illegitimate child or to either parent in the case of legitimate offspring. In the same year, Ontario barred those less than twenty-five years of age, the single, widowed, and divorced in most circumstances, and male adopters of girls.

Despite such restrictions, agencies across the country were facing increasing pressure to place the mounting numbers of children who were in public care. Newspaper advertising of Crown wards in the 1960s and 1970s, like the initiation of groups such as the Open Door Society beginning in Montreal in 1959 and Saskatchewan's AIM (Adopt Indian Métis) from 1967, attempted to promote adoption as exemplary citizenship.[79] In much the same vein, Ontario's 1965 Child Welfare Act required 'every children's aid society' to 'endeavour to secure the adoption of Crown wards, having regard to the individual needs of each ward.' Such societies had one year after the committal of a ward to report on efforts.[80] Successful placements promised to relieve provincial coffers and remove youngsters to more deserving parents.

By the 1970s, legislators had set the fundamental terms for the modern transfer of children. These envisioned the surgical separation of first and subsequent families. They frequently appeared to regard birth kin as untidy postscripts to better relationships. Records were increasingly unavailable to birth parents and adoptees. At the same time, legislators were prepared to narrow the conditions of acceptability of adopters. To an unprecedented degree, mature heterosexual couples were identified as the proper custodians of offspring. Birth parents, notably young unwed mothers, would be relieved of responsibilities in order to make better choices. Neglectful and dangerous parents and kin would be shunted far into the background, hopefully to disappear forever, and, in any case, not to inflict their shortcomings on a new generation. Increasingly diverse groups of adoptees would thus secure a new lease on life. Shorn of suspect antecedents, they could join the respectable and the industrious as good citizens.

Connecting Past and Future: The 1970s to the 1990s

In the last decades of the twentieth century, confidence in new beginnings was clearly waning. The reports of the Royal Commission on New Reproductive Technologies and the Royal Commission on Aboriginal Peoples both highlighted adoption as a public concern, albeit very differently. Evidence of abuse and prejudice, the identification of fetal alcohol spectrum disorders and other drug-related conditions, the collapse of the availability of babies from unwed mothers, the sight of Canadians joining a dragnet of the developing world for healthy children with vulnerable birth families, an Aboriginal redress movement, and 'searchers' who spoke of 'primal wounds' and stolen histories, all increasingly supplied a disturbing backdrop for legislation. Largely unprecedented attention to Native children and communities made it very clear that adoption by mainstream families was no shortcut to the just society. The demands of gay and lesbian Canadians for equal access to adoption further challenged long-standing assumptions about what constituted the 'good' family. Laws grew increasingly elaborate as they tried simultaneously to address a variety of demands and to maintain adoption as a viable solution to the expense and tragedy of growing numbers of children-in-care. Mention of registries and openness reflected the complicated connections that Canada's diverse families have regularly tried to maintain on an informal basis.

While the transformation wrought in the last decades of the twentieth century is striking, much legislation was relatively familiar. In 1972, New Brunswick reconfirmed the drive for secrecy in an amendment to its Adoption Act: 'Notwithstanding the Rules of Court ... the court may direct that statements and evidence that may be detrimental to the welfare of the child or the interests of the applicant be omitted from the notice of application and, where substituted service of the notice is to be effected by public advertisement, shall direct that the names of the child and of the adopting parents be omitted from the notice of application.'[81] A year later, Alberta amended its Child Welfare Act to give the province the right to determine when a statement of religious preference ceased to be valid. In 1974, Nova Scotia and Manitoba allowed the adoptee to be identified in the application solely by a birth registration number. Jurisdictions still deliberated about the appropriate period after childbirth before adoption orders could be issued. Inheritance continued to perplex. Manitoba's Child and Family Services Act assured residents in 1986 that adoption did not alter the right to inherit from birth kindred. After 1988, Newfoundland extended the rights of adoptees so they could inherit from their adopted kin. Much else regarding consents, confidentiality, and eligibility likewise remained familiar.

Reconsideration was nevertheless very much in the air. Intensified concern with the rights of children was critical to this shift. In the 1970s, official guardians (Ontario) and children's advocates (Alberta, Manitoba) appeared to guarantee new protection. While approvals of transfers from those over twelve, and sometimes as young as ten, had regularly been mandated, the consent of younger children was increasingly required. After 1970, Ontario courts could consult youngsters seven and older. Adolescents also gradually won the option to reject name changes. The status of illegitimate offspring began to improve dramatically with the elimination of distinctions between those born in and out of wedlock (in, for example, Ontario in 1977, New Brunswick in 1980, Yukon in 1984, and the Northwest Territories in 1987).

Children's rights were specifically embraced in the growing proclivity of legislatures to define 'best interests' as the operative principles of child welfare. In 1979, Manitoba rather typically interpreted the former to include mental, emotional, and physical needs, opportunity for parent–child relationships, and the need for continuity as well as for permanency. In 1980, New Brunswick's Preamble to the Child and Family Services and Family Relations Act began with a reference to a national standard:

> WHEREAS children have basic rights and fundamental freedoms no less than those of adults; a right to special safeguards and assistance in the preservation of those rights and freedoms and in the application of the principles stated in the *Canadian Bill of Rights* and elsewhere; and a right to be heard in the course

of, and to participate in the processes that lead to decisions that affect them and that they are capable of understanding . . .[82]

In 1985–6, the Statutes of Manitoba set out a 'Declaration of Principles' for the Child and Family Services Act that proclaimed the 'family' as the 'basic unit of society', with a 'right to least interference'. At the same time, acknowledging long-standing hardships, it credited families with legitimate claims to 'preventive and supportive services' and singled out Indian bands as deserving programs that respected 'their unique status'. The province's 'best interests' guidelines now included the child's 'cultural and linguistic heritage'.[83] In 1992, PEI legislation defined best interest at length and added that 'an adopted person has a right to non-identifying information concerning his or her background and heritage' as well as a variety of circumscribed entitlements to identifying documentation and reunions.[84] Five years later, the Northwest Territories recognized that 'decisions concerning children should be made in accordance with the best interests of children, with a recognition that differing cultural values and practices must be respected in those determinations' and 'each community has a role in supporting and promoting the best interests of the children and the well-being of families in the community.'[85] All these provisions paid unprecedented attention to the child and to the relationships in which he or she was embedded prior to and after adoption.

Enhanced attention to youngsters' histories was further confirmed by renewed preoccupation with consents. As the 1970 Yukon Ordinance to Provide for the Welfare of Children emphasized, surrendering adults had to have surrenders 'fully explained' and attest that they 'freely and voluntarily understood'.[86] Appropriate times to dispense with parental consents were spelled out more clearly. In 1980, New Brunswick waived the necessity in cases, not only of neglect and of the failure to maintain, but when original custodians had 'not had an ongoing parental relationship with the child and a delay in securing a home for the child would be detrimental to the best interest of the child.' And as was also familiar, here and in other jurisdictions, judges could always dispense with consent by invoking 'best interests'.[87] In 1983, Nova Scotia insisted that consent be accompanied by professional counselling and increased the time before agreement was valid. Growing conflict over consents was also signalled by that province's regulation that 'No action may be taken and no damages may be awarded against a person who does not give a consent or confirm a consent for adoption notwithstanding any representation by the person that the consent or confirmation would be given.'[88] At the end of the 1980s, Saskatchewan set the time limit as three days from birth while also demanding that birth mothers receive 'independent advice'.[89] In 1998, the Northwest Territories refused consents before the eleventh day after childbirth and specified that 'a parent shall be presumed to have demonstrated the intent to forego the rights and responsibilities of parent in respect of the person of the child where the parent . . . in the case of a newborn, has failed to communicate with or visit the child or the person with whom the child has been living during the six month period before a petition is issued.'[90] Such preoccupation with consent reflected the frequency with which it emerged as a key issue in many end-of-the-century court cases.

If legislatures continued long-standing interest in setting conditions for true consent, they also paid unaccustomed notice to persons, biological kin and otherwise, having meaningful associations with youngsters. In 1972, the Northwest Territories required the superintendent of child welfare to give preference to a grandparent providing a suitable home. In 1978, Ontario expanded the definition of a parent to include

> a person who has demonstrated a settled intention to treat a child as a child of the person's family and a person who is not recognized in law to be a parent of a child but (i) has acknowledged a parental relationship to the child and has voluntarily provided for the child's care and support; (ii) by an order of a court ... or a written agreement, is under a legal duty to provide for the child or has been granted custody of or access to the child, or (iii) has made a written acknowledgement of the fact of his or her parentage to the adoption agency or licensee.[91]

Six years later, Yukon legislated the preference 'where practicable' to place children with families of their 'own cultural background and lifestyle preferably in their own community.' Only if such placement could not occur within 'a reasonable time' were youngsters to go elsewhere.[92] In 1985–6, Manitoba's Child and Family Services Act allowed natural parents to place offspring with kin without prior notification or approval of the director of child welfare. Four years later, in 1989–90, Saskatchewan ordered that 'a birth parent or another person may have access to the child if each adoptive parent consents' and offered some protection to access orders of biological parents in step-parent cases.[93]

Such legislative shifts across Canada confirmed the long-standing observation that blood kin often wished to continue contact even after children had been formally transferred. It also responded to the willingness of relatives, perhaps more than ever, though that is impossible to determine, to litigate their rights. In 1982, for example, the Ontario District Court in Thunder Bay granted paternal grandparents access to grandchildren who had been adopted by the biological mother and her new husband. They were now deemed to fall within the definition of persons who had rights with respect to children.[94] When the 'best interests' doctrine was invoked, relatives might fare better than parental claimants in the courts. Such was the case in the Northwest Territories in 1985, when a mother lost an appeal for custody of her child, whom she had not seen for sixteen months, to her aunt and uncle.[95]

In the era's heightened concern with biological kin, fathers became especially visible. In 1987, British Columbia responded to a decision of the provincial supreme court, which concluded that under the Charter of Rights and Freedoms, unmarried fathers had a legal relationship with their children, by legislatively allowing for their consent.[96] In 1995, the province's Adoption Act provided for the creation of a Birth Fathers' Registry and set forth a social as well as a biological definition of paternity that included previous custody, guardianship, or support. Two years later, Manitoba's Adoption and Consequential Amendments Act raised the issue of the consent of 'birth fathers'. Such initiatives recognized how far the century had come in reconsidering fathers, especially as parents of children previously designated as illegitimate. Since the nineteenth century, Canadian legislators had been accustomed to attempting to force seducers and other presumed reprobates to pay for their pleasure through the acknowledgement of paternity. By the end of the twentieth century, however, greater acceptance of common-law unions and of the value of fatherhood more generally perhaps spurred some men to seek greater control in the lives of children. Canadian law-makers heard from a noisy fathers' rights movement, which sometimes appeared especially preoccupied with punishing women and reducing financial obligations but which also suggested some reconception of roles.[97] Heightened sensitivity to fathers had nevertheless to address familiar tragedies, as in one 1992 Ontario case when a court had to decide whether the consent of a rapist, if he could be located, was necessary for a baby's placement: the court ruled it was not.[98]

Growing numbers of step-parent adoptions, the majority of which involved the husbands of biological mothers, also prompted some 'natural' fathers to seek official sanction for continued contact. In 1979, Manitoba responded by allowing former spouses to apply for access when a step-parent adoption was contemplated. A 1985 decision by the same province's courts supported the 'gradual reintroduction of the father' into the life of a nine-year-old, whom he had seen infrequently but for whom he had paid support, after her adoption by her step-father. This decision, like others, was supported by 'an expert' who stressed the 'importance to an adopted child of knowing about her parents of origin.'[99] In 1984, Yukon allowed step-parents custody rights without eliminating contact with the natural parent. In 1990, Nova Scotia established that courts facing applications for step-parent adoptions could 'in the best interests of the child, grant an order for joint custody of the step-parent and the father or mother rather than an order for adoption.'[100] The kinds of complications that could bedevil law-makers were captured by an Ontario court case of 1990: here a step-father, despite the breakdown of his marriage to the biological mother, wished to continue the adoption of a child who did not know of the lack of a blood connection.[101]

The issues raised by step-parent adoptions constituted only one instance of relations that needed consideration in a period when there was unprecedented recognition of former injustices. Indigenous protest, especially during and after the 'sixties scoop' of youngsters into state care, put the abduction of status and non-status youngsters front and centre. By 1980, child welfare authorities cared for 4.6 per cent of all status Indian youngsters in Canada, compared with .96 per cent of all children. In some regions, such as Northern Ontario's Kenora district, the CAS caseload was 85 per cent Native.[102] Such numbers operated in concert with diverse rulings by Canadian courts to move relations with First Nations parents and communities to the forefront of adoption debates. While interpretation of the 'best interests' doctrine readily privileged adopters, commonly whites, and state authorities only slowly acknowledged the cause of conditions that undermined Native parents, there were indications of progress.

In 1975, the important BC case *Natural Parents v. Superintendent of Child Welfare et al.* before the Supreme Court of Canada directly raised the question of the retention of Native status. By confirming that Aboriginal children did not lose status upon adoption, the decision undermined decades of legislation promising a break with the past.[103] Continuing entitlement to official Indian status, like step-parent adoptions, fundamentally challenged secrecy by anchoring children to preceding worlds. While the economic benefits of access to treaty funds and entitlements were obvious, courts also gradually recognized cultural inheritance. In the 1979 case *Fitzgerald v. Sagiaktook,* the benefits of exposure to Inuit culture encouraged the court to give custody to the mother.[104] The uncertainty of judicial decisions and the continuing advantages of adopters were, however, highlighted in 1990 by the inability of the mother of a two-and-a-half-year-old of white–Squamish heritage to revoke her consent by stressing the value of Aboriginal culture. The court 'granted the adoption on the assurance of the adoptive parents that they would encourage the child to be proud of her native ethnic background.'[105] Key provincial investigations—in the 1970s by Judge Thomas Berger in British Columbia and in the 1980s by Judge Edwin Kimelman in Manitoba and Dean Ralph Garber in Ontario—nevertheless signalled changing times with their insistence on involving Native communities in discussions regarding the adoption of youngsters.[106]

Legislators slowly responded. In 1973, British Columbia pioneered in accepting that adoption did not affect 'the status, rights, privileges, disabilities, and limitations of an adopted Indian person acquired as an Indian under the *Indian Act* (Canada) or under any other Act or law.'[107] In 1979, Manitoba required that the adoption order of a status youngster had to be forwarded to Ottawa for registration. By 1984, Ontario was requiring that the 'best interests' approach acknowledge 'the uniqueness of Indian and native culture, heritage and traditions' and the value 'of preserving the child's cultural identity'.[108] Bands were to be informed of, and have opportunity for input into, placements. 'Customary care' practices were gradually recognized, as was the right to Native child and family service authorities. Equally important was emerging provision for subsidized care as well as other family support services, including special needs agreements and emergency houses. As one expert concluded in 1985, at least one province had taken 'a bold step': 'in spite of the confusion over the jurisdictional issues, and the lack of sensitivity or effort in some situations, there is no doubt that Ontario's *Child and Family Services Act* has signaled the beginning of a new era in child welfare protection for native children. The *Act* is far from perfect in terms of its response to native concerns, but is a vast improvement.'[109]

By the mid-1980s, legislative adjustments were increasingly nationwide. Alberta's 1984 Child Welfare Act required that the federal Department of Indian Affairs be informed of Native adoptions, and it directed child welfare authorities to cooperate with bands on guardianship agreements and to inform children of their status when they were old enough. In 1985–6, Manitoba's Child and Family Services Act confirmed that bands were entitled to services acknowledging their unique cultural heritage. In 1988, Alberta included adult band members as potential interveners in decisions regarding apprehended youngsters. In 1989, the Northwest Territories statute on adoption made its first explicit reference to 'Aboriginal' youngsters by requiring consultation with Native organizations. In

1990, Nova Scotia's Act Respecting Services to Children and Their Families formally acknowledged the special role of the MicMac Family and Children's Services of Nova Scotia. In 1994, the Saskatchewan Act to Amend the Child and Family Services Act authorized agreements with bands to protect children.

In 1995, British Columbia's Adoption Act required the superintendent of child welfare to 'make reasonable efforts to discuss the child's placement' with a band or Aboriginal community. Revealing of complications, it also stated that this requirement lapsed if a child over twelve or birth parents or guardians objected.[110] The difficult balance of rights and obligations was further suggested by other legislative provisions such as the section in Yukon's 1986 Children's Act that ordered pregnant women believed to be abusing alcohol or other drugs to be supervised or counselled to reduce the 'serious risk' of 'foetal alcohol syndrome or other congenital injury'.[111] Such legislation did not necessarily translate into action or change. One expert observer of British Columbia concluded that there was only 'lip service in the Family and Child Service Act regarding notification to a Band of child welfare proceedings of a Band member. However, to coin a phrase, no policy is a policy position, since natives are exposed to differential treatment because of their racial characteristics.'[112] As welfare budgets and justice agendas met neo-conservative Canadian governments in the 1980s and 1990s, Native children continued to be disproportionately taken into care, usually in white families.

Transracial adoption in Canada frequently involved Native boys and girls, but the unprecedented welcome by white parents to African, Asian, and mixed-race girls and boys also slowly emerged to challenge the pretence to familial normalcy.[113] The presence of those whom Karen Dubinsky has dubbed 'hybrid babies',[114] plus the growing insistence of adult adoptees on recovering pasts, forced legislatures to begin to re-examine old assumptions. In 1975, Nova Scotia pioneered, amending its Vital Statistics Act to permit adult adoptees access to original birth certificates. The provision was almost immediately repealed, a foretelling of future controversies.[115] Three years later, Ontario's Act to Revise the Child Welfare Act signalled shifts, with provisions giving children fourteen years of age the right to chose or reject name changes and creating a voluntary registry for adoptees at age eighteen and birth parents. If both registered, they were informed, and the agencies that had been involved were to supply counselling. Manitoba and New Brunswick soon followed along much the same lines. Typically, underage adoptees were constrained from acquiring information, but 'special circumstances' and appeals were permitted, if not encouraged.[116]

The pace of change accelerated in the mid-1980s with the coming into force of section 15 of the Charter of Rights and Freedoms, which promised Canadians equality of protection and benefit before the law. In 1984, the Yukon Children's Act both reconfirmed secrecy and finality and permitted application for non-identifying information by adoptees and adopters. It also added that 'upon the application of any person and subject to any regulations that may be prescribed, the Director may disclose to the applicant any particulars of the adoption that he has in his possession, including information identifying the parents by birth or other kindred.'[117] Other jurisdictions began to establish rules that curtailed as much as they opened up opportunities for reconnection with original kin. Manitoba's 1985–6 statutes required the consent of adopters to the release of any birth information. In 1985, Alberta permitted only the release of non-identifying material and a voluntary disclosure system. Two years later, British Columbia created a voluntary Adoption Reunion Registry for adults. Matches had to occur before information could be exchanged, and adopters' identities were not to be recorded. After significant outrage from adoptees, biological parents, and even adopters when it seemed that Ontario planned to close down access even to non-identifying files in 1984–5,[118] the province appointed the dean of the University of Toronto's School of Social Work to investigate the question of access. In 1987, Ontario specified restrictions on researchers and further ordered that the Freedom of Information and Protection of Privacy Act, 1987 did not apply to adoption information. It did, however, maintain access to non-identifying material and permit enquiries by birth grandparents and select others. Registrars did not, however, have to cooperate if they believed that disclosure threatened 'serious physical or emotional harm.'[119]

In the last decade of the twentieth century, politicians continued their slow and uncertain acknowledgement of responsibility to searching adults. Saskatchewan statutes of 1989–90 mandated a Post-Adoption Registry and services, including counselling. By 1990, Newfoundland allowed adoptees aged nineteen and older to apply for non-identifying material but nothing else, unless the individuals sought agreed. British Columbia's 1991 statute provided for a passive registry, whereby the province supplied information when adult adoptees and birth relatives both applied, and for an active registry that allowed the superintendent of child welfare to undertake discrete enquiries on behalf of adoptees, birth parents, or siblings. Unless a veto had been placed, reunions could be assisted. In 1992, Prince Edward Island decreed that everyone's 'choice of anonymity should be respected' but confirmed that adoptees had a right to non-identifying data. A Reciprocal Search Register was to match applicants with a 'significant relationship'. The island's director of child welfare, nevertheless, maintained the right to determine what information was in the 'best interests' of applicants. Responding to a widespread problem that undermined any willingness to break old codes of confidentiality, the province's legislators rather belatedly also demanded 'reliable records'. They also allowed access for genealogical or historical research after all parties were believed dead for twenty years and no harm was likely to those alive.[120] In 1994, Alberta was unique in permitting private 'licensed search agencies' to handle disclosures and look for blood relatives.

In 1995, British Columbia provided that, if the superintendent of child welfare believed the best interest of an Aboriginal child was served, authorities could, with the consent of adopters, disclose information to enable contact by an Indian band or community. Despite the federal Freedom of Information and Protection of Privacy Act, that province's adoptees and natural parents could issue disclosure vetoes and no-contact orders. In 1996, Nova Scotia's Act to Provide for Adoption Information established a Passive Adoption Register and criteria and controls for reunions. Information remained highly restricted. Both adoptive and natural parents could refuse consent to identifying information and, while the province had to inform Ottawa if a child had Native status, it did not have to disclose this to adopters, adoptees, or anyone else.

In 1996, Prince Edward Island continued to allow the director of vital statistics to alter original birth registrations in the case of adoption, but, for the first time, it allowed the maintenance of the original at the request of adopters and with the agreement of birth parents. Manitoba provided for contact and disclosure vetoes by adoptees and natural parents in 1997. It maintained a Post-Adoption Registry, which required reasonable efforts to locate members of the adoption circle and allowed applications by birth siblings. In 1998, the Northwest Territories legislated an Adoption Registry to maintain records and histories and facilitate reunions. Grandparents and other blood relatives could add their names, and social workers were to encourage adopters to inform children by age twelve that they were named in the registry. All members of the adoption circle were enjoined to make available up-to-date personal histories. A 1999 amendment to Alberta's Child Welfare Act granted sixteen-year-olds living independently the right to apply for information, and adult adoptees, with consent from the biological parents or verification of their death, to obtain original birth certificates. Notably, this section pertained only to children adopted on or after 1 January 2000.

In addition to setting up both passive and active registries, legislators began to recognize openness in the very course of formal adoption. In 1980, New Brunswick's Child and Family Services and Family Relations Act allowed parents to learn more about prospective adopters, with the consent of the latter. In 1992, the PEI legislature envisioned the possibility of continuing contact between adoptive and natural families, although arrangements had no legal force without a formal written agreement and independent legal advice.[121] Five years later, Manitoba allowed openness agreements 'for the purpose of facilitating communication or maintaining relationships . . . between an adoptive parent or prospective adoptive parents' and birthparents, the extended birth family, or anyone who had established 'a meaningful relationship with the child', including birth siblings and Indian bands.[122] Limits to connection were equally visible. British Columbia's 1995 Adoption Act observed that a 'failure to comply with an openness agreement is not grounds for the court to revoke a consent to adoption.'[123]

Demands for greater openness grew. In 1985, Alberta recorded 6,400 names on its registry waiting list, despite the legislature's stated worry that the privacy of birth mothers be jeopardized.[124] The overall legislative tone nevertheless remained, for the most part, unsupportive of ready disclosure. Substantial fines sometimes warned against unauthorized access. Saskatchewan's Act Respecting Adoption embodied the pervasive unease:

> No action lies or shall be instituted against the minister, the department, a peace officer or any officer or employee of the department or agent of the minister, where the minister, department, peace officer, officer, employee or agent is acting pursuant to the authority of this Act, the regulations or an order made pursuant to this act, for any loss or damage suffered by a person by reason of anything in good faith done, caused, permitted or authorized to be done, attempted to be done or omitted to be done, by any of them, pur-

suant to or in the exercise of or supposed exercise of any power conferred by this Act or the regulations or in the carrying out or supposed carrying out of any order . . .[125]

When changes failed to come swiftly enough, claimants for information turned increasingly to the courts, albeit with little sign of success.[126]

Standing against demands for greater openness was the persisting desire for absolute finality. After 1970, legislatures continued to endeavour to put a permanent stamp on adoption agreements. In that year, Yukon ordered that no action could set an order aside unless it had been achieved by fraud and its dissolution was in the interest of the child. Three years later, Saskatchewan provided that a 'Court of Appeal shall not set aside an order of adoption by reason only of a defect or irregularity in matters of procedure.'[127] In 1984, Ontario declared orders for the most part 'final and irrevocable' and not to 'be questioned or reviewed in any court'.[128]

Even as legislators strove to affirm the permanence of new relations, they also demonstrated new flexibility in enlarging the pool of prospective parents. In 1970, Yukon permitted unmarried persons or couples over twenty-one and other applicants justified by blood relations or other circumstances. The Northwest Territories and Saskatchewan shortly followed with similar sections in their acts. The Canadian Charter of Rights and Freedoms meant that legislatures also joined Yukon with its 1984 Children's Act that proclaimed: 'There is no presumption of law or fact that the best interests of a child are, solely by virtue of the age or the sex of the child, best served by placing the child in the care or custody of a female person rather than a male person or of a male person rather than a female person.'[129] Growing willingness, as in Newfoundland at the beginning of the twenty-first century, to allow 'natural' parents officially to choose adopters also broadened the field, even as it acknowledged new respect for the unwed. At much the same time, judicial challenges forced jurisdictions to accept same-sex couples, a shift that merely echoed a long-standing reality for earlier generations of Canadians.[130]

The introduction of adoption subsidies in the 1970s further diversified those who could consider adding youngsters to their households. By 1985, Alberta, Ontario, Manitoba, Saskatchewan, and Yukon, as well as Quebec, had passed supporting legislation and others slowly followed. Saskatchewan's early 1973 initiative promised financial assistance when 'reasonable' efforts to place the child had failed because of their 'special needs'. Funds could pay for 'initial and continuing expenses'.[131] In 1986, Yukon authorized the payment of 'medical, surgical or other remedial care'.[132] While racial minorities, those with mental or physical disabilities, or those who were part of sibling groups were singled out in some legislation, so too sometimes were adults whose resources could not readily sustain adoption expenses.[133] Although, as one social work investigator has pointed out, subsidies were far from automatic or sufficient, they opened the door for some 'special needs' youngsters and some prospective adopters, Natives among them.[134]

In more than a hundred years of legislation, Canadians had sometimes included reference to immigrant children and to the Second World War British guest children in provincial child welfare legislation, but legislators were preoccupied largely with domestic placements. By the end of the twentieth century, however, courts increasingly adjudicated claims regarding children from elsewhere[135] and legislatures endeavoured to regulate the movement of girls and boys across frontiers. In 1979, Manitoba forbade youngsters' adoption outside the province without special permission. In 1984, Yukon inscribed in its Children's Act the UN Convention on the Civil Aspects of International Child Abduction. In the 1990s, provinces began referring to the The Hague Convention on the Protection of Children and Co-operation in Respect of Intercountry Adoption. Rising numbers of international adoptions encouraged legislatures to join the commitment of the federal government to these international conventions that prioritized placements in original homelands and recognized children's rights to cultural and other heritages.

Such principles should have been familiar. They greatly resembled those demanded in child welfare by First Nations opponents of interracial adoption. In both cases, however, provinces and territories at the end of the twentieth century showed little capacity to live up to legislative promises. As we shall see in later chapters, Native and international adoptions supplied plenty of controversy in these years while eager would-be mothers and fathers readily sidestepped attempts at regulation.

Their actions were familiar. Despite a century and more of legislation, Canadians have never wholly regulated adoption. Some adopters and some birth parents have always wished to conduct their business beyond the public eye. The private market remained vigorous in most jurisdictions, despite some legislative efforts to regulate maternity homes and adoption professionals and agencies. Most notably, intra-family transfers of children remained, as always, largely unexamined by authorities. The recurring lack of attention to step-parent adoptions, at least until the emergence of a fathers' rights movement, signalled the commonplace assumption that the state ought to intervene as little as possible in family life. Ironically enough, the legal recognition of custom adoption served much the same purpose. By the end of the twentieth century, the transfer of babies was especially likely to be handled privately, rising from 22 per cent of all such adoptions in 1981 to 59 per cent in 1990.[136] As one British Columbia social worker critically noted, this trend was driven by the shortage of 'healthy white infants available through the Ministry' and the emergence of more 'aggressive' demand from 'many couples, particularly those who have deferred parenthood in favour of establishing careers and gaining financial security.' They were 'unaccustomed to allowing others to make decisions for them and may have little faith in the ability of a government department to solve their particular problem.' In contrast, the only way she could explain the attraction for single mothers was 'the illusion, if not always the reality, of greater choice.'[137] While Canadians might oppose governments proposing to withdraw all scrutiny from private adoptions, as Alberta suggested in 1984,[138] they continued to demonstrate considerable ingenuity in forging their own relations, both domestically and internationally.

Although the Canadian provinces and territories have jurisdiction over adoption, as with child welfare more generally, the federal government plays a role in taxation and employment policies as well as in international adoptions. In 1975, it set up the National Adoption Desk to coordinate some provincial efforts and to negotiate international agreements, but the bulk of activity remained at the provincial level. In the last decades of the century, adoptive parents began to campaign for paid adoption leaves to match those for biological mothers and, later, for fathers as well, for tax credits for adoption-related expenses, and for improved consular support and equal claims to citizenship for international adoptees. By 2000, much remained to be done. Adoptive parents received fewer weeks of insured employment leave than their biological counterparts, had yet to receive tax benefits, and were still forced to sponsor their child as a permanent resident before they could apply for citizenship. The continuing necessity for such campaigns invokes adoption's recurring status as a private initiative without public consequences. In fact, the acquisition of children by any method is ultimately a profoundly social act with implications for many aspects of community life, as the provinces and territories had decades to discover.[139]

From 1970 to the end of the century, Canadian legislators began to provide greater access to information and to foresee greater openness in adoption as they confronted a changed world where alternatives to the heterosexual nuclear family were increasingly presumed legitimate. Yet, fears of knowledge and ongoing contact continued to shape adoption laws. Tensions were embodied in two end-of-century reports. One, the Royal Commission on New Reproductive Technologies, saw adoption as a positive, albeit too limited, response to the dilemma of Canadians confronting infertility. The other, the Royal Commission on Aboriginal Peoples, condemned a history that had devastated entire communities. Both issues were visible in the legislation as it evolved from 1873 to 1997 and equally too in the drop in domestic adoptions from 5,376 in 1981 to 2,836 in 1990 to 2,710 in 1999.[140]

Canada's overall legislative record in adoption is complicated. It reminds us that state efforts to manage populations must take into account traditional pathways by which citizens and others endeavour to assert their own preferences. In a democracy, policies must also pay some attention to a variety of voices. As legislators negotiated the principles to inform the transfer of children among families during the nineteenth and twentieth centuries, they variously took into account the predicament of birth parents and communities and the desires of potential adopters. Just as with immigration, suspicion and hope loomed near the surface of many debates. Too often, impoverished birth parents, mothers in particular, were further victimized as objects of legislative regulation. Increasingly, however, lawmakers struggled to admit the legitimacy of various family forms and to permit connections between old and new worlds. In their search for more inclusive and open adoption at the end of the twentieth century, they were effectively exploring the meaning of official commitments to multiculturalism and equality more generally. Ultimately, laws, for all their power, can only hint at the realities of class, gender, and race that shaped Canadians' experience of adoption over some hundred and more years. These issues are the concern of subsequent chapters.

Class Matters

Children are very rarely transferred to the care of others when the material circumstances of biological kin are good. What exactly has gone awry has, of course, differed sharply among individuals and over time. Adults in legislatures, judiciaries, or child welfare programs who have been involved in making new arrangements for youngsters have sought to explain child casualties. A few have pointed to the structural factors that make parenting so difficult for so many. In 1963, Mary King, long-time superintendent of child welfare for British Columbia, observed:

> The need . . . is to help families provide a sound, healthy environment in which their children may grow to physically and emotionally healthy adulthood. This means families having work and adequate incomes, living in healthy communities, and having their own needs met sufficiently well to enable them to give loving and understanding care to their children. It requires emotional maturity and great strength of character to meet the daily stress and frustration created by lack of work, marginal income, poor housing, ill health, and lack of wholesome recreational and social activities. Yet many families who are least well equipped emotionally and physically to raise their children amid such frustrations must try to do so.[1]

While King's sensitivity to the forces that undermine family life has been shared by many commentators on adoption, it has rarely been powerful enough to offset the commonplace preference for focusing on a litany of failures or individual failures: bad luck, bad choices, bad times, bad genes, or bad drugs. Those in authority have frequently preferred to sidestep rather than confront questions of power.

The subjects of scrutiny, adults separated from offspring, have rarely been in a position to offer their own version of events. As likely losers in many of life's battles, they have had most often to accept little more than uncertain hearings for their pain, anger, confusion, and shame. Individuals commonly designated failures at a task—parenting—that most Canadians have taken for granted have been hard put to explain their own predicament in structural terms. Class consciousness, when it has existed, has been more likely to be associated with public life, notably the labour market, rather than with private spaces.

Class—and, as we will see in the next chapters, gender, religion, and race—has been only uncertainly identified as constructing adult options in relations with children. Indeed, recognition of class's influence in setting life's perimeters has regularly been significantly less likely than acknowledgement of the repercussions of being male or female or of membership in a religious or racial group. As one 2000 international study put it, 'class is one of the silent dynamics of adoption.'[2] Like others elsewhere, notably but not only in the United States, Canadians have regularly failed to consider how class has structured and continues to structure child exchange.

This survey of over one hundred and twenty-five years of legislation, policy, and practice cannot ignore how child transfer and adoption have reflected the location of some families near the bottom of Canada's social and economic hierarchies and of others higher up. Access to what has been termed the 'male breadwinner wage' or the 'family wage', and better has always been limited.[3] Economic well-being, if not a prerequisite for good parenting, has always been a substantial asset. Adults who cannot afford comfortable homes, healthy food, and respite from caregiving, and who have seen little hope for themselves, have been extremely hard put, however much they might wish or struggle, to support daughters and sons. Canadians should be surprised, not when they occasionally fail, but that they so often succeed.

Racialized minorities, from the First Nations and blacks for much of Canada's history, to the Irish in the nineteenth century, or southern or eastern Europeans or Asians for periods in the twentieth century, have been especially likely to find themselves at the base of a system of class relations that has often, but never always, corresponded to racial hierarchies. They have never been alone, as we are reminded by the pithy observations of Sam Slick, the Yankee peddler invented by pre-Confederation writer Thomas Chandler Haliburton, on the sale of Nova Scotia paupers, including children, to the lowest bidder: 'I guess you need'nt twitt me with our slave-sales, for we deal only in blacks; but blue nose approbates no distinction in colours, and when reduced to poverty, is reduced to slavery, and is sold—a *White Nigger*.'[4] Close to one hundred and forty years later, a short-lived amendment to British Columbia's Protection of Children Act, proposed initially by Thomas Berger's Royal Commission on Family and Children's Law, similarly conveyed the interconnections of class and race. Any 'concerned party' in family court proceedings could request two lay persons 'to sit with the Family Court Judge to hear neglect cases' in order to 'neutralize class bias among judges and contribute to their knowledge of the cultural background of families.'[5] Despite protests from Native organizations, this provision was eliminated after the Social Credit Party defeated the New Democrats in 1974. While Natives had their own social and economic hierarchies and have been distributed in a variety of social locations in the larger society, their particular opposition reminded observers that they have been disproportionately located at the bottom.

Canadians of many hues and origins have found themselves with insufficient resources to secure a minimum standard of living. Facing limited options, they have been hard put to maintain respectability, plan for the future, or postpone gratification, all behaviours that commonly contribute to successful parenting. Not surprisingly, those at the base of the Canadian vertical mosaic have always supplied the bulk of youngsters surrendered to others. My investigation of adoption also suggests that, as the adage 'women are only a man away from welfare' implies, positions within Canada's social and economic hierarchies may shift dramatically over a lifetime, and family members may fall within different classes. Such apparent fluidity should not blind us to the reality that many generations of some families have struggled with poverty. This group of citizens has no ready label. Terms like the poorest of the poor, the disreputable or unrespectable working class, welfare mothers, paupers, the disadvantaged, and the lumpenproletariat appear inevitably stigmatizing. I have chosen, for the most part, to employ simply 'the disadvantaged' or 'the poor'.

Canada's vertical mosaic, which includes stratification among the diverse communities themselves, has always featured large numbers of disadvantaged children at its base, as the recurring pledges to eliminate child poverty remind us.[6] First Nations children attending residential schools or caught up in the 'sixties scoop', like other girls and boys consigned to industrial schools or the arms of non-kin, were vulnerable in the first instance because their parents' command of material resources was less, often much less, than those mothers and fathers who could send offspring to Upper Canada College, psychiatrists' couches, elite camps, or other sites where their needs, and those of their parents, might be met. Adoption legislation's long-standing preoccupation with matters of inheritance largely missed the point: adoptees hardly ever came from circumstances that permitted any realistic hope of material benefits.

In 1971, *The Real Poverty Report* summed up the situation that had long stalked Canada's class system:

> To be poor in our society is to suffer the most outrageous kinds of violence perpetrated by human beings on other human beings.
>
> From the very beginning, when you are still a child, you must learn to undervalue yourself. You are told that you are poor because your father is too stupid or too shiftless to find a decent job; or that he is a good-for-nothing who has abandoned you to a mother who cannot cope. And as you grow up on the streets, you are told that your mother is dirty and lazy and that is why she has to take money from the welfare department. Because you are poor, the lady from the welfare office is always coming around asking questions. She wants to know if your mother is living with a man, and why she is pregnant again.[7]

In other words, impoverished youngsters have been embedded in the larger context of family disadvantage. This reality flew straight in the face of much insistence that wealth did not matter, since 'love', 'the rightful dower of all children', flourishes without regard to material circumstances.[8]

While the history of adoption must pay close attention to youngsters, it is misleading to focus on them alone. As Jane Pulkingham and Gordon Ternowetsky have rightly argued, singling out children too often 'plays into existing distinctions between the "deserving" and "undeserving" poor. It obscures the extent to which the process of labour market and welfare restructuring is gender-, race- and class-based' and the demands on 'improperly constituted families' to 'reconstitute a traditional family form.'[9] Adopters of prospective offspring from Canada or abroad have then been readily characterized as 'rescuers', innocently unconnected to the structural relations that position them to the advantage of others.[10] The causes of poverty, 'a basic contributor to dependency, neglect, and abuse,'[11] regularly become someone else's responsibility, commonly that of surrendering adults. Society's losers in the high stakes game of class have been held responsible for failure to maintain children suitably and winners congratulated for their good fortune and presumed industry in achieving preferred standards.

This chapter describes some of the ways in which class operated to distinguish those considered the worthy and the unworthy custodians of the nation's children. It begins with a discussion of how economic ranking has been visible in adoption laws and judicial decisions. Next, it considers surrendering communities and individuals. Just who lost youngsters? It then moves to an examination of Canadians whom authorities have assessed as suitable guardians for Canadian girls and boys. Foster and adoptive parents are singled out for separate attention as two important, sometimes sharply distinguished but always closely associated, constituencies of adult caregivers. While the class differences of adults in children's lives preoccupy this chapter, it also attends to the ways that girls and boys have been designated as more or less valuable by reason of their class origins and how this has affected their distribution in adoption's hard markets.

Legal and Judicial Acknowledgements of Class

As was suggested in chapter 2, legislators were long preoccupied with property and only relatively recently with what else, such as racial and family histories and statuses, might be inherited. To be sure, requirements for religious matching invoked a complicated history of inter-group relations, but for much of Canadian history the Protestant–Catholic divide coincided to a significant degree with the line between the more and the less well-to-do. Legislative preoccupation with property reflected even more explicitly the interest of more prosperous classes in adoption as one means of securing property through the generations. It also helps explain why legal confirmation had to struggle against the appeal of informal arrangements in which inheritance was only a minor concern. Only as the modern state increasingly regulated its citizens, and as citizenship came to include rights to some measure of social security, did the attractions of formal adoption come to the fore. Once pensions, such as those stemming from war or industrial service, and benefits, as with the federal government's programs of family allowances or child tax credit after the Second World War, touched the mass of Canadians, the completion of legal formalities began to offer unprecedented economic advantages.

Mounting financial benefits were accompanied by the appeal of legally enforceable boundaries between new and old. Where the exchange of children long involved some degree of knowledge, obligation, or reciprocity among families, attachments in the modern world increasingly raised the prospect of unknowable, suspect, or even unsavoury pasts to which connections should be sharply curtailed. In the days before racial boundaries were questioned, potential newcomers might not be readily physically distinguishable from adopters. Confidentiality and secrecy promised to disguise certain types of class strangers, something they could not later guarantee for racial strangers to new households. Effectively then, such provisions in much twentieth-century legislation functioned to obscure the role of class in determining domestic vulnerability.

Right from the beginning, adoption laws took the normality of the middle-class or propertied household as their fundamental yardstick. Children and parents who came under the auspices of these laws were to be caught up in a net of regulation, or what Michel Foucault has termed 'disciplinary regimes', that increasingly set appropriate standards of behaviour for all concerned.[12] Although the disciplining of the poor has been most obvious, adopters who wished state confirmation of rights had also been increasingly obliged to submit themselves to supervision and probation. While many did, and do, buy themselves out of much regulation by their privileged access to resources, those desperate for progeny have found themselves subject to the home studies and character checks that otherwise generally dogged those tagged as less worthy. No wonder one of the sure signs of middle-class and better status has been grumbling about state investigation of 'their' private affairs. By the closing years of the twentieth century, advantaged Canadians facing small numbers of healthy infants available domestically, and not always matching age, sexuality, and other standards for approval, frequently looked elsewhere.

In time, efforts at regulating the global trade in children—as with provincial legislatures' inclusion of United Nations' codes dealing with adoption, trafficking, and abduction—slowly began to catch up with the increasingly international market in sons and daughters. Only the very rich or well positioned continued to be allowed the virtually free rein that had distinguished Canadians such as the novelist Mazo de la Roche and her cousin Caroline Clement in their acquisition of two British children with the assistance of future British prime minister Harold Macmillan or the more anonymous Christian missionaries who returned from Asia with domestic reminders of the reach of empires.

While always significant, the power of privileged classes to order children on demand has always been informed by persisting allegiance to the authority of blood and faith in parental, most often maternal, sentiments. The checkered history of consents in Canadian courts has told complicated tales of conflicts in which class clearly played a role within families and within larger communities. Judges' decisions were never predictable. Richer and poorer claimants might be variously supported in their applications for children.

More prosperous adopters often won the day. In the case *Re Grafasso*, before the Ontario Supreme Court in 1916, an unwed mother left her baby with the family in which she was nursemaid to another infant. Some six years later, while working as a domestic in a boarding house, she applied to recover her daughter. The judge, citing the 'stain' of illegitimacy, the uncertain prospects of domestic service, and the comforts of the adopters whose name the child bore, albeit without legal entitlement, refused to authorize return.[13] In the same year, the Ontario Supreme

Court ruled against a father's application for a daughter whom the Toronto CAS had determined to be 'neglected' and handed over by indenture to 'an approved foster home'. Despite the birth family's bettered circumstances, including savings and a home, their history of apparent abandonment and criminality could not withstand the promise of Nipissing foster parents to attend 'to the physical, the moral and religious upbringing of their ward.'[14]

The economic calculations made by many judges were set out even more explicitly in the case of an Albertan Protestant mother who endeavoured to regain her daughter in the 1920s. Another couple wished to adopt the child; the mother went to the courts for relief. One judge in the appellate division of the province's Supreme Court argued the mother had done nothing to lose custody but had in fact ensured the well-being of the child by handing her over to others. Permanent loss of her daughter would be 'not only an injustice, if not a moral wrong, but an invasion of the natural primal rights of humanity.' His colleague, however, in siding with the majority, insisted that a mother earning only some $25 to $40 a month as a domestic was hardly in a position to support the child. Another agreed, noting that the prospective adopters were 'well-to-do' and 'in a much better position to maintain the child.'[15] In 1948, the Ontario Court of Appeal upheld an original judgment against an unwed Kingston stenographer who was appealing the adoption of her daughter. The original judge had noted approvingly that the new parents had spent some $1,500 for clothing, medical services, and other matters and that 'while the rich and poor have an equal right before the courts in the respect of custody of children, the "welfare of the child" must involve some consideration of the educational opportunities offered.'[16]

Would-be parents who were, for the most part, middle class, older, settled, and had male breadwinners most clearly embodied the ideals favoured by authorities. This was the constituency so frequently offered a lock on the past in the twentieth century. The presence of adopters in the Conservative cabinet of Ontario premier Frank Miller in 1985, when it prepared to refuse all information to searchers, was only one reminder of who in the adoption circle was well-positioned to exert influence.[17]

The judiciary nevertheless regularly supported poorer biological families against more well-to-do claimants. In 1926, the Nova Scotia Supreme Court favoured a male labourer whose sixteen-year-old daughter had been designated a 'neglected' child. The judges noted the unfair conduct of proceedings against the family and ordered her release.[18] In 1953, a young Dutch couple overwhelmed by the demands of immigration, and living in cramped quarters, surrendered twins through their doctor to a husband and wife 'considerably better off', 'both in their middle thirties and childless.' With improved circumstances and family support, the birth parents soon appealed for restitution. They lost the original decision but won on appeal, when one judge concluded that the children had a right not to be alienated 'from their own flesh and blood'.[19] In 1966, the BC Supreme Court allowed the appeal of a natural mother against would-be adopters of her daughter. Despite previous promiscuity, desertion, and uncertain employment, the mother, then in a relationship with an older man with a home in Toronto, was determined to have shown sufficient maturity not to have her consent dispensed with.[20]

Over many decades, legislation and court decisions attempted to juggle pasts and futures in which class functioned to promise different outcomes. If the 'best interests of the child' was regularly interpreted to the advantage of potential adopters, other forces were also at work. Neither legislators nor judges could dispense casually with the rights of those left behind by formal adoption. Canadians' long-standing investment in blood ties, maternal love, and, it should be said, in the notion of property in children, was not easily overcome. A somewhat romantic but also realistic recognition that biology mattered and that material well-being was not the be-all and end-all of human relations has always served to hold in check otherwise powerful demands to shift custody to the economically more powerful.

Surrendering Communities

The unfortunate youngsters who thronged Canadian institutions throughout the nineteenth and twentieth centuries were always disproportionately recruited from the nation's poorest families. Fragility, like wealth, was likely to be inherited. Instances of Horatio, or Horatia, Algers always existed, as did scions of millionaires who ended up on the street, but the dice have always been loaded. For those at the bottom, even if they shared racial and religious histories with their economic superiors, something—a mentor, a particular combination of brain and brawn, or an unusual opportunity—had to tip the scales if they were to escape.

Canadian fiction is filled with portraits of orphans who providentially secured places in the heart of middle-class beneficiaries. The options were matter-of-factly set out in a 1875 novel that featured little Tommy adopted by a colonel's wife, who explained, 'I shall grow too fond of the child to make him into a servant.'[21] Escape from his class roots was also the fate of E. Pauline Johnson's Buck, a young Barnardo servant taken in by a kindly Canadian doctor and his angelic daughter. By saving his benefactress from ruffians, he justified his salvation and elevation into the respectable classes.[22] Author Nora Tynan's short story 'The Christmas Baby', from 1907–8, featured a well-to-do British bachelor lawyer retrieving a child from the streets, only to discover that she not only possessed 'golden curls' but was the daughter of his beloved sister, who had emigrated to Canada and died.[23] J.T. Stirrett denied such rescue, albeit regrettably, to the suggestively named Blossom Criglet, who 'was one of those often encountered in the slums, for which no reason can be given beyond ascribing it to some freak of Nature. In the midst of a family which had few agreeable traits, this child blossomed in person as well as in name. Like a pure white flower growing in a bog, she was so wonderfully beautiful and fragile that her continued existence seemed to be a miracle.'[24] These storybook children, like their more famous exemplar, Anne of Green Gables, traversed the pages of early Canadian fiction, regularly singled out as atypical of their kind. Anne, like the youngsters above, stood out from the suspect boys among whose number Marilla and Matthew Cuthbert had expected to recruit an addition to their household. Like golden nuggets, such children shone. Others were not so lucky.

While the vast majority of newcomers to Aboriginal North America had fled poverty, or what they viewed as unacceptable economic conditions in original homelands, white girls and boys thrown up on new shores by hard-hearted fate as cholera orphans in the 1830s and 1840s, or as 'home children' later, were not readily taken to the bosom of colony or nation. Such youngsters met much the same welcome as the poor did in Britain and Europe. If they could labour for a pittance, they might be given house-room. Canadian householders never readily took in those who could not pull their weight.

When their numbers multiplied with the addition of offspring of German and French parents dying en route to the colony in the late eighteenth century, Halifax's orphans were consigned to the poorhouse and Canada's first orphanage. Many other relatively recent arrivals evidently felt little sense of obligation to the children of others.[25] Inmates of Maritime poorhouses were farmed out to the lowest bidder as apprentices or household help. In 1916, Nova Scotia still had to report that '76 children classed as normal are being cared for in various country [Poor Law] institutions.' By then, authorities were concluding that 'it is manifestly impossible for these children to have the care and attention which is to develop the traits necessary to good citizenship.'[26]

Upper Canada, later Canada West, then Ontario, never had poor laws, choosing to provide for desperate youngsters in a variety of adult institutions, including prisons and hospitals, as well as orphanages and infant homes. Ethnicity shared with the powerful guaranteed little protection. In the 1890s, a Scottish-Irish washerwoman, who was described as beaten by her husband and let down by 'layabout' adult sons, saw her daughter consigned to a shelter with a host of others.[27] The offspring of such impoverished city-dwellers provided the bulk of girls and boys to be transferred across domestic boundaries. Of particular concern from the mid-nineteenth to the mid-twentieth century were those termed 'home children', youngsters sent abroad by Britain's philanthropic agencies. For many Canadian householders, such additions were counted among the discardable dross of humanity. Joy Parr in *Labouring Children* and others have chronicled in detail the often brutal reception of youthful migrants.[28] Philanthropists hailed such economic refugees as 'snatched from pinching hunger, fluttering rags, and all the squalor of gutter life' to be 'lifted up into some task for decency and cleanliness.' Such a child, 'trained in the school whose first and last lesson is to fear neither God nor man,' had to be 'taught the beginnings of Christian faith and duty' and be 'borne away to the free spacious regions of the western hemisphere.'[29] Not surprisingly, many adults who received such migrants believed them suitable only for serving those lucky enough to have arrived earlier and to own property. While Canadians were slowly reconsidering ideas about child labour, they long reserved such reappraisals for their own offspring.

In 1882, Ontario's Walpole Township council protested the entry of 'home children', concerned that the country would become 'the dumping ground for the indigents of the old world.'[30] While sympathy built up over the years, such newcomers regularly raised suspicions. Despite the arguments of the imperially minded that immigrant children represented 'a really great and beneficial piece of

Empire building,'[31] rebuttals always surfaced. In 1922, one Progressive member of Parliament from Alberta voiced persisting sentiments: 'Nobody but degenerate parents would want to part with children to send them away to work in a distant country.' Given such progenitors, he confidently predicted 'the grossest discrimination will be displayed against the unfortunate immigrant child.'[32] Three years later, a leading Canadian clubwoman and internationalist spoke bluntly: 'Our experience would indicate that the percentage being brought up as actual members of the family and receiving a share in the family's resources, ultimately, is very small. The others, the great majority, who come in, come in definitely to work.' A leading unionist was even more to the point: 'In Canada we know full well that the children who have been brought out have been exploited by those who have received them, by those who have no children of their own, by those who use them to save their own.'[33] Young refugees from Britain's poorest homes might allow the release of householders' prized progeny for schooling and pursuits that would confirm their advantage for another generation.

Residential schools for Aboriginal students shared significant histories with other provisions for impoverished youngsters. At first indistinguishable from, and sometimes one and the same as, the industrial and reform schools that housed the offspring of the poor more generally, they increasingly aimed to segregate indigenous students to be remade as brown workers in respectable homes and farms. Initially, when education to some degree comparable to that of other Canadian pupils appeared to be promised, Native elites often welcomed schools for their own children and for others in their communities. By the beginning of the twentieth century, however, it was increasingly clear that residential education was decidedly inferior and frequently disastrous. Elite Natives, such as the family of E. Pauline Johnson, who had once chosen options such as the Mohawk Institute at Six Nations for their offspring, sought safer guarantees of education and opportunity. The loss of a constituency that had sufficient cultural and other resources to make other arrangements left residential schools, like industrial schools and orphanages, increasingly sheltering the most disadvantaged Native youngsters.

Despite mounting opposition, Indian Affairs and churches, aided and abetted by the RCMP, as the national police force was known after 1920, continued to search out pupils. Their efforts, when combined with the increasingly desperate position of Aboriginal families, especially during the Great Depression of the 1930s when their wage-earners might well be first fired,[34] maintained registration until the last school was closed in the 1990s. Widows and widowers, after unsuccessfully canvassing relatives for support, might well turn to the schools for help, as did unwed mothers and other kin who could or would not feed additional mouths. As Susie Doxtator, a pupil at the Mohawk Institute from 1930 to 1941, remembered, 'I ran away once and I came home to my aunt's, but they were so poor they couldn't look after anybody else either.'[35] Many students, as the alumnae of two Ontario schools—Mount Elgin and the Mohawk Institute—reported, knew that they had been sent 'because their parents died or separated, or were too poor to keep them.'[36] Authorities largely ignored the dire straits that forced communities to see their most vulnerable members in foreign institutions. As historian John Milloy has concluded, 'the official view seemed to be that the need for welfare and residential placement was not a product of economic circumstances but of parental moral shortcomings.'[37]

Whether Aboriginal or newcomer, children with ties to only one set of parental kin to draw on in emergency have always faced particular jeopardy. Single, sometimes unwed, mothers have frequently been economically vulnerable. In both the nineteenth and twentieth centuries, their offspring might well disappear into healthy communities, there to be sheltered relatively anonymously by kin and neighbours whose own histories might also include the absence of church-going to confirm marital ties. When birth registrations were uncertain and demand for birth certificates infrequent, knowledge of bastardy might well not be widely communicated nor even considered especially important.

Reports like those from the Toronto Infants' Home and Infirmary in the 1870s that enumerated infants deserted and 'exposed on the streets' were commonplace into the twentieth century.[38] Even when they wished to help, biological kin were themselves sometimes in desperate circumstances. Such was the problem for 'Kenneth M.' who was forced to leave his fourth foster home in the 1950s. As a sympathetic Vancouver social worker reported, 'the foster mother was the natural mother's aunt. These people loved the child and wished to keep him but because of their housing situation and their financial position were forced to give him up. Kenneth was very upset when he was moved from this home.'[39] Like many families around the country, his maternal relatives lived too close to the margin to enlarge their household.

Unmarried mothers coming to the attention of welfare authorities were especially likely to have limited resources. In 1970, the Newfoundland Department of Public Welfare reported that, of the 613 unmarried mothers in its records, only 35 were educated above Grade 12, while 44 had less than Grade 6, and 298 Grades 6 to 8. Among their numbers were 197 domestic servants, 23 factory workers, 19 nursing assistants, 5 cooks, 59 waitresses, 16 telephone operators, and 125 unemployed. Somewhat higher up on the social scale were 3 registered nurses, 34 salesclerks, 22 stenographers, and 68 students.[40] Given discriminatory wages, few such women easily supported themselves, let alone others.

The options facing unwed mothers depended not only on the support they found from kin and neighbours but also on their calculation of their own and their offspring's future. If they, and their families, had hopes that respectability could be regained and that schooling or ordinary life could be resumed, then daughters and sons were more likely to be surrendered. If offspring matched the desires of would-be adopters, then birth mothers could also console themselves with the prospect of bettering their children's chances. Such were the hopes of a middle-class Grade 12 student in 1966, who trusted that the child she had produced with a 'graduate engineer' would benefit from her 'profoundly unselfish act' and be nurtured by two loving parents.[41]

Poorer and negatively racialized women had fewer illusions that homes would be found. Patients at Halifax's Grace Maternity Hospital in the mid-1960s were typical. Black mothers overwhelmingly kept their infants while middle-class white women opted for surrender.[42] Children who could count only on mothers hobbled by racist and sexist moralities and economic discrimination started lower on life's slippery ladder. They found few sheltering arms. No wonder one historian of the seduced in Canada has concluded that 'child servants in the late eighteenth and the early nineteenth centuries were orphaned, abandoned, or poor children who were apprenticed by parents, guardians or magistrates in order to provide for the maintenance of the child.'[43]

While offspring of parents without partners were always especially vulnerable, two-parent families have never entirely escaped distress. Structural under- and unemployment, insufficient wages, and unchecked cost of living kept many below the poverty line. Orphanages and child welfare programs have helped biological families retain youngsters, and such retention became the leitmotif of much modern work in social security. Even then, significant numbers of adults found no way to reconcile their own needs with maintenance of children.

Mothers and fathers unable to care for children have often appeared to be especially poorly integrated into their communities. They have frequently stood at the margins, often with complicated histories of neglect and abuse. Recurring judicial and criminal investigations often place their tragedies near the centre of public memory when it comes to considering the transfer of children. In British Columbia in 1995, the Gove Commission drew attention to Verna Vaudreuil, who was physically and sexually abused and a foster child in many homes before she became an unwed mother at nineteen. In 1992, her son, five-year-old Matthew died at her hands.[44] A modern roll call of death chronicled by public reports of various kinds would include Kim Anne Popen in Sarnia, Ontario, in 1976, Vicky Star Ellis in Toronto in 1977, and John Ryan Turner in Saint John, New Brunswick, in 1994.[45] In October 2004, a muck-raking *Globe and Mail* reporter introduced her description of an unemployed Toronto couple's abuse of their infant son and his subsequent release for adoption with a reference to Charles Dickens's *Tale of Two Cities*. This link to a past chronicler of abused and desperate children provided an apt reminder of how the depths of the social order provide fertile grounds for abuse. Yet that larger context went ignored and the writer, as she had done with previous cases of child murder in her city, contented herself with pillorying the undeniably appalling parents.[46] Many more child tragedies have escaped even this limited assessment.[47]

Brutal and inadequate parents have been regularly vilified, their frequent economic distress regarded as yet more proof of their overall inadequacy. In 1890, the Anglican periodical the *Canadian Churchman* typically summed up 'the causes of poverty' in ways that contemporaries and those to follow would find familiar: 'primarily sloth and intemperance'.[48] Welfare workers often preferred a different vocabulary, but their assessment could be very similar. In 1953, a University of British Columbia social work professional reported on the adoption placement of legitimate children. Despite the obvious economic distress of much of his sample, he emphasized that 'causative factors were primarily of a subjective psychological nature.' These included immature spouses, interfering mothers-in-law, and any woman who 'failed to make a satisfactory identification with a female figure, and who has failed to accept her sex, giving birth to the child, and the duties which she is called upon to perform in the care of the child . . . a tremendous blow to the defenses which she has set up to deny her femininity.'[49] Almost twenty years later, a *Maclean's*-Goldfarb poll reported that some 50 per cent of Canadians believed that poverty was 'chosen' by those afflicted.[50]

Explanations for neglected and abandoned children have also regularly cited substance abuse of various kinds. In the nineteenth and twentieth centuries, alcohol was the favourite culprit. Drink regularly threatened family safety. Boozers consumed family income, and their violence and irresponsibility threatened children. Such was the case of a Polish immigrant whose behaviour attracted police raids in First World War-era Toronto. His wife escaped with a babe-in-arms, whom she then left with the Catholic Children's Aid Society 'with a note pinned to its clothing' in 1917.[51] After the Second World War, another so-called hyphenated Canadian, Victor Malarek, remembered a home destroyed by his labourer father's drunken assaults.[52]

In the last quarter of the twentieth century, hard-drinking Native women have been particularly identified with fetal alcohol syndrome disorders. There is evidence that too ready labelling may offer opportunities for mainstream observers to sidestep, as anthropologist Jo Fiske reminds us, 'concerns expressed by Aboriginal organizations with respect to "cultural genocide", racism, and loss of identity as causal factors in Aboriginal behaviours and social alienation in the dominant society.'[53] In the same years, other intoxicants were also spreading ruin and preoccupying critics. An epidemic of so-called hard and soft drugs supplied new, again sometimes problematic, answers for high levels of children in public care. American popular, often neo-conservative, commentators appeared especially preoccupied with 'crack babies', 'ice babies', or 'meth babies', all seeming products of bad mothers. In response to a widespread moral panic, Canadian and American child health experts joined together to insist that cocaine exposure in the womb was rarely the real problem, all the more so because the placenta seemed often to act as a barrier: 'We are deeply disappointed that American and international media continues to use a term that not only lacks any scientific basis but endangers and disenfranchises the children to whom it is applied.'[54] Such hard facts had stiff competition from the continuing appeal of individualized explanations for parenting failures.

As these latter examples demonstrate, sympathy for hard-pressed birth parents has been, at best, uncertain. Their social and economic marginality was frequently visible before, and was only further confirmed by, the loss of youngsters. Limited resources made it harder for them to parent, sometimes helped drive them to brutality, and gave them little opportunity for respite. Whatever kinds of people they might have been, they could only with difficulty meet standards for childcare that were increasingly informed by notions that children should not labour, should not be subjected to significant corporal punishment, and should remain innocent and dependent. Such childcare strategies were most easily embraced by those higher on the social pyramid. Authorities would seek them among foster and adoptive parents, with varying degrees of success.

Foster Parents

Canadians and their records have not always distinguished between foster and adoptive parents. Well into the modern period, as a study for one 1960 'Conference on Children' lamented, even the distribution of children among adoption, foster, and group homes has not always been clear.[55] Imprecision has been all the greater because, as the Alberta Child Welfare Commission reported in 1968, 'the dividing line between the child in a foster home and an adoption home is indefinable (which can be attested to by the many foster home parents who have adopted the child originally placed in their home on a foster home basis).'[56] Despite the imprecision of records, the numbers involved in foster care have been large. Canada's major study of adoption in 1980 put foster children at some 68 to 80 per cent of all those in care in the previous twenty years, 'making foster homes the single most important child care resource.'[57] As Alberta authorities had already acknowledged in 1943, 'a foster home program is the steel framework of any child welfare structure.'[58]

When Ontario's first superintendent of child welfare, J.J. Kelso, searched for adults to assume parental responsibilities in the 1890s, he followed long-standing traditions in seeking free care. He rejected institutional solutions and preferred the fostering out that typified the Scottish child welfare system and that, in the guise of apprenticeship and indenture, had a long Canadian history. Turn-of-the-century waifs and strays were to be succoured in family homes. Kelso's hopes rested on 'respectable' householders' willingness to welcome unrelated youngsters. In 1893, he stated:

> As these children are taken in nearly every case from the poorer classes, they will be more at home and more likely to thrive among working people of modest pretensions. It is very essential that in the homes of foster parents habits of cleanliness and tidiness should prevail, that truthfulness should be strictly observed and bad language be forbidden. With such conditions, and a genuine love for the child, the lack of a bank account is of small importance.[59]

More than three decades later, he was still hopeful of taking children out of 'sordid surroundings,' preferably transferring them from urban to rural settings. He also continued to hold out hopes for free homes:

> We frequently find that when we endeavour to place a child in a foster home we are asked how much we are willing to pay a week.... There are many fine, healthy boys and girls who should be placed permanently in free homes, and we are firmly convinced that these free homes can be found if reasonable effort is made and the work elevated to the high plane of Christian and patriotic service. In the first few years of Children's Aid work, when there was no thought of payment, many fine people opened their homes gladly to the needy child, and they should be encouraged to continue this noble service.[60]

Such sentiments counted on the appeal of young children at least as much as on the nobility of the service.

A home-finder for Toronto's Infants' Home in 1934 described the desired meeting of foster child and adult: 'We then go to a smaller home and see a tiny baby sleeping peacefully in a carriage on the front porch. Everything about the baby is sweet and clean. We are invited in by a young woman who proudly shows her little home; her husband is a street car conductor. They have no children and are "crazy" about this one, but do not want to adopt her because they hope some day to have one of their own.'[61] Separation did not always occur. As an earlier observer had cheerfully noted:

> It frequently happens that when a child has been in a home it so attaches itself that the family feel they cannot give it up and they either adopt it outright or the visit goes on indefinitely. In many ways these free adoptions are the more satisfactory. No one is under any obligation, the authorities can keep a closer jurisdiction over the child, and it seems probable that this plan will get more children out of institutions and into good homes, if even for a few months, than the system of regular adoptions alone would do.[62]

Thrifty British Columbia, like other jurisdictions, long remained hopeful regarding the potential of free homes. Only in the early 1930s did it begin to pay maintenance for all foster children, not only infants.[63] Alberta's long-time superintendent of child welfare, Charles B. Hill, resisted anything but free homes. Like others, he trusted that 'the interests of good citizenship' and the 'zeal for the cause of wayward youth' would offer sufficient recompense.[64]

The response of most modern professional social workers was much less sanguine. Robert Mills, the head of the Children's Aid Society (CAS) of Toronto and the author of the chapter on child protection and child care in a major study of welfare in Alberta in 1947, was scathing in his dismissal of unpaid care. Hill's methods were damned as dangerous and old fashioned. Mills pointed out that 'free homes' almost invariably meant the girls and boys were taken as 'farm labour or domestic help' and not to meet 'their need for homes in which their personality can unfold along lines of happiness to themselves and acceptability to the community in which they will some day play an important part.' In effect, the five hundred 'free foster homes' claimed by the province were really 'work' placements for those designated 'non-adoptable, whether dependent, neglected or delinquent.'[65] The hardy fondness for homes without payment nevertheless proved extremely handy for tax-payers. Every jurisdiction was eager to download obligations.

Relying on free homes as a solution to children in care drew on romantic notions of adult–child, especially mother–child, bonding. Maternal love would compensate for shortcomings in budgets for girls and boys. Free homes also ignored a long history of households' exploitation of children and drew on observations of the willingness of the nation's working families to shelter additional members when the need arose. Only too revealingly, very few hopes for foster parents rested on application from the middle class, which was presumed to be little interested in the offspring of disadvantage. They depended instead on the hospitality of those whose modest means placed them above most offending households but securely in the working class.

A post–Second World War assessment of Toronto's foster families would not have appeared unusual anywhere in English Canada. The great majority were married couples, often with children, home-owners, British, between twenty-five and fifty-five years old. Few had post-secondary education and most had far less. Most were 'self-supporting but with incomes less than $2,500 a year. Husbands were mainly engaged in skilled or unskilled labour.' 'Very few had people other than immediate family in their homes' and most 'desired children, especially girls, between the ages of six and twelve.'[66] That preference signalled an age when children might be handy but present fewer demands than infants, toddlers, or teens. Revealing too, it was an age range that households considering emigrant children often preferred. The gender preference was also commonplace, a reflection of the faith that girls were less challenging.

As adoption laws increasingly encouraged some adults to pluck selected girls and boys permanently from state and private care, distinctions between fostering and adoption became clearer. In general, more prosperous households were to welcome candidates who presented fewer problems. Proposed additions were likely to be younger, healthier, and more of a match with the ideal children of the middle class. Another group of families was needed to care for children who could not find permanent new associations, either because they had not been released legally by birth parents or because they could not meet the aspirations of potential adopters. These latter households, sometimes called 'boarding' but more often 'foster' families, were expected to make limited rather than life-long commitments. Unlike adopters, they were to share children to some degree with both welfare personnel, who were charged with guaranteeing standards, and with birth kin, whom it was trusted many children might eventually rejoin. Foster parents, overwhelmingly mothers, were paid for these duties, but the general undervaluing of domestic work meant that such compensation was as minimal as could be managed.

From the outset, the situation of foster mothers was almost impossible.[67] They were to be badly paid for 'labours of love' that tradition marked as done most appropriately without material reward. Their duties were stigmatized because money entered the picture. Their predicament was all the worse because they were to share children at a time when the mark of the mature and successful adult and household was autonomy and privacy. Not surprisingly, observers of foster parents regularly noted that 'acceptance of the biological parents is perhaps the single greatest strain in the foster parent function.'[68]

The centrality of foster care to child welfare and the difficulty of the work ensured that recruitment remained a problem throughout the twentieth century in all regions of the country. In 1944, a home-finder for the Toronto Infants' Homes told of desperate efforts to find 'some new and arresting form of advertisement.' This included six weeks of 'newspaper advertising, radio spots and movie splashes.' But 'only a full-page advertisement with a child's picture donated by one of the large department stores brought an immediate and unexpected response.' Typically, very few applicants, about 3 per cent, met standards for care and accommodation. The Infants' Homes then resorted to canvassing the clergy and circulating letters to foster mothers, offering to the latter 'a financial award to those bringing in the largest number of satisfactory homes.' This, too, proved unavailing.[69] Respectable Canadians with other options normally looked elsewhere for occupations. As one Albertan noted in 1965: 'Due to prevailing community attitudes, foster parents do not enjoy much status. Foster homes are mostly concentrated in the poor sectors of cities and at marginal income levels.' She further had to admit that 'it is known that prior to 1958 due to the desperate need for foster homes, the policy was to accept almost anyone who applied.'[70]

The persisting shortage of foster homes owed much to bad pay and low status. It also reflected the fact that most Canadian homes had limited space. Children and parents have regularly doubled up in bedrooms and had limited bedding and provisions even for family members. Working-class households, such as those in the area of downtown Montreal dubbed 'the city below the hill' by one urban reformer in 1897, were already largely full up, and over-crowding was much the same elsewhere.[71] Payments for foster children hardly allowed for securing more space. Foster care programs also relied on mothers being at home and meeting standards at least minimally satisfactory to child welfare authorities. Few households could make such commitments or sacrifices.

Continuing problems in finding caregivers led welfare agencies to experiment with broadening the pool of acceptable candidates. While most legislation theoretically permitted single adoptions, acceptance was always quite limited and not open for public discussion before the 1970s. Foster parents, however, might well be single. After the Second World War, a Toronto social worker reflected on the need to increase foster placements. While insisting that the 'normal' home consisted of two parents and that many female applicants were at least somewhat duplicitous and/or psychologically maladjusted, she concluded that widows or spinsters must be suitable if they appreciated the need for male influence and were 'mature' people who did not expect the children to answer all needs. As she noted, all the agencies within the Welfare Council and Community Chest of Greater Toronto employed such women, but the 'investigation' was 'very thorough' and they were 'used mostly for girls or infants.'[72] While some such foster mothers shared responsibilities with other adult women, not until 1994 did Toronto's CAS invite same-sex couples to apply.[73]

The need to address the limited pool of applicants for fostering's hard tasks also encouraged the turn to kinship foster care that, by the last decades of the twentieth century, was increasingly seen as an important resource.[74] Some child welfare workers hoped to tempt middle-class citizens into fostering, but enthusiasm rarely produced more than paper.[75] As Robert Van Krieken's important study of child welfare programs in Australia has argued, the initiation of foster care systems relied heavily on the emergence of a 'respectable' working class that wished and was able to keep mothers/wives in the home. Such inmates were to devote energies to raising children and modelling the industry, discipline, and cleanliness that the middle class believed true of itself and wished for others. Australians, and Canadians too, seeking to affirm respectable status often embraced just such qualities. As Van Krieken further explained, 'artisans and skilled workers had for centuries attempted to distinguish themselves from the casual labouring poor, even if, in fact, they were poor themselves, and the boarding-out of children was premised on that distinction. It was only respectable working-class families that children were boarded-out to—feelings of moral hostility towards the "lower orders" were not confined to the bourgeoisie.' Values relating to children established a critical difference between the 'respectable' and the 'rough'.[76] Foster children were likely to come from families on the extreme margin; white foster families stood closer to the centre, where they were likely to share 'a range of familial morals with the middle class.'[77]

Respectable working-class families ready to take on the task on resocializing surrendered children depended on a male breadwinner's wage for stability. Yet this was always in short supply. When times were especially difficult, households might turn to fostering to tide them over. British Columbia's experiments with paid care began in the interior of the province, in the East Kootenays, and the province soon discovered 'the problem of families in receipt of public relief requesting foster children as they saw a means to help family finances.' Such applications were rarely accepted, but authorities could not always be choosy.[78] In 1988, a report for the Ontario Association of Children's Aid Societies pointed to the continuing importance of supplementary funds to many foster families with less than the average provincial income.[79]

Increasingly, working-class opportunities and maintenance of respectability came to depend on wives and mothers taking waged jobs outside of the home. Full employment and reduced barriers to equity, as during the First World War, inevitably attracted those who might otherwise foster.[80] This trend was especially obvious by the 1950s and 1960s and came to embrace middle-class households as well. The numbers of women at home to take on the tasks required by child welfare authorities were rapidly dwindling. When youngsters directed to the foster care system were increasingly likely to have significant problems, the attractions of alternate ways to sustain budgets was all the greater. Interest in or even love for non-related children could after all be satisfied by less taxing, if similarly under-paid, employment in the daycare arrangements, both formal and informal, that Canadians increasingly constructed in the last decades of the twentieth century. That such problems also afflicted both the United States and Great Britain by the 1920s was no consolation to children or those who cherished them.[81]

The persisting shortage of foster homes aligned with prejudice to create special problems for some girls and boys in care. British Columbia was typical for many years in accepting that Native children were rarely favourites in the foster care lottery. In 1939, the province's Division of Neglected Children cautiously experimented with home placements, rather than the more common institutionalization, for mixed-race children. With the goal of producing 'better citizens', it planned to place such 'boys and girls from the Industrial Schools in foster homes on the request of the psychiatrist and the School Principal.'[82] Three years later, it had to report that finding foster parents 'who like Indians and think like Indians is an almost impossible task.' It did, however, discover a few 'half-breed homes of a lower standard than we usually ask in our foster-homes' and observed that 'the children have adjusted well. They are well-fed and well-clothed and attend school

and church.' While their caregivers were reckoned inappropriate for white children, they seemed 'to give security and a sense of "belonging" to the half-breed
child who becomes bewildered and unhappy when surrounded by too many of
the amenities of civilization.'[83] By 1949, the same province's Social Welfare Branch
was congratulating itself on situating a 'few selected children who showed ability
and wished to continue their education beyond the grades available to them on
the various Indian reservations. The results have been gratifying to all concerned.'
These chosen few went on to university and vocational training.[84]

By 1955, West Coast authorities were trusting that 'more welfare workers' would
be 'available to encourage better home conditions on Indian reserves' and ultimately more foster homes.[85] In 1958, the Vancouver CAS and its Catholic counterpart set up a 'home-finding' committee for 'part-Indian children'.[86] At much the
same time, the province's Child Welfare Division and the Federal-Provincial Welfare
Committee on Indians in British Columbia cooperated to prepare an 'attractive
booklet entitled "In Search of Indian Foster Homes."'[87] Yet, by the third quarter of
the century, well-meaning BC social workers had to admit to being largely side-
swiped by 'the shortage of adequate housing on the Reserves.' Sympathetic
observers cited a survey of Lytton, a small interior town, which discovered an average of 12.5 individuals per home, to point out that 'at present, an extended family
is overwhelmed when a relative's child is placed with them for a few days.'[88]

While the difficulties of First Nations children have always been marked across
the country, others were also considered to pose substantial challenges that many
foster parents were not prepared to confront. Teens were a recurring constituency
of the unwanted. Everyone reported cases where long-term foster parents ultimately returned youngsters 'who have been unable to cope with problems which
came to a head during the child's adolescent period.' Children with handicaps of
any kind, which included physical or mental disabilities, membership in sibling
groups, or encounters with the law, were always harder to place. Boys stood out in
every category, but even girls could present a puzzle, as with the case in Toronto
of 'a little girl from the Children's Hospital where she had been intermittently for
nearly a year. She was a serious diabetic and to complicate matters she was a Gypsy
with a colourful and devoted family connection.'[89]

While acceptable youngsters were shunted off into adoption, foster parents were
regularly expected to deal with youngsters less in demand. By the end of the twentieth century, tasks had become daunting even for the brave. Ironically, efforts to
support birth families sometimes contributed to later problems in fostering. The
problem was well summed up by a leading Canadian critic in 1980:

> It is thought that children now come into care from much more serious sit-
> uations. . . . The current emphasis on providing services to children and fam-
> ilies in their own homes means on the one hand that some of the less serious
> problems are resolved without apprehending the children; but on the other
> hand, paradoxically, this 'last resort' approach can prolong the length of time a
> child remains in a crisis situation and thereby increase the emotional and psy-
> chological damage to the child.[90]

Another well-informed observer bluntly appraised a too common situation: 'Where foster parents were once mother and father substitutes, they are now required to be surrogate therapists.'[91]

Foster parents' frequent financial marginality, the commonplace lack of respect for their work, and the difficulty of the tasks set the stage for frequent failure. Throughout the twentieth century, caregivers moved in and out of fostering. Their frustration with the system sometimes attracted headlines. Sympathy has often been in short supply for caregivers who violate cultural norms by accepting money. In 1997, an article in *Maclean's* typified coverage of foster parents in its title 'The Horrors of Abuse', by an unknown author whose only recommendation was tougher laws and sentences for abusive adults.[92] Sometimes, however, there were signs of sympathy for society's parental proxies. In the early 1960s, an Ontario Protestant foster mother campaigned publicly to adopt two Catholic sisters long in her keeping and found significant sympathy in her battle with officials, although perhaps more for her religious affiliation than anything else. Soon, however, brushes with the courts by three of her birth children told against her.[93] In the 1990s, Ontario foster parents trying to keep children of an Aboriginal mother, again in opposition to welfare authorities, attracted kudos. Ultimately, unlike the earlier case, they appeared to have won because their position coincided with common suspicions about Native parenting.[94] In 1997, local sentiments were mobilized when a BC ranching household ran afoul of the Ministry of Children and Family. A reporter allowed the long-time foster father to point out the commonplace dilemma: 'We take the given-up-on kids.' The 'tough love' response, always a favourite for adolescent males in particular, was also emphasized by the surrogate father, clearly confirming his mainstream masculinity: 'The boys receive love, clear and consistent house rules, and a grounding in good work habits.' Foster parents' frequent confidence in their practical skills and their often associated scepticism about professionals were also visible when the head of the province's Federation of Foster Parent Associations was quoted as blaming policies 'developed by people who are, and have for some time been, removed from the reality of child care' and, in particular, from hard-to-handle abused and neglected children.[95] In 2004, a letter to *Maclean's* again took issue with the commonplace slighting of foster parents:

> I was surprised to read your assertion that, 'The vast majority of the remaining [unadopted] children grow up without the love and security they'd get from committed parents.' My wife and I have been foster parents for five years and have had 24 children pass through our home, in addition to our two biological children. We take kids from ages 4 to 10 and we raise these children like our own. We are loving, committed, and a lot of children who have passed through our home and family have wished to return. Ask the kids, they'll tell you.[96]

This last writer embodied the pride that many foster families took in their contribution, but the job was rarely sufficiently appealing to produce needed recruits among the working class or to reach into the middle class.

Not surprisingly, Canadian social workers were regularly desperate for solutions to the recurring foster care crisis. This helps explain why they generally welcomed white foster parents for Native youngsters or any foster or adoptive parents for those with disabilities. When it appeared that affections might become permanent and formal adoption seemed in the cards, they sought ways to stem 'foster care drift.'[97] Because they readily appreciated that some people fostered for pay because they could not otherwise afford to have children, especially those with special needs, they also favoured the move to subsidized adoption that slowly began in the 1970s. This, it was hoped, would expand the pool of adopters and provide permanence for more youngsters. Anxiety that money would somehow undermine adoption's privileged status as 'like our very own', not to mention penny-pinching governments, always undermined support. As the Alberta Association of Social Workers put it, 'any possibility of a suggestion that parents adopted for monetary reasons could only be detrimental to the child's welfare.'[98] British Columbia similarly worried about 'adverse psychological effects' if girls and boys believed they were paid for.[99] Nevertheless, by the end of the twentieth century, initiatives such as subsidies suggested that adoption and fostering were to some degree again converging.[100] A few poorer Canadians found new opportunities to add children to their households.

Adopters

Citizens who best approximated cultural ideals started off with tremendous advantages if they wished to add to families through adoption. Faith in the superior qualifications of certain women was widely taken for granted. As Patricia Hill Collins has observed in the United States: 'Through their ability to transmit national culture to the young, middle-class and affluent White women allegedly remain superior to all other groups in socialising White youth into naturalised hierarchies of race, gender, age, sexuality and social class.'[101] Others were suspect. Few critics were as unequivocal as one leading child psychologist and head of the Institute of Child Study at the University of Toronto. He quite straightforwardly proposed that 'unless a child's natural parents can prove that they are the best persons to care for him—and sometimes they are not—they should be forced to give him up. . . . We must assess parents and take children away from those who are incapable of providing them with the minimum essentials, emotional as well as material, for their healthy development. . . . Human welfare must take precedence over individual freedom.'[102] If his bluntness was unusual, his assumption that some Canadians were more entitled to offspring was commonplace.

Early advocates of adoption rarely minced words when they described preferred applicants. In 1896, J.J. Kelso explained that 'where the reputation of the family in church and society is well known, almost no supervision is needed. It has to be remembered that the people who adopt children are doing a great public service for which they are not paid, and they would naturally take offence if approached in an unreasonable spirit.'[103] In 1911, Ontario trusted that 'some of the best homes in the Province have opened their doors to friendless, homeless children.'[104] Not surprisingly, such applicants were also likely to go to the front of the line when it came to choice of offspring. In 1945, the Victoria CAS typically appreciated full well that middle-class requests were best situated for success when 'applications for babies do outnumber, by far, the available "baby supply."' In such high stakes, education, money, and powerful ethnic and racial identities made a difference.[105]

Child welfare authorities have always tried to recruit the 'best' homes for their charges. What this has meant is an often realistic preference for economically stable households. Such stability has largely been the prerogative of the middle class, the great majority of whom have been of European origin and often Protestant. More often than not, such adults have been home-owners with higher than average levels of formal education. This has been the group from whom the bulk of legislators, policy-makers, and social workers have also been drawn. However much they might otherwise differ, they often shared assumptions about what constituted suitable upbringing. While many understood that the poor could be good parents, and indeed they often judged them based on just this expectation, they frequently credited their own class with special abilities. Those conclusions helped drive policies and practices that effectively discriminated against the less well-to-do. Even where resource economies thrived on workers' capacity to move in search of employment, for example, cultural ideals of normalcy often meant that 'mobile homes such as house trailers were rarely considered desirable adoptive homes.'[106] Applicants who could not measure up to economic and social indicators of well-being were, sometimes fairly enough, not easily accepted as guaranteeing happy outcomes for girls and boys.

Not surprisingly, the cheery tales paraded for public consumption have been likely to profile the middle class in a flattering light. Consider these stories of rescue. The first comes from J.J. Kelso, who attempted to counter prejudice by insisting that 'many children taken from the lower strata of life, when placed in good environment, develop mentally and physically and become good citizens.'[107] In 1919, a journalist in turn cited Kelso's arguments with enthusiasm as she approvingly described the trend to adoption in the aftermath of the great flu epidemic that orphaned so many youngsters. While it was natural, she suggested, to worry about birth 'parents and their ancestors for seven generations back', 'a difference of environment' would shift the balance in favour of youngsters.[108] Fiction writers drew much the same moral. In 1933, readers of *Chatelaine* learned about the lovely Iona Wilcox, who, unknown to herself, had been adopted from an infants' home by her well-to-do parents. She was the fiancée of Tom Norwood, who had previously sworn he'd never risk marrying someone of unknown ancestry. Loving adopters protected Iona's secret, and she was free to marry the superior Tom. She soon became joyfully pregnant but lost the infant at birth. Wild with grief, Tom took his wise mother-in-law into his confidence and substituted a girl born to parents who conveniently died without leaving relatives. Readers were left to imagine that the new daughter would prove as satisfactory as the new mother and to take for granted the rights of middle-class couples to society's 'spare' children.[109]

Two years later, the same magazine offered the tale of a real-life social science experiment. An author and his wife set out to test the value of their assets by adopting a toddler as company for their young daughter:

We had a mutual belief that environment, if not quite so important as hered-ity—and we had an open mind on that, too—plays a vital part in the develop-ment of human character. We believed that, given the right background, train-ing and affection, a very young child might be persuaded to grow up into a happy and personable being, whether he was your own child or the child of other parents. . . . It was therefore not too absurd to imagine, surely that the child of someone else unformed and plastic in character, might be influenced quite beneficially by ourselves.[110]

Like its counterparts in a host of publications, this serialized account of a boy's suc-cessful integration into the middle class took the family's entitlement for granted.

The inauguration of polite behaviours in newcomers was critical in integrating class, as well as other, strangers into middle-class family circles. One mother of a newly adopted son described the delicate balance sought in acceptable masculinity.

His first day at school I waited anxiously for him to come home. He was late. His new sister told me he was rolling in the gutter winning a fight with the toughest boy in the grade.

It was good news. Having had one boy, I knew this was the surest way to social acceptance among eight-year-olds. His opponent has been his good friend ever since.

While she had been warned 'a child with his unsettled background would lie and steal, to say the very least,' her greatest problems proved otherwise: 'after a year, there are no more double negatives or misplaced pronouns.' Nor was this all:

Table manners were another small problem. I like dinner time to be relaxed so that the children will talk and tell us about their day. Suddenly I found myself continually nagging at this new child on my left.

It is difficult to sit quietly and watch a child holding his fork in his fist and jabbing the meat as though it were alive. After a couple of tries though, he discovered that our method of using a knife and fork was not only quieter, it was more efficient.

Report cards provided still better proof of escape from unfortunate origins: 'The one he brought with him is a crime sheet of the first order; John was not always honest, did not tell the truth, was not reliable, nor polite and his marks were low. The report he brought home last week might be for a different boy. We rejoice over the A's and the comments on his good behavior.'[111] Such assimilation into the middle class fulfilled many hopes.

To be sure, progressive observers and moments when there appeared to be plenty of young candidates for new homes sometimes encouraged consideration of adopters beyond the idealized white middle class. Such was the faith of an upbeat group of British Columbians, including the liberal Catholic bishop Remi De Roo, settling down to discuss 'the history and practice of adoption' in their province in Canada's centennial, 1967. They argued that prospective fathers and mothers were appropriately 'diverse in their national and racial origin and economic status.' They hailed prosperous, 'well-established' Natives, 'Asiatics' who were 'respected and well-liked by their Caucasian neighbours,' and 'Negroes' whose numbers were unfortunately too few to be 'a resource for the part negro child.' They approved of permanent paid foster homes and subsidized adoptions for those on 'limited incomes'. They applauded a Native adopter who 'could not read, write, or speak English but she did embroider a pair of moccasins for her expected baby' and claimed to be 'more favourably impressed' than they were by the more well-to do.[112] Some decade later, the same province's child welfare ministry articulated similarly inclusive sentiments. It reported that 'hard-to-place' parents, including a paraplegic logger, a blind mother, and a couple who had reversed traditional gender roles, were given serious attention as prospective parents.[113]

In the 1960s, social workers facing increasing caseloads and inspired by the progressive spirit of the age often sought to enlarge the pool of parents by de-emphasizing bureaucratic barriers and material constraints. According to one representative of the Ottawa CAS,

> there have been many changes in Ottawa's adoption practice in the previous decade. A gradual move away from actual and detailed family histories. A diminishing concern with factors like home ownership, bank balances and conformity to narrow, middle class community norms. We became more concerned with family relationships, attitudes towards adoption (telling, infertility, illegitimacy, etc.), expectations of children, and preparation for placement and adoptive parenthood.[114]

The pragmatic benefits of greater diversity were noted by Alberta's Committee on Adoption. In 1965, it concluded, albeit rather reluctantly, that, given the numbers of children in care, the province ought to be flexible about 'working' mothers, especially for older youngsters. It trusted that policy change 'might lead to placements in an appreciable number of excellent homes in the lower income group.'[115]

Even when new candidates for parenthood were included, some youngsters could not readily generate interest. In 1932, a Montreal nun aptly summed up the recurring problem of supply and demand that generations of welfare workers understood to structure the adoption market:

> The crux of the problem is a shortage, not of children but of the type of children adopting parents want. Most people seeking to adopt children come from the better educated and more well-to-do part of our population, while most of the children come from very average homes. The parents want children in perfect health, with physical characteristics akin to their own, with freedom from hereditary taint, and with intelligence high enough to meet their educational ambitions. If they were having children of their own they would have to be satisfied with unalterable characteristics; but since they are choosing their child, they have already decided exactly what these character-

istics are to be, and nothing will make them change their minds. . . . In a surprising majority of cases, 'it must be a girl.' . . . No one wants a boy who is wearing glasses: nor a girl who has bandy legs that will need a great deal of care until they are straight; nor a wee maid with a wry neck.[116]

Given recurring reservations about seemingly less than perfect kids, like would-be parents who did not match cultural ideals, adoption's hard markets sometimes seem to have brought together two groups with at least some degree of competitive disadvantage.

Women and men who wished to parent and who had resources to support their desires have not been easily deterred. Those who could not readily meet official requirements or overcome official prejudice commonly turned to private arrangements. Such was the solution of the numerous Jewish and older would-be parents who flocked to Nova Scotia's Ideal Maternity Home and other such institutions. In such nurseries they could troll for youngsters to match their requirements. With money in their pockets, they need not face rejection.[117] By the end of the Second World War, middle-class citizens had grown accustomed to receiving children who were guaranteed as coming 'from a good family' and 'decent people' and possessing 'no bad blood.'[118]

Some Canadians, such as an older Toronto mother and her advertising executive husband who welcomed an eight-year-old boy in the 1950s, and a dentist and his wife with seven adopted kids who had become 'local celebs', were confident enough to count heavily on new environments. In the latter case, quite typically, 'religion' formed 'the strong steady core of the household.'[119] Such optimism, while it never overcame the steady preference for infants, was a powerful force, especially in the decades immediately after the Second World War. Later, race-based challenges, complaints from searchers, and panics over genetic predispositions and maternal addictions made confidence harder to sustain, and some children more likely to remain with temporary custodians.

As they crowded adoption waiting rooms in Canada and around the world in the last decades of the twentieth century, middle-class adopters discovered new constraints upon their freedom to parent. They found their credentials subject to 'red tape', waiting periods, 'intensive intake interviews, get-acquainted sessions, references, one-on-one interviews,' and home visits, just the practices the clients of the emerging social welfare system had to learn to accept.[120] In response, they questioned the credentials of interrogators. The activist climate of the 1960s and 1970s further encouraged, as one critical social work observer noted, an 'increased willingness to use political and advocacy activity.' This, 'in combination with the class position occupied by most adopters, led to increased pressure being brought to bear on the state to expand the supply of adoptees.'[121]

Signs of such determination can be seen as early as the 1950s with the assault on religious matching. Many would-be parents became obsessed with the idea that an abundance of attractive Catholic kids were available if only they would be released to Protestants. A 'Mrs Brisbin' was a typical complainant in her testimony before Alberta's commission reviewing adoption in 1965. She cited cases of

Catholic abuse and Protestant probity in insisting 'I do not think religion should enter into it at all. There are many people outside the church who would make wonderful parents and religion should not be a bar, it should not be considered to adoption, only a home for the child is what should be considered.'[122] She went further still in making the connection between social background and entitlement. As she told the committee, her son, a United Church minister in Hamilton, Ontario, had told her of the success of a female missionary in bringing home a ten-year-old from India. Brisbin also reflected upon the power of different kinds of distinctions in concluding that, although this single Protestant deaconess had encountered major hurdles, 'I don't think race makes as much difference as religion.'[123] In short, she appeared to brook no bars, religious or racial, to the acquisition of offspring.

By the 1960s, questions about the suitability of so-called working mothers, and, in effect, preferences about the class of adopters, also began to come to a head. Alberta's committee provided a forum for the debate. The representative of the province's Welfare Council pointed out that daycare would keep some hard-pressed families together, especially those headed by single mothers, and prevent the necessity of offspring coming into public care.[124] One commissioner expressed doubt, wondering, if parental responsibility was delegated to any agency, 'how far is this removed from, say the communistic structure, where the child is cared for by the state?'[125] She appeared to have missed the point that the lack of daycare meant that mothers could not find full-time employment and could not support offspring, who then ended up with Alberta Social Services. The chief commissioner noted that a questionnaire sent to Albertans who had adopted in the preceding two years (some 2,200 were sent out and over 1,500 returned) discovered 'unanimous' opposition to full-time paid maternal employment.[126] The speaker from the Welfare Council interjected revealingly: 'I suspect that the questionnaires that you got back are from middle-class families where adopting children go because the tendency has been to place children in this category. Therefore, you do not reflect the thinking of a mother who may come into a lower class family. I think that is one of the problems. Where economic security is sufficient, you do not have the mother working but in a lower class family, it may be necessary for the mother to work.' As a social worker, he further observed,

> one of the things you look at is economic security and one thing you are more likely to do is find an adoption placement in an income group that provides this. What would happen if you extended the spectrum, so to speak, of placing children in more wealthy families and poorer families, relatively speaking, I do not think we know the answer to that one yet. . . . The question in my mind would come up, if I was a person placing a child for adoption, if I knew a mother had to do work, would I do this. Maybe it is unfair of me but I do not think I would do this.[127]

The chief commissioner agreed, arguing that children in care were already likely to be 'pushed about a bit and rejected already. This is one of the arguments that the department uses against placing a child with a working mother.' Full-time maternal care was the only cure.[128]

The representative from the Calgary CAS acknowledged that more and more wives were entering the labour market but that the 'ideal, happy home would be one which has sufficient income, where there is enough money coming in, where the mother is happy to be in the home, to be a housewife, to be a mother and to look after the children.' He had to admit, however, that this scenario was 'not exactly the society that we are living in today' and that day nurseries hadn't seemed to harm Europeans.[129] In the course of the spirited and, it seems, often emotional discussion, even defenders of working mothers, such as one female physician, were forced to suggest children were better off when mothers were at home.[130] In fact, as Alberta's welfare experts had to admit, despite their official discrimination against working mothers, they had in fact 'no control over what the mother does after the one year supervisory period in adoptions.'[131] Notable in these discussions was the absence of attention to prospective fathers. Mothers always stood front and centre in discussions of who could appropriately parent.

Those determined to parent increasingly did more than merely lobby for consideration. In the last three decades of the twentieth century, many Canadians in search of babies deserted the public adoption system to resort to private agencies and intermediaries where they hoped to be more in charge. In 1981, 22 per cent of all infant adoptions were arranged privately; in 1990, this has leapt to 59 per cent.[132] The difference in the birth mothers using the two systems was closely related to this shift. Native and more disadvantaged mothers in general, whose offspring were often termed 'special needs', were far more likely to remain within the state system. As they waited on public rolls, their offspring were most often those who grew steadily older and thus still more unattractive to the vast majority of would-be parents.

Private adoptions most often involved different participants. Healthy and often young Caucasian birth mothers, with their especially prized babies, faced an active market that they might well hope could better guarantee their offspring a good life. Yet if the parties to private transactions often shared racial identities, they were nevertheless hardly on a level playing field in having their needs met. As two of Canada's leading authorities have recently concluded, 'as private adoptions account for an increasing proportion of all adoptions, the focus on the best interests of the child is called into question. As prospective adoptive parents become the paying consumers of an adoption service, there is the potential for the needs, desires, or expectations of the adopting couple to once again supersede the needs of the child.'[133] Once they surrendered children in private exchanges, birth mothers lost their ultimate trump card. When it came to ensuring that agreements be honoured, their resources were unlikely to match those of their replacements.

By the closing decades of the twentieth century, privileged Canadians were increasingly willing to broaden their searches. As healthy infants became increasingly hard to get domestically, the ground had been prepared to look elsewhere. Newspaper accounts and personal confessions regularly highlighted assumptions that sweeping the world for supposedly unwanted children was a very good thing.

Sensitized by decades of coverage by the press and a broad spectrum of aid groups to international disasters with young casualties, the hearts of Canadians were readily stirred by appeals such as that by the 1964 ad from the Christian Children's Fund that urged them: 'This year—give a child for Christmas.'[134] Foster Parents Plan and a host of agencies cultivated the well-springs of often genuine concern by connecting donors to real children in impoverished situations around the world. In 1997, the *Toronto Star* was not unusual in extending the tale of rescue of an 'orphan pulled from gutter' to include removal to Canada itself.[135]

Even as social security for impoverished families in North America shuddered under neo-conservative assaults in the 1980s and 1990s, Canadians, like Americans, turned to Asia, Europe, and Latin America to engage in a 'a particularly privileged form of immigration that is facilitated because the right to form families is a consecrated middle-class imperative.'[136] As a submission to the federal Committee on International Adoptions from the group Families for Children put it in 1974, 'government officials do not tell citizens whom they can marry—neither should they dictate arbitrarily a country of origin.'[137] Canadians who might be reckoned too old or missing a heterosexual partner or otherwise disqualified for domestic adoption, or who were merely unwilling to endure lengthening waiting lists for infants, employed their resources to disregard barriers. Such was true of Renaldo's parents. Rejecting 'drug-damaged Canadian children', these British Columbians sought healthy offspring from Peru. There, much to their dismay, they also encountered bureaucracy and unexpected and lengthy resistance from Renaldo's birth mother. While resources clearly made all the difference, they denied they had 'bought Renaldo': his mother, they insisted, was more moved by the promise of photos than money or, presumably, their determined pressure. They justified every tactic in their baby-seeking arsenal because otherwise, 'we'd never have known Renaldo, our bright laughing boy, our son, his skin like silk, so smart, so affectionate, a brother for Carl.'[138] By the end of the twentieth century, would-be parents had learned of questionable practices and desperate birth parents from Romania to Peru and back again. As the executive director of the Child Welfare League of Canada observed in 1995, 'people are prepared to pay money for children—that fact alone raises moral issues.'[139]

Canadian experience affirms how often adoption involves the assertion of class privilege. The desired result was set forth quite straightforwardly by Ontario's superintendent for neglected and dependent children in 1925, when he assessed the results of the 1921 Adoption Act: 'The best homes in the Province have been thrown open to welcome these unfortunate children and to-day the child from the home of penury is not infrequently transported to a state of comfort and even affluence.'[140] The result has sometimes meant tremendous advantages for children. As one survey noted, the outcomes for 'intellectually handicapped' youngsters improved as a result of 'the superior social class position of the adoptees.'[141] Another international study concluded, typically, that a move up 'the socio-economic scale from their family of origin' brought emotional, social, and educational benefits.[142] Despite such positive assessments, as we shall see in chapter 8, the searching and

Native repatriation movements have foregrounded losses. Pain and alienation have been very much part of the larger story. Nevertheless, searchers and Native champions have sometimes admitted the material and other advantages that improved their individual chances. Ironically, they, like many more silent adoptees, sometimes provided one variant on the North American dream of social mobility.

In summary, then, the history of adoption offers one expression of what John Porter famously described as the 'vertical mosaic.'[143] The transfer of children from less advantaged to more advantaged populations has directly invoked the politics of class in the domestic realm. Struggles over the possession of girls and boys, the nation's fundamental resources, ultimately often stand alongside the conflicts conventionally acknowledged between capital and labour. Just as in pitched battles on picket lines and at negotiating tables, outcomes were never entirely certain. Power and resistance were never uncomplicated or entirely predictable in their benefits or their costs. Ultimately, however, adoption, like much else in the Canadian polity, demonstrated that class mattered, from the nation's bedrooms to its legislatures.

Gendered Lives

Gender, unlike class, has always been openly and specifically articulated in the course of the transfer of youngsters. Throughout Canadian adoption history, women and men, boys and girls, have been regularly marked as distinctly gendered. Performing in the context of powerful normative expectations that frequently pandered to the celebration of difference, female members of the adoption circle have been likely to be associated with nurture and emotion, and males with toughness and reserve, qualities they were also believed to demonstrate in the public realm. To be sure, alternative roles and voices, such those embodied by Matthew and Marilla Cuthbert in *Anne of Green Gables* and late-twentieth-century campaigners for gay and lesbian adoption, have persistently challenged narrow conception of what it has meant to be male and female. The fact, too, that multiple influences have shaped all individuals—including those of class and race, which ebb and flow over lifetimes—has meant that gender has never operated alone. Ultimately, however, whatever the particular intersection of identities, both Natives and newcomers have commonly presumed that gender made a difference in adoption.

This chapter examines how that difference worked to construct options and perceptions. It does this in three stages. First, it concentrates on the female adults involved in the transfer of children, notably both birth and adoptive mothers. Second, it suggests how gender frequently operated with regard to the youngsters to be incorporated into new homes. Girls and boys often faced different expectations and met somewhat different fates. Finally, it shifts to an examination of biological and social fathering. Adults confronted a variety of choices about what it meant to be male. In every instance, notions of femininity and masculinity helped set the stage for what happened in the course of the adoption tale.

Mothers to the Nation

Mothering, both biological and social, has never been far away from roles deemed most appropriate for women in Canada's various communities. The salvation of Aboriginal and settler nations has regularly been tied to women's acceptance of reproduction and nurture as basic to their lives. As the report of the Royal Commission on New Reproductive Technologies also made clear, parenting has been tremendously important to the vast majority of Canadians, but women have been among the most committed. Infertility has triggered 'complex and powerful emotions', 'a loss of self-esteem mixed with feelings of grief, anger, and sometimes guilt about the source of the infertility', and 'a sense of isolation from family members and friends.'[1] Such sentiments are not new. Women share a long history of desperately seeking to guarantee successful pregnancies, including subjecting themselves to potentially harmful surgical and drug therapies.[2] As one modern adopter explained, she could get over not having a husband, but she 'couldn't get over never having a baby.'[3] A Salish heroine depicted by Métis writer Lee Maracle put it similarly when she reflected, 'She was not hungry for a man at all, but hungry for her daughters.'[4] The strength of such sentiments sometimes led women far afield. On Christmas Eve 1981, the *Globe and Mail* described four Quebec women who had been imprisoned in Guatemala in the course of efforts to adopt. Despite incarceration, one of them summed up her experience: 'I'd go through it all over again in order to get that child.'[5]

To be sure, maternity has never been the desire of all women. Enthusiasm has been fostered or undermined by times and associations. Directives to reproduce have nevertheless been hard to avoid. Patriarchy has assessed all women as naturally responsible for childbirth and rearing. Capitalism has hoped to profit when the labour force and consumer market grow. Racialist thinking, one part of a larger eugenic discourse,[6] has always, however, presumed a hierarchy of preferred babies and mothers. Only too often, white middle-class women have been pressed to procreate, poor white women, especially the unwed, pressed to surrender offspring, and racialized minorities pressed to restrict their supposed excess fertility. Such assumptions have been far from rudimentary or inconsequential as women everywhere try to make sense of who they might be as individuals and as members of the larger community. As Patricia Hill Collins has cogently observed in the case of the United States, 'ideas about idealized and stigmatized motherhood within family rhetoric contribute to links among family, race and nation. As a result, the issue of who will control women's mothering experiences lies at the heart of state family planning decisions.'[7]

The fact that 'the pursuit of happiness' for women, and for very many men, has been regularly defined in terms of successful offspring frequently detracts, as Elaine Tyler May has recognized, from substantive engagement in public life.[8] Good citizenship for women in Canada, as elsewhere, has readily been reduced to 'good parenting' rather than as one possible expression. Such commonplace reductionism has made access to parenting opportunities as the supposedly fullest expression of gender authenticity all the more critical. While men's civil capacity has been likely to be judged by some reference to their military or economic contributions, women unable to give birth or to rear offspring have regularly been viewed as failing a significant test of citizenship. In contrast, those women who assumed maternal responsibilities have frequently won social approbation whatever else they do. This varied reception has loomed large in all discussions of the transfer of youngsters.

Birth mothers unable to support progeny have also been regularly, if sometimes uncertainly, grouped into two camps. There have been those generally accepted as unfortunate or simply unlucky. They have often been married women who lost the support of male breadwinners through death or some shortcoming perceived as unrelated to the women involved. Such 'blameless' mothers have been likely to be considered worthy of private and public support. The second category has included mothers who failed to demonstrate sobriety, industry, and sexual respectability and, until the late twentieth century, all unmarried women. The plight of the 'blameless' group generated Canada's first experiments with social security. Beginning during the First World War, mothers' pensions or allowances were designed to aid the respectable in maintaining youngsters in hard times.[9] Ironically, this was just the group among whom adopters often wished to recruit. Repeated yearning for off-spring who had decent parentage and were of 'good people', such as that revealed in ads offering and asking for children in the Methodist *Christian Guardian* and the Anglican *Canadian Churchman* into the early years of the twentieth century, depended in large measure on limited options for the respectable poor. The further expansion of the welfare state in the decades immediately after the Second World War offered an increasing number of mothers designated as deserving an unprece-dented, albeit all too fragile, security. While state funding never matched a bread-winner wage,[10] it supplied indispensable support, in the process rescuing many chil-dren who otherwise might have entered the formal or informal adoption market. Slow improvements in maternal health, occupational health and safety, and social security more generally, as well as new opportunities for birth control and abortion, also operated over the course of the twentieth century to ensure that fewer girls and boys entered the market for new parents.

Though significant numbers of youngsters were no longer available for adop-tion, or exploitation, demand continued to flourish. The Royal Commission on New Reproductive Technologies suggested that infertility has likely remained rel-ative steady over time, at about 7 per cent of couples.[11] This figure measures only one part of demand. One-child families have not always been preferred. In some periods, notably but not only the 1950s, adoption has been employed to create larger households. Many Canadians have also often longed for both daughters and sons, a balance that adoption might grant, as the couple in the article 'A Son of Their Own at Last' admitted.[12] Too, some single Canadian adults, notably but not only women, have always sought progeny without testing their own fertility. Partners have not been essential to adults' desires for children. Finally, politics has sometimes made a difference: some would-be parents worried about global over-population or believed it preferable to rescue those already born than to reproduce themselves. Whatever the reason, modern Canadians nevertheless commonly shared a sense of entitlement to offspring, whether by adoption or by birth, and their assumptions had considerable weight.

The removal of some girls and boys from the adoption market in the course of the twentieth century's expansion of social security encouraged reconsideration of possible donors. As Claudia Nelson has suggested of the United States, 'the rheto-ric of adoption occasioned both tributes to motherhood and the examination of feminine failings.'[13] Unwed mothers supplied a case in point. While the distinc-tions were never absolute, in the nineteenth and early twentieth centuries single women producing offspring were generally considered morally reprehensible, especially by authorities, if not always by their own families and communities. As

Karen Dubinsky has demonstrated in her study of sexual assault, girls and women were always likely to be blamed for non-marital intercourse. They, not seducers and rapists, frequently faced ostracism and notoriety. The commonplace discovery of dead infants and maternal deaths as a result of abortion confirmed a harsh reality.[14] When the unwed and their offspring resorted to public or private charity, they might well be spurned or sheltered only on sufferance.

As Andrée Levesque has concluded in her careful assessment of Montreal's major Catholic institution, unwed mothers were treated punitively because they were regarded as moral and, indeed, spiritual failures. Whatever the specifics of their condition, all were likely to be condemned as temptresses who had succumbed to the pleasures of the flesh.[15] The Protestant shelters that also emerged in the late nineteenth century might well be equally censorious. Illegitimacy tarred offspring, who in their turn commonly faced rejection by those with starched consciences. One modern-minded critic summed up the past practices that haunted the vulnerable into the twentieth century: 'Many settlements with Puritanical religious beliefs required that the unmarried mother confess her sins before the congregation. She might be publicly whipped or placed in stocks, or imprisoned. To help her or her child, it was believed, would only increase the number of illegitimate births. This attitude has, of course, been modified through the years but it has not entirely disappeared.'[16] For years, many religious and lay child welfare workers encouraged single women to keep their children. Offspring might offer a ready reminder of sin and the need to sin no more. Yet pressure for retention acknowledged the fact that many potential adopters were reluctant to take immorality's tainted products into their households, and there was little substitute for mother's milk. If such progeny did not remain with those who gave them birth, they might well face extended periods of institutionalization, a sure threat to survival, especially before the ready availability of commercial baby foods, such as pablum.

Feminists have been prominent among Canadians challenging such one-sided morality. In 1923, during legislative debates regarding the introduction of an act to protect the children of unmarried mothers, Alberta suffragist MLA Irene Parlby voiced evolving sentiments: 'I believe that any girl who has the moral courage to bear the social stigma to face the world and keep her child, has expiated her sin: and by so doing she merits our support and sympathy.'[17] In Toronto, one female neighbour championing a seventeen-year-old unwed mother condemned to the province's mental hospital in Orillia drew even more damning conclusions in 1933:

> She is not the first young girl who has been betrayed by a man . . . and this fact does not make her a mental case or a moron.
>
> From my own observations I know the girl is capable and able to fill a useful place in the outside world. I believe that she has been simply railroaded into a mental institution to satisfy the ego of paid social workers and busy bodies who themselves are labouring under the delusion that by placing girls in mental institutions they can right a social condition that has persisted since the dawn of history and will persist to the end. The solution to the problem does not lie in the insane asylum. To my mind the treatment accorded

Georgina Washington is on a par with the burning of witches in less-enlightened times.

Social work experts, themselves sometimes feminists, might also be sympathetic. In 1945–6 Saskatchewan's director of child welfare reflected upon the 'intense emotional experience' of unwed mothers and suggested they not be asked to make decisions before the passage of six weeks. With careful support, such young women could be rehabilitated. Provincial mothers' allowance would permit them to raise their child, albeit—like married women or widows in the same position—with considerable difficulty. Saskatchewan's study of recipients of such assistance concluded that 'an unmarried mother who elects to keep her child does so because she is ready to accept the responsibility and the child in spite of certain obvious handicaps can live a normal life.'[19]

At issue, of course, was the social construction of what constituted normality. A 1949 report on unwed mothers by the Montreal Council of Social Agencies conveyed the recurring contradictions found in public discussions. On the one hand, most unmarried parents were reckoned 'disturbed' transgressors of 'social laws', as the 'family unit is still the accepted pattern in our society.' On the other, the report recommended 'greater social acceptance', especially because some 'unmarried mothers are able to provide a fairly normal home for their children.'[20]

Despite recurring sympathy, as well as families and communities that might shelter the unmarried, harsh judgments remained commonplace for many years. In 1948, Newfoundland's child welfare authorities reported that 'some people in this country still feel that unmarried mothers have committed a crime against society that can never be effaced and they are inclined to condemn their children to eternal ostracism.'[21] Even as moralistic censure slowly lifted, environmental and psychological explanations emerged to stigmatize the unwed yet again. By the 1940s and 1950s, such women were increasingly assessed as expressing unresolved conflicts, most often with their own mothers. In 1946, the *Canadian Mental Health Journal* described the case of the unmarried Louise, who resisted placing her infant, Michael, for adoption. Only a hard dose of therapy, including repeated visits to a psychiatrist, convinced her to focus on her supposed psychological shortcomings, particularly a lingering emotional attachment to the birth father. Timely intervention was portrayed as helping a disturbed young woman fast forward into maturity. Louise's transfer of Michael to adopters, along with a gift of baby pictures and a silver spoon, signalled the modern resolution of an old problem.[22]

In 1949, Montreal's Council of Social Agencies drew similarly on contemporary social science to conclude that 'in almost all cases an unmarried mother is a disturbed person and that her transgression of social laws contributes to further disturbances with her.'[23] Ten years later, a representative of the Unmarried Parent Department of the Children's Aid Society (CAS) Toronto reported:

> We now see this particular problem as a symptom of a troubled personality, or of a young person caught in the confusion of changing social mores. . . . Our clients come from a cross section of the community, no longer are they

the 'servant girls', 'immigrants', or girls from the lower socio-economic group, and we therefore have to face up to the fact that we are all involved in this particular social problem. Of course she has done wrong and incidentally no one knows it better than the girl herself. But does this make her wholly bad? I think this is the difference in our attitude today, and what enables workers with unmarried mothers to be concerned for them as people, with their strengths and weaknesses just like the rest of us. . . . It may surprise you to hear that some girls have little or no sense of guilt about what has happened to them: but should it really surprise us when we look back just a few years to the way many of them have been brought up. I sometimes think of them as 'war casualties'—they are the children whose fathers were overseas, mother working and perhaps having an extra-marital affair of her own, about which the children were aware to a greater or lesser degree; and then when father returned from a war, perhaps separation of parents or constant bickering.

And in the present phase of our culture, what could be more confusing than the popular emphasis on glamour and sexual attraction. Look at many of our TV programmes, advertising posters, movies, etc.[24]

Again, in 1960, Manitoba authorities endeavouring to assist clients similarly turned to psychological explanations: 'hostilities, conflicts and insecurities arising out of her background and life experiences all contribute toward the out-of-wedlock pregnancy.'[25] Four years later, the Fredericton CAS lamented the fact that they did not 'have adequate facilities' to treat pregnant women and girls with 'complex personality problems'. It also pointed to the role of the environment, as the most vulnerable were those most likely to be 'denied the social pretence their more fortunate cousins have of a visit to grandmother in the west.'[26] In 1967, a supposed epidemic of the unwed inspired Vancouver journalist, later member of Parliament, Simma Holt to write 'about illegitimate children and the other unwanted children who have ended up as murderers, habitual criminals, or lost people wandering through our world, unloved, alienated, indeed despised . . . fated for a life of loneliness and rejection, a life spent largely in prisons and mental hospitals.' She further concluded that it 'is usually the poorest type of girl who attempts to keep her child.'[27] As a writer concluded in an article for the *Alberta Medical Journal*, the best outcome was the creation of the 'normal family' by way of the 'rehabilitated unmarried mother and an adopted child.'[28]

The coincidence of the rise of psychological explanations for unmarried mothers with the emergence of 'illegitimate children' as 'practically the sole source of adoption by people unrelated to them' did not go entirely unobserved. One critical contributor to the leading professional journal, *Canadian Welfare,* was deeply disturbed by the embrace of prejudicial American trends. As she observed:

The picture of the unmarried mother has been built up on the basis of characteristics common among the group seeking social agency aid. A high proportion of these girls are teenagers, and since teenagers are generally apt to feel that their parents don't understand them, it's not hard to imagine how a girl in such a predicament would view her relationships with her parents—

particularly her mother. When we are in a corner we naturally try to find a scrape goat.

Young mothers were so pressed to surrender that, as she argued, they had in effect 'no choice'.[29]

This damning appraisal of much Canadian practice was, however, repudiated in the same issue by the superintendent of the Unmarried Parents' Department of the Toronto Children's Aid and Infants' Home. Without apparently skipping a beat, this official returned to an insistence upon the neuroses of the unwed.[30] As Rickie Solinger has observed of the United States, the spread of psychological explanations after the Second World War encouraged 'white unwed mothers to relinquish their illegitimate babies . . . grooming them to resume the roles of normative young womanhood—coed, coquette, and bride.'[31] Despite the persistence of continuing reservations, much the same development seems to have occurred in Canada.

Native mothers, unwed and otherwise, have had special difficulty in winning respect from newcomers. As early as New France, Jesuits singled out eastern Aboriginal mothers as likely to be overly indulgent and thus neglectful. Later in the course of contact, different styles of parenting supplied one source of conflict between European traders and their Aboriginal 'country wives'. Settlers in the Canadian West, like those before and after, readily dismissed Aboriginal women as immoral and sexually promiscuous, both incompetent and inferior maternal material. While First Nations champions such as the Mohawk-English performer and writer E. Pauline Johnson rejected the epithet of squaw and celebrated Native mothers for their ingenuity, industry, nurture, and self-sacrifice,[32] they were hard put to counter pervasive calumny. No wonder that legal scholar Marlee Kline concluded it has been well nigh impossible for indigenous women to be regarded as 'good mothers' by representatives of the Canadian state.[33]

Increasingly, social workers and social critics clearly understood that many mothers forced to contemplate loss of offspring have been victims of poverty, unscrupulous men, and uncaring communities. The Great Depression, and economic downturns in general, were especially likely to generate recognition of larger predicaments. In 1932, one journalist writing for *Chatelaine*, Canada's leading women's magazine, portrayed candidates for adoption as

> handed out of the window before the fire reached them, by the owners, who, having themselves been badly burned by other fires of immorality or poverty, desired that these very precious bundles of merchandise might escape a similar fate.
>
> These particular goods mostly take the shape of babies born of unmarried mothers. They are given up voluntarily—although that isn't the right word—by girls who walk into your office very bravely but without the baby, and tell you of the bitter struggle they have made trying to get along and keep the baby properly. But because of unemployment, sickness, or in most cases the failure of the child's father to help, they have to give up. . . . They have sinned but their punishment is great.[34]

Later, British Columbia's child welfare workers typically described how birth mothers cried for months and sobbed every year on children's birthdays. Far from uninterested, these unfortunates intended rescue for their offspring and in the process demonstrated 'true mother love'.[35]

Moralistic rhetoric nevertheless lingered. Such was the case with a 1962 appeal to Vancouver readers on behalf of three-month-old Mary, who was reckoned the 'sin' of those who gave her life but who could be fully rehabilitated by adoption into a 'good family' that would cloak her 'at last, with respectability.'[36] As child welfare services slowly professionalized across the country, a process that was not to be complete until well after 1945, environmental and psychological explanations for unwed parenthood grew stronger. Real sympathy persisted, but an older morality that allocated blame firmly to women was never far away.

The promise that they could rejoin the ranks of the respectable if they 'chose' to surrender offspring influenced many unwed mothers well into the 1960s and beyond. It also inspired social workers all too aware of the economic and social dilemmas confronting clients who kept babies. While authorities regularly insisted that they applied no pressure and allowed clients to formulate their own plans,[37] they also dealt daily with the reality of widespread poverty among mother-headed families. As one Child Welfare Commission reported in 1968: 'We believe that there is a direct relationship between the unmarried mother's decision as to whether she keeps or surrenders her child and the availability or lack of community resources such as subsidized daycare nurseries. The extreme lack of such resources and facilities in all of Alberta, particularly in the smaller centres, makes it difficult if not impossible for many unmarried mothers to keep their children.'[38] While newspapers featured lifestyles of famous single mothers like Mia Farrow with twins, social workers understood that few had the resources to match such choices.[39] They also knew from painful experience that later apprehension was only too common and that older children glutted adoption's hard market.

As unwed mothers came to be assessed increasingly hopefully as sources of suitable infants, concern grew over their efforts at retention. After 1945, a raft of studies, often associated with Canada's schools of social work, identified 'keepers' as frequently ill-prepared, weak, selfish, and often less intelligent and goal-oriented than 'donors'. The unfavourable comparison was clear in one Toronto social worker's report to an international conference in 1959: 'Over the past few years, we have found that the more emotionally healthy unmarried mothers are the ones likely to relinquish their children: not because they do not love them, but because they care enough to want this child to have the love and protection of two parents, who will cherish and nurture him in a normal home setting.'[40] Demographic comparison of the two populations fuelled damning observations. In 1975, a report on the situation in Edmonton, Alberta, observed 'that the tendency is increasing for the younger, less mature woman to keep her child while the older woman, who appears to have more concrete goals for herself, surrenders her baby.'[41] Eight years later in Ontario, the chairman of Durham Region's Welfare Committee described 'kids' having babies and ending up on welfare, which provided both with only a wretched existence. No wonder he believed that 'young mothers would be further ahead to give their babies up for adoption, get back to school again, get a good schooling, start a new life and get into the work stream later on.'[42] Worse fears sometimes still further encouraged such preferences. In 1968, for example, Alberta's Child Welfare Commission insisted 'that there is a direct relationship between cases of the battered child and the fact that the mother did not want the child, and the child was unwanted from the beginning.'[43]

By the 1980s, Canada's New Right found convenient targets in single mothers, who were readily deemed social parasites contributing to the national debt.[44] Moral conservatives were, however, rarely fans of women controlling their own bodies. Their opposition to abortion and sex education supplied a case in point. Debates in the Canadian House of Commons revealed important connections. In 1987, a Progressive Conservative MP from Niagara Falls, Ontario, insisted that Canada had no unwanted children: 'I cannot tell you how many times I have been in my law office with young couples who have told me of their difficulties in adopting children. People in tears have told me there is nothing they wanted more than to adopt a child but they could not do so because of the abortion laws.'[45] A little more than a year later, a Liberal MP from Quebec voiced similar views, urging 'a massive effort' encouraging 'more women to complete their pregnancies, to give those couples who want a child, or hope for one as many chances as possible of adopting one.'[46] He was joined by the Conservative representative from BC's Fraser Valley East: 'There are so many couples trying to adopt children that many agencies cannot take any more names. Yet, 60,000 babies are aborted each year. It is a crying shame.'[47] Like Birthright, an international anti-abortion, pro-adoption organization begun by Louise Summerhill, a mother of seven, in Toronto in 1968,[48] such speakers tied out-of-wedlock pregnancies firmly to production for the adoption market. No wonder a priest writing for the *B.C. Catholic* in 1988 was able to hail a young woman's 'courage, goodness and generosity' in giving a baby up for adoption.[49] Such sacrifice ensured redemption.

By the close of the twentieth century, moral outrage increasingly focused on failures to provide 'good parents' with 'wanted' children. This worked hand in hand with long-standing anger about the costs of social welfare to stigmatize many poor mothers. Such women were all the more condemned when they produced offspring physically and mentally tainted by apparent maternal failings, be these AIDS or alcohol and drug abuse. Proposals to incarcerate pregnant women who failed to match acceptable standards promised healthier babies but did little to address the real tragedy. By the end of the twentieth century, babies once assessed as inadequate were eyed increasingly enthusiastically. Adopting parents were now the good mothers who deserved the production of other loins.

Birth mothers had, of course, their own stories to tell as they dealt with shifting views of their offspring and themselves. Their frequent rejection of the role of producers of offspring for others emerges most clearly in the voices of searchers and in the numerous court cases where they sought to revoke consent. At the end of the twentieth century, opposition found collective expression in groups such as the Canadian Council of Natural Mothers (CCNM) (established in 2002 as an affiliate of Parent Finders) and Origins Canada (part of an international group that began in Australia).[50] As a related website declared, birth mothers 'were being continu-

ously re-traumatized each time so-called experts and health professionals mini-
mized and invalidated the severe emotional anguish, trauma, and grief left in the
wake of their adoption experience.' One president of the CCNM similarly summed
up 'adoption' as 'all about loss for adoptees and natural parents.'[51] As indicated in
chapter 8, separated biological kin regularly insisted upon the centrality of blood
ties and rejected any charge of earlier immorality or psychological shortcoming.
Instead, they readily assumed the identity of 'victim', of their gender for the most
part but also sometimes of their class and racialized position in Canadian society.
Searching birth mothers also regularly prided themselves on never relinquishing
maternal feelings, and they sometimes explained the entire trajectory of their subsequent life in terms of unfulfilled maternal longings.

Native women rarely joined formally with activist white birth mothers. They
were likely to locate their losses within the larger framework of western colonialism that denied them humanity in many aspects of their lives. The novel *Daughters
Are Forever,* by Lee Maracle, provides a dramatic and disturbing account of the
struggle of Marilyn, a Salish mother and social worker, to understand both her previous abuse of her own children and far worse neglect by her Aboriginal clients.
Her reflections are dogged by guilt and despair. Eventually, Marilyn is able to take
responsibility for former failures while concluding, as she did in her master's thesis, that racism and colonialism had set the stage for 'the historic condition that had
birthed massive child neglect among Native families.'[52] Other First Nations
accounts have similarly tended to situate maternal vulnerability firmly within the
context of racism and to demonstrate sympathy for birth fathers. Such men may
have failed to protect offspring or mothers, but they themselves have often been
traumatized by racism.[53] Such support for biological fathers has little equivalent
among other groups of birth mothers and their sympathizers.

As the emotional debates over the choice of appropriate adjectives such as
'birth', 'natural', 'original', or 'first' as appended to 'mothers' or verbs such as 'surrendered', 'gave', 'transferred', 'stolen', and 'abducted' have suggested, the right to
'mother' is contentious. While women connected by blood to offspring have regularly insisted on priority, their claims have been challenged. 'Adoptive', 'adopted',
'social', or 'actual' mothers have contested any designation that smacks of the sec-
ond-rate. Louise De Kiriline, the nurse who cared for the Dionne quintuplets,
who were born in 1934, through their first difficult months, set out the common
refrain. A birth mother herself, she assessed the unfortunate Elzire Dionne—who
was especially suspect, at least among English-speaking urbanites, as rural and uneducated as well as French Canadian—as ill-equipped in her 'indiscriminate
mother love' to live up to her high calling. Championing all of her sex who took
on responsibilities for the progeny of others, De Kiriline described a 'love very
nearly akin to and, I venture to say, fully as unselfish and strong as the love of any
woman who bore her own child.' While accepting 'the intangibly intimate bond
between child and mother,' she concluded it was

> most unfair to allege that a woman, unfortunate enough not to have a child of
> her own, is incapable of love for a child as sublime as that of a mother. Let the

mother who dares say that of another woman ransack her own heart for errors committed against her own children, which might cast a doubt upon the genuine quality of her mother feelings, before she utters so thoughtless an allegation.

The Dionne babies did not lack love during their first year of life, despite their privation of mother's care and presence.[54]

Such observers emphasized that good mothers were ultimately made, not born. As Julie Berebitsky has convincingly demonstrated for the United States, adoption thus offered an increasingly approved way to join the 'normal' community of women, for whom maternity was deemed *de rigueur*.[55]

Adoptive mothers often reiterated, and even celebrated, the idealized construct of motherhood. Such was the case of a PEI woman who went abroad when artificial insemination failed. Determined to acquire a newborn, she refused a six-month-old infant and concentrated on the offspring of a seventeen-year-old in Lima, Peru. When she claimed to recognize him instantly as her son, she allowed her need to overwrite his biology. Too, as is so often the case when laying claim to possessions of others, she renamed him, in this case David, or 'beloved'. This was only the beginning: she and her partner also planned to adopt a Guatemalan girl, because 'family is the most important thing in life.'[56] Yet, despite efforts to insist upon the normality of the drive to parent, particularly to mother, such initiatives challenged narrow definitions. 'Families' were much more than products of biology; they were ultimately social creations. Throughout their history, voices of adoptive mothers helped expand the maternal ideal well beyond blood to include ties of care and commitment.[57] Nor were they necessarily alone. Grandmothers have also been identified as particularly supportive of integrating youngsters into established kin networks. In extending families through adoption, both mothers and grandmothers could play the nurturing roles deemed so essential to female identities in the nineteenth and twentieth centuries.[58]

Popular literature, which readily feeds the dreams of female readers, has maintained an active discourse celebrating maternal adopters. Early reports from Ontario's superintendent of neglected and dependent children supplied typical acknowledgement. The evocatively titled poems 'The Wicked Little Babies' and 'Nobody's Child' shared sentiments with another contribution, 'The Foster Mother'. This latter prototype lamented the loss of one child while finding consolation in the arrival of another. The conclusion of the protagonist—'I am thy mother still'—hinted at the complicated range of emotions that might well greet newcomers to bereaved households.[59]

Empty-nesters supplied fodder throughout the decades for Canada's fictional representations of the adoption story. In 1965, *Chatelaine* published 'The Boy Nobody Wanted'. Unlike infants, who readily won hearts, here was a ten-year-old Métis resident of Edmonton's children's shelter for 'victims of neglect, mistreatment or illegitimacy.' A modern child psychologist assessed him as worth redemption. This expert's mother, evocatively named 'Nan', a popular short form of Nana or Grandmother, proved ready to follow up her daughter's modern diagnosis with old-fashioned love. Not so incidentally, empty-nester Nan would be rescued from a life without apparent meaning or occupation.[60] In 1999, the volume that received the Hugh MacLennan Prize for fiction and was shortlisted for the Governor General's Award for fiction featured the intriguing 'Mother: Not a True Story'. In a fascinating reminder of the 1900 Ontario poem mentioned above, it featured an adopter who felt like a lottery-winner. When her daughter asked if she had thought she was saving a child's life, the adoptive mother offered a poignant reply: "'No,' she repeated again. "I thought you were saving mine."'[61]

Official reports regularly confirmed the commonplace assumption that married life was empty without girls and boys by the fireside. In 1950, Newfoundland's regional welfare officer for the west coast area described a local beneficiary's response, which counterparts across the nation would have echoed:

> One particular mother said to me: 'before you gave me this child I used to bowl, play cards, and go regularly to the movies, to help drive out the monotony. Now I cannot be bothered for Junior supplies all the enjoyment I want, and friends who would see me come to the house. Is he not a little darling?'
>
> Yes, I have seen like conditions in many homes, life has taken on anew meaning and given such parents a definite purpose.[62]

Where childless middle-class women might, for much of Canada's history, have had much to occupy them, whether this involved responsibilities for household production or young and old kin, after the Second World War some experienced the sense of uselessness that Betty Friedan chronicled in *The Feminine Mystique* (1963). New youngsters offered essential opportunities for justifying and renewing old roles.

Even in the closing decades of the twentieth century, women working for wages outside the home were rarely considered ideal adopters and were routinely rejected. Commonly assessed as selfish, they were viewed as generally poor maternal material. As more wives entered the labour market, such prejudices were difficult to sustain. Alberta's 1965 Committee on Adoption devoted considerable attention to reviewing the standard response as it heard from and about professional women, especially doctors, who had found a variety of ways to sidestep restrictions. Shifts in opinion were signalled by the committee's recommendation that Alberta 'as a matter of policy' should accept 'working women' as 'suitable' parents and in fact provide 'extensive day care centres'.[63] That battle remained far from won for many years. In the 1990s, the struggle continued but increasingly focused on the provision of equal access to the paid maternity and paternity benefits that also extended possibilities for adoption.

So-called working wives were not the only women to seize opportunities to parent from sceptical authorities. Both fiction and non-fiction early on recognized the recurring longings of the unmarried. Bessie Marchant's pre–First World War novel *Daughters of the Dominion: A Story of the Canadian Frontier* profiled Nell, who adopted three female orphans and set about making a thrifty living running a 'food shop' in a small mining town.[64] Marilla Cuthbert in *Anne of Green Gables* might have been initially reluctant, but she too took her place along the host of tough-minded but ultimately maternal spinsters who saved themselves as well as young-sters. By 1958, when *Chatelaine* featured still another such tale, Canadians were very familiar with the rescue theme. Forty-year-old Rose found herself the sav-iour of eight-year-old Lori. This youngster, the daughter of a mother who, while 'not uncaring, not drunken,' was 'mentally deficient' and might have appeared ini-tially unprepossessing, but as 'a Canadian child of British ancestry in a land of peace and plenty' she had potential to be unlocked. Ultimately, despite early reser-vations, Rose could not resist the appeal of the youngster knocking on her door, admitting, 'Lori is mine and I am certainly and forever hers.'[65]

The fact that writers, like other professional women, have often been better positioned to assume the role of single parent has sometimes contributed to the literature invoking parenting. Mazo de la Roche's adoption of youngsters has been judged to have influenced her work.[66] The stories of best-selling children's author Jean Little, whom adoption directly touched as an aunt and great-aunt, are infused with concern about how children fare.[67] Equally revealing are poet Ethelwyn Wetherald's reflections on acquiring a toddler, Dorothy, and that daughter's own loving memoir. Wetherald's sixth book of poetry, *Tree Top Mornings*, was dedicated to Dorothy, and 'As Good as a Throne' explicitly set out new priorities:

> Here is a thought as good as a throne
> I am my own, yes wholly my own,
> No burdensome parent and nobody's wife
> I can simply do as I choose with my Life!
> True I have millions of human brothers,
> But they have no claim on me at all,
> I certainly shall not live for others
> Nor an imagined duty's call.
>
> So I stretched out my feet, as women will,
> To the open fire, for the day was chill;
> When, swift as the rush of running water
> Burst in my little adopted daughter.
>
> She wanted ice cream—the half of a brick
> She wanted help in arithmetic
> She wanted to know the reason why
> I had not made a blueberry pie.
> She wanted sympathy, candy and ink,
> She wanted a dress of rosy pink,
> And help in collecting leaves and barks–
>
> At this, with a few sarcastic remarks,
> My Ownness arose and wished me 'Good Day?'
> And all in reply that I could say
> Was, 'Thrones are no good anyway![68]

Wetherald's inclinations were similarly demonstrated in the 1930s, when she took in a poor neighbour's child, thus ensuring that he could go to high school. This foster son might have shared the benefits of 'Uncle Will', the poet's brother, whom Dorothy remembered as possessing 'a wonderful knack of being able to relate to a child.'[69] The daughter herself dedicated a volume

> To my birth mother Mary, who unselfishly shared her child to give me oppor-
> tunities that would otherwise have been impossible.
>   To my adoptive mother Ethelwyn Wetherald who, even in the early 1900s
> taught me to not 'follow the crowd' but to be my own person and follow my
> dreams.[70]

Such adoptions have always occurred. Few jurisdictions ever completely barred single candidates from consideration, and private arrangements have been far from unusual, although they subsequently have often been forgotten by public memory. In 1938, the *Victoria Times* reported that 50 single men and 130 single women had taken home youngsters between 1920 and 1935.[71] Wartime losses fuelled demand. In 1943, the *Vancouver Province* wondered about the options for 'unmarried women in good circumstances' who faced 'diminishing hopes of matrimony'. The city's CAS, however, remained largely uninterested, claiming only two cases of such adopters, both in 'unusual circumstances'.[72] Indeed the reality, if not the fiction, of single parents remained largely invisible for many years. Only as the numbers of provincial wards grew did signs of greater acceptance slowly appear. In 1959, Vancouver Island's Isobel Wilson applied to adopt a two-year-old girl she had cared for since birth and was 'forced to wage a long and expensive legal battle for her right to single parenthood.' Later, a forty-year-old Vancouver secretary similarly overcame initial rejection to become 'as excited as any young woman' who 'expected her firstborn'. Both inspired imitators, but other forces were also at work. By 1968, a provincial social worker admitted that worries over the rise in the numbers of illegitimate children had produced some acceptance of single adopters.[73]

In Alberta, a forty-one-year-old anaesthetist was equally committed to overcoming the odds. In 1968, the *United Church Observer* favourably chronicled her adoptions, first privately of an 'Asian-Caucasian' baby and then through the provincial system of a Métis girl and a white boy.[74] Three years later, the *Star Weekly* sympathetically profiled a United Church minister from Bathurst, Nova Scotia, who chose two daughters, one of Aboriginal ancestry.[75] In the same year, Montreal supplied similar reports of single female adopters. The manager of a downtown clothing store parented a six-year-old girl of black and white ancestry hailing from Nova Scotia. In defending their approval of such arrangements, Montreal's adoption experts carefully distinguished between successful candidates for motherhood who had 'freely chosen to adopt a child because they want one' and their unmarried clients who were 'forced into becoming a single parent because of circumstances.'[76] Special competence was similarly credited to a thirty-five-year-old director of nursing for BC's Cancer Control Agency and to a fifty-two-year-old Grade 1 teacher from Victoria whom the *Globe and Mail* identified in 1978 as adopting, respectively, a two-year-old Korean orphan and two daughters, each diagnosed with disabilities. These independent-minded women possessed homes, savings, and good jobs. In the era of rising divorce rates, a man, as they suggested, was no longer crucial.[77]

By 1985, a Nova Scotia master's thesis in social work surveyed a range of provincial practices. Crediting the Los Angeles Bureau of Adoptions as a pioneer in accepting single adults in 1965, it sifted through Canadian evidence from the 1970s. While the non-discrimination requirements of the 1982 Canadian Charter of Rights and Freedoms inspired caution, jurisdictions such as the Northwest Territories, Ontario, and Nova Scotia reported few such placements and then 'only in special circumstances'. Yukon child welfare authorities observed that single applicants were discouraged because so few youngsters were available. Alberta claimed to judge single and married applicants on the same basis. In the context of an increasingly competitive adoption market, however, it admitted that success stories among the unmarried were increasingly unusual. In Nova Scotia, only two of eleven agencies accepted single adopters. The Halifax Children's Aid admitted previously placing mixed-race siblings aged six and seven and an eight-year-old with emotional problems separately with two female university professors. One Nova Scotia agency dealing solely in infants explained that birth mothers themselves insisted on two parents. If it handled 'older, hard-to-place children', the agency felt, however, that it 'would be much more interested in placements of this type.' Nine of the eleven single parents interviewed for the thesis held jobs as nurses, teachers, or childcare workers. Most were older, white, and relatively well educated. They explained their determination to have daughters and sons: 'I've always wanted children—from the time I was a little girl. . . . As I grew older I decided to adopt as a single parent if I didn't have children by the time I was 32.' 'I really missed them [children] just terribly and didn't realize that there was anything you could do about it until someone that I knew told me that in Ontario and California single parents had adopted. . . . I still remember the day I was told that.' And 'I was continually "borrowing" my sister's kids and hated taking them back.'[78] The absence of husbands proved no fatal deterrent to women who prized maternal roles.

Reports from across Canada indicated that the situation for single adopters was most favourable when there was a glut of state wards. While heterosexual couples always stood at the front of any line when it came to the adoption of healthy white babies, they were much less likely to compete for other kids. In 1965, Alberta's Adoption Committee pointed to a professional woman who had adopted 'two children who otherwise would have been hard to place.'[79] By 1982, the same province's authorities agreed that single applicants were especially suited for older youngsters in state care.[80] This was not unusual. Everywhere across the country, single women regularly enlisted as the mothers of 'special' girls and boys. Children who were older, racialized, or credited with disabilities were routinely paired with adults who were likewise viewed as less than ideal. As one progressive social worker noted, the rising tide of illegitimate children in the 1960s prompted British Columbia to accept single applicants. She also noted that such open-mindedness did not extend to provision for daycare or subsidies.[81] While Julie Berebitsky has argued that 'virtually no single women adopted' in the United States by the 1920s, this may be less true of Canada. Certainly it is not true to suggest that 'by the 1950s, child welfare professionals were united in their opposition to single women.'[82] While often forbidden 'blue-ribbon' babies, single women emerged as fully paid-up members of the corps of Canadian mothers taking on the jobs and children few else wanted.

Even single adopters were likely to be privileged in a variety of ways when compared with those who surrendered offspring. Finances, age, and social situation underpinned their determination to parent. The fact that many adopters, both single and married, were drawn from the same social groups as the professionals and volunteers who arranged placements proved a tremendous advantage on countless occasions. Child welfare workers might well understand and sympathize with their peers' desire for children. Such would-be parents were all the more welcome because they supplied the 'happy stories' that punctuated the commonly tragic narratives of less-wanted kids.

Yet, whether married or single, adoptive mothers were never viewed entirely unproblematically, especially as psychological theories that emphasized female vulnerability to maladjustment took hold in the caring professions over the course of the twentieth century. Like birth mothers, if somewhat differently, adoptive mothers too might be judged wanting. In 1928, Ontario welfare experts obsessed about seemingly over-possessive women who tied sons and daughters to apron strings and who would not sponsor independence. Their efforts were rejected as not 'love but selfishness'.[83] Female candidates could also sometimes take the blame for infertility. In 1955, the *Bulletin* from Toronto's Academy of Medicine identified a 'murderous mother complex' in women who claimed to desire offspring yet who were said unconsciously to reject them with 'repeated abortions and functional sterility.' No wonder such unnatural creatures were also suspected of abusing unfortunate adoptees.[84] In the next decade, the journal *MD of Canada* characterized patients with repeated miscarriages as often 'either immature, unable to accept the responsibility of motherhood, or independent and frustrated, conditioned to the rewards of the male world and viewing maternity as unsatisfying.'[85]

Single women were especially vulnerable to charges that they violated deeply held notions of propriety for their sex. While traditions of family adoption had always included spinsters and widows, the professionalization of child transfer in the twentieth century, with its preference for the heterosexual couple, undermined, even when it could not entirely overcome, long-standing legitimacy. The transition was summed up in the negative conclusions of a senior social worker from Toronto's CAS and adviser to the League of Nations, Robert Mills:

> Some organizations are fairly definitely opposed to the placing of a child with an unmarried person, whether spinster or bachelor. This is based in part upon the need of two parents, but more particularly upon experience which has shown that the relationship developed is nearly always highly abnormal. While the relationship may not be homosexual, yet the mere presence of a child in

such a home often indicates an adult in need of compensation to assist in overcoming poor adjustment to life. The child is not treated as an individual searching for wholesome interest, good friends and natural independence, but is considered unconsciously as a satisfaction for a craving which should have been met in a more normal manner.[86]

A colleague of Mills and a leading child welfare reformer, Charlotte Whitton could be similarly homophobic.[87] Even the essentially sympathetic observations by Benjamin Schlesinger, one of Canada's leading scholars of single parenthood in the last decades of the twentieth century, embodied the commonplace implication of abnormality: 'Some women, percentage unknown, may actually find married life uncongenial and contrary to their predispositions but accept marriage as a neces-sity, although unwanted, prerequisite for parenthood. Given a socially sanctioned avenue to parenthood through single-parent adoption may enable such women to be mothers without having to accept the status of wife.'[88]

When lesbian and gay adults won the right to adopt in many provincial juris-dictions late in the twentieth century,[89] opponents, such as BC's REAL Women, repeated old accusations in their campaigns to advance the heterosexual family. Self-professed critics of 'dominant women', they had, however, to steer a careful course. On the one hand, they saluted 'the thousands of single moms and dads who are doing a heroic job in raising their children to become productive and respon-sible citizens' while at the same time fiercely opposing children adopted by single adults with 'family situations where there are such greatly increased risks of not thriving mentally, emotionally, spiritually, financially, and educationally.'[90]

Once they surmounted the various hurdles in their paths, adoptive mothers appear to have behaved much like their biological counterparts. This has often meant that their family roles differed from male parents. All the more so as they were regu-larly credited with initiating adoption, these women appeared likely to take particu-lar responsibility for the household's emotional well-being. This has usually included the 'telling' of the adoption story. As one 1948 social work thesis concluded, most mothers made the decision if, when, and how to tell the truth of origins. The writer also observed that women felt that 'men were so much more possessive than women' that they could not bear dealing with their children's prior history.[91] Years later, Marie Adams, an adoptive mother who interviewed other parents who shared her experience of difficult, often tormented, relations with their children, also summed up recurring gender differences. Mothers, she found, were much more likely to blame themselves if children became anti-social or criminal. Tragic outcomes were interpreted as condemning women and their 'childrearing practices'. In response, mothers readily lost confidence and 'became emotionally distraught'. Adams pointed, in contrast, to fathers' ability to distance themselves from responsibility and their 'unwillingness to talk about their sons as much as the mothers wanted to.'[92] Such differences would not have distinguished adopters from very many Canadian couples. The great majority of such studies ultimately drew heavily on mothers' ver-sions of events. The fact that experts and would-be experts in child welfare were also likely to be female has always privileged one perspective on adoption.

As many scholars have observed, the exchange of youngsters has persistently involved networks of women. One Toronto adopter, then an art director for a major publisher, credited her ability to secure a child to just such support. Not only did she work through adoption agencies, such as Families for Children, run largely by women, she depended on female kin. With her mother, who had years previously been assisted in adding a son to her household both by her own sister and by the *Toronto Telegram*'s Helen Allen, editor of 'Today's Child,' she forged 'a partnership of women so strong that though it might be stretched at times, it could never be broken.'[93] Bridget Moran, an outspoken social worker in Prince George, BC, who became a legend helping women and children in the adoption circle, summed up lessons that were sometimes learned: 'I was also politicized by my experiences as a female in a world that seemed to carry the warning, "For men Only." . . . I had never ever wanted to be a man but I passionately wanted to share some of the freedoms men enjoyed.'[94]

Pink-Ribbon Babies

Gender differentiation continued among adoptive youngsters. Girls and boys were for the most part sharply distinguished. Even before adoption became popular, gender made some youngsters more or less attractive to new households. In 1896, the *Canadian Churchman* noted that the CAS had many unfilled applications for young girls but few for boys. Mindful of those who stayed longest in shelters, readers were urged to 'try and make some sacrifice, if necessary, and take a boy,' such as '"Jack," a boy of two, with auburn hair and blue eyes, a bright, lively little fellow.'[95] In British Columbia, as elsewhere where children were often wanted for their labour, applicants in search of domestic help considered girls while those who wanted outdoor labourers preferred boys. Both sexes regularly complained of overwork, uncomfortable housing, and poor clothing but they also showed some sharp differences. British Columbia's male wards were reckoned perhaps seven times as likely as their female counterparts to die, a statistic that reflected the nature of their toil, the often harsh physical conditions in which they lived, and greater indifference to their welfare. Girls, who were likely to remain in contact with kin and connections from the past, appeared more likely to find anchors of care and concern.[96]

To be sure, girls did not always get off lightly. Those who did not readily match the desires of the adopters of their day were markedly vulnerable. Such was the case of one 'Colored girl' who was sent to a foster home by an Ontario CAS in 1906. When she ran away, she was recaptured, assessed, ominously, as demonstrating 'the usual characteristics of her race,' and placed in an institution.[97] At the beginning of the twentieth century, her gender, like that of her First Nations counterparts, ultimately did little to improve her prospects.

While there have been occasional dissenters,[98] most reports suggest that Canadians, like adopters in the United States and the United Kingdom, have preferred daughters, increasingly the younger the better.[99] Philip Hepworth's benchmark study on foster care and adoption in Canada pointed out that, although statistics have regularly ignored gender, authorities always noted the popularity of girls. More boys always remained in state care.[100] Even the patriotic appeal of soldiers' orphans after the First World War did not alter the prevailing preference. In 1921, Ontario's Soldiers' Assistance Commission noted that although it had successfully arranged adoption for seventy-one youngsters 'into good families,' 'for some reason or other most of these have been girls.' Equally disconcerting was the fact that further applicants remained largely unsatisfied because nine out of ten requested daughters.[101]

Gender favouritism has been much analyzed. In summary, girls have been identified as additionally valued because they have been endowed with attractive 'natural' qualities such as obedience, gentleness, and affection. They also appeared less threatening to patrilineal families, as they were presumed to lose both name and independent identity upon marriage. Some analysts have argued that prospective mothers preferred children of their own sex. Social work scholar H. David Kirk suggested, however, that the apparent preference for daughters was part of wives' strategies for gaining consent from reluctant spouses. They were prepared to accept either boys or girls as long as they got a child, and they were willing to acquiesce to male preferences for daughters, who wouldn't inherit family names and who were more likely, with their supposedly natural qualities, to confirm rather than threaten paternal masculinity.[102] The 1948 case of a middle-class couple living in a Toronto suburb revealed how spouses might act out just the understanding that Kirk described. As the interviewer discovered, 'they adopted another girl because Mrs T. smiled, her husband loves girls, big ones and small ones and Mrs T. loves all children so that really didn't make a difference.'[103]

Whatever the sources of predilections, gender provided a mainstay of both fictional and real adoption stories. Anne of Green Gables was far from the first girl to reward those who took her in. The best-selling novel *The Adopted Daughter or the Trials of Sabra; A Tale of Real Life* featured a girl who, unlike her family's biological offspring, all boys it should be noted, mourned her loving adoptive mother and named her own child in her honour. In 1862, officials of Halifax's Protestant Orphanages grumbled about placing boys who regularly became 'restless after a few years' but congratulated themselves on seeing 'more contented' girls likely to create 'homes of their own, [and] continue to write, expressing gratitude to the Committee who cared for them in their youth.'[104] Ontario's J.J. Kelso summed up similar sentiments at the beginning of the twentieth century: 'Boys after they pass the age of four or five are not usually very attractive, while their chief accomplishment consists in their ability to wear out clothes, and creating a good deal of noise and confusion.'[105] Some decades later, the same theme mobilized a woman writing to the *Globe and Mail* in 1951: boys were aggressive, noisy, and destructive, but girls were more easily handled, naturally helpful, and a comfort to those who took them in.[106] In the 1990s, one single adoptive mother put her choice even more simply: 'I thought it would be easier for me to raise a girl alone than a boy.'[107]

It proved very difficult to shift gender preferences. Even advertising was not always successful. In 1957, Ontario initiated province-wide ads for the wards of the CAS, but, as one despairing welfare worker reported, 'everyone wants a blue-eyed gold-haired girl under the age of 6 months,' and 'it's difficult to place the poor kid-dies who aren't made to order.'[108] In editing the influential 'Today's Child' in the *Toronto Telegram*, Helen Allen began her campaign with a female youngster, an obvious ploy to ensure success for the larger group, the majority of whom were boys, for whom she hoped to find homes. In the last decades of the twentieth cen-tury, international adopters continued long-standing preferences. The Chinese child that the *Globe and Mail* identified in 1961 as the first refugee adoption was, hardly surprisingly, a girl.[109] She was the first of many. She and her sisters inspired a series of children's books, the *Autumn Jade Mystery Series*, that demonstrated once again girls' centrality to the national adoption narrative.[110]

The special appeal of girls has sometimes encouraged child welfare profession-als to hope that gender would counter other possible liabilities. In 1955, the BC social welfare branch reported attracting parents for a four-year-old with 'charm and potential'. Careful cultivation of her adopters was clearly essential because, although this little girl held 'the promise of the daughter they longed for,' she was also her 'part-Indian'.[111] In 1964, home-finder Helen Allen profiled the well-named 'Hope', a picture-perfect '15-month-old girl of partly negro and white background with sparkling brown eyes and curling dark brown hair. A delightful child with a happy outgoing nature' and 'high intelligence', she 'loves other chil-dren'. Placed like many of her counterparts in the 'Women's Pages,' she was the poster-child for the disadvantaged who had already failed to find takers.[112]

Hope's prospects were not unusual. In 1965, a member of Alberta's Committee on Adoption reported that Protestant 'negro' girls could always be placed, as could sibling groups, if the youngsters were under five and 'if at least one of them is a girl.' Among Catholic children, who regularly found greater difficulty than Protestants in finding new homes, the same pattern emerged, especially for those 'aged 2 to 10 years.'[113] When Jewish refugee youngsters arrived in 1947, few Canadians wished to parent the great majority, who were male adolescents. Overwhelmingly, they requested girls under five, a group that had rarely survived the Holocaust.[114]

Not only were girls more likely to get snapped up, some evidence has suggested that birth parents may also have also more reluctance to part with them.[115] Both biological and adoptive kin had often reported finding boys harder to raise.[116] In the decades that established adoption as a significant way of creating families, some agencies went so far as to deny adopters more than one girl or even demanded they take a son as the price of acquiring a daughter. In the case of one tragic inter-national adoption that drew much attention in the 1990s, the Canadian mother was forced to take a Mexican brother in order to access his sister. Once home, she soon dispatched him to the Toronto CAS and decamped with her new daughter.[117] While the mass circulation *Star Weekly* might occasionally hail a little blond boy as 'Canada's Champion Baby', most social workers knew full well that his sister was likely to be the real winner in the adoption sweepstakes.[118]

If girls supplied their share, and perhaps more, of good news stories, they some-times remained vulnerable. Until the middle years of the twentieth century, some householders sought them from orphanages and emigration societies for hard labour and sometimes for sexual exploitation. Child welfare authorities encountered abuse regularly enough to be especially protective. The death of a child supposedly adopted by her tormenters inspired Montreal's Protestant Orphanage to withdraw for the most part from such placements.[119] The motives of even the seemingly most charitable of applicants often had to be closely examined. When the Canadian Jewish Congress at long last won its crusade to admit child refugees in 1947, it had to guard against members of its own community who offered accommodation for girls 'which, upon investigation, turned out to be veiled schemes to secure domestics.'[120] Fears of girls' special vulnerability also appeared to have influenced proclivities to apprehend. Ontario's superintendent of neglected and dependent children typically justified taking 'more' girls in care because they were believed 'exposed to special dangers and temptations.'[121] In such cases, protection went hand in hand with the greater regulation that regularly shaped female prospects.

Daughters' attractions have clearly often resided first and foremost in the mind of prospective adopters. Some studies have also suggested that children's gender helps explain individual reactions to dislocation and transfer. It remains difficult, however, to generalize beyond the observation that girls have appeared somewhat less likely to work out their pain and anxiety through aggression against others.[122] Ultimately, it seems fairest to conclude with one Canadian observer that 'although it is easier for girls to meet society's expectations generally, there is no reason to believe they are less affected emotionally by the loss of their family.'[123]

Boys have clearly often promised something different to the adults who considered their qualities. Canadians have regularly been reassured by reminders, such as those by Ontario officials in 1895, that 'wayward boys, if taken at the right time and in the right way, can be converted into first-class men.'[124] The alternative was ominous. After the Second World War, the *Calgary Herald* blew the lid off the type of scandal that most often seems to have involved the mass mistreatment of male children. Its article 'Children in Iron Cages' described years of abuse during which the 'Edmonton Children's Aid Department, and with the full knowledge of officials of the Child Welfare Branch' had been restraining eight- to eighteen-year-old boys 'in a basement, in steel cells, similar to the ones used in police lock-ups throughout the country.' Inmates 'slept on steel shelves without mattresses, had no exercise, or schooling or recreational facilities, for periods up to two weeks at a time.'[125] Like those who similarly crowded the halls of institutions like St Vincent's and Mount Cashel in Newfoundland and elsewhere, Alberta's youngest citizens were hardly prepared to fulfill hopes for the next generation. Not surprisingly, worries about boys left on the shelf frequently spurred the search for homes.

Social workers learned to think strategically as they faced disproportionately male caseloads. As early as 1932, one such expert provocatively described tactics that commonly proved effective in moving hard-to-place children:

> The salvage firms, consisting of such groups as Children's Aid Societies and Infants' Homes, are reputable firms, and take pride in delivering goods in as near a perfect shape as possible. Not always able to fill the exact orders received they will make substitution at times, with the consent of the customer, and

often the order for a little girl is filled by the dispatch of a little boy who is sent 'on approval'. But generally the goods remain sold and very few come back for re-sale. Some of the salvaged goods are not damaged at all.[126]

When child welfare authorities moved heavily into advertising in the 1960s, they tried to profile boys in ways that caught readers' eyes. 'Today's Child' was typical in mustering attractive portraits. Helen Allen emphasized the positive attributes of Robert, a 'blond, handsome 10-month-old baby boy, affectionate and alert,' of 'healthy' Joseph, 'an attractive little boy, one-and-a-half years old . . . [with] good ability and . . . full of mischief,' of 'happy', 'responsive' Leslie, and of William, at almost sixteen the oldest candidate over the first two years of the column, with his 'fair skin' and interest 'in sports, especially hockey and sports cars.'[127] A year later, the presentation of four-year-old Alan testified again to the significance of gen-der-typing. With his 'merry smile and twinkling eyes,' he was 'a very active child, who throws himself into roughhouse games with other children and has guns and trucks as his favorite toys. He carries these lively tastes into TV watching for he likes cowboy programs.' 'Nice manners', however, also reassured prospective par-ents that this 'Indian-Scottish-Irish' lad could channel his innate masculinity and become a fine son.[128] Male siblings received similar treatment. In 1965, Allen appealed on behalf of 'three young brothers [who] want to stay together.' Jack aged ten, Ralph nine, and Harry nearly eight emerged as 'active young sportsmen, play-ing baseball and hockey . . . All enjoy fishing. All are enthusiastic bicyclists. They are proud of prizes won for perfect Sunday School attendance. Harry can hardly wait for his birthday so he can join his brothers in Cubs.'[129]

The *Tely*'s efforts were matched nationwide. In 1968, the *Vancouver Sun* told the story of 'Little Scottie.' This 'blue-eyed wonder with a ready smile, turned out to be a ham who'll stop at nothing to win the hearts of the ladies,' who proclaimed him 'all boy'. Equally pointedly, he was declared to have 'the build of a miniature football player.' Aided only by the 'prop' of a child's broom, he readily became a 'weightlifter'. In fact, he embodied a world of athletic prowess. In one 'instant he was Mickey Mantle hitting an invisible flyball out to left field' and in the next 'Arnold Palmer getting a birdie on the first.'[130] The *United Church Observer* offered similar testimony with its description of Michael, 'of mixed Anglo-Saxon and negro background,' who 'loves to play games and can pitch a ball like a regular "pro".'[131] Readers would be hard-put to miss the message of male potential.

Even if they did not initially succumb to boyish charms, prospective adopters sometimes made strategic compromises in order to parent. When Alberta's Adoption Committee surveyed 1,547 provincial couples who had taken young-sters between 1963 and 1965, it concluded that many deliberately applied 'for a male child on being told that there could be a longer waiting period for a female placement.'[132] Would-be mothers and fathers learned how to advance on crucial waiting lists. As the numbers of healthy Caucasian infants available for release declined sharply in the last decades of the twentieth century, choice of gender might appear less significant and applicants more interested in sons.

Boys' options have not, of course, always been entirely bleak. Some Canadians sought them out. After the Second World War, masculinity sometimes had an especially positive purchase on community feelings. Some groups could be notably sympathetic. As one investigator in Halifax discovered, 'a strong male preference is found among the Navy couples.'[133] Other factors could operate more generally across the country. One father spoke for many parents who wished boys to complete a family with only female biological offspring. They found young 'Colin irresistible'.[134] When, many years later, gay men were approved as adoptive parents, they too might well hope to make the difference for youngsters who found fewer takers than their sisters. The determination of two white men from BC's Lower Mainland, both of whom prided themselves on being good dads to a two-year-old African-American son born prematurely in Chicago, held promise.[135]

Adoptees' gender continued to make a difference as they got older. As we shall examine more closely in chapter 8, the majority of adult searchers for birth parents have been women. Despite this commonly observed fact, Canada has been distinguished by a number of highly visible male searchers. Torontonian Barry Stevens made an award-winning film, *Offspring*, about his search for his sperm donor. Vancouver journalist Rick Ouston wrote his compelling *Finding Family*. In general, however, such efforts, like the majority of Canadian films dealing with searching, have far more often emerged from women's needs.[136]

Casual Fornicators, Delinquent Dads, and Determined Fathers

The place of fathers in the adoption circle has traditionally been viewed as biologically central but socially marginal. Unmarried men have frequently disappeared at or soon after conception, and male adopters have rarely been as audible or vocal as their female counterparts. Perhaps not surprisingly, most reflection and research have addressed the lot of women and girls.[137] In fact under-reporting and under-examination have been true of Canadian fatherhood in general. Fortunately, this is changing. Historian Cynthia Comacchio has suggested that modern fatherhood took shape in the face of the preoccupation of child study experts with mothers and panics about the supposed decline of 'better stock'—white Protestant Canadians. This meant that fathers have often been invisible or largely a source of a worry. Whatever criticism men faced, they were nonetheless likely to be forgiven or more commonly taken for granted as long as they supplied the financial needs of children and families. For all Canadians' intermittent references to emotional ties between modern dads and their offspring, fostered notably through leisure activities, 'the reality was that fatherhood came to be associated almost exclusively with its material aspects.'[138]

Measured by the standard of economic support, biological fathers in the adoption circle have been commonly deemed irresponsible, casual, and slackers in the hard work of fatherhood. Their absence or some other failure has been viewed as key to precipitating children and their mothers into the hands of private and public authorities. Such sperm donors were considered at best casual fornicators and often their failings were worse.[139] When sexual intercourse, casual or not, was succeeded, as it has been in many cases, by apparent financial delinquency, birth fathers have understandably been liable to harsh judgments.

Until the late twentieth century, unwed parenthood placed men in a unique legal position regarding offspring.[140] Whatever the reason for failing to marry the women giving birth, they had only one legal connection to their offspring, the obligation of financial support, and that was only if paternity was acknowledged or could be proven. The mother alone was the legal guardian. Only her consent was necessary for the surrender of youngsters. In most instances, mothers and children could inherit from one another, but fathers had no equivalent relationship. One scholar succinctly summed up the common relationship: 'You have no rights, only obligations.'[141] Frequently adversarial relations between biological parents further undermined whatever abilities and willingness to parent may have existed. Decades of Canadian adoption experience has nevertheless provided repeated proof of the conclusions reached by Saskatchewan's Division of Child Welfare in 1952 when considering confirmation of paternity: 'We realize how important it is for any child to know his heritage.'[142]

Knowledge has not always been available. Throughout history, women and men have brought a variety of assumptions to sexual relations. Some men have been no more than sperm donors. One Ontario case in the early 1990s made just this point. The equality demands of the Charter of Rights and Freedoms had raised the question of whether the consent of a 'natural' father was needed for adoption. Rejecting this proposition, the birth mother pointed out that the baby resulted from rape. Not surprisingly, the courts ultimately dispensed with paternal agreement, concluding that 'the remote chance that a rapist might wish to acknowledge and assume responsibility for the child he fathered, bears no realistic proportion to the government objective of providing an expeditious and final adoption.'[143]

Disparity between the relative power of women and men has been especially visible when it involved the military, the institution that most fully embodied collective masculinity. Canadian and American bases in Newfoundland during and after the Second World War, like those elsewhere across the nation and around the world, presented a special challenge to local women hoping for more than a brief fling.[144] As the film *Seven Brides for Uncle Sam* (1997) movingly conveyed, Americans at Fort Pepperrell became experts at loving and leaving. Newfoundland authorities quickly came to reckon the costs in unwed pregnancies. As they learned, 'putative fathers are largely Servicemen, and herein lies the greatest problem, because nearly all of them have departed and have been discharged,' leaving behind mothers and children to 'become public charges'.[145] Such desertions were not unique to military men, of course, as a study in Hamilton, Ontario, makes clear. Men who regarded their sexual encounters as casual were likely to view any resultant offspring as little more than potentially expensive encumbrances. For such reluctant parents, adoption provided one more way of sidestepping responsibility for conception.[146]

Canada's most extensive study of adoption, Paul Sachdev's *Unlocking the Adoption Files,* placed men firmly on the margins of the adoption story. First of all, researchers found records deficient on biological fathers. While acknowledging their 'principle' role on the path to adoption, Sachdev and his assistants largely shared informants' assessment of them as a 'phantom figure[s].' One birth mother summed up the commonplace indictment: 'Birth father is not a person in my estimation.' In general, adopters, adoptees, and birth mothers 'were either opposed [to] or ambivalent' about releasing information about adoptees to biological fathers.[147] The responses of Sachdev's Newfoundland sample reflected widespread assumptions about men's irresponsibility and lack of interest. As one authority has noted, Canadians have generally been convinced that it was 'unnatural' for any woman to wish to surrender a child and that it was equally peculiar for unwed dads to want to parent.[148] Much custom as well as law underpinned court decisions, such that by the BC Court of Appeal in 1927, which ruled against the right of an unwed father, about to be deported, to take a child from the mother, and another many decades later involving an unmarried New Brunswicker who tried to recover an illegitimate infant surrendered by the mother for adoption.[149]

Challenges to tradition and law increased dramatically after the 1960s and 1970s. Child welfare authorities grew more and more concerned, beyond their familiar interest in financial support, in putative fathers.[150] By 1975, BC's Royal Commission on Family and Children's Law acknowledged unmarried fathers' efforts 'to have a voice in planning for their children.'[151] Nineteen years later, the province's panel to review adoption legislation agreed that birth fathers needed legal recognition.[152] And in 1999, Newfoundland, like other jurisdictions in the same decade, first made legislative reference to 'birth fathers'.[153] Like those in Australia,[154] Canadian courts also increasingly pondered the extent of paternal rights. In 1986, in the case of *O'Driscoll v. McLeod*, the BC Supreme Court concluded that 'a natural father and his child born in and out of wedlock shared a legal relationship from which legally enforceable rights and obligations flowed.' A year later, the same province produced the ruling that legislation's failure to require paternal consent to adoption contravened the Charter of Rights and Freedoms.[155] In 1988, the Ontario Divisional Court debated and then rejected claims by a biological father that the Charter guaranteed him equality in custody.[156] Five years later, however, the BC Supreme Court allowed an unwed father the right to 'apply for custody, guardianship or access in spite of the mother's refusal to allow him to acknowledge paternity.'[157] Such varied decisions evoked the complicated nature of individual cases but also displayed unprecedented consideration for the rights of unwed birth fathers.

In the last decades of the twentieth century, a fathers' movement emerged to campaign for paternal rights.[158] As Canadian legal scholar Susan B. Boyd has usefully noted, such demands readily became weapons to assail feminists and women in general. They are frequently more about asserting male power than about taking day-to-day responsibility for children's overall care.[159] Despite such tendencies, some men have always been deeply committed to meaningful roles in parenting. While, according to Barbara Melosh's 2002 study, the United States has not produced 'a single birth father [who] has published a full-length memoir, and few men claim the name "birth father" publicly' Canada, again like Australia, has supplied several examples.[160] In 1989, BC journalist and former member of the provincial legislature Barrie Clark described searching for a daughter he and his university girlfriend had given up in 1952. Registered under Ontario's first reunion registry, he and the birth mother demanded the opening of adoption records.[161] In 2003, Randy Shore, the deputy chief news editor of the *Vancouver Sun* revealed his experience as a teen dad surrendering a child in 1981. When the birth mother began to search many years later, Shore supported her and discovered a happy outcome.[162] Revealingly, both men were distinguished by maintaining at least some limited contact with their earlier partners. The precise meanings of such stories is not always clear, but they, in conjunction with court cases and the fathers' rights' movement, suggest that some men were increasingly interested in pursuing an active role in the lives of offspring.

Male adopters have supplied their own perspective on fathering. To be sure they too have often been far from visible. The explanation for their failure to attract notice, however, has seemed rather different than that for birth fathers. Good would-be dads have largely been presumed to supply the critical material foundation for parenting. For the most part, they have been considered likely to be both more rational and less directly engaged in the exercise than their spouses. Once they had, as became increasingly necessary over the twentieth century, subjected their economic credentials to home study, they thereafter generally stepped to the sidelines in the larger public drama.

By their relative silence, men have frequently been judged more reluctant to welcome new offspring. Some degree of paternal reticence might well have originated with shame over infertility. As one adopter explained to his adult daughter, 'No man likes to think that he's infertile. It makes him less masculine. It's nice to know you can procreate.'[163] A 1961 study of twenty-seven new adoptive fathers 'ranging in background from bus driver to university professor' typically identified their wives as both inspiration and driving force. One man stated quite starkly: 'Most adoptable children are illegitimate and the idea of nurturing someone's else's mistake repelled me.' Agencies told repeated stories of husbands who insisted on harder-to-get girls lest the family name be tarnished by an 'outsider'. The author of the study tried to reassure his audience, insisting that 'agencies had no perfect babies so they don't expect to find perfect fathers.'[164] Reservations nevertheless regularly lingered. Some clinical assessments have concluded that male adopters have also felt less close to and successful with youngsters and needed more assistance than their biological counterparts.[165]

Whether moved by their wives' desires or their own, many Canadian men have ultimately proved determined to parent youngsters born to others. As Canadian historians such as Cynthia Fish, Jack Little, and Robert Rutherdale have demonstrated, fathers have often invested strong emotions in paternal roles.[166] Many male adopters shared just such feelings. Sometimes this was intensely practical. The Second World War brought forward a host of servicemen who endeavoured to complete adoptions in order to receive dependant's allowances.[167] Like the fictional well-to-do bachelor lawyer who was portrayed rescuing a Canadian niece before the Great War, adopters might well feel that youngsters heralded 'light and joy and laughter'.[168] The determination of one BC father in the 1970s to continue involvement in the life of a child whom his wife brought into and then took out of marriage with him similarly conveyed the value accorded adoptive ties.[169] By the end of the twentieth century, many signs suggested the increasing popularity of adoptive fatherhood. One British Columbian celebrated his new status by inaugurating a set of stories celebrating the daring of Chinese girls like his daughters. In the process, he demonstrated just how fiction and fact might combine to convey heartfelt emotion.[170] Adoptive fathers were part of the larger male community among whom there were many who always took parenthood very seriously.

Within the adoption circle, mothers and fathers, daughters and sons, however acquired, have been very likely to experience fertility, parenting, and filial relations in at least somewhat distinctive ways. Women and girls frequently emerge as the key players, both the subjects and the objects of desire. Men and boys, as often less desiring and less desirable, stand somewhat to the side, although this may be changing in recent years. This domestic portrait in which women and girls stand to the forefront and men and boys to the rear constitutes the mirror image of much in the public realm. Just as women have often had to challenge traditions that deny them appropriate qualities for entry into good waged employments and political life, men have had to counter pervasive assumptions that presume a domestic deficit on their part. While it remains impossible to disentangle how culture and biology have contributed to these gendered scripts and outcomes, both appear implicated. Ultimately, whatever the precise cause, gender emerged as a persistent feature of adoptive, as well as public, relations within Canada.

Today, as in the past, preference and recruitment do not occur in isolation. Blue-ribbon adoptees have matched some long-standing preferences of mainstream Canada for immigrants generally. Although adult European males, with a variety of skills, have always stood at the front of the line for full citizenship, women of the same background have also been favoured, albeit frequently as something of an afterthought. In one revealing instance, however, women, like girls, have had priority: they have regularly been actively recruited as domestics. When it comes to interacting with others, female adults and children have both been presumed to be better bets. Yet, by the mid-twentieth century, preferred candidates for household service, as for adoption, were decreasingly available. Immigration policies, like hearts and homes, had to contemplate racialized strangers. Caribbean and Philippina workers succeeded earlier recruits from Britain and Europe and encountered additional restrictions and compromised opportunities for full citizenship. They have been considered, as Abigail B. Bakan and Daiva Stasiulis so revealingly put it, 'not one of the family.'[171] The disabilities imposed on foreign nannies and household workers correspond to the persisting failure to grant automatic citizenship to youngsters adopted internationally and the frequent prejudice experienced by interracial families. Girls and women might sometimes be favoured in adoption, as in immigration, but gender was ultimately only one part of what was evaluated as they entered hard markets for labour and loving. Canadians have weighed many considerations as they constructed families and a nation. Gender might be an asset, but other markers always mattered a good deal. Ethnicity and race, as we shall see next, supplied a somewhat different purchase on the hearts and minds of Canadians.

Religion, Ethnicity, and Race

Notions of religion, ethnicity, and race have regularly bedevilled adoption. In the decades after the first adoption laws, Canadians demonstrated a variety of responses to this 'triumphirate' of difference—which often meant the foregrounding of culture and skin colour—that contemporaries regularly summed up as 'racial'. 'Race' was a fluid, socially constructed category, which allowed plenty of room for diverse prejudices. The sheer size of Canada also set the stage for a broad range of scenarios about what constituted meaningful difference. Sometimes characterized as a railway station where people have entered, mingled, and departed, Canada has also provided a site for sexual congress that contributed to the long-standing mixing of the world's peoples. Métissage of every kind, in fact, has made a mockery of racial essentialism, but racial vocabulary and politics haunted the exchange of youngsters.

For many years, distinctions among peoples of European origin mattered a good deal. Common parlance through the mid-twentieth century regularly hailed the Scots, the Irish, the Welsh, and the English as 'races'. At the same time, Canadian mainstream Protestant households frequently considered Catholic, Jewish, and non-Anglo-Celtic European ancestry as problematic. Asian and African origins were viewed as suspect still longer. This chapter considers the shifting views on racial difference, the evolution of controversies over religious matching and assessments of Canadian children of European (non-British) and Asian and African ancestry. Slowly and uncertainly, some youngsters formerly deemed outsiders were brought into the multicultural fold. While the particulars of racial hierarchies shifted over time and among regions, Aboriginal peoples ultimately stand out as European Canada's consummate 'Other', but they too, as we shall see in chapter 6, are not readily reduced to a single portrait or experience. Finally, as chapter 7 suggests, international adoptions raised their own issues of race.

Calculating Difference

Canadians past and present have employed 'race' variously to signify differences of religion, ethnic origin, or skin colour and to justify unequal treatment. While certainties have been claimed, confusion over terms and their meaning has been rampant. Adoption records have been packed with distinctions between 'them', variously racialized as different and commonly inferior, and 'us', in the first instance the Anglo-Celtic mainstream and eventually by extension all those of European

Table 5.1   Are the adopting parents of the same groups as the natural
                  parents?

Group	Yes	No	Unknown
Racial	23	99	14
Social	89	26	21
Educational	68	25	43
Religious	117	10	9

SOURCE: BC Superintendent of Neglected Children, *Annual Report* (for the year ending 31 March
          1939).

origin. As Canadian scholars Frances Henry, Carol Tator, Winston Mattis, and Tim
Rees have pointed out in *The Colour of Democracy: Racism in Canadian Society*,
assumptions of biological and cultural superiority as well as practices of individual
and institutional racism have conferred advantage and disadvantage in all aspects
of life. Any investigation of the child welfare system, where authorities have been
overwhelming white and clients have been disproportionately drawn from non-
dominant groups, reveals 'the development and maintenance of policies and practices based on the marginalization, exclusion, segregation, and domination of
Aboriginal peoples and racial minorities.'[1] Adoption itself, with its promise of
domestic intimacy, has variously involved rejection, assimilation, and integration
for various categories of youngsters. Those choices from the nineteenth to the
twentieth century demonstrated how race has regularly mattered a good deal.

   Calculation of difference has been fluid. In 1939, British Columbia's superintendent of neglected children captured the recurring dilemma of definition and
the social nature of supposedly biological categories. He struggled hard to explain
statistics in his annual report that compared the background of that year's natural
and adopting parents (see table 5.1):

> There is shown a great difference between the racial background of the
> adopting parents and the children they have taken into their homes. These dif-
> ferences would not be nearly so noticeable if English, Irish and Scots were not
> tabulated as separate racial strains, for the majority of our adopting homes and
> our children represent a mixture of these strains with a large percentage of
> Canadians who have had several generations born in Canada and are not cer-
> tain what their racial strain is. The ten placements made in a different religious
> group were made by the natural parents themselves and were placements with
> which no social agency had anything to do. The large number of 'unknowns'
> is due to the fact that very often we are unable to get detailed information
> about the natural father.[2]

As this bureaucrat's confusion suggested, religious, ethnic, and racial identities
could not be easily summed up. They might well be multiple, more or less import-

ant, or even shift significantly from one place or time to another over the lifetimes of individuals and generations. Ignorance, convenience, and prejudice all informed the process of identification. Too, as with all matters concerning adoption, deception added to the puzzle of discovering 'true' identities. Surrendering parents and adopters have been regularly tempted to construct personal stories, which resemble the truth in varying degrees.

Yet, if uncertainty dogs efforts to appreciate the religious, ethnic, or racial makeup of the adoption circle, other matters have been much more clear. In particular, those beyond English Canada's dominant European group—Protestant Anglo-Celts—have frequently entered the circle with disadvantage. Any trace of Catholic, non-Christian, or non-Caucasian beginnings, most particularly skin colour other than 'white', has regularly marked youngsters as less adoptable. Unlike 'blue-ribbon' babies with the right histories, who always found takers among the mainstream, others have struggled to find welcome when they 'matched' only the much smaller pool of adopters from minority populations. Persistent affirmation of distinctions between 'us' and 'them' regularly channelled excluded youngsters to institutions, foster homes, and earlier labour. Until well after the Second World War, the introduction of racially stigmatized children into middle-class households was rarely considered. As the director of Toronto's Children's Aid Society (CAS) concluded in 1939, matching his overwhelmingly Protestant British applicants with similar children forestalled unfortunate outcomes such as interracial marriage.[3] Such preferences were tenacious. As late as 1954, the National Film Board's *Chosen*[4] took for granted the benefits of Canadians' keeping to their own kind. Mainstream Canadians were to be spared the heartbreak of one couple whose adopted baby 'began to show Negroid tendencies.'[5]

Colour-Blind Liberalism

A 1957 Canadian social work thesis suggested that old prejudices were in retreat. The author applauded the shifts revealed between the Child Welfare League of America's first and second workshops, 'Adoption Practices, Procedures and Problems.' In 1949, representatives from Canada and the United States had stressed the need for matching and the danger of placement before children's authentic nature, racial and otherwise, could be assessed. By 1952, a paradigm change was evident. That year's delegates de-emphasized the protection of adopters and recommended placements as close to birth as possible. Such experts, and the student author, agreed with an American anthropologist who stressed youngsters' capacity to model on new families and deplored 'the fact that particular personality and psychological characteristics are attributed to certain races.'[6] Such conclusions encouraged mainstream adopters to reconsider previously suspect candidates. While white babies continued in highest demand, girls and boys with other antecedents increasingly joined their ranks. Progressive-minded Canadians, like their American counterparts, moved from what Ruth Frankenberg has termed '"essential racism", with its emphasis on racial difference and biological inequality' to a faith in 'essential "sameness", popularly referred to as "color-blindness"' or, less sympathetically but more accurately, '"color evasiveness" and "power evasiveness."'[7]

Unprecedented confidence in the possibility of integrating cultural and racial strangers into the family circle sprang directly from the revived liberalism and radicalism of the age. Variously rooted in faith, notably among religious liberals, optimism about the power of environment, hatred for the atrocities committed in the name of racial and religious superiority, and inclinations favouring international cooperation, 'colour-blind' sympathies motivated many child welfare professionals and would-be parents. These were much the same citizens—women and men such as Janet and Pierre Berton and Aline and Jean Chrétien—who supported the Canadian Bill of Rights in 1961, official bilingualism in 1968, multiculturalism in 1971, and the Canadian Charter of Rights and Freedoms in 1982. An essentially progressive trust in the politics of integration transformed adoption politics after 1945 and contributed to a significant, although ultimately incomplete, challenge to Anglo-conformity or what has been dubbed 'the symbolic order of the Canadian nation.'[8]

Such liberalism remained influential throughout the twentieth century, but its reign has never been uncontested. Mixed-race families always encountered hostility. Long-standing racism and religious bigotry or essentialism denied full humanity to some groups of children and abjured the crossing of religious and colour lines. Canadian advocates of eugenics or fascism, or milder forms of reactionary politics, remained determined opponents of enhanced social diversity. Such opposition was not the only criticism of the colour-blind agenda. In the last half of the twentieth century, critics from what Himani Bannerji has termed 'the dark side of the nation'[9] pointed increasingly to the structural underpinnings of racism. Many black, Catholic, and Native commentators condemned the transfer of children from the more vulnerable to the more powerful. What liberals hailed as the triumph of tolerance and equality, minority populations have sometimes judged mere assimilation on Anglo-Celtic terms, or even cultural genocide. Frankenberg has identified this position, with its renewed emphasis on racial difference, as 'race cognizance'. It represents a third, and so far incomplete, paradigm shift in race relations. As she explains, 'where the terms of essentialist racism were set by the white dominant culture, in the third moment they are articulated by people of color. Where difference within the terms of essentialist racism alleges the inferiority of people of color, in the third moment difference signals autonomy of culture, values, aesthetic standards, and so on. And, of course, inequality in this third moment refers not to ascribed characteristics, but to the social structure.'[10] All three positions have been variously and sometimes simultaneously visible in the evolution of adoption politics and procedures. While liberalism dominated the last half of the twentieth century, it has had to share influence with two very different kinds of racial politics, the first oppressive and the second ultimately liberatory.[11]

Liberal hopes rose steadily in the decades that constituted what was hailed as 'the century of the child'. The activist Adaline Marean Hughes, wife to James, Toronto's well-known inspector of public schools, spoke for many early child-focused reformers. In 1900 she presented her optimistic vision to students at the Presbyterian Ewart Missionary Training Home and Women's Foreign Missions Society in Toronto: 'Child-life is the same everywhere, whether the child be born in Canada, in India, in China or in the South Sea Islands. It makes no difference what blood flows in his veins, savage, semi-civilized or the bluest that civilization can produce. Child-life and child-nature are governed by the same laws in every land under the sun.'[12] A Baptist couple from Richmond, BC, who set out to foster 'five coloured children' in 1957, would have been in full agreement with such sentiments. Their rescue mission was brought right up to date, however, by the timely newspaper story, 'Little Rock Could Learn a Lot', with its reminder of racial segregation in the American South.[13] Steinberg's, a major Canadian grocery chain, summed up a brighter day in hailing the United Nations' Cooperation Year in 1966. Its newspaper ad picturing four boys, one Black, one Asian, and two seemingly white, featured the caption 'We sincerely and deeply believe that every year should be the year of co-operation and brotherhood.'[14]

Insistence on common humanity and resistance to racial essentialism ebbed and flowed during twentieth century. It found secular expression in the modern social sciences, with their frequent commitment to renewed family life. From the 1920s on, the child-study movement stood in the forefront of greater faith in the possibilities of domestic rehabilitation. Before the tragic outcome of their experiments in the 1930s and 1940s with the Dionne quintuplets became clear, experts produced a string of seeming success stories. In 1956, the Neil McNeil Home, Toronto's last Catholic orphanage, provided young subjects for an astonishing longitudinal study. Social scientists and child welfare professionals, led by Canadian child-study expert Betty Flint, tested, placed, and followed up an initial sample of eighty-five youngsters. While four decades of monographs testify to persisting pain, dislocation, and trauma, researchers, bolstered by unprecedented resources, including paid and voluntary assistance, remained publicly optimistic about prospects for rescuing youngsters who started life with tremendous disadvantage.[15]

In 1967, when British Columbia's child welfare specialists and champions assembled in the first provincial conference devoted to adoption, the Sunday prayer of Bishop Remi De Roo caught the expansive mood: 'In Christ You have adopted us as members of your heavenly family. We are Your adopted sons, Your children, brothers and sisters of Christ and in Christ. . . . We have come together in fellowship to further the work of adoption in the Province of British Columbia. We know that in Your kingdom there is no class distinction, no prejudice, no discrimination. Your Son Jesus Christ taught us that love and love alone can make all men one.' Reflecting the ecumenical spirit of the times, 'Red' Remi was followed in short order by Dr Sydney Segal from Vancouver General Hospital. He proved an equally passionate advocate of 'children whose social problem is not of their own making and who are full fledged citizens like anyone else.' This Jewish pediatrician and noted neonatologist found ready sympathizers in condemning barriers to integration as 'all a bunch of Rs: Race, Religion, Resources.'[16]

A flood of articles and testimonials in the 1960s celebrated Canadians who were prepared to embrace tolerance at their own firesides. Such was the case with one family with eight children, seven of whom, whose backgrounds were 'Scottish, African, Ukrainian, French, East Indian, and possibly Spanish,' were adopted. Self-defined 'ordinary' and 'average' Canadians, the parents of these children condemned racial discrimination as a 'great evil' and requested hard-to-place children of any race: 'For we have learned, and our children are learning, too, that all men are created equal under the skin; that color and hair, like the shades of flowers, are merely added variety and charm.'[17] A United Church minister and his wife similarly cited their hatred for 'unfair' and 'un-Christian' racial prejudice as one reason to embrace a seven-month-old mixed-race daughter. The adoptive mother summed up her commitment in verse:

> Not of my flesh,
> Not bone of my bone,
> Yet miraculously still
> My very own.
> Never forget
> For a single minute
> You didn't grow under my heart
> But in it.[18]

Teachers and social workers regularly joined Protestant ministers as interracial adopters. Secular apostles, such as two Maritimers celebrated in the *Star Weekly* in 1973, might give birth to children, but they also wanted to express their commitment to a transformed politics within an expanded family circle. In this case, they adopted a 'Negro' son while they lived in New Glasgow, Nova Scotia, and knew 'quite a bit about him'. Next they acquired Faith, a white-'MicMac' daughter, through New Brunswick Social Services' Add-a-Child program. They later added two Vietnamese youngsters to their family and enrolled as foster parents to others living in the Philippines, India, and Brazil.[19] Such practical advocates of racial and religious inclusion took for granted membership in an expanding worldwide liberation movement. Another adoptive father, a professor at Ottawa's Carleton University, linked his personal actions to the assault on South African apartheid and, moreover, insisted that integration worked both ways: blacks should be able to adopt white youngsters.[20] Realistically, this was rarely possible. As one BC study, *New Families for Young Families,* acknowledged in 1967, despite the presence of 'prosperous' and 'respected and well-liked' Chinese, Japanese, East Indian, black, and 'native Indian' households, they could not succour all youngsters of similar origins who were in public care. Even well-established Native families who fished and logged were rarely 'interested in adopting through agencies', and, just as significantly, they could be every bit 'as demanding and discriminating about the child's background as some Caucasian families.'[21] Progressive white families had to take up the slack.

Some cross-racial adopters emerged from Canada's professional and intellectual elite. Such was the case with Janet Berton, who became actively involved with Toronto's Committee for the Adoption of Coloured Youngsters (CACY) in the early 1960s. Already well-known for their embrace of progressive cultural causes, this western-bred but Toronto-based homemaker and her husband, Pierre, integrated a infant girl, Perri, of mixed African European ancestry into their family of two sons and four daughters in 1965. While her father recalled Perri encountering 'very little prejudice,' he also cited incidents when she was hailed as a 'nigger,' 'the little darky girl,' and 'the little pickaninny'.[22] Like the Liberal minister of Indian Affairs and Northern Development, Jean Chrétien, who with his wife, Aline, included a Native son in their family, the Bertons hoped to make personal contributions to a brave new world. More Conservative representatives of the Canadian professional elite, such as CBC broadcaster Barbara Frum and her husband, Murray, were also sometimes caught up in the swell of support for Native adoption. Their son Matthew joined them in the 1960s, but, like many others, later struggled to reconnect with his roots.[23]

In 1969, a popular article titled 'A Daughter—or a Symbol?' flagged issues raised by whites' enthusiasm for interracial adoption. The author, while initially reluctant, ultimately followed his wife's lead in agreeing to add a daughter to their one-son family. Trumpeting his lack of 'any racial prejudice', this journalist believed himself very much in the spirit of the age, citing the Beatles' song 'All You Need Is Love.' What he possessed, in addition to arrogance and naïveté, as his confessional reflection made entirely clear, was a host of influential connections. Among his doctor, Vancouver CAS workers, colleagues, relatives, and neighbours 'who flooded' them with gifts, he found ready supporters and concluded 'though we weren't typical, we weren't extraordinary either.'[24] Such lucky citizens had a head start when seeking to parent the offspring of surrendering mothers to whom the times regularly denied birth control, abortion services, and employments that might have sustained different choices. Better-placed citizens were just those Canadians whom a social worker writing in *Canadian Welfare* in 1956 wished to attract: 'In getting to know these families, who are white, we have arrived at the comfortable conclusion that they have the background and attitude to be successful parents to . . . special children.'[25]

By the closing years of the twentieth century, optimism remained in some quarters but it was also hard-tested. As Canadian governments retreated from the promise of equality-seeking in the course of the neo-conservative retrenchment of the 1980s and 1990s, optimism about racial politics of every sort seemed to ebb as well. Liberalism, for all the generosity it often embodied, was ill-equipped to tackle the structural foundations of child apprehension or to understand the resistance of racial outsiders to the apprehension of their children. Ultimately, it sometimes proved easier to search for progeny abroad.

Religious Barriers

Canadian progressivism, like that elsewhere, long conducted a running war with religious credentialing, whether this was required for the franchise, education, or adoption. Up to the third quarter of the twentieth century, legislation, policy, and practice regularly imposed sectarian qualifications on adopters. Protestants were to adopt Protestants, and Catholics Catholics. Jews endeavoured to administer their own institutions and claimed their own youngsters from the public system. Child welfare authorities often served sectarian clientele and nurtured close ties with religious leaders. As Canadian society grew more secular and more diverse, such requirements seemed more and more out of step. Jews, agnostics, and atheists were among the many who found themselves badly served. Lying, misrepresentation, and border-crossing, as with Jewish-American families who sought offspring in Nova Scotia's Ideal Maternity Home, were relatively commonplace as would-be parents scrambled to sidestep bars of faith.

Still more influential in fuelling demands for reform was English Canada's recurring discrepancy between supply and demand. Surrendering and receiving families were often distinguished by religion, a distinction that frequently corresponded to a difference in material prospects. Generally speaking, Catholics, a substantial Christian minority in English Canada, were likely to be poorer, both less able to adopt, and somewhat more likely to contribute offspring to the care of private and state child welfare agencies. As Karen Balcom has noted, the Quebec church was so self-conscious about the mismatch between 1945 and 1960 that it actively emigrated young wards to waiting American homes.[26] The so-called 'surplus' was also visible elsewhere. An adoption reformer in Alberta in 1965 reported that Catholic applicants always had 'a wider choice of children for adoption.' In contrast, Protestant adults supplied the largest unmet demand, especially for infants, and proportionately fewer progeny in the care of others. As the Albertan reformer noted, 'there are very few White Protestant girls in the 2-to-10 year age group available at any time and at the date of this survey there were none.'[27]

Demands to uncouple religion and placement grew over the course of the century. In 1916, English Canada's leading popular magazine, *Saturday Night,* voiced typical liberal outrage in profiling an exemplary childless Unitarian, 'a certain prominent lady of Toronto', who rescued an infant from the city's CAS. Her daughter proved so frail that only 'care and lavish attention' ensured that she thrived 'like a green baby tree'. In all the excitement, however, and no doubt because the new mother belonged to the city's elite, formalities of transfer were initially ignored. Some months later, sponsored by the daughter of the premier of Ontario and the chief inspector of Toronto's public schools, the Unitarian couple applied for, only to be denied, permanent custody on the grounds of their faith, or perceived lack of such. The outraged journalist denounced the CAS for denying Unitarians 'status in the fold of the all-embracing Creator' and pronounced the 'situation ... as preposterous as it is silly.'[28]

Such judgment was not unusual. Numerous court decisions overturned requirements of religious matching, citing instead the best interests of the child. In *Re Grafasso* in 1916, the Ontario Court of Appeal decided against an unwed Catholic housemaid seeking to recover her daughter from Protestant householders. In *Re Taggart* (1917), the Supreme Court of the same province prohibited a Catholic widow from recovering her eldest child from her Protestant sister-in-law. In *Cullen v. Kemp* (1925), the court upheld the adoption of a child assigned by his birth father to a Catholic orphanage but surrendered to a Protestant couple. In 1933, the BC Court of Appeal in *Bland v. Agnew* supported Protestant applicants against the Victoria Catholic Children's Aid and the local bishop. In the same year, that court ruled similarly in *Re Ward Dill v. Children's Aid Society of Catholic Archdiocese of Vancouver.*[29] As these cases suggest, practice might well contradict regulations. In particular, agencies eager to shift responsibilities could well favour whichever applicants possessed the material resources to assume financial and other duties. In English Canada, Protestants were simply more likely to be better positioned to afford children and to ignore Catholic grievances that 'to permit a Catholic child to be brought up in a non-catholic home and atmosphere—no matter how much good will is intended—is almost in the realm of premeditated theft: the future theft of that child's possession—his faith.'[30]

While Catholic 'losers' appeared common, they were not alone in their vulnerability. Jewish Canadians might work out individual arrangements with state child welfare authorities, but they too worried about losing young adherents. The Holocaust provided ample opportunity for anxiety. In June 1945, the *Globe and Mail* reported the remarks of one rabbi who believed Europe's young survivors were in danger of being 'spiritually kidnapped'. He called for a 'proclamation by the various Governments that children do not become the property of their rescuers and cannot be deprived of their Jewish heritage.'[31] Such concerns were relatively unusual. Much more common were the recurring difficulties faced by Jewish families seeking sons and daughters.

It remains difficult to know whether Jewish citizens took the lead in demanding an end to religious matching in Canada, as Ellen Herman suggests they may have done in the United States.[32] After 1945, the assault was widespread. Like burgeoning support for interfaith marriages,[33] the transfer of children to religious strangers was embraced as emblematic of a new age. At least as powerful was the strong demand of a 'plethora of willing applicants' among both Protestant and Jewish couples who readily felt deeply aggrieved by a presumed pool of inaccessible Catholic youngsters.[34] Such eager applicants applauded an Ontario judge whose 1961 ruling in favour of Protestants was hailed as a 'blow delivered to all religious, racial, color, national and ideological bars. . . . A true blow against the religio–legal obstinacy resulting in the denial of many hundreds of children of a home with adoptive parents.'[35] That decision also sparked a flurry of letters to the *Globe and Mail,* as readers raised issues of theft and abduction but also the interests of children.

In 1963, the *Star Weekly* summed up liberal arguments in an editorial entitled 'The Dark Ages Are Over.' Criticizing provinces that did not permit interfaith adoptions, it claimed to defend Catholic children who thereby lost loving homes. It also lambasted the contradictory logic by which biological parents surrendered all rights, except that of designating religious placement. Why, it asked, did the religious relic survive when modern adoption eliminated former names and identities?[36] The shifting sentiments of the 'Age of Aquarius' were again summed up in a 1964 Symposium on Interfaith Adoption. Champions insisted that deference to the 'best interests of the child' required early placement in good homes regardless of religion. Rabbi Gunther Plaut outlined the need for updating old regimes. Although Jewish tradition had little to say specifically on adoption, times, he observed, were changing. He accused child welfare authorities of two-dimensional thinking: Canada's religious communities were far more than merely Catholic or Protestant. Keeping in mind the thrust of the modern transfer of children, he concluded, in an echo of the earlier *Star Weekly* argument, 'it is contradictory for a parent who gives up a child for adoption, to give up the *person* of the child, but retain determination of the child's *spiritual future*.'[37]

Such arguments did not persuade Catholic leaders such as Coadjutor Archbishop Philip F. Pocock of Toronto, who attacked 'crossfaith' adoptions as 'a sellout to authoritarian statism.'[38] A social worker from the Toronto Catholic CAS cited the authority of the UN Declaration of the Rights of the Child from 1959 in appealing for recognition of the significance of spiritual development.[39] In addition to sending children to same-faith American homes, the hierarchy joined with the Catholic Women's League to sponsor Adoption Sundays and a Catholic Adoption Year in 1963. Such resistance, however, flew in the face of majority power.

In 1964, the report of Ontario's Advisory Committee on Child Welfare considered a range of options to reduce the expense and the tragedy of the growing numbers of children in care. It tackled the role of race, disability, and religion in limiting options and cited the UN's declaration to signify its commitment to the best interests doctrine. While the main report made no specific mention of the Aboriginal children in care, its authors clearly listened to the raft of witnesses protesting religious matching. The final recommendation 'that there is no denial of a good home to a child because of the religion or lack of religion of the adopting parents' signalled the victory that Protestants and their allies had long demanded.[40] A year later, the Alberta committee examining adoption likewise found itself in the midst of heated debates over the prospects of Catholic youngsters. While one Catholic social worker condemned the pervasive 'bias against religion',[41] he was hard put to prevail. While agreeing that spirituality was extremely important, Rabbi Klein and the Edmonton Jewish Council ultimately sided with Protestant critics to insist that girls and boys not be left in limbo when no suitable same-faith adopters turned up.

The passion and prejudices evoked by the religious controversy were evident in the interjections of one female witness before the Alberta Committee on Adoption. She invoked long-standing Protestant prejudice in recounting the tragic tale of an eight-year-old 'beaten and physically disabilitated [*sic*] by a Roman Catholic family.' The little girl was rescued only when a good Protestant family rushed to her aid. According to the storyteller, no one of the child's own faith was prepared to save the youngster. No wonder this speaker urged that 'religion should have nothing to do with adoptions.'[42] In response to hard questioning from a Catholic member of the committee as to whether godless families should be permitted to apply, a Calgary United Church minister captured the dominant opinion emerging across the country: 'Well, I think we would at least say this, that they ought to be given much more sympathetic consideration than probably what they get now.' This witness went on to add that Canada had become a 'pluralistic society' composed of Christians, Muslims, Buddhists, and Jews, and he drew on his and his wife's personal experience of fostering a Japanese Buddhist baby in arguing for recognition of diversity.[43] With debates on the subject regularly disturbing the hearings, the final Alberta report concluded, not surprisingly, that 'the most significant problem in adoptions in Alberta at this time' was 'the matter of interfaith adoption'.[44]

As the numbers of children in care mounted steadily in the 1950s and 1960s, pressures to relax regulations proved increasingly successful. In 1961, Manitoba allowed natural mothers to stipulate that they had no religious preference. In 1966, Alberta's Child Welfare Act did the same. It also specified that a religious preference lapsed if twelve months' worth of efforts to place the child with adopters of the same faith failed. A year later, Saskatchewan amended its legislation to waive the need for religious matching if an otherwise suitable adopter was available. As Alberta's Department of Child Welfare cheerfully noted in 1967, 'the statistical record shows that the primary interest of an unmarried mother when surrendering her child is that he be placed in a secure adoptive home.'[45] In 1975 BC's Royal Commission on Family and Children's Law agreed. It concluded that 'permanence at the earliest possible date is paramount' and that no transfer should be delayed more than three months for religious reasons.[46] While religion continued to trouble the courts for some time,[47] the value of early transfer increasingly trumped sectarian preferences.

Religious matching had been enshrined in Canadian adoption practices for close to a hundred years when it largely, although never entirely—as the continuation of religiously affiliated agencies across English Canada suggested—succumbed to growing secularism and to the demands of prospective adopters for access to a greater range of youngsters. Where, once, religious difference had provided a line that few Canadians would readily cross in constructing their households, its authority had significantly receded by the 1950s and 1960s. By that time, liberals had also begun questioning other distinctions that divided communities.

Ethnic and Racial Boundaries

The substance of debates about sectarian matching, with their reference to origins on the one hand and the best interests of youngsters on the other, often closely resembled arguments over the merits of crossing other boundaries. Ethnic and racial identities had always been powerful determinants of the fate of Canadian youngsters, but they were rarely explicitly cited in formal regulations. They were, however, very much part of the 'common sense' of the age, so much taken for granted that guarantees in legislation were barely thought of. Only when an anti-racist 'equality talk' surfaced in the closing decades of the twentieth century was 'race', in the particular form of Aboriginal rights, to find a home in legislation.

For many Canadians, challenges to ethnic and racial boundaries involved commitment to a 'colour-blind' liberalism that placed its hopes in the eclipse of race and ethnicity. This commitment often involved the deliberate denial of the heavy hand of history and ongoing discrimination. The trend to secrecy and confidentiality of records from the 1920s to the 1960s was in just this vein. It permitted some cultural strangers, who, by virtue of physiology and colouring and European roots, could pass as homespun, to integrate into Anglo-Celtic households almost on the sly. Secrecy might well camouflage their origins from the public eye.

Just as in the reception of immigrants more generally, candidates of non-British European origins remained problematic for many in the mainstream well into the twentieth century. The continuing uncertainty about their acceptability was obvious in the pages of the *Toronto Telegram* in the mid-1960s. In its first two years of publication (1964–6) 'Today's Child', edited by crusading journalist Helen Allen, conveyed English Canada's uncertain embrace of cultural diversity. Often suspect French-Canadian ancestry, marking some 20 per cent of the more than four hundred girls and boys advertised in these years, was singled out for attention by English readers. Such history clearly still gave some prospective parents pause. It was also increasingly appraised in the light of new national expectations. 'Active, lively' seven-year-old James, with his 'French-Canadian background' and bilingualism, was an attractive 'lad'.[48] As Allen pointed out, 'Many families want their children to be bilingual in Canada 1965.' Two 'pretty sisters, 10 and eight years old', with a 'French-Canadian background, with French as their first language,' presented the 'opportunity for parents to have two bilingual daughters' and 'would no doubt encourage other children to do so too.'[49] In a decade that saw the beginning of French immersion in English-Canadian public schools, such arguments were newly persuasive.

If Canada's 'two solitudes' were being reconsidered, so too were English Canada's views of other European nations. Some 40 per cent of Helen Allen's kids during 1964–6 were credited with European origins—Italian, Polish, Belgian, Irish, German, and Maltese, among others—that the mainstream would previously have regarded with caution. Like two-year-old Joey, with his 'fair hair and dark eyes', 'Polish and Italian' background, and 'superior intelligence', they were newly promising candidates for full inclusion in the Canadian family.[50] Four- and five-year-old sisters of French, Scottish, and Italian origin, promised to become 'affectionate and co-operative' daughters.[51] Ukrainian ancestry was just one part of what made eight-year-old Ken 'an active youngster with a good sense of humor', who 'could carry on a conversation with any one' and very much wanted 'to be adopted so he will have parents of his own like the other boys at school.'[52] Although such ethnic origins had characterized Canadian newcomers previously termed 'strangers within our gates', they offered promise in a nation that, in the 1960s, was about to embark on official multiculturalism.

In Canadian family and national politics, religion remained closely allied to race and ethnicity. Divisions among the French, the English, the Irish, and the Scots, not to mention other European peoples, and often those between rich and poor, have traditionally been reinforced by Catholic–Protestant distinctions. The predominance of Catholicism among the children advertised in the *Tely*, especially Native youngsters, evoked familiar histories of disadvantage. Two Jewish girls profiled in 1964–5 were highly unusual. They can best be explained by apparent medical problems. The mother of five-month-old Lisa suffered 'from a nervous disorder', although 'other family members are normal and above average in intelligence.'[53] Three-year-old Ellen offered 'the coloring and delicacy of a Dresden doll' but she was marred, at least in some eyes, by 'feet [that] turned in.' 'Disability' was at least as important as religion in making such girls outsiders to the Canadian mainstream.[54]

While gentiles might sometimes regard Jews as a distinctive race, that categorization was increasingly reserved for others. Children whose ancestry hailed from

Africa or Asia, or from North America's Indigenous peoples, were Canada's pre-
eminent racialized minorities. Colour was, above all, the key marker of race in the
twentieth century. Yet, for such groups too, religion often remained a significant
distinction.

Asian and African Ancestry

Canada's child welfare authorities have always encountered minorities whose skin
colour announced racial disadvantage. In 1895, the Guelph CAS reported 'a colored family is still before us to deal with, it being very difficult to find homes for
colored children.'[55] In 1897, the Anglican *Canadian Churchman* asked for 'good
Christian couples' to adopt a number of boys, including 'James S', who possessed
'curly hair, dark complexion, black eyes . . . some African blood . . . one of the
brightest boys in the Shelter and a general favorite.'[56] In 1931, Ontario's superintendent of neglected and dependent children lamented an ongoing problem:

> It is hard enough to get good foster homes for children of Anglo-Saxon race
> but when it comes to mixed nationality, especially when there is half Chinese
> or half negro blood, the difficulties become infinitely greater. However, in an
> almost miraculous way suitable homes have been found for even these appar-
> ently hopeless babies. A mulatto child, for instance, was gladly adopted by a
> coloured railway porter and his wife, while a Chinese baby was placed in the
> home of a wealthy Chinaman through the kind assistance of a mission
> worker. Two months ago an application for a child was received from a well
> to do Indian farmer and the next day a letter came from the north describ-
> ing a baby that fitted in exactly.

He further reflected on a difficulty emblematic of uncertain categories: 'A red-
headed baby was reported as difficult to place and the next day a fine red-headed
man came along looking for just such a baby.'[57] Such observations in the early
public record were relatively infrequent. In most years and certainly before the
1950s, the vast majority of children coming before public and private agencies
were European in origin, and commonly Canadian-born.

The near invisibility, for much of the century, of youngsters with Asian or
African heritage did not mean that they were not in need. More than anything
else, their absence signified pervasive mainstream indifference to their disadvantage. Many institutions, such as the Vancouver CAS, regarded 'children of colour' as
unplaceable and for many years resisted accepting them. White couples might seek
servants among marginalized populations but rarely progeny. Not surprisingly,
minority parents and communities often tried desperately to make their own provision for protecting girls and boys.

Black citizens had a long history of self-help. Local single parents were especially
dependent on support from kin and neighbourhood, as the Halifax Infants' Home
refused for many years to accept non-white children.[58] One study from the mid-
1960s calculated that 'only 29 per cent of the Negro girls are referred to agencies

whereas 69 per cent of the lower and middle-class White mothers have sought help or are referred.... About 75 per cent of the Negro unwed mothers keep their babies; very few consider adoption.' Part of the difference could be explained by the greater likelihood of relatively stable common-law unions in the black community but, as this researcher failed to acknowledge, it also sprang from long-standing traditions of community assistance and hard-won knowledge that black babies won fewer takers.[59]

Additional responsibilities could overwhelm mothers and families, and tragedies prompted local white liberals and black activists to support the founding of the Nova Scotia Home for Coloured Children (NSHCC) in 1921. Operating like many child welfare institutions, it combined instruction and labour. Black girls and boys were directed to domestic and farm employments, for which they were commonly believed most suited. Relatives often remained in touch, sometimes retrieving youngsters in better times and other times agreeing to their surrender to other households as servants, labourers, and, more occasionally, family members. In 1958, one Halifax study concluded that black children were likely to be institutionalized because of overcrowding in 'negro homes'. They also stayed significantly longer than their white counterparts. Over a three-year period, the latter were far more likely to find at least the promise of better times in family placements.[60] Like many other residential institutions, the NSHCC eventually faced charges of sexual and physical abuse from former inmates. It remains impossible to know whether such exploitation was more or less frequent than that which occurred in family settings.[61]

Institutions devoted to such racialized children survived well into the twentieth century but their day gradually waned. As the leader of the Co-operative Commonwealth Federation insisted in Parliament in 1954, discrimination against Asians, blacks, and Natives was simply unacceptable. There was, he argued, no 'difference in individual aptitudes or intelligence because of the colour of the skin.'[62] While Canadians had sometimes prided themselves as being more tolerant than Americans, post–Second World War social critics were increasingly likely to question such complacency. A 1958 editorial in the *Star Weekly* summed up a much less favourable comparison when considering Canadian sympathies for the school integration campaign in Little Rock, Arkansas, concluding, 'let's expend that indignation in cleaning our own backyard.'[63]

The nation's social workers often stood in the forefront of progressive efforts to confront racial prejudice. By mid-twentieth century, their operations were slowly expanding to include more remote areas and, still more slowly, Indian reserve communities. In the course of outreach, which often extended over hundreds of kilometres and included unmanageable caseloads, as Bridget Moran described so poignantly in her memoir, *Little Rebellion*, many childcare workers became even more acutely sensitive to diversity and poverty, as well as to their all too limited resources.[64] The activist-minded began regularly to condemn the discrimination faced by Asian, black, and Aboriginal citizens and drew on personal observation in describing the hard costs paid by individual youngsters. In 1951, a sympathetic BC welfare worker described the case of eight-year-old Teddie, whose background was

'East Indian' and white. This little boy from Vancouver took up hours at weekly conferences as many months were devoted to finding a suitable home. Eventually, to general relief and delight, this 'attractive and lovable' child became the '"son" of extremely proud and happy East Indian parents' elsewhere in the province.[65]

Outcomes were not always so fortunate. Three years later, BC's Social Welfare Branch described an eleven-year-old Anglo-Chinese child, who had never found a permanent home. This failure upset those who knew him as 'a promising boy of whom any parent could be proud. He ranks high in his school class, is a leader in community groups, and is to have the signal honour of representing his church club at an international conference in London, England, this summer.'[66] While social workers believed that attitudes had changed sufficiently in 1954 so that parents would have accepted this mixed-race youngster if he had been an infant, this was little consolation for their growing client or his champions.

When they endeavoured to assist racialized boys and girls, social workers first set out to match them with similar families. Efforts spurred wide-ranging searches and inspired collaboration among child welfare groups across the country. By the 1950s, British Columbia was negotiating with Ottawa, other provinces, and the Canadian Welfare Council to arrange for cross-boundary placements that would allow youngsters to be sent to prospective parents anywhere they might be found. Such efforts were typical of many jurisdictions. Children unwanted in one region might well find happy outcomes elsewhere. British Columbia reported early success. Three wards of partial Japanese ancestry were dispatched to adopters with a similar background east of the Rockies. In turn, a local 'negro' family was assisted in locating suitable offspring in an eastern province.[67] In 1956, the province's Social Welfare Branch congratulated itself on finding a good home with 'parents of a similar racial origin' in Montreal for a three-year-old girl.[68] Four years later, it shipped seven wards outside the province, one each to Ontario, Manitoba, and Alaska, and four to Yukon. The superintendent of child welfare urged the Catholic CAS to explore options in Oregon, where Catholic babies were believed much in demand.[69] Such long-distance deliveries were reckoned fortunate for several reasons: 'From a financial standpoint, thousands of dollars of taxpayers' money have been saved in this one adoption placement alone. No price can be placed, however, upon the savings in human values which resulted from the effort and joint planning of the several workers involved for a child who, to them, had a right to parents of her own.'[70]

Jurisdictions sometimes observed that mixed-race children, who often appeared more regularly in care than those identified with a single ancestry, met an uncertain welcome from marginalized groups themselves. In 1959, BC's Department of Social Welfare placed eight children of part Chinese or Japanese background, four of them with 'adopting parents of full Chinese or Japanese parentage.' This was considered noteworthy, as social workers believed that Asian, including 'East Indian', communities resisted mixed-race offspring.[71] At the same time, BC social workers found that 'wholly Oriental' children, like those who were identified solely as white, much more readily found new parents in their particular communities.[72]

Going largely unmentioned in British Columbia and other provinces were the

Table 5.2   Children of interracial origin and racial origin other than white placed for adoption by BC Department of Social Welfare according to sex during the fiscal year 1961–2★

	Male	Female
Native Indian and white	17	21
Negro and white	2	2
East Indian and white	–	2
Chinese and white	2	4
Japanese and white	1	1
Chinese and Native Indian	–	1
Syrian and white	2	1
Arabian and white	1	–
Native Indian	8	11
Japanese	1	1
Chinese	–	1
Totals	34	44

★ The ethnic/racial categories for tables 5.2 to 5.6 are those used in the original.

SOURCE: BC Department of Social Welfare, *Annual Report* (for the year ending 31 March 1962), 53.

small size and economic vulnerability of marginalized groups. Such disadvantage helped ensure that there would be sons and daughters for white adopters who increasingly considered partial Asian descent quite acceptable, even attractive, in off-spring. This choice reflected commonplace racial thinking that characterized Asians as smarter and less trouble than many other youngsters. As this preference frequently involved girls, gender was also at work. The observations of an Alberta familiar with the adoption politics in her province in the 1960s were familiar across the nation: 'Protestant negro girls can be placed just as soon as received. . . . As to Protestant negro boys, these can be placed fairly easily as infants. . . . However, once a negro boy reaches school age, there is little hope of adoption.'[73] African Canadian boys easily aroused racist fears that meant early and continuing marginalization.

By the end of the 1950s, appropriate placements for growing numbers of racial minority children had become a major problem for welfare authorities. Rejection was increasingly viewed, however, as the relic of bad times. Moreover, racial essentialism was nearly impossible to monitor, not to mention appearing even more demonstrably absurd as distinctions and recombinations multiplied. In the 1960s, BC's Department of Social Welfare invoked the scale of the dilemma when it tried for a brief six years to track racial histories. The results are shown in tables 5.2 to 5.6. Such diversity, so carefully and ultimately uselessly chronicled, made obvious mockery of efforts at matching.

Table 5.3   Children of interracial origin and racial origin other than white placed for adoption by BC Department of Social Services according to sex of the children and religion of the adopting parent during the fiscal year 1962–3

	Sex			Religion of adopting parent			
					Roman		
	Male	Female	Totals	Protestant	Catholic	Confucian	Total
Native Indian and white	16	19	35	28	7	–	35
Negro and white	1	3	4	3	1		4
Chinese and white	4	5	9	8	1		9
Japanese and white	2	2	4	4			4
Native Indian and East Indian		1	1	1			1
Native Indian and Chinese		1	1	1			1
Native Indian, Negro and white	1		1	1			1
Native Indian	14	9	23	16	7		23
Japanese		1	1			1	1
Chinese	1	3	4	3		1	4
Totals	39	44	83	66	16	2	83

SOURCE: BC Department of Social Welfare, *Annual Report* (for the year ending 31 March 1963), 56.

Table 5.4   Children of interracial origin and racial origin other than white placed for adoption by the BC Department of Social Services according to sex of the child and religion of the adopting parent during the fiscal year 1963–4

	Sex of child			Religion of adopting parent		
	Male	Female	Total	Protestant	Roman Catholic	Total
Native Indian and white	18	20	38	31	7	38
Negro and white	2	5	7	7		7
Chinese and white	4	1	5	5		5
Japanese and white	1	4	5	5		5
Eskimo and white		1	1		1	1
Maori and white	1		1	1		1
Syrian and white	1		1	1		1
Native Indian	1		1		1	1
Arabian and white	1		1	1		1
Chinese	2		2	2		2
Negro and Chinese		1	1	1		1
East Indian	1		1	1		1
Japanese	3		3	3		3
Totals	35	32	67	59	9	67

SOURCE: BC Department of Social Welfare, *Annual Report* (for the year ending 31 March 1964), 56.

As these tables suggest, Canada's West Coast, like other regions, had its own demographic character. Native children, as we shall see, were increasingly common in British Columbia after the Second World War, and the province always reported the largest percentage of youngsters with Asian origins. In contrast, it counted relatively few of African ancestry, though a small vibrant group had arrived in the province in the mid-nineteenth century. Black girls and boys were much more likely to contribute significantly to caseloads in certain parts of Ontario and the Maritimes, where long-established and relatively large African Canadian communities existed. By the 1950s, these had won somewhat better access to the social services available to other citizens. At least as important in determining demands for child welfare was the presence of relatively new arrivals, notably domestic workers entering from the British West Indies under federal immigration schemes. Lonely young women proved especially vulnerable.[74] While it is not yet clear, it seems very possible too that the presence of an American military base, Fort

Table 5.5   Children of interracial origin and racial origin other than white placed for adoption by BC Department of Social Welfare according to sex of the child and religion of the adopting parent during the fiscal year 1964–5

	Sex of child			Religion of adopting parent			
	Male	Female	Totals	Protestant	Roman Catholic	Buddhist	Totals
Native Indian and white	56	40	96	78	18		96
Negro and white	2	3	5	4	1		15
Chinese and white	3	4	7	7			21
Japanese and white	2	3	5	4		1	14
Indian, Mexican and white	1		1	1			3
Mexican and Spanish		1		1			2
Syrian and white		3	3	3			9
Native Indian	1	8	9	6	3		27
Hawaiian and white		2	2	2			6
Chinese		1	1	1			3
East Indian and white		3	3	2	1		9
Japanese	2			2			4

SOURCE: BC Department of Social Welfare, *Annual Report* (for the year ending 31 March 1965), 56.

Table 5.6   Children of interracial origin and racial origin other than white placed for adoption by Department of Social Services and CAS according to sex of the child and religion of the adopting parent during the fiscal year 1965–6

	Sex of child			Religion of adopting parents				
	Male	Female	Total	Protestant	Roman Catholic	Sikh	Buddhist	Total
Department of Social Services								
Native Indian and white	22	34	56	39	17	–	–	56
Negro and white	2	2	4	4	–	–	–	4
Chinese and white	5	4	9	8	1	–	–	9
Japanese and white	4	3	7	5	2	–	–	7
Native Indian and East Indian	–	1	1	1	–	–	–	1
Indian, Mexican and white	1	1	1	1	–	–	–	1
Arabic and white	1	–	1	1	–	–	–	1
East Indian and white	1	–	1	–	1	–	–	1
Native Indian	2	6	9	8	1	–	–	9
East Indian	1	–	1	1	–	–	–	1
Japanese	–	1	1	–	–	–	1	1
Chinese	–	2	2	2	–	–	–	2
Hawaiian and white	1	–	1	1	–	–	–	1
Subtotals	38	56	94	71	22	–	1	94
Vancouver CAS								
Native Indian and white	1	8	9	9	–	–	–	9
Negro and white	1	2	3	3	–	–	–	3

Table 5.6   *(Continued)*

	Sex of child			Religion of adopting parents				
	Male	Female	Total	Protestant	Roman Catholic	Sikh	Buddhist	Total
Chinese and white	1	2	3	3	–	–	–	3
Chinese	1	1	2	2	–	–	–	2
East Indian and white	3	–	3	2	–	1	–	3
Polynesian and white	–	1	1	1	–	–	–	1
Subtotals	7	14	21	20	–	1	–	21
Catholic CAS of Vancouver								
Native Indian and white	1	2	3	–	3	–	–	3
Native Indian	1	1	2	–	2	–	–	2
Fijian	1	–	1	–	1	–	–	1
Subtotals	3	3	6	–	6	–	–	6
Victoria Children's Aid Society								
Native Indian and white	1	1	2	2	–	–	–	2
Negro and white	–	1	1	1	–	–	–	1
Chinese	1	–	1	1	–	–	–	1
East Indian and white	1	–	1	1	–	–	–	1
Subtotals	3	2	5	5	–	–	–	5
Grand Totals	51	75	126	96	28	1	1	126

SOURCE: BC Department of Social Welfare, *Annual Report* (for the year ending 31 March 1966), 57.

Pepperrell, near St John's, Newfoundland, from 1941 to 1961 contributed to the appearance of mixed-race infants in that province.[75]

Children with African ancestry had occasionally been fostered in white Canadian homes in the early decades of the twentieth century, but short- or long-term parents were always 'hard to come by', even when eager social workers reminded audiences that '"different" looking children had the needs of all children', and that 'we know too that as they are happy and productive, society is enriched; as they are unhappy and it is impoverished.'[76] Reconsideration of what Karen Dubinsky has termed 'hybrid babies' attracted a good deal of attention, even though there were relatively small numbers of such children. More than offspring who 'matched' the dominant community, the girls and boys of such stigmatized others raised important questions about families and Canada itself.

Debates and initiatives were nationwide, but Montreal's efforts caught the national and international spotlight. The city's Children's Service Centre (CSC), a reincarnation of the old Protestant Children's Home, pioneered in the 1950s to find homes for mixed-race babies. In the first instance, as elsewhere, it endeavoured to match black youngsters with similar families, but the latter's numbers proved insufficient. A hierarchy of preference that favoured children with Asian or Native ancestry over those with African backgrounds further handicapped efforts. As tables 5.7 and 5.8 indicate, demand for 'coloured' children of any sort did not keep up with the numbers coming into custody. Since it wanted homes rather than institutions, the CSC worked hard to attract white parents.

The CSC's revolutionary attack on prejudice was greatly assisted by the closely associated Montreal's Open Door Society (ODS), founded in 1959. Led by progressive-minded English Montrealers, the ODS quickly transformed itself from a local support group for parents involved in interracial adoption to a champion of interracial families and civil rights. It inspired imitators across North America, including in cities and towns like Toronto, Ottawa, Vancouver, and Nelson, British Columbia. The ODS's ties to a continuing tradition of evangelical rescue were suggested by the appeal by one of its founders, Margaret Edgar, in the pages of the

Table 5.7   Applications for non-white children received by the CSC of Montreal, 1951–62

Year	Number of applications	Year	Number of applications
1951	1	1957	3
1952	1	1958	4
1953	1	1959	8
1954	2	1960	14
1955	2	1961	26
1956	3	1962	29

SOURCE: Miss Gallay, 'Interracial Adoptions', *Canadian Welfare* 39 (November–December 1963): 248.

Table 5.8   Children designated as other than 'white' placed for adoption by Montreal CSC, 1951–May 1963★

Racial identification	Number
Negro	5
Negro and white	66
Negro and Canadian Indian	1
Canadian Indian	1
Canadian Indian and white	20
Oriental	1
Oriental and white	19
East Indian and white	2

★Includes one child from Ontario, one from Alberta, and ten from Nova Scotia. The ethnic/racial categories are those used in the original.

SOURCE: Miss Gallay, 'Interracial Adoptions', *Canadian Welfare* 39 (November–December 1963): 250.

United Church Observer 'for general acceptance of children of mixed race.'[77] Not surprisingly, a social worker identified a 'strong expression of religious and humanitarian motivation' among one hundred applicants for such children. As sixty of these families already had biological offspring, sterility was less of a factor than reform sympathies.[78]

While Montrealers appear to have begun their efforts slightly earlier, their counterparts in Toronto were similarly active. During the 1950s, the city's two Children's Aid Societies claimed to have secured families for five or six black children a year, the first with white adopters in 1952.[79] By 1954, the CAS of Metropolitan Toronto reiterated its commitment to matching by assigning one employee special responsibility for attracting 'Negro' applicants. Newspaper publicity and contacts with individuals and groups were undertaken, but results proved disappointing: only seven children found such parents in 1954 and only two in 1955.[80]

When homes could not be discovered within, they were sought outside the province's black community. From 1959 to 1961, the CAS of Metropolitan Toronto placed thirty-two 'Negro' children for adoption, thirty in white homes. In 1960 and 1961, the Catholic CAS made similar arrangements for four youngsters. Such initiatives did not begin to meet the need. By 1962, both agencies reported some 150 children in care and asked the city's Social Planning Council to help develop community educational programs to recruit more would-be parents.[81] The adoption consultant for the Children's Welfare Branch of Ontario believed the moment ripe, arguing 'the public is so much more accepting than we anticipate—sometimes social workers are too hesitant to punch at it.'[82] Continent-wide efforts augmented local publicity drives. Beginning in 1968, the Adoption Resource Exchange of North America (ARENA) sought homes wherever they could be located. Such institutionalized border-crossing reflected the faith that homes could always be found, if the right efforts were made.

The Montreal ODS inspired the creation of Toronto's CACY in 1962. Its membership included representatives of the city's liberal Jewish and Protestant, white and black elite. They included Dr Daniel Hill, an America-born PhD graduate in sociology from the University of Toronto and the first full-time director of the Ontario Human Rights Commission; Mrs Wilson Brooks, the wife of the city's first black public school principal; Bernard Berger, a Jewish philanthropist; Dr Norma Ford Walker, a medical geneticist from the University of Toronto; and Janet Berton, housewife and writer. A sympathetic contemporary emphasized the importance of 'the inter-racial character of the project's leadership, which' encouraged widespread black support and 'insured that the approach to the recruiting of white parents has remained soundly based.'[83]

The Toronto CACY's campaigns nevertheless produced mixed responses. Despite its biracial leadership, some black critics resented the preoccupation with black children, worrying lest it reinforce negative associations of their community with illegitimacy. And in a foreshadowing of concerns later expressed by the American Association of Black Social Workers in 1973 and indigenous critics about children from their own communities, some black citizens raised the possibility that youngsters might lose their 'Negro heritage'. Overall, however, the African Canadian response was reckoned positive. 'As one elderly man observed thoughtfully "I never thought I would live to see the day."'[84] The CACY also worked hard to generate white support. Its strategy relied on canny reminders of basic human rights and of money to be saved. Younger people were credited as more enthusiastic and less fearful than their elders, who were more like to recoil at the possibility of future mixed-race marriages. Many white observers, however, in encountering black leaders and issues, often for the first time, claimed to be excited and committed to ending racial discrimination. Overall, the CACY believed 'the prevailing climate seems to be that the expression "prejudice" is no longer socially acceptable.'[85]

Between 1963 and 1965, members pitched their plea at some ninety meetings, with attendance judged at close to 3,000. It is impossible to estimate CACY influence, but over much the same period Toronto's CASs placed ninety-three children with African ancestry—seventy with whites and the rest with black families—and an additional eight youngsters of Asian and/or Native background with families who had originally requested a black child. The CACY also took some credit for the *Toronto Telegram*'s success in securing parents for eighteen 'Negro' children portrayed in 'Today's Child' in 1965.[86]

That column provided a revealing picture of how interracial placements might be encouraged. In the case of Matthew, 'a beautiful boy nearly a year old,' exoticism was clearly part of the appeal of a 'heritage' that was 'Spanish and French with the possibility of negro blood several generations back.'[87] Other adopters could win the opportunity to rescue an intelligent daughter, Lisa, who, at six and bravely 'flashing dimples', was having to make sense of Indian, white, and 'Negro' ancestry on her own.[88] Still another column produced the commonplace liberal credo, 'a child is a child—no matter what his race or color.' It also pointed to the fact that Ontario's black families were doing their share and more of adoptions. It was time for white families to step up to the plate. The progressive sympathies of most adopters were reaffirmed when the new mother of a four-year-old agreed that they would "'take advantage of all opportunities for Jeanie to meet other Negro children" and added "but we think the main thing is to teach her that the color of the skin doesn't matter.'"[89] In face of such testimonials, Helen Allen readily found a rich faith:

> Shining through them all is the warm-hearted knowledge that every child needs a home and parents, and that the presence of a child makes any home richer.
> Nowhere is there the slightest hint of racial prejudice. Though each child's background has been spelled out, most letters do not refer to it. Others dismiss it casually as something quite unimportant.[90]

Assumptions that race could be washed away by tolerance were common across the country. The sister of two adoptees in Vancouver at the end of the 1960s remembered that her fair-complexioned parents welcomed a daughter who was 'black, Aboriginal and Mexican Indian as well as white' with little preparation or support beyond the conviction that such an adoption was a good way to enlarge the family without contributing to world population pressures.[91]

One 1966 assessment identified significant distinctions between white and black adopters. The former frequently, as with the Bertons, encompassed much larger families: only some 5 per cent were without offspring when they applied. Two-thirds had three or more children at home. In contrast, close to 40 per cent of black applicants were childless, and only 12 per cent had three or more offspring. Whites were also likely to be significantly better off, with a median income at $7,200 compared to $5,600 for blacks. Before adopting, a third of whites reported no contact with the African Canadian community. Yet, inspired by a combination of religious faith and a commitment to civil rights, all resolved to raise offspring 'with an awareness of his negro background, as well as of his adoption.' Revealing of their hopes, many anticipated that, by the time their children were adults, 'inter-racial dating and marriage' would no longer be an issue.[92]

Montreal and Toronto appear to have offered the best prospects for placing youngsters of African ancestry. Elsewhere opportunities seem to have been slimmer. A Nova Scotia social worker beginning her practice with a rural child welfare agency in 1968 recollected the need to send such children, unwanted in the province, to black families in Montreal and the West Indies. She and others slowly began to consider white applicants elsewhere. In 1969, she placed a two-year-old with white Quebecers, already active in the ODS and parenting a black son. In the 1970s, as fewer white babies became available and West Indian outlets seemed to 'dry up', Atlantic welfare agencies began to consider local white as well as black families.[93]

In 1987, the first generation of Nova Scotia's white adopters was appraised as frequently university educated, church-going, and already parenting biological offspring. Many revealed family histories of adoption, sometimes 'transracial'. The majority of respondents reported encountering some racism, including a 'friend' who accused one couple of '"baby snatching" from the black race', but overall white Nova Scotians were judged pleased with their choices. The same study suggested that representatives of the province's black community harboured more reservations. The influence of the Black Power movement was palpable, with two speakers opposed to white families on any grounds and nine assessing black adopters as preferable.[94]

Other investigations raised issues that regularly troubled transracial adoption. Adults who would have had difficulty meeting contemporary qualifications for adoptive parenthood sometimes surfaced. One young African–Nova Scotian woman who went home with Montrealers in the 1960s observed that the age of her parents—her father was sixty and her mother forty-seven—meant that she was one of the few youngsters available to them. And indeed transracial adopters were commonly older. Nor did racism and racial ranking disappear. Young residents of the NSHCC readily observed how 'light-skinned and mixed-race children tended to be preferred by foster and adoptive families, making the darker-skinned peers feel unwanted.'[95] Concerns about what was happening to its charges prompted the NSHCC to establish a committee on interracial adoption. Its 1971 report contained an exchange between the black chairman and the province's white director of child welfare. While the latter took clear pride in the unprecedented tolerance of white applicants, he was also obviously uncomfortable when forced to admit that black families would not be permitted to adopt white youngsters. Not surprisingly, his interrogator wondered 'whether psychological and racial genocide is being practiced.'[96] Such conclusions help explain the shift in the home's board of management from a majority of white men in the 1970s and the appointment of the first black president in 1974.

Some whites were clearly sensitive to shifting perceptions. One progressive Haligonian, a law professor at Dalhousie and later founder of the university's Mi'kmaq Law Program and executive director of the Nova Scotia Human Rights Commission, favourably invoked a 1963 Montreal study, supervised by H. David Kirk, Canada's leading exponent of mixed-race adoption. He reassured readers that youngsters 'demonstrated no ambivalence or confusion about their colour' and that 'being raised in a white family did not generate negative feelings about their own race.' He felt confident enough to conclude that 'perhaps the importance of being raised in the black culture has been over-emphasized.'[97] The NSHCC's 1979 investigation of placements was less sanguine. It found adopters regularly failed to provide cultural supports and rarely successfully managed black hair and skin. Those researchers were all the more disconcerted to discover that adoptees were likely to 'label themselves as "colored", "brown", and even "white"' and that 'white parents don't even tell their children that there are differences among people.'[98] Such observations seem hardly surprisingly. Many liberal adopters embraced a colour-blind politics that offered little insight into the operation of race and racialization.

By the 1990s, however, scholarly studies were reporting positively about interracial adoption.[99] A significant group of adopters committed themselves to maintaining the cultural connections of their children. By 2005, the Adoption Council of Ontario was rather typically hosting an Interracial Adoption and Discussion Group and including on its website a 'Transracial Adoptees' Bill of Rights' that epitomized Frankenberg's third category of 'race cognizance':

Every child is entitled
- to love and full membership in his or her family.
- to have his or her heritage and culture embraced and valued.
- to parents who value individuality and enjoy complexity.
- to parents who understand that this is a race-conscious society.
- to parents who know their children will experience life differently from themselves.
- to parents who know that belonging to a family is not based on physical matching.
- to parents who have significant relationships with people of other races.
- to parents who know transracial adoption changes the family forever.
- to be accepted by his or her extended family members.
- to parents who know that if they are white, they experience the benefits of racism because the system is organized that way.
- to parents who know they cannot be the sole transmitter of the child's culture when it is not their own.
- to grow up with items in the home environment that are created for and by people of their own race or ethnicity.
- to have places available to make friends with people of his or her race or ethnicity.
- to have opportunities in his or her environment to participate in positive experiences with his or her birth culture.
- to opportunities to build racial pride within his or her own home, family, school and neighborhood.[100]

Such statements vividly conveyed the distance some Canadians had travelled to embrace a more inclusive, race-sensitive politics in adoption, as in other matters in the dominion. Unfortunately, voices from Canada's racialized communities, other than First Nations, have been rarer in communicating their collective opinion of surrenders. Donor nations, in contrast, have sometimes chosen to slam doors shut. Yet given the choices available to disadvantaged children, as to other newcomers, it may well be that, as one Quebec adoptee, born to white mother and a black father, concluded, adopting parents 'did the right thing'.[101]

Wherever the particular process or outcome of decisions that took them from Canada's and the world's poorer communities, girls and boys have regularly struggled with what philosopher Charles Taylor has termed the 'politics of recognition'. On too many occasions, even with the support of progressive and supportive parents, children, racialized as strangers to the dominant group, have been denied dignity, respect, and recognition of their value as individuals with unique histories.[102]

As the president of the Ottawa Open Door Society readily stressed in 1974, much work remained to be done: 'We know that socio-economic and ethnic discrimination is very real in Canadian society. We can work to improve the situation and in the questioning of the use in our schools of texts with prejudicial content.' Unless adopters were able to 'help a child discover and have pride in his heritage,' 'whiteland' might, he understood, undo all the intended good.[103] Injury has been possible even when individual lives have been materially improved and the nation as a whole experimented with unprecedented inclusion by the end of the twentieth century. Canada's continuing difficulty in confronting long-standing prejudice was all the more visible when, as the next chapter demonstrates, Aboriginal children and communities confronted the mainstream.

Native–Newcomer Contact

In Canada, First Nations children have often aroused special interest from new-comers. In the seventeenth century, Samuel de Champlain and Catholic religious orders hoped to transform indigenous communities by remaking youngsters. So long as Native societies remained largely intact, such initiatives reported little success, all the more so when Native peoples realized that the exchange of children was not reciprocal. As they expanded west and north, white settlers, governments, and churches undermined Aboriginal families and cultures. That disaster hit some communities particularly hard, but none was immune. By the mid-nineteenth century, white authorities readily turned to residential and industrial schools, which they also favoured for disciplining working-class youngsters, to secure their dominion over indigenous lands and bodies. Church-run institutions became favourite tools for remaking recalcitrant Native children. Not until well after the Second World War were some Aboriginal youngsters perceived as suitable candidates for white homes.

Although institutional segregation commonly reflected racial essentialism, and adoption drew on liberal hopes for full integration, both frequently aimed to produce 'apples': such children might be Indian or 'red' on the outside but their commitment to European values made them 'white' on the inside. By the closing decades of the twentieth century, liberal confidence in assimilation faltered in response to well-publicized tragedies and Native resistance. This chapter examines the shifting provision for Aboriginal youngsters whose birth parents could not, or were not allowed to, care for them. That complicated story, before it turns to residential schools and the evolution of views on adoption, properly begins with a reminder of the diversity of Native societies and the unequal vulnerability of children.

Native Societies: Diversity and the Care of Children

As with other groups, fostering and adoption by kin and community were commonplace in Aboriginal societies. The transfer of children might serve symbolic and practical purposes. Girls and boys could become war captives and peace offerings. Their shift among clans and other groups could promise survival for populations decimated by disease and losses to residential schools. Grandparents and older relatives might gain caregivers in old age.[1] Custom and practice varied tremendously across the country and were further diversified with the appearance of extensive mixed newcomer-Native communities, some of which identified as Aboriginal. Preoccupation with the desperate situation of some families in the course of imperial contact has frequently obscured this diversity. Today, as in the past, Native nations have had access to a variety of resources and traditions in their encounter with whites. A few were destroyed; some came close to extinction; most struggled for equilibrium. The fate of youngsters was ultimately tied to that of their societies.

Individual community members might well benefit from differing levels of resources. Traditional and mixed-race elites wielded authority through their control of cultural capital and through frequently privileged access to employments and opportunities presented in the course of contact. Although they encountered fewer opportunities than their settler neighbours, Natives too have been 'distributed across the range of class sites within Canada.'[2] George Martin Johnson, the father of the writer E. Pauline Johnson, the son of a clan matron, a translator for the Anglican Church and Indian Affairs, a Scottish Rite Mason, the husband of a middle-class English Quaker, the employer of servants, and a Mohawk chief, had equally advantaged counterparts across the country on territories whose leaders managed, often with the assistance of missionaries and federal bureaucrats, to cobble together additional sources of power. While smaller bands and tribes lacked the same capacity for sharply distinguished roles and ranks, Ontario's Six Nations have been far from unusual in supporting a significant social hierarchy.

Privileged access to and knowledge of Native cultural capital, whether this be potlatches, sun dances, or wampum, strengthened Aboriginal elites, even if it could not make them invulnerable to white incursions. And if many First Nations were desperately poor, some were materially successful. One 1960 study, for example, reckoned some BC Native seine boat captains wealthy, as were a few ranchers, including one individual in the Okanagan whose total assets were estimated at 'more than $500,000'.[3] While often undermined by credit restrictions, some canny Aboriginal entrepreneurs found ways to make money. The same investigator from 1960 concluded, 'Indian investment in income-earning capital is, proportionate to their incomes, perhaps larger than that of Whites. . . . Large numbers of fishermen, farmers, trappers and loggers have bought expensive equipment and the payments on these purchases often leave a very slim margin for personal needs.'[4] Fifteen years later, William Stanbury's *Success and Failure: Indians in Urban Society* differentiated sharply between the Aboriginal unemployed and employed, noting that 'a higher degree of cultural identity appears to increase the probability of success (obtaining a job) in the labour market.'[5] Just as revealingly, the more highly educated of his sample of 1,090—those with Grade 12 or better—were significantly more likely to belong to Indian organizations, attend Indian ceremonies, read one or more Indian publications, and visit reserves.[6] In short, some Native families always found strength in traditional values or Christianity, sought out formal and informal education, cooperated to oppose white claims, and resisted drugs, including alcohol. Whether in Metlakatla on the west coast or Oshweken in Six Nations, they counted themselves, and were often considered, respectable.[7] Such Aboriginal elites were also likely to share certain sensibilities with European intruders. They too might well embrace discipline, education, and sobriety, just those 'family values' that commonly distinguished the respectable from the rough in more mainstream populations.

Divisions were never hard and fast. Families everywhere slipped back and forth between disaster and prosperity. As in the white working class, Aboriginal survival was often precarious, dependent on uncertain health and unpredictable and regularly insufficient resources. Every community counted marginal members. Unlike Aboriginal leaders, the less fortunate were likely to lack traditional authority, 'good' names, high status, or connections to white power-brokers. It was one thing to be on the fringe of thriving Native communities in good times, quite another to have limited resources in the face of a determined assault by newcomers. Such rankings had implications for children as Native societies struggled to cope with contact.

The proportion of Aboriginal youngsters in residential schools or in care has varied markedly among bands and over time and space. Some families and communities lost large numbers. Those more susceptible to the impact of Europeans disease, resource extraction, or population pressure were frequently hard put to protect members from any stratum of life. Although they have not been systematically studied as to their cultural and economic resources within Aboriginal communities, apprehended children and their families often appear especially marginal and most injured by drugs, including alcohol. Young products of relatively casual Native–white liaisons, which undermined still further critical kin connections, including claims to band membership, often seemed especially vulnerable.[8]

Those least connected to the successful in their communities were more hardput to evoke sustained expressions of solidarity. At the beginning of the twenty-first century, the situation of two young sisters, born of a Squamish band member in thrall to addictions and apparently long absent from her reserve, and a white partner, evoked only a seemingly formulistic defence. BC's Squamish Nation spent an estimated $200,000 to defend its right to repatriate the youngsters from Ontario but could not produce any band member willing to take responsibility for their day-to-day well-being. Even within a First Nation that had won a significant degree of autonomy and prosperity, solidarity clearly had real limits.[9] In contrast, in 1980, the Spallumcheen campaign to return children apprehended by BC child welfare services appeared to have been immeasurably strengthened by the fact that apprehensions had included elite youngsters, among them the chief who led the resistance and his brother.[10]

As in non-Native communities, some children appeared simply less valued than others. Much as implicit assumptions about the relative worth of various youngsters help explain why the Canadian state has moved slowly and incompletely to confront poverty, so too they may suggest why the Assembly of First Nations (AFN) and other Aboriginal leaders have rarely prioritized children's well-being. The distinction between girls and boys who have been particularly at risk and those for whom First Nations families and communities have been more successful in mustering the resources to retain or quickly reclaim evokes the differences scholars have identified between the 'rough' and the 'respectable' among the working class or in society more generally.[11] The former, especially wounded by violence, addictions, and the worst of unemployment and poverty, have disproportionately lost progeny. Such was the case with a mother-led family from BC's Vernon Indian reserve, where a maternal grandmother, in her desperate efforts to pick up the pieces, 'preached about being proper when we grew up.'[12]

Those apt to exert collective leadership and express solidarity, promote cultural awareness, and value industry and discipline, have more often been able to retain daughters and sons. As Jo Cain pointed out in her fine master's thesis in social work in 1985, 'traditional' families were often readily distinguishable from the 'marginal'. In Vancouver's Downtown Eastside, the former benefited significantly from

> a growing number and variety of services, offered through native organizations which are culturally sensitive to native needs, the Marginal families appear to be as alienated from these services as they are from the range of social services traditionally offered through mandated child protection agencies. Often raised in care or extremely impoverished, chaotic and violent circumstances, the Marginal group may present as having a negative attitude towards natives—possibly because their own low self-esteem is a reflection of mainstream racist attitudes to which they have been exposed with no opportunity for them to be offset by positive native values.[13]

Recognition of different levels of risk has been hampered by the prevalence of what might be termed the 'classical family of Native nostalgia', which commonly contrasts modern Aboriginal vulnerability with the situation believed present before European landfall. Modern First Nations speakers and sympathizers typically invoke a pre-contact age when families and children flourished without institutional discipline, corporate punishment, or violence. Romantic images of bygone times, part of what Jo-Anne Fiske and Claudien Herlihey have termed 'the discourse of identity', have been clearly intended to inspire and provoke: the solutions to the dilemmas of the here and now are believed to lie in recapturing some part of the past.[14] Like most essentially political discourses, utopian visions have some roots in reality. An abundance of newcomer and Native commentators have contrasted Native and newcomer childrearing practices, with the former routinely emerging as more flexible, tolerant, and affectionate. Utopian dreams have, however, been problematic in their dismissal of abuse and violence as essentially foreign and modern and their essentialization and homogenization of experience across time and space.[15] Ultimately, they appear to be more fighting creeds than proven reflections of past times. As such, they can both inspire and disable.

Resort to a supposed golden age has evolved in the face of racist assessments of traditional Native childrearing practices. Missionaries and state bureaucrats often linked early socialization to later savagery, promiscuity, intemperance, and indolence.[16] This condemnation had a counterpart in many middle-class assessments of the working classes. The poor, and paupers in particular, have routinely been dismissed as lacking the moral fibre for success and civilization. Disadvantaged white children, whose homes offered few comforts and for whom the streets promised employment, excitement, and camaraderie, emerged in Canada as elsewhere as the moral equivalent of North American 'savages'. Parental failings in the realms of sobriety, cleanliness, and industry, rather than inherited disadvantage, uncertain economies, and recurring illness, were seen as handicapping offspring from a variety of marginalized groups. Sent to institutions or to new families, such girls and boys were expected to find incentives to assimilate to middle-class ideals, although rarely to the comforts of that status.

Given the strength of familial ideologies and the real value of kinship, it is no surprise that the majority of Canada's Aboriginal children—whether status Indian, non-status, Metis, or Inuit—have, like working-class youngsters, always grown up within their own families, both nuclear and extended. In 1910, for example, 'residential schools catered to but one-fifth (19.7 per cent) of school-age Indians and Inuit' and at their height they housed 'about one-third' of eligible candidates.[17] In British Columbia, status children in care, including those placed in residential schools for 'family reasons', were estimated at 4.43 per cent of the Native population aged 0–19 years in 1972, 3.25 per cent in 1966, and 2.84 per cent in 1962. The comparable proportions for the non-Indian population revealed the same trajectory at 1.14 per cent, 0.98 per cent, and 0.84 per cent respectively.[18] In 2001, Aboriginal children made up about 40 per cent of Canada's 76,000-odd youngsters in care. The great majority of the 33 per cent of the Aboriginal population as a whole—that is, about 323,960 children—who were under fourteen were, however, in their own homes.[19] Statistics necessarily supply but a snapshot in time. Many more youngsters experienced some time in care. But this has been true of all populations. Most girls and boys in all communities never lived with non-kin. If nuclear families could not manage, then relatives and neighbours frequently offered shelter, whether good, bad, or indifferent.

Many grandparents were called on when mothers and fathers hit hard times or found it impossible to parent. A sense of common jeopardy may also have increased 'the importance of mutual help and self-reliance . . . after contact with Europeans.'[20] Such arrangements appear similar to those observed among the poor in general. As Anna Davin has observed of nineteenth-century London and Lynn Abrams of nineteenth- and twentieth-century Scotland, kin and neighbours, many not so far removed from destitution, frequently provided the first line of defence for families in difficulty.[21] Many Aboriginal adults were also likely to shelter relations and neighbours in need, on a scale unmatched in settler society. In contrast, child welfare authorities always found it difficult to recruit Native foster parents. Social workers, the vast majority of whom were of European origin, knew little of reserves or Native people and sometimes shared mainstream prejudices. Aboriginal groups themselves were suspicious of agencies they associated with abduction and genocide.

Often forgotten is the fact that Native families occasionally assumed responsibilities for white youngsters. Evidence so far is scanty but nevertheless suggestive. In the 1940s, one unidentified Six Nations woman mothered Tom Blackthorne after he escaped an abusive adoptive home. As he remembered, she offered 'the only real family he had known to that point.'[22] Some twenty years later, welfare authorities were much more inclined to intervene, as in the case of two-and-one-half-year-old Bridget, 'a child with ivory white skin and light gold hair' found living in 'tender, all-enveloping care' in which she thrived with Tom, who had served overseas with the Canadian Scottish regiment, and Sarah Tait, both members of the Bulkley Valley's Carrier Nation. Bridget's mother, living common law with a Dutch immigrant, sought respite from caring for several preschoolers when she gave her daughter to the Taits, parents of a good friend. When she died in childbirth soon thereafter, her male partner demanded the return of his daughter, who was then committed to the child welfare authorities. The Taits, who had lost children to illness and had adopted another, wished to keep Bridget, but this was not about to be allowed in such a community that was described by journalist Simma Holt as 'both gentle and harsh, loving and dangerous'.[23] For all their value, the resources of care and generosity represented by the Taits and others should not be over-estimated or romanticized. No room was available for significant numbers of girls and boys in disadvantaged communities all around Canada.

Industrial and Residential Schools

In Canada, various child welfare programs evolved as a capitalist state endeavoured to manage diverse populations. Both critics and supporters of the First Nations have been preoccupied, not unexpectedly, with the distinctions of race. In fact, the treatment of Aboriginal girls and boys was one part of larger modern project that aimed to refashion a range of youngsters so that they, unlike their progenitors, would cause little trouble to those in authority. First Nations families encountered European imperialism in the context of precedents and ongoing child-rescue ideologies that 'identified the parent as a danger to the child.'[24] No sharp line divided institutional and domestic placements or abductions. Both represented exercises in social welfare that aimed both to discipline and to rescue. The supposed malleability of youth, in which the modern child-rescue movement put great stock, encouraged some optimism about apprehended youngsters, whatever their origin.

Modern schooling, increasingly lengthy and compulsory, was one solution to the breakup of traditional communities, the potential instability of heterogeneous societies, and the expansion of empires. It set out to bring students into imagined communities where they would be assigned by virtue of their race, gender, and class, not to mention other characteristics, to appropriate roles and obligations. Yet indoctrination was always uncertain, compromised as it was by the mixed motives of educational champions, which often included at least intermittent commitment to equality and democracy as well as meritocracy, and the resistance, often strenuous, of clients.

Right from the beginning, a variety of institutions delivered education. Working-class children were disproportionately assigned to industrial and reform schools and Native youngsters to industrial and residential schools. Luckier girls and boys escaped to day and public schools, where kin supervision of their well-being was much more likely. It was no coincidence that both working-class and Native youngsters were first directed to industrial schools, whose very name signalled dedication to vocational labour. The daughters and sons of those designated marginal and appropriately subordinated were allocated overwhelmingly to domestic and agricultural employment. While provinces dedicated training or reform schools to the reconstruction of delinquent or 'pre-delinquent' working-class youth, the federal government empowered Catholic and Protestant churches to employ residential schools to refashion Natives. Indian agents were especially likely to consign youngsters they considered neglected and abused.[25]

Isolated settlements and jurisdictional responsibilities helped dictate that option, but so did the commonplace racism of mainstream institutions. Native youngsters might well be barred from orphanages, private and public children's homes, and public schools. The attitude of the Vancouver Children's Aid Society (CAS) was typical. It might pity poor Native youngsters, but it long resisted attempts at integration. As an official reported after the First World War, 'if they have been brought up as Indians, . . . certainly they are not fit to be in our Home.'[26] Until well into the twentieth century, only the mixed-race youngsters who could pass as members of the dominant community were likely to be apprehended for assignment to mainstream facilities.[27]

Until they were closed—the last one, Saskatchewan's Gordon Residential School, in 1996—residential schools served as omnibus, multi-function institutions, especially for children from reserve and remote communities. A 1953 survey designated 4,313 of 10,112 inmates as welfare cases.[28] Another assessment the next decade concluded that 'many neglected children of school age are still sent to residential schools owing to the absence of proper child care services in the provinces.'[29] The proportion of welfare cares rose over time. The Great Depression of the 1930s, for example, forced Ontario's Mount Elgin Indian Residential School to restrict intake to orphans and destitute youngsters.[30] As Aboriginal communities learned of the shortcomings of residential schools, those with resources often chose, when they could, to keep offspring at home. Should elite daughters and sons nevertheless attend, they might well benefit from internal hierarchies that confirmed those in Native nations themselves. As J.R. Miller has pointed out, high-caste Tsimshian students 'had to be exempted from menial chores' performed by others.[31] In contrast to those judged their social betters, the offspring of marginal community members seemed more susceptible to extended stays, bullying, and the worst of residential schools.

In many instances, gender was clearly important to schooling, just as it was in fostering and adoption. As anthropologist Jo-Anne Fiske has observed of the Lejac Residential School in northern British Columbia, girls, more than their brothers, might discover mentors and find the training helpful for later employments.[32] Beverly Hungry Wolf of Alberta's Blackfoot Nation suggests that something similar happened at St Paul's Anglican Residential School.[33] At age twelve, the future poet Rita Joe asked to attend the Shubenacadie Residential School, founded in 1930 to 'provide for the "underprivileged Indian child of Nova Scotia and the other maritime provinces," including "orphans, illegitimate and neglected children."'[34] For all its shortcomings, it promised something better than the neglect and brutality she had suffered being passed around Mi'kmaq families after her mother died.[35]

In the nineteenth century, advocates of child welfare began condemning orphanages and reformatories for failing to protect or stimulate. Residential schools out-lasted many other institutions. Their survival owed much to churches' determination to maintain their hold, to the isolation of many Native communities, and to mainstream indifference and racism. By the mid-twentieth century, however, Aboriginal and non-Aboriginal critics were increasingly influential, spatial segregation and racial prejudice embarrassed a modern nation, and expanding urban Native populations required different responses. Disadvantaged youngsters increasingly became the target of authorities eager to solve the Native problem in new ways.

The Mainstream Discovers 'Citizens Minus': 1940s–1970s

For many years, provincial child welfare authorities largely ignored indigenous children. As Jessa Chupik-Hall has effectively argued, Indian families in trouble before the mid-twentieth century had little recourse but tight-fisted aid from federal Indian agents and residential schools.[36] Provinces, already stingy with the white poor, moved slowly to address Native distress. Their early observations and remedies sometimes appeared little different than those addressed to more mainstream families. During the Great Depression, for example, Ontario's superintendent of neglected and dependent children reported on a case from the Temiskaming District, where a couple with four children nearly froze as they 'camped on the bare ground with only the canvas between them and zero weather.' The nearest CAS officer located the youngsters 'comfortable quarters' so that the Native parents could 'rest assured' that they 'would be well looked after' until the winter trapping was finished.[37] Such comments, with their underlying assumption that Natives too had rights to aid in bad times, were rare. For the most part, authorities said little and probably did less.

As time passed, provinces reluctantly assumed duties that they generally felt were properly Ottawa's. In 1939, BC authorities typically concluded that 'when faced with incest, contributing to juvenile delinquency or physical abuse,' they had little choice but to apprehend. In such circumstances, the province preferred to ask relatives to take over, but it also experimented with 'white foster homes which were believed free of "racial prejudice."'[38] A year later, the province's superintendent of neglected children returned to the problem, citing the case of 'half-breed' siblings identified by a sister as starving and ill. A plane was sent to bring them south to Prince George, where one little girl was admitted to hospital with spinal and pulmonary tuberculosis and her brothers handed over to a Children's Aid Society. Such tragedies prompted growing criticism of federal educational and welfare programs.[39]

The plight of Aboriginal youth was further highlighted when they turned up in criminal justice institutions already housing so many of their working-class contemporaries. As Joan Sangster has reported of Ontario Native girls, 'by the 1960s, they were being incarcerated in alarming numbers disproportionate to their small percentage of the overall population.'[40] In British Columbia, the Willingdon School for Girls similarly found itself the custodian of unprecedented numbers of

Aboriginal youngsters. Soaring illegitimacy rates provided further cause for worry and reconsideration of existing policies, notably residential schools.[41]

As Canadian social workers increasingly encountered evidence of Native hardship and poverty in the 1940s and 1950s, they counted on expert intervention and, ultimately, assimilation. BC's superintendent of child welfare argued that unless Canadians were willing to have 'the whole question of the Canadian Indian investigated by an authoritative group of experts, free from racial prejudice, and objective in their outlook, we shall continue to have the disheartening situation we have today, where within our provincial borders we have large racial groups, who are not even expected to conform to the minimum social standards which we require from the rest of our citizens.'[42] Officials favoured success stories that embodied the promise of integration. In the 1940s, with the cooperation of the federal Indian Affairs Branch, BC's welfare authorities experimented with foster placements for a 'few selected children who showed ability.' Unable to continue their education on reserves, a handful of Native teens were assisted in attending high schools, vocational programs, and the University of British Columbia, seemingly on the same basis as other students.[43] The clear message was that integration solved the white problem with Natives.

The same well-intentioned, if naive, hopes for full integration and common services prompted the Canadian Welfare Council and the Canadian Association of Social Workers to present a joint brief to the 1946–8 Joint Committee of the Senate and House of Commons considering the revision of the Indian Act. They condemned policies that did not give Natives equal services, that allowed unqualified Indian agents to administer welfare, and that employed residential schools for neglected youngsters. More particularly, they pointed to 'loosely conceived and executed' adoption practices that were 'usually devoid of the careful legal and social protection afforded to white children' and that 'simply absorbed' children 'into the homes of relatives or neighbours without any legal status.'[44] At long last, advocates argued that care for Native youngsters should match that promised their white contemporaries.

More than ever, Aboriginal peoples became the subject of 'equality talk'. This could obscure the special circumstances of Aboriginal peoples. Such was the case in the 1940s, when Alberta child welfare started classifying all neglected children as simply 'Canadian'. The result, as a critical study sponsored by the Imperial Order Daughters of the Empire (IODE) noted, might 'be politically acceptable; in social practice it is handicapping to find 36 half-breed children neglected one year, 14, 15, 16 delinquent in 3 years and then none at all,' as that racial category disappeared.[45] Such omissions reflected that acknowledgment of race was increasingly equated with inequality and segregation, and thus was to be avoided. The leader of the Co-operative Commonwealth Federation (CCF) in the federal parliament spoke for many Canadians in 1954 when he opposed residential schools and endorsed integration. He argued:

> We shall find the Indian child has just the same kind of ability as the average white child. I do not believe there is any difference in individual aptitudes or intelligence because of the colour of the skin.

> I am quite sure that in the past we have not given the Indian child the opportunity that child should have had to live a full and decent life. . . . After all, the Indians are the original occupants of this country and have a culture of their own.[46]

In the 1950s and 1960s, the BC Advisory Committee on Indian Affairs, composed of civil servants, public-spirited citizens, and representatives of the First Nations, articulated similar hopes for racial partnership. A nation whose prime minister, Lester B. Pearson, had recently won the Nobel Peace Prize had no excuse not to confront long-standing inequalities:

> With the present focus of world attention on the less advanced races of the earth, Canada is aware as never before of her responsibilities to her native citizens. The Indian people, also, are becoming increasingly conscious of the contribution required of them in an era of rapid social and economic change, and are seeking to align the responsibilities of citizenship with their cultural heritage of the past. With pride in their birthright, and in their increasing population and growing contributions to this country, the Indians of to-day may well say in the words of their Indian poetess Pauline Johnson, 'We are the pulse of Canada, its marrow and its bone.'[47]

Demands that Natives receive the same treatment as other Canadians frequently recognized prejudice as the enemy. But critics of old arrangements also readily slipped into condemning supposedly infantilized clients. In 1959, a report from Manitoba's Department of Agriculture and Immigration endorsed the extension of provincial child welfare services, which it credited with higher standards than those of federal authorities, to reserve populations. It anticipated improving services by ending segregation. It also condemned 'paternalistic' federal governments for fostering dependency in Aboriginal clients. The latter were tartly summed up as 'conditioned to white gifts' and 'exploiting the White man'. Only when supervised by well-trained provincial social workers and expected to behave like everyone else would Natives develop the proper strength of character to survive in the modern world. Despite the Manitoba report's occasional admission of prejudice, its version of equality largely ignored long-standing material exploitation and cultural needs.[48] Six years later, the Alberta Women's Liberal Association was kinder but voiced many of the same sentiments. Its members discussed a resolution asking Indian Affairs to 'launch a more vigorous campaign encouraging Indian parents to allow the separation of their children from home when this might be necessary for their education.' As a reporter for the *Edmonton Journal* approvingly noted, in a typical expression of liberal colour-blindness, 'eventual integration and equality is the goal.'[49]

The 1950 transfer of the Indian Affairs Branch from the Department of Mines and Resources to the Department of Immigration and Citizenship signalled shifting federal views. Native peoples were moving, at least symbolically, from the category of exploitable resource to responsible citizen. At much the same time, Indian

Affairs social workers began sponsoring Homemakers Clubs and leadership courses for parents, initiatives designed to encourage imitation of settler-family models. **Failures** frequently continued to be blamed on the shortcomings of Aboriginal individuals and cultures rather than any fault on the part of newcomers. It is hard not to agree with Hawthorn's study that the 'most elementary and important point about the welfare policies of the Indian Affairs Branch is the consistently low status they have enjoyed.' Ultimately, they appeared 'little wanted', 'poorly suited', and 'handled poorly'.[50]

Ottawa also very much hoped to download unwelcome responsibilities. In 1951, it amended the Indian Act to permit the extension of provincial welfare services to reserves but, significantly, without additional funding. Ontario and British Columbia worked out the first agreements with Ottawa. In 1953, officials in the west coast province spoke of cooperating with Indian Affairs to usher in a wide variety of benefits, including services to unmarried mothers. Native youngsters were hailed as 'future citizens' who deserved all the advantages offered to others.[51] A year later, Ontario produced a report, *Civil Liberties and the Rights of Indians in Ontario*, endorsing agreements between Ottawa and the Children's Aid Societies. While other arrangements slowly followed, policies remained at best very uneven. As Jessa Chupik-Hall has noted, 'ensuing struggles over cost-sharing agreements and responsibility delayed the extension of child welfare services in most provinces for fifteen to twenty years.'[52] Penny-pinching and short-staffed provincial bureaucracies were ill-equipped to supply services.

For all their obfuscation and sidestepping, governments could not always ignore Native distress. Changes in communication brought Aboriginal and other Canadians in closer proximity across the country. While isolated communities still existed, news of tragedies increasingly seeped out, and cities housed growing numbers of Aboriginal residents. One outspoken social worker in Saskatchewan remembered the result in the 1950s and 1960s. Despite the province's official policy against providing services to reserves,

> it became increasingly difficult to enforce this policy because children were suffering and in some cases dying because of neglect. Child Welfare, therefore, did increasingly take emergency action. An agreement was made with the federal government that they would pay a per diem rate for all children who came into care who were Indians. But no over-all agreement has been reached between the senior governments which would assure child welfare services for all families who need them. It would, in its initial phases, need much more staff and more financial backing than the provincial government has available. [53]

As social welfare costs mounted, governments rarely became enthusiastic about assuming additional responsibilities. Not until 1989–90, for example, did Saskatchewan's Act Respecting Adoption mention 'status Indians'. And yet, less than two decades later, in December 2004, Canada's 'national' daily would hail that province as nearing an Aboriginal majority.[54]

Possibilities for extending services were especially likely to be explored for Métis children in the two decades after the Second World War, but every kind of assistance was limited. Problems were essentially three-fold. First, social services were already hard-pressed to meet the needs of urban white populations, few of which received the ideal assistance desired by social workers. The personal, financial, and drug counselling, housekeeping services, daycare, and decent jobs that might have kept many biological families intact were noticeably absent everywhere in Canada. Social workers always struggled with enormous caseloads and limited resources. When Aboriginal youngsters entered the system, their needs were likely to be still greater than those of their white counterparts and all the harder to address. Immediately after the Second World War, before doing very much for Aboriginal residents, Saskatchewan's director of child welfare already sounded overwhelmed by the

> difficult conditions under which the field staff operate. The districts are too large, necessitating much of their time being spent in traveling. The average caseload of the rural worker is over 200 cases, which means that it is possible to do little but emergencies. . . . It is the worker in the field who meets the brunt of the criticism. Far harder, though, for the workers to accept than the criticism and dissatisfaction of the public is the fact that they cannot provide the service which they know is needed. It is difficult to refuse help to people in need, to have to close your eyes to home conditions which are not satisfactory for children, to work mainly on an emergency level when the crisis could have been avoided in many cases if it had been possible to give a preventive service earlier.[55]

In 1955, BC's Provincial Advisory Committee on Indian Affairs believed that more Indian foster homes could be found but acknowledged that no additional welfare workers were available to recruit them. Nor, given 'the present complement of staff', could the Family Counseling Service could be extended to reserves.[56] A year later, the committee complained that existing caseloads could not expand to include to reserves.[57] In 1963–4, Saskatchewan's director of child welfare sounded eager to provide assistance in 'the traumatic transition from the simple life of the Indian to the more complex life of the non-Indian', but provision had hardly improved from the years immediately after the Second World War: as always there was 'a serious challenge to resources'.[58]

Native critics have sometimes believed that a much better deal existed for non-Aboriginal families. The common lack of appreciation of the general failure of child welfare services spurred survivors like BC Native Ernie Crey to complain that 'for status Indians like my mother, there were none of the social services a white family in crisis might have received. For her, there were no homemakers, no preventive family counseling services, no funded day-facilities. There was no respite at all from the day-to-day drudgery faced by an uneducated, widowed mother of six trying to survive on welfare.'[59] Whatever the promises of politicians and bureaucrats, neither white nor Native families were generously or adequately served. For all the good intentions and efforts of social workers, child welfare rarely offered much beyond minimal assistance. Even when Indian foster and kin homes on reserves were found, as they were for mixed-race Mary Lawrence and several of her siblings in British Columbia in the 1960s, cultural support aside, they too might not be able to address the need of traumatized children. Wherever they landed, such children were likely to shift from pillar to post.[60]

The second challenge to extending services for Native children was the debate among social workers regarding the standards that should be applied to families, biological as well as foster and adopting. To be sure they had preferences. Many—especially, one suspects, the least experienced, who dealt most often with Aboriginal clients—had firm and frequently naive opinions on what constituted good homes. When they entered reserves, they often rejected the foster homes used by Indian Affairs as materially and otherwise inferior to the best available elsewhere. Not surprisingly, Native families might well predict such assessments and be all the more reluctant to apply.[61] Nevertheless, even before many professional social workers considered Native clients, the majority also understood that they regularly had more children to dispose of than applicants for them. They also, however, feared the damage of institutional life.

Given the resources at their disposal, most social workers preferred to keep girls and boys with biological parents. This preference was clear in the lengthy debate in Nova Scotia between F.B. McKinnon, the regional Indian Affairs Branch supervisor and a social worker himself, and Helen E. Gruchy, the director of Nova Scotia's CAS of Colchester County, over whether to apprehend six children in an impoverished Native family. The latter defended the parents as doing their best in face of considerable adversity, but she could not keep them together. In 1961, the parents lost permanent custody and subsequently separated. Just as Gruchy feared, the two youngest children went to non-Aboriginal homes.[62] In Saskatchewan just slightly later, the director of child welfare extended to Native families the principles he professed with respect to more mainstream clients: 'The punitive aspect of the older laws has given place to the deep-rooted belief that the needs of children are best met through maintaining and respecting parents' rights.'[63] Much the same reluctance to break up households was reported in Alberta, where authorities were aware that they could 'attempt only minimal protection services on reserves, and since facilities for placement of Indian children are limited, they are apprehended only as a last resort.' Recognition of the prevalence of poverty, large families, common-law unions, and the perceived resistance of some Indian nations like the Blood to accept other Aboriginal youngsters ineligible for band benefits helped make experienced professionals all the more loathe to remove youngsters.[64]

The third problem with extending child welfare services to Native peoples was the extent of racism in Canada, something many child welfare workers appreciated. In Vancouver, the Catholic CAS had regularly encountered special problems in placing mixed-race charges. More often than not it had no choice but to house them in institutions, though this was never considered satisfactory. In many provinces, case workers desperately sought foster homes for youngsters who were 'usually quite "Indian" in appearance' but found few who would 'accept them and give them the love and security' they deserved.[65] In 1945, Saskatchewan authorities apprehended Métis youngsters they believed were 'wandering uncared for in the isolated wooded country of Green Lake' in the northern part of the province. A new shelter in the area eventually housed more than forty-five inmates, but staff turnover, problems with co-ed housing, and high costs led to the 1951 decision to close. As the consultant hired to assess the resulting dilemma reflected, 'the biggest obstacle encountered was the reluctance of communities and individuals to accept metis children. We encourage people to think about these children as children, and not as classes or colours, and helped to see that their wants and needs were the same as those of children the world over.' Only 'where it was possible to get this interpretation across' were 'the great majority of people able to accept the metis child.'[66] A similar impasse occurred in northwestern Ontario in the same years, and, in 1955, provincial welfare workers in the Kootenay region in southeastern British Columbia cited mainstream unwillingness to foster Aboriginal youngsters as one reason for their reluctance to extend services.[67] In particular, social workers everywhere regularly observed that 'negative attitudes toward the Indian appear to exist strongest in the communities of closest proximity to the reservations.'[68] Recurring placement problems led authorities to send Métis youngsters to other jurisdictions, including the United States, where prejudice was counted less corrosive. The Canadian alternative for these children was likely to be institutionalization 'for many, many years'.[69]

For all the many failures and shortcomings, which are very easy to document, the shift in thinking about Aboriginal people from the 1940s to the 1960s was nonetheless significant. That somewhat better day was best captured by the conclusions of the monumental *Survey of the Contemporary Indians of Canada: A Report on Economic, Political, Educational Needs and Policies* written by anthropologist Harry Hawthorn, political scientist Alan Cairns, and other social scientists. Indians were no longer mere subjects of the Crown but Canadians. Their special dilemma was pithily summed up in the influential phrase 'citizens minus'. As the report suggested, the solution lay in bringing Aboriginal peoples into full rather than incomplete fellowship with other Canadians. A classic liberal document, it espoused consultation and common services.

Alan Cairns, who many years later in the context of growing Native protest would publicly worry about 'citizens plus', wrote the social welfare section. He was scathing about the Indian Affairs Branch: 'An analysis of Branch welfare policy in the immediate post-war years reveals comparisons with the Elizabethan Poor Laws. The insistence on kinship obligations, payment in kind, and service from the able-bodied reflected a continuing adherence to assumptions which, under the impact of pressures from the social work profession, were rapidly disappearing in the White community.'[70] He applauded provincial child welfare services for attempting to ensure at least 'minimum availability'. While 'neglected children of school age are still sent to residential schools owing to the absence of proper child care services in the provinces,' the arrival of provincial services on many reserves represented 'one of the most significant achievements in the elimination of discriminatory treatment between Indians and non-Indians in the field of welfare.' Cairns credited this transformation partly to politicians' sensitivity to suffering, but hailed the attitude of social workers as more significant: 'The humanitarian ethic and professional values of social workers are positive factors facilitating the extension of child welfare services when recalcitrant problems of staff and finances can be overcome.'[71]

Cairns also acknowledged Native resistance to white initiatives and discovered 'antagonism when Indians are adopted by non-Indians.' He recommended 'cautious and patient effort' to address long-standing suspicions. He counselled social workers to develop Aboriginal foster homes and to listen to Aboriginal identification of issues. He nevertheless concluded that problems were rarely unique:

> There are never enough foster or adoption homes; persons with child welfare problems seldom present them directly to the agency; each ethnic group has its own kinship system; and finally, social workers have never had an easy job in establishing unguarded relationships with other groups and classes. We conclude therefore that there is no uniquely Indian aspect to the problem of Indian–social worker relationships which constitute a major barrier to services. The habituation of the Indian community to child welfare services with the passing of time, and the accumulation of experience by sensitive social workers will undoubtedly reduce the apprehensions which are products of uncertain initial encounters. The appointment of Indians to Boards of Directors of the [Children's Aid] Societies, and consultation with the chief and council would undoubtedly contribute to improved relations between the Societies and Indian communities.[72]

Unlike some critics of existing relations, Cairns also favoured retaining 'special status' while at the same time offering Natives the same services as other citizens.

The political scientist's conclusions were in keeping with federal and provincial legislative tendencies of these years. In the early 1960s, the Canadian Bill of Rights and British Columbia's more innocuously titled Public Accommodation Practices Act typified heightened determination to end racial and other forms of discrimination and to bring disadvantaged groups into fuller citizenship.[73] The change was summed up in *Adoption and the Indian Child*, a pamphlet circulated by Indian and Northern Affairs Canada in cooperation with the Adoption Desk of Health and Welfare Canada and the provincial and territorial departments of social welfare in the early 1970s:

> The Indian people faced the second half of this century feeling they were strangers in their land, they were regarded as second class citizens, and that they were discriminated against in their efforts to live a normal life and earn a decent living in the general Canadian society. . . . They may or may not choose the Indian way. They may decide not to accept all Canadian values. They almost certainly will adopt values which have a basis in Indian culture. They will walk with more pride and more confidence. They will continue to meet discrimination, but will challenge it as unworthy. They will become

equal partners in this land, the land which their proud ancestors agreed—by binding treaty—to share with the newcomers.[74]

Such well-intended statements were a considerable improvement upon the mean-spirited racist narratives that previously dominated public discourse. Unfortunately, in Canada, much like in Australia and New Zealand in the same years, 'equality rhetoric' ironically 'became a significant factor contributing to the overrepresentation of indigenous children in the child welfare system.'[75] Families that were rarely judged comparable to middle-class households might well forfeit youngsters.

The Liberal Turn to Fostering and Adoption

In the 1960s and 1970s, authorities increasingly prided themselves on policies 'of non-differentiation between Indian and non-Indian and of treating all equally.'[76] As child welfare workers encountered more and more Aboriginal children in the course of increased apprehension—what has been dubbed the 'sixties scoop'—many continued to question detentions, just as they did with other families. Alberta's 1965 *Report* of the Committee on Adoption heard from 'certain senior welfare workers in the Department [of Welfare]' who 'expressed the view that perhaps the Department had been too hasty both in accepting surrenders from Métis mothers and in seeking to apprehend Métis children.' They concluded that, 'as a rule, the incidence of serious neglect of children among Métis is not any more pronounced than among the general population.'[77] Some conclusions also supported long-standing preferences for matching, which, not so incidentally, albeit ironically, often corresponded to racist preferences. Public records made regular references to efforts to place Natives with Natives. When British Columbia's superintendent of child welfare placed four children with Indian parents in 1961 and hoped 'that more and more Indian families will open their homes to accept a child through adoption,' the province's Advisory Committee on Indian Affairs commented favourably.[78] In the 1960s, Alberta badly wanted Métis homes and was 'not averse to providing subsidies.'[70] Between 1964 and 1968, Ontario's Kenora CAS flew some eighty wards to remote northwest Native homes in an effort to better match their clients.[80] Such efforts often responded to Native initiatives, such as a resolution from the Saddle Lake Band in Alberta that asked that 'children be placed with Indian families in other communities, other than "white" homes' because 'this will enable these children to retain their culture and heritage' and that 'the Chief and Council of the Tribe concerned be consulted before these apprehensions are made.'[81] In Ontario, initiatives such as the 1977 creation of a CAS office in Ohsweken in Six Nations were similarly designed to improve communication.[82] A year later, as part of a federal initiative, the CAS of Fort Frances in the province's northwest corner hired Moses Tom from the Big Grassy nation, himself the grieving and conscience-stricken father of four apprehended children, to try to keep youngsters with their families. His commitment to this cause eventually led to his reputation as the 'father of repatriation'.[83]

Table 6.1   Adoptions of Indian children (includes all provinces and the
Northwest Territories), 1968–80

Year	By Indian people	By Non-Indian people★	Total
1968	55 (25.8%)	158	213
1969	79 (27.2%)	212	291
1970	37 (16.2%)	192	229
1971	45 (16.1%)	235	280
1972	48 (15.1%)	269	317
1973	100 (23.4%)	328	428
1974	104 (28.5%)	261	365
1975	99 (28.6%)	247	346
1976	114 (26.6%)	381	428
1977	127 (24.8%)	385	512
1978	111 (23.9%)	354	465
1979	156 (26.5%)	433	589
1980	131 (23.2%)	435	566

★ Includes non-status Aboriginal adopters.

SOURCE: Department of Indian Affairs and Northern Development, Headquarters in Child Care Task Force, *A Report on B.C. Indian Child Care* (Program Evaluation Branch, Indian Affairs and Northern Development, Appendix IV (May 1982), 1.

Natives sometimes applied to authorities for youngsters. Although the number is difficult to know precisely, as the category 'non-Indian' included non-status Aboriginal adopters, it regularly failed to meet high hopes, as Table 6.1 suggests. Unfortunately, it is impossible to evaluate the relative merits of different placements.

When they could not match Aboriginal youngsters with adults, some social workers endeavoured to link charges with previous histories. Such was the case with Suzanne, who at age two had been placed by an Ontario CAS with middle-class white adopters. When she had difficulty in adolescence, the agency set up a 'visit to an Indian reservation and discussion with some of its admirable residents' and provided literature to study the history of the Ojibwa tribes, all of which was intended to provide 'an opportunity to understand some of the strengths of her background.'[84]

Child welfare authorities slowly moved to cooperate with Native communities. British Columbia's Advisory Committee on Indian Affairs supplied numerous reports on collaboration in the 1950s and 1960s. In Canada's centennial year, it celebrated bands who contributed 'energy, planning and funds, in establishing small-group receiving homes.' On northern Vancouver Island, collaboration included 'a management group made up of all segments of the community but initiated by the Indian people.' The same folks 'established a day-care centre which is aimed at eliminating the cultural and cognitive deficit that seems apparent in many of the individual children progressing into the general school system.'[85] A year later, the Cowichan band was applauded for establishing a receiving home that offered 'temporary and emergency care to Indian and non-Indian children.'[86] In keeping with such spirit, child welfare authorities three years later worried about the 40 per cent of children in care who were Native—'future citizens' who, for want of proper placements, 'stand in jeopardy of losing not only their right to a rich and noble cultural heritage but also their rights to their own identity and sense of purpose.'[87]

Recurring recognition of the value of cooperation and Native heritage surfaced along side the insistence that all human beings shared the same needs and that good parenting did not require matching. David Fanshel's *Far from the Reservation*, with its optimistic assessment of the Indian Adoption Project (IAP) run from 1958 to 1968 by the US Bureau of Indian Affairs and the Child Welfare League of America, embodied liberal hopes. While IAP advocates suggested that the first objective was to offer 'the opportunity for a good life within their own family, or at least a family of their own tribal heritage,' 'transracial adoption' soon emerged as the mainstay of the program.[88] Although babies of African ancestry remained largely unwanted by whites, Indian children, especially in areas remote from large concentrations of Native Americans, were often 'regarded with unabashed admiration as truly the "first Americans" or the only "real" American.'[89] Although Fanshel did not interview birth mothers or children, and nowhere indicated this might be a problem, he remained cautiously optimistic. He did not appear to worry overmuch about the 42 per cent of birth mothers who were identified as having serious drinking problems or the 45 per cent described in 'terms which indicated that they suffered from quite severe personality disorders.'[90] In the days before fetal alcohol syndrome disorders (FASD) had been clinically defined and regularly, though sometimes inappropriately, applied to Native youngsters,[91] he provided an 'interim report' that concluded that adoptions would result in positive experiences for the new parents and secure placements for girls and boys.[92] He also issued a warning: 'It may be that Indian leaders would rather see their children share the fate of their fellow Indians than lose them in the white world. It is for the Indian people to decide.'[93] In fact, mounting criticism by Native Americans helped lead to the US Indian Child Welfare Act in 1978, prohibiting adoption of Native children by whites. In 2001, the Child Welfare League officially apologized for the IAP.

The immediate successor to the IAP was the Adoption Resource Exchange of North America (ARENA), in which Canadians and Americans collaborated in placing Aboriginal children in white homes. In Canada, Saskatchewan was in the forefront of such initiatives with its AIM—Adopt Indian Métis—program beginning in 1967. By the mid-1960s, provincial child welfare authorities, increasingly worried about unmet Aboriginal needs, frequently concluded that 'a concentrated educational program must be developed in order that the community no longer turns its back on the Métis and Indian child. The 32.3 per cent of children in care who are of Métis or Indian extraction have proven they are no different from the other 67.7 per cent, except for the colour of their skin. All children have one common denominator, they need secure homes. These children are being denied that basic human right.'[94] Matching, that long-standing guiding principle of adoption professionals, did not matter as much as good parents of any kind.

Affirming the 'permanency planning' emphasis of many agencies, AIM ran photographs of Native youngsters in local newspapers and canvassed widely to move wards from institutions and foster homes. Criticism was almost immediate, with one Native woman condemning the initiative as resembling nothing more than 'advertising for a pup'. Opposition to American adoptions was particularly intense. Saskatchewan was forced to modify its advertising and in 1973 provided a subsidy to establish a Native-run group home in Saskatoon.[95] The mounting numbers of Native girls and boys in care, however, meant that many continued to go to white families, who had fewer and fewer 'blue-ribbon' babies from whom to choose. As Alberta's report on adoption observed in 1965, prospects for adopting infants other than Indian were effectively nil.[96]

AIM was far from alone. The Open Door Society (ODS), created in Montreal in 1959, and its imitators across the country committed themselves to crossing racial boundaries of every sort. Their shared credo held that children should not be barred from family life and love because of outmoded, and presumably racist, preferences for racial matching. Shortly after its Quebec founding, the ODS opened shop in British Columbia's Adoption Placements Section as a direct effort to deal with the backlog of Native wards, estimated at some 39 per cent of children in care.[97] The United States remained a favoured destination. In 1971, twenty-five of forty-three children of Native ancestry listed by ARENA were Canadian, and British Columbia's adoption authorities maintained a 'longstanding working relationship with the State of Washington' in the same years.[98] Saskatchewan-born Cree folk singer Buffy Sainte-Marie ended up in the United States because of similar connections. Such transfers continued to draw fierce fire. When Alberta sponsored television commercials featuring twenty-five wards, several of whom were First Nations, it attracted familiar criticism from the president of the province's Métis Association, who asked, 'Would you want to see your child advertised on television like a used car which is up for sale?'[99]

Despite protests, ads remained a commonplace strategy of child welfare authorities facing large caseloads of Native children, who were increasingly designated, in the parlance of the late twentieth century, 'special needs'. In 1964, 'Today's Child' in the *Toronto Telegram* typically embraced the cause of interracial adoption. In efforts to counter older narratives that judged the First Nations too alien to be incorporated into the future, Helen Allen, like many other adoption champions, painted positive portraits, arguing that 'most Indian children' are 'friendly, amiable youngsters, who get on well with adults and other children.'[100] Or that they were 'gentle, pleasant, cooperative', and 'easily [made] friends' or that they showed 'the typical Indian child's gentle disposition.'[101] The intelligence of Native youngsters was readily singled out to tempt prospective parents who hoped for academic ability in their offspring.

Allen advertised only those youngsters who had been circulating in the welfare system without offers. The first week, in 10 June 1964, brought Leslie, an 'appealing little boy', to the attention of readers. He was quickly followed by twenty-one-month-old Anne, 'a bright, brown-eyed little girl of Indian background' and the 'petite' and 'shy' 'Joanne who 'loves to be cuddled'.[102] By November 1964, optimism was sufficient to see potential adopters asked to 'happily accept' the 'Indian heritage' of the 'attractive 18-month-old' Bruce who, like all good boys, loved 'rough and tumble games'.[103] By February 1965, new parents were expected to foster the pride of Phyllis, 'a lovely baby', in her Indian heritage.[104] A few months later, 'Today's Child' demanded for Terry—'a lovable little boy with an appealing personality . . . ahead of his age mentally,' who understood 'English and French, and speaks both well for such a young fellow'—'Roman Catholic parents who will make him proud of his Indian heritage, and will provide stimulation for his above-average intelligence.'[105]

Such positive introductions were challenged elsewhere. One-year-old Anthony was presented as both Indian and French but, revealing of fears, was described as without 'Indian characteristics'.[106] Eighteen-month-old Alex had a 'North American Indian background', but readers were reassured that he was 'often mistaken for southern European'.[107] Such qualifications suggest on-going reservations. A year into her crusade, Helen Allen claimed that many of 'these descendants of Canada's first citizens have been adopted, all by white couples.' At the same time, she highlighted a request from an Indian woman for one of the *Tely*'s children and suggested that 'in the far north . . . Indian men and women [were] standing in a line to ask if a child might be available to them.' Yet she regularly profiled Native children in ways that downplayed histories that might compromise reception by white readers.[108] Even then, she frequently had to re-advertise. Her column nevertheless signalled a sea-change in attitude. The desires of 'one couple seeking to adopt Leslie, the little Indian boy,' and their claim that 'the only thing we could possibly be more interested in is twin Indian boys,' had never been voiced in a public forum.[109] For all their naïveté, such hopes communicated views on race that contradicted the worst of the past.

Although white adopters never took more than a minority of Native children offered, mainstream parents, from the 1950s on, nevertheless supplied a constant stream of human interest stories for the Canadian press, usually serving as proof positive of the good intentions of both individuals and the country itself. Public evidence suggests that such adopters often had strong feelings as they crossed the colour line. Many were not easily deterred. One doctor testifying before Alberta's hearings on adoption in 1965 conveyed the common desire to rescue, as well as middle-class authority:

> When my husband & I applied for the first child, this is two years ago, we didn't specify Métis. We asked for a child who would be hard to place, either because of mixed race or because of a physical handicap, and it was the department's decision to give us a Métis child. . . . This is rather unfair, perhaps, to say but I had learned how to bully the department by the time I came

> to my second adoption and I waited a suitable length of time in each stage
> and then phoned and jogged their memory and this appears what you have
> to do if you want to get going. We put our application in, our form in on the
> 11th of December and we got the child. . . . He was born the 17th of
> December and we got him six weeks to the day so it was roughly seven
> weeks.[110]

Later that day, she elaborated her position as she rejected the arguments in favour
of matching by the representative of the Catholic CAS who saw traces of 'white
conceit'. Her reply was simple: 'The eventual idea is to assimilate them, isn't it, so
it is all one society. . . . Unfortunately, I think it is true to say, that the average Métis
family in Alberta today is not really in a position to assimilate them. I agree with
you this would be much better but this is really not a fact.'[111]

White adoptions were presumed to supply 'good news' stories. In January 1965,
the *Edmonton Journal* profiled the case of a Yellowknife couple who adopted first
'a little girl of negro and Eskimo descent' and then an Indian infant son.[112] Some
two weeks later, it celebrated a Canadian Press story about an 'Eskimo' toddler
given as a daughter to a federal civil servant in northern Quebec.[113] At much the
same time, in Prince Rupert, British Columbia, John Cashore, a United Church
minister and his schoolteacher wife, adopted the newborn daughter of a white
teenager and Native adult.[114] In 1973, the *Star Weekly* reported on Sackville, New
Brunswick professionals who had adopted a Mi'kmaq daughter through the
province's Aid-a-Child program.[115] In 2000, a Bloc Québécois member of
Parliament recalled with pride before the House of Commons his adoption of a
Native son some eighteen years earlier.[116] 'Like our very own', such youngsters
went on to a range of good and bad outcomes.

As with all adoption statistics, exact figures on placements of any sort are impossible to know. Jurisdictions published information irregularly, often failed to com-
pile it at all, used different criteria to determine racial status, did not know the
background of youngsters, or never received relevant information from front-line
agencies. As the outstanding study by Patrick Johnston, *Native Child and the Child
Welfare System,* rightly concluded, gathering and comparing meaningful statistics
is at best an uncertain enterprise. Tables 6.2 to 6.7, however, offer a broad sense of
the situation in the last half of the twentieth century.

The statistics provided in these tables cannot adequately convey the range of
problems facing children and families. Even when liberal hopes were rising, signs
of trouble were apparent. One adoptive father, himself a former inmate of an
orphans' home, gave heartfelt evidence before Alberta's committee investigating
adoption in 1965:

> We have had many complaints from our neighbors for adopting a Métis
> child. . . . She is still not old enough to realize and we are a little bit worried,
> when she gets old enough, when she is a few years older, that she will realize
> that maybe being an Indian wasn't the greatest thing that ever happened to
> her, or being part Indian and we are doing our best to make her feel proud

Table 6.2   Adoptions of Indian children by province* and territory, by characterization of the adoptive parents, 1971–7

	BC	Alta.	Sask.	Man.	Ont.	Que.	NS	NB	PEI	NWT	Yukon	Total
1971												
Indian adopters (IA)	14	5	3	3	12	2	–	–	–	5	1	45
Non-Indian adopters (NIA)	83	5	49	29	62	–	–	–	–	2	5	235
Total	97	10	52	32	74	2	–	–	–	7	6	280
1972												
IA	18	6	6	3	9	1	1	–	–	4	–	48
NIA	91	8	39	57	51	2	–	1	–	8	12	269
Total	109	14	45	60	60	3	1	1	–	12	12	317
1973												
IA	16	5	10	15	16	3	1	–	–	34	–	100
NIA	69	5	59	65	100	2	–	–	–	21	7	328
Total	85	10	69	80	116	5	1	–	–	55	7	428
1974												
IA	11	9	12	21	15	9	2	2	–	23	–	104
NIA	11	13	73	76	44	2	–	–	–	29	13	261
Total	22	22	85	97	59	11	2	2	–	52	13	365

Table 6.2   *(Continued)*

	BC	Alta.	Sask.	Man.	Ont.	Que.	NS	NB	PEI	NWT	Yukon	Total
1975												
IA	10	16	6	11	29	11	2	–	–	13	–	99
NIA	16	11	82	82	38	–	–	1	–	13	5	247
Total	26	27	88	93	67	11	2	1	–	26	5	346
1976												
IA	25	8	4	17	29	5	4	1	–	21	–	114
NIA	116	19	72	101	38	–	1	1	–	20	13	381
Total	141	27	76	118	67	5	5	2	–	41	13	495
1977												
IA	24	11	7	18	35	14	4	2	–	12	–	127
NIA	113	14	71	105	48	3	–	–	–	17	14	385
Total	137	25	78	123	83	17	4	2	–	29	14	512

* Newfoundland is not included in the original table, but no explanation is given.

SOURCE: Margaret Ward, *The Adoption of Native Children* (Cobalt, ON: Highway Book Shop, 1984), 39, table 1. Statistics were supplied by the Registrar, Department of Indian and Northern Affairs.

Table 6.3   Native children placed for adoption as a percentage of all children placed for adoption in British Columbia, 1976–9

Year	Total children placed for adoption	Total Native children placed for adoption	Native children as % of all children placed for adoption
1976–7	865	247	28.6
1977–8	654	169	25.8
1978–9	720	189	26.3

SOURCE: Charlene Mignacco, 'Towards Native Control of Child Welfare: The Nuu-Chah-Nulth Tribal Council "A Case in Point"' (MSW thesis, University of British Columbia, 1984), 9, table 3.

Table 6.4   Manitoba children placed out of province, 1981

	Number placed	% of total
Registered Indians	52	48
Indian (other)	4	4
Metis	37	34
Non-Native	15	14
Totals	108	100

SOURCE: Lawrence J. Barkwell, Lyle N. Longclaws, and David N. Chartrand, 'Status of Métis Children within the Child Welfare System', *Canadian Journal of Native Studies* 9, no.1 (1989): 44, table 3.

Table 6.5   Status Indian children in care as a percentage of all children in care of New Brunswick's Department of Social Services, 1978–81

Year	Status Indian children in care	All children in care	Status Indian children in care as % of all children in care
1978–9	80	2,270	3.5
1979–80	75	2,059	3.6
1980–1	81	2,028	3.9

SOURCE: Patrick Johnston, *Native Children and the Child Welfare System* (Ottawa: Canadian Council on Social Development, 1983), 48, table 22.

of her heritage but, the fact remains, if these people are going to make fun of her, or look down on her for this, it is not right and we find that she is not any different than any other white girl or any other child, she acts exactly the

Table 6.6   Status Indian children in care as a percentage of all children in care of Yukon's Department of Health and Human Resources, 1976–81

Year	Status Indian children in care	All children in care	Status Indian children in care as % of all children in care
1976–7	119	194	61.3
1977–8	103	189	54.5
1978–9	109	194	56.2
1979–80	104	158	65.8
1980–1	82	134	61.2

SOURCE: Patrick Johnston, *Native Children and the Child Welfare System* (Ottawa: Canadian Council on Social Development, 1983), 53, table 29.

Table 6.7   Status Indian children in care in Canada as a percentage of all status Indian children, 1979–80

Province/territory	Status Indian children in care as % of all status children 0–19 years
Atlantic	3.8
Quebec	4.0
Ontario	2.2
Manitoba	4.3
Saskatchewan	4.8
Alberta	7.3
British Columbia	5.9
Yukon Territory	7.7
Northwest Territories	1.8
Canada	4.6

SOURCE: Patrick Johnston, *Native Children and the Child Welfare System* (Ottawa: Canadian Council on Social Development, 1983), 57, table 31.

same. . . . I think there is a very large segment of the population who do look down on these people as second class citizens. . . . Now, I was a patient in a hospital where there was a nurse and she was an Indian and I do not think I ever had a nurse who was better nurse than her. . . . She did twice as much work as any other nurse on the floor and everybody liked her, all the patients thought the world of her. . . . This girl was raised off the reservation, or so called. She was adopted and raised in a private home by adoptive parents.[117]

This speaker was far from alone in his concern. Social workers shared his front seat in assessing results. Many, like Prince George social worker, Bridget Moran, understood the ultimate dilemma:

> Our aim, we were told, was to keep children with their natural parents, and to remove them from their homes only when their mental or physical well-being was threatened. . . . In practice we had no resources that might conceivably have helped to keep families together, and children in their natural homes. We had no mental health facilities, no family support workers, no treatment centres of any kind. . . . The result was that when we discovered a child at risk in his own home, we had no recourse but to move him into a foster home. This often meant putting children in any home that would take them, whether or not that home had been approved or even investigated. . . . It was not always doom and gloom in the welfare office. We rescued many children from impossible home situations, facilitated the return of many more children to their natural parents, and placed lovely babies with happy adopting parents.[118]

By the early 1970s, the BC ministry responsible for child welfare, liberated by the election of a NDP government more sympathetic to social programs, also acknowledged unmet challenges:

> Nowhere is the need for prevention more obvious than among our Indian people. Statistics show that Indian children, once removed from their family and cultural roots, remain in care for longer periods and are frequently lost to their tribe. The past year has been one in which there have been frequent meetings and discussions with the Indian people to plan with them toward the provision of a better child welfare and family service on the reserve. . . . Protective services to children must focus on the rehabilitation of the family and the eventual restoration of the child to his natural parents.[119]

As another outspoken child welfare veteran, Joyce Timpson, has pointed out, field workers were going public with their worries long before many others showed interest. Front-line experts used the *Journal of the Ontario Association of Children's Aid Societies* to express developing reservations. Many contributors captured 'the dilemma of CASs caught between recognition of cultural differences and the need to provide protection. It reflected sensitivity to cultural differences. This literature was never referenced by the critics of CAS workers.'[120]

Bridget Moran resigned her position over lack of support from BC politicians: the profession was generally well-known for chewing up members who could not accept the terms of employment or the burnout that commitment entailed. This appeared especially true of those with significant Aboriginal caseloads. Social workers, whom one observer rightly labelled Canada's 'dirty workers',[121] nevertheless continued to endure the brunt of criticism from Aboriginal and non-Aboriginal critics for the deeper failure to deal fairly with the First Nations.

Race, Rights, and Reaction, 1970s–1990s

In the last decades of the twentieth century, First Nations people, already addressing the consequences of a century and more of residential schools, were increasingly angry and outspoken about provincial child welfare regimes. Even supposed adoption successes, such as folk singer Buffy Sainte-Marie, went public to question whether the 'adoption of native children into non-native families is a good thing.'[122] They spoke out eloquently before public investigations,[123] cooperated with progressive policy-makers, and forged their own instruments for addressing the distress of children in their midst. Canadians in general found new opportunities to learn about the downside of Native–white adoptions. Prize-winning fiction, such as Mary-Ellen L. Collura's *Winners* (1985), with its story of Jordy Threebears who ultimately survived some dozen foster homes in the course of negotiating the experiment with transracial placements, and Richard Wagamese's *Keeper'n Me* (1994), which featured former foster child Garnet Raven coming to terms with return to his Ojibwa home, joined older stories like *Anne of Green Gables* to provide a very different perspective on the transfer of youngsters. Raven signalled the change when he charged white authorities with failing to appreciate the

> extended family concept. When you're born you got a whole built-in family consisting of everyone around. So it was natural in my parents' eyes to leave us with the old lady while they were out trying to make a living. But the Ontario Children's Aid Society had a different set of eyes. . . . We wound up in a group home on a farm outside of Kenora. . . . Put in another home . . . it looked like the land just swallowed me up. . . . I disappeared completely from the Indian world. Everywhere they moved me I was the only Indian and no one ever took the time to tell me who I was, where I came from or even what the hell was going on. . . . With no one pitching in any information I just figured I was a brown white guy. . . . The most popular way of learning about Indians was television . . . then there was books. Indians never got mentioned in any of the schoolbooks except for being the guides for the brave explorers busy discovering the country . . . heathen devils . . . or simple savages. . . . I was embarrassed about being an Indian.[124]

One Aboriginal woman from Atlantic Canada summed up Native feelings equally viscerally in a poem 'The Honour Song of the Micmac':

> A child of Abduction
> I am a child of many colors,
> I am a child of different cultures.
> I am a child of abduction.
> I am not yours to keep.

You cannot ease the pain of the families torn apart.
You cannot wipe the tears or
Mend their broken hearts.
You cannot call me your own for
I am not yours to keep.

I am a child of your lies.
I am a child of your deceit.
I am a child of abduction.
I am not yours to keep.[125]

In the last decades of the twentieth century, such accusations haunted all discussions of Native child welfare.

In 1974, in response to a request from the province's Department of Human Resources, the Union of BC Indian Chiefs (UBCIC) presented a brief on adoption and welfare services. Noting that 39 per cent of all children in care in 1965 had Indian ancestry and that the situation might well worsen given the high proportion of children in the Native population, the authors acknowledged that 'during the years 1963–1969 there is considerable information to indicate the Adoption Placement Section has also made a number of attempts to encourage and facilitate the development of an increased number of Indian adoptive homes of both status and non-status origination.' Local implementation nevertheless remained a major problem. The UBCIC judged knowledge of Native customs and languages and culturally sensitive procedures to be in short supply when social workers set out to work with bands. A good part of any solution had to lie with supporting local expertise and initiative. As the brief insisted, 'leadership must be allowed to emerge from the Indian population. We are in a new era and must adjust to the changing society accordingly.' The authors recommended the appointment of two persons, preferably Native, responsible to the UBCIC to deal with fosterlings.[126] A year later, the ministry's annual report, newly subtitled 'Services for People', hailed the previous year for its cooperation with the UBCIC and the appointment of BC's Family and Children's Law Commission, chaired by Provincial Chief Justice Thomas Berger, as a 'milestone of hope for children'.[127] The election of an NDP government headed by social worker Dave Barrett and his appointment of social worker Norm Levi as minister of Human Resources set the stage 'for a significant revamping of social programs and social service delivery.'[128]

Matters were especially urgent because, in response to Aboriginal parents contesting a placement, a key case, first known as *Birth Registration No. 67-09-02227* and then as *Natural Parents v. Superintendent of Child Welfare,* was winding its way through the courts. In 1973, the BC Supreme Court ruled that the Adoption Act did not apply to Natives as it compromised Indian status. Up to this time, adopting parents were simply advised of a child's Indian status and told to inquire further of the federal Department of Indian Affairs (DIA). When the adoption was formally completed, the provincial superintendent of child welfare notified DIA, which was supposed to record the child's original band and the name of new parents. This practice assumed that status remained unaffected. The 1973 decision, which upheld the parents who opposed adoption by white applicants, threatened such placements of status youngsters. In response, the superintendent applied to the provincial Court of Appeal, which reversed the decision. This ruling was appealed to the Supreme Court of Canada. In summer of 1974, white adopters of Native children had reason to fear that permanent placement might not be possible, and the ministry itself strengthened efforts to locate Aboriginal homes.[129]

In the last decades of the twentieth century, *Natural Parents v. Superintendent of Child Welfare* was one of many to debate the 'best interests' of Native children. In the 1980s, judicial decisions had to address this issue within the context of Aboriginal rights as framed within the Canadian Charter of Rights and Freedoms. Were youngsters' interests best protected by recognition of Native traditions and biological parents or by consignment to non-Aboriginal adopters who were almost always reckoned materially and psychologically stronger? In the 1960s and 1970s, as we have seen, customary or traditional adoption was recognized by courts and increasingly enshrined in legislation, a clear victory for Aboriginal rights-seekers who wished the dominant legal regime to entrench 'custom'. On the other hand, traditional practice, as sometimes interpreted for the courts by Native leadership, might not benefit modern Native women whose lives resonate in response to needs that their ancestors could not have imagined. As Jo-Anne Fiske has well noted, 'in the struggle for decolonization, a victory for one group may imply defeat for another.'[130] Women may not be empowered when custom that has often made them the primary caregivers is reified in modern legal codes.

Native women's dilemma is all the more acute when racist stereotypes in the dominant society regularly deny their capacity as good mothers. The important intervention in the best-interests debate by feminist legal scholar Marlee Kline emphasized the cultural construction of good parenting, especially good mothering, as overwhelmingly favouring mainstream women.[131] When such prejudice combined with legitimate concerns about the safety and well-being of girls and boys, the result might well be rulings like that in December 2004 by a Saskatchewan court against the government policy to refuse placements without band permission.[132] As has been often said, such decisions failed 'to give due weight to the reasons why the parents were unable to care for the child temporarily and to the long-term interests of the child being deprived of his/her heritage.'[133]

In October 1975, the Supreme Court of Canada ruled that youngsters did not lose status in adoption. This was especially important for two reasons. First, it meant that adoption did not eliminate past connections. Aboriginal children would not be entirely 'our very own' in new families. Second, the decision also allowed placements to continue. Not surprisingly, the potential for conflict was enormous. Despite efforts by provincial child welfare officials, the UBCIC, and the BC Association of Non-Status Indians to communicate, relations were troubled. Cooperation crumbled when both Native organizations, according to the Ministry of Human Resources, withdrew from all governmental-funded projects in May 1975.[134]

Initial hope for improved relations resided with the appointment in December 1973 of the Royal Commission on Family and Children's Law. Acknowledging the centrality of Aboriginal concerns to his mandate, Justice Berger consulted extensively with Native communities. The final report in 1975 discussed in detail cultural insensitivity, corrosive economic preconditions, the need for continuing consultation with bands, and re-education of social workers. It recommended recognition of custom adoption and formal consultation with and notification of bands. It discovered that some Aboriginal mothers wished to deny bands the knowledge of their children and affairs, and it supported their right to do so.[135] The election of a conservative Social Credit government in December 1975 limited the province's ability to act on Berger's recommendations. Not until 1979 was a Child Welfare Review Planning Committee set up with the cooperation of Native groups. Progress remained intermittent. The passage in 1982 of a new Family and Child Service Act required that band chiefs or managers be notified of applications for wardship, but it 'made no provision for involvement of Indian people in child welfare processes affecting their children. And much to the consternation of Indian organizations, earlier legislation providing for a panel system, including community representatives, in child neglect hearings was repealed.'[136]

Across the country and at much the same time, the Department of Indian Affairs and Northern Development (DIAND), Ontario, and that province's Aboriginal organizations were reviewing welfare agreements. The well-titled report, *A Starving Man Doesn't Argue*, underscored the unevenness and inadequacy of services to Native families. Typically, CASs with large Native populations, such as those in Northern Ontario, were not funded to address geography, caseloads, or cultural differences. Unlike municipalities, bands had no standing with the CAS or input into their decisions and no authority to deliver their own services. Too often, CASs appeared indifferent to Aboriginal concerns. The report emphasized the need to involve Natives in all aspects of planning, control, and delivery of services.[137] In the same year, another report for DIAND, while admitting some improvements at the level of administration, similarly condemned the powerlessness of bands to design programs.[138]

By the early 1980s, Native advocates were increasingly vocal, but DIAND continued to insist it had no duty to guarantee status and rights to adoptees. This position was strongly resisted by critics who pointed to the potential loss of educational, health, and other benefits. Band payments and annuities, held in trust, were to be paid only upon application. In effect, as one scholar noted, adoptees were involuntarily enfranchised. In response to federal recalcitrance, First Nations communities took action. Alberta's Yellowhead Tribal Council, with some 3,100 members in five bands, initiated searches for some seventy children who could be deprived of significant oil and gas royalties. In December 1983, the president of the Assembly of First Nations (AFN), Chief Dave Ahenakew announced plans to ask all jurisdictions to inform youngsters of their status. If necessary, the AFN would challenge confidentiality rules under the Charter of Rights and Freedoms.[139]

Such warnings helped prompt Ontario to ask Ralph Garber, the dean of social work at the University of Toronto, to investigate adoption disclosure. Pointing out that 78 per cent of status youngsters between 1969 and 1979 had been adopted by non-Natives, he argued that the Child and Family Services Act should both notify bands, allowing them the opportunity to make alternative arrangements, and find ways to ensure that urban Natives gained the same option. Like Berger before him, Garber worried about the consent of birth parents:

> The needs and rights of bands in respect of their members has to be balanced against the needs and rights of their members as individuals, independent of their association with the band. In making this assertion, I give full recognition and appreciation to the facts of Indian experience in Canada . . . [and their] harmful, unfortunate, and prejudicial treatment. . . .
>
> As individuals, birth parents (or more typically birth mothers) have recourse to the Charter to affirm their rights. On the one hand an Indian birth mother might indeed be as concerned as her band that the band is in danger of losing its future if her children were to be adopted outside of the band. She would therefore readily consent to have the band notified of her plan to relinquish the child for adoption. On the other hand she may have left the band to live elsewhere and prefer, for her own reasons, that the child not be cared for by the band. Either wish should be respected. *I recommend therefore that except where the child is a Crown ward, the birth parent's consent be required for notification to an Indian band or Native community.* . . . Since a majority of Indian children placed for adoption are in fact Crown wards, the requirement for birth parent consent should have minimal effect on Indian bands.

Ultimately, he concluded 'the individual's rights are paramount.'[140]

Many of the same issues troubled Manitoba, with its still larger proportion of Aboriginal children in care. Until 1977, that province had no Aboriginal-controlled child welfare agencies. That year, the Manitoba Indian Brotherhood and the governments of Canada and Manitoba agreed that Indian child welfare needs should have 'immediate and urgent priority' and that each reserve should have indigenous staff to address problems.[141] In 1981, the Manitoba Métis Federation successfully campaigned for a moratorium on out-of-province placements and demanded greater Aboriginal involvement in child welfare.[142] That same year saw the creation of the Dakota Ojibway Child and Family Services (DOCFS), which became Canada's first Indian child welfare agency to deliver legally mandated child and family services to members on and off reserve. The situation, however, remained far from ideal on many reserves and in the cities. Two faculty members in social work from the University of Manitoba summed up the situation at the beginning of the 1980s as nothing less than 'colonialism'.[143]

By the middle of that decade, some Native nations had clearly targeted child welfare as a central issue. British Columbia's Spallumcheen Band seized control over child welfare after a well-orchestrated march on the home of the minister of Human Resources. Four Alberta bands similarly employed child welfare bylaws to avoid provincial interference. Such initiatives directly challenged trilateral agreements among Ottawa, the provinces, and Aboriginal leaders that had committed bands to working within provincial child welfare regulations.[144]

Continuing to respond to Native pressure, Manitoba's NDP government placed a moratorium on out-of-province placements in 1982. Two years later, the province negotiated with the Winnipeg Urban Indian Coalition to help establish the Ma Mawi Wi Chi Itata Centre, which was intended to sidestep the Winnipeg CAS with its recurring apprehension of Native youngsters. Manitoba also established a committee on Aboriginal adoption, chaired by Edwin Kimelman. His exhaustive report, *No Quiet Place,* did not mince words in identifying 'cultural genocide'. Like Berger and Garber, Kimelman visited Native communities, received briefs, and listened to a wide range of speakers.

The director of permanent planning for the CAS of Western Manitoba, who had been with the agency since 1955, suggested to the Kimelman inquiry that no status Indian children had appeared in care before 1962 but that a large, albeit unknown, number of non-status youngsters had been apprehended. Little thought was originally given to placing them with new families. As she explained, 'in fact in 1962, adoption placement was not considered likely for most children over three years nor for any child where there were [*sic*] any question of physical problems or delayed development or mixed race.' Apprehension was rarely attempted because fostering and adoption were unlikely. In the early 1970s, however, policies shifted dramatically, with the large numbers of children coming into care. The director described attempts to cooperate with bands and to find Native homes, observing, 'I vividly recall a worker I supervised who used to ask families requesting placement for their children whether they couldn't suggest a relative or neighbour on the reserve and was regularly told that they wanted their children in a white foster home—that Indian parents were "bad" parents. That attitude on the part of Indian families has changed but it was a very frequent reality in the 60's.' She reiterated that, despite efforts to recruit reserve families, 'the majority we have had offered their homes for specific children, usually relatives.' When asked about kinship care, she was also ambivalent. While it often appeared to work, it sometimes resulted in multiple placements, and 'children we have known to come out of that and it has been very clearly harmful. The child doesn't know where he or she belongs.'[145]

She found a happier story elsewhere. Americans had proved eager to take a wide range of youngsters, including those with emotional and physical disabilities. She told the story of a ward, seriously abused by his mother, who had been registered with the National Adoption Desk in 1979 and appeared in a local newspaper column, 'Children Who Are Waiting,' and in the *Tely's* 'Today's Child' in 1980. All interest faltered in face of the child's significant needs. Only then was he offered to Americans, and she claimed the agency received regular reports on his well-being. She cited other such cases in the course of insisting that 'many of the American families with whom we were placing especially [in the] 1969–1975 period, had at least some Indian in their background. In fact one child who would have been placed with an American Indian family in the States was placed instead with an Ontario white family because [of] a temporary provincial policy refusing permission to place out of Canada in 1976.' She went further in defending such choices, pointing to children who refused to return to reserves.[146]

The director was also cautiously optimistic about new options. Conditions on reserves had improved. Fewer girls and boys suffered major health problems. While the closure of a residential school had produced an 'abrupt increase in children admitted to care' and instances where one grandparent was struggling to cope with twenty-seven grandchildren in a two-room house, its termination was applauded as avoiding 'the splitting of families and has given parents the experience of parenting their school aged children and provided children with parenting models.' She also believed that the 'keener awareness of Indian culture' by American adopters had inspired greater sensitivity on the part of Canadians. 'The American families were the first to say "give us written material so that we can tell the child about Sioux background or his Ojibway background". I think we learned a lot from the American adoptive families in what we can provide the children.'[147]

A representative of the Advisory Committee of the Winnipeg CAS next outlined a recurring dilemma. Native women wished to surrender babies but protested efforts to return them to the reserve. She asked for advice, but received none, at least in public, from Native witnesses.[148] Another social worker from elsewhere in the province described considerable success in cooperating with Native child welfare services. In fact, he couldn't remember placing any wards outside the province. He enthusiastically endorsed local control. He also pointed to parents who required that placements occur in distant reserves 'because they fear interference by relatives or people they know.'[149] A brief from the CAS of Central Manitoba returned to the need for permanency, arguing that Native opposition to transracial adoption was not universal. It defended white adopters:

> White families who adopt trans-racially, regardless of their residence, generally value the differences among family members and try to help each child find his own way. Global assumptions about non-native adoptive parents voiced by the opponents of trans-racial adoption, smack of racism and paranoia. . . . However, we do not believe that children need to find their identity only in their race. . . . The children now in our care are waiting for families they can claim as their own. . . . [They] do not have time to wait while policy organizations quarrel over them and community resources are—perhaps too hastily—developed for them.[150]

This agency was willingly to plan with the DOCFS but wished to make final decisions. Not surprisingly in view of such recalcitrance, this CAS damned any separate welfare system as both expensive and contrary to the Charter of Rights and Freedoms. Self-confidence, indeed, arrogance, dripped from the last line of the brief: 'We simply want to get on with the job of planning permanently and responsibly for the children in our care, without restriction.'[151]

White adopters also appeared before the Manitoba inquiry. Some defended authorities, condemning Native critics for provoking 'racial confrontation' and endorsing 'racial purity'. They insisted that cultural issues were over-rated. From this point of view, the original failure lay with Native communities that did not care for their own. Children's ultimate well-being depended on white homes.[152] One adopting couple insisted that 'refusing to allow Caucasian or other racial groups the right to adopt or foster Indian and Métis children is discrimination and against human rights.'[153] Twelve adopters associated with the Native Ministry Board of the United Church were more conciliatory. They recommended improved social work training and compulsory training in Aboriginal issues, subsidized adoptions for Native parents, greater CAS attention to local communities and to the recruitment of Native adopters who should be offered ongoing support. Finally, they accepted responsibility for educational work with their own adopted Native children.[154]

Not surprisingly, Native witnesses often provided an especially damning perspective. As the representative for the DOCFS observed:

> The agencies that care for children are looked upon as policemen, not as a helping agency. If you sit in my shoes, when people come and take and kidnap your people that is not a helping agency. . . . Our definition of family, relative, adoption, long-term foster care are very different. . . . We do not have a great concern about confidentiality, about placing children, or adopting them. . . . We all in our family in the reserve look after our children. . . . Every child care situation in the reserve is not necessarily because of a broken family, because of a social structure breakdown or anything like that. It is, many times, a positive understanding of bringing up a child. . . . Nobody ever asked us to adopt a child until the Indian organizations came into being and we at no time had applications from the reserve to adopt Indian children.
>
> It was just impossible in the eyes of Indian parents to adopt children at all, even though some did and some adopted other than Indian children.[155]

Much the same argument came from a spokesperson from The Pas Indian Band, which lacked a legal mandate as a child welfare agency but which had been operating a foster parent program with federal cooperation for some years. He asked for a complete range of services to be located on band territory.[156] The staff economist for the Manitoba Métis Federation pointed out that US Native leaders credited the continuing surrender of the province's children to American families with compromising their own campaign against transracial adoption.[157] Some Native representatives, such as a witness from the Alcohol Council of Manitoba and Children of the Great Spirit, condemned both the devastation attendant on state intrusion and the creation of welfare dependence.[158] The speaker from the Thompson Native Women's Association acknowledged the good intentions of many white adopters but recommended training more Native workers, increasing efforts to recruit Native adopters, and instituting reserve group homes.[159] A less accommodating view was evident in a member of a northern band and a victim of a residential school, who hailed Indian Affairs personnel as 'my bitter enemy'.[160]

In testimony before the Manitoba inquiry, a brother and a sister described a 'good' adoption by Americans who supported their desire to return home. They concluded, 'although we were fortunate to have a good experience in our adoptive home, we feel we have lost some of our identity as Indian persons.'[161] Unfolding at much the same time was the revelation of an adoption with a far worse outcome. Efforts, eventually successful, were afoot to repatriate Cameron Kerley, born on the Sioux Valley Reserve of Manitoba in 1964 and jailed in Kansas for the 1983 murder of a sexual predator, posing as a good father.[162] The suicide of Richard Cardinal, a Métis youth who hanged himself after a lifetime spent tossed among sometimes abusive foster homes, reaffirmed the tragic message that few could avoid.[163]

In the face of such evidence, and while not uncritical of Aboriginal organizations, *No Quiet Place* sided largely with Native critics. Kimelman denounced welfare policies as culturally insensitive and social workers as well intentioned but largely ignorant: 'The miracle is that there were not more children lost in this system run by so many well-intentioned people. The road to hell was paved with good intentions, and the child welfare system was the paving contractor.'[164] He recommended greater investment in culturally appropriate services, the education of Native social workers, more use of the extended family, commitment to reconnecting adoptees with their heritage, and placement in non-Native families only as a last resort.

No Quiet Place proved something of a wake-up call. By 1999, the province's Aboriginal Justice Inquiry was able to point to considerable progress: 'Over 45,000 Indian people on reserves, and more than 28,000 off-reserve status Indian people, are now served by Aboriginal agencies. As a result, in 1987, 840 of the 1,200 Aboriginal children in care in Manitoba, or about 70 per cent, were under the care of Aboriginal agencies. There are now more than 900 foster homes in Aboriginal communities and over 300 Aboriginal professionals who have been trained to deliver culturally appropriate child and family services.'[165] Other jurisdictions also occasioned hope. In British Columbia, two Coast Salish families successfully used the provincial court system to negotiate shared care for a two-year-old. The judge consulted with First Nations advocates, bands, and families. Eventually everyone agreed that a Council of Elders should recommend a solution under the authority of the Family Relations Act. The result gave the father custody but also offered the grandparents and the child's aunt, to whom the deceased mother had assigned custody, reasonable access. In the process, as one sympathetic Aboriginal observer noted, 'a tradition of centuries was changed so the courts have a record of the proceedings of the Elders' Council. . . . Our traditional methods are demonstrably consistent and compatible with as well as complementary to the existing legal system.'[166] Elsewhere across the country, Native families similarly experimented with combining Aboriginal traditions of child transfer and mainstream legal confirmation.[167] In 1989, British Columbia introduced a new Native adoption policy that mandated provincial social workers to work with bands. If a white placement could not be avoided, the new parents had to commit themselves to educating the children about their heritage and, 'where appropriate', allowing contact with the band. Still more indicative of new preferences was the province's delegation of complete authority in child welfare to social workers in an Indian-managed program, that of the Nuu-chah-nulth.[168]

Many bands experimented with forms of self-government that often included some responsibility for child welfare. Aboriginal-run programs were also increasingly available to off-reserve populations. Thus, as a 2000 study concluded, 'in a relatively short period of time, the changes in child welfare administrative and program delivery procedures have had some positive impact on band, community, and family relations. In particular, participation by and consultation with First Nations peoples have provided avenues for raising and responding to critical issues in a manner sensitive to local needs.'[169] For all such positive signs, many investigations after the Berger, Garber, and Kimelman reports documented the painfully slow response of state welfare systems. In many cases, as Kimelman had noted, patterns of institutionalization continued to lead straight from the welfare to the criminal justice system. Continuing barriers to progress were well summed up by Charlene Mignacco in her study of the Nuu-chah-nulth Tribal Council:

> Through my personal experience as a band social worker, I found that the lack of community resources on all levels was a major contributing factor to the problems facing Native families and children. One might argue that resources such as day care centres, counseling services, crisis homes and group homes are culturally inappropriate for Native reserves because in fact they are white middle class institutions. This is true to some extent, but it must be appreciated that the traditional patterns of child welfare management are less intact today because of social disintegration. While it is essential to try to strengthen the traditional patterns, there is also a need for extra services to help families cope with the stresses of modern life. It is also essential to note that services and resources that are developed will be staffed by Native people according to their values and norms. . . . It is therefore more reasonable to try and salvage what worked in the past and integrate it with what works in other areas of child welfare.

While she acknowledged some improved services, such as the federal government's Guardian Financial Assistance Program, recurring emphasis on short-term solutions, the lack of Native involvement in planning, and provincial-federal disputes handicapped initiatives. Much more was needed to support communities and agencies such as the Gitksan-Carrier and the DOFCS in their blending of modern child welfare strategies with 'traditional cultural ways'.[170]

Nor were white-ruled governments and bureaucracies the sole cause of failures. A 1991 report commissioned by British Columbia's United Native Nations pointed out that 'the grantsmanship practices within the Native Indian community have their own regrettable aspects, as various groups contend for funds, engage in take-over attempts, and partake in flagrant nepotistic practices.'[171] Natives were not always well served by the 'domination of local elites'. Patrick Johnston noted in his comprehensive study that child welfare often received attention only when Native women forced it on the agenda of the largely male Aboriginal leadership. Like their non-indigenous counterparts in legislatures, Indian leaders sometimes appeared more addicted to talk than action.[172] As one critic observed, 'allegations that political considerations outweighed concern about child welfare . . . surrounded reports in 1987 of child abuse result from improper placement of children by the Awasis

Agency into homes on reserves in Northern Manitoba.'[173] At the very least, it sometimes seemed that many Aboriginal communities and agencies were not well equipped to take over duties that began to come their way in the 1980s.[174] This has made long-standing problems harder to tackle, and Native children continue to die tragically, even when bands select kin as foster parents.[175] Alcohol and other drug addictions as well as endemic violence in many Aboriginal communities constitute further threats to optimal child development.[176]

Reports in the 1990s summed up many continuing dilemmas. The Aboriginal Committee of British Columbia's Community Panel on Family and Children's Services Legislation Review produced *Liberating Our Children, Liberating Our Nations* in 1992. Affirming the unfavourable comparison between pre- and post-contact Native societies, it supported the maintenance of a moratorium on white adoptions of Native children.[177] The panel itself agreed that First Nations people should determine policy, including who was properly to be counted Aboriginal. In response to the commonplace complaint from white critics that Aboriginal child welfare policies were themselves racist in too often valuing Native over other heritages, it concluded:

> No one in the aboriginal community who spoke to the Review Panel advocated viewing a child's non-aboriginal heritage as less important than aboriginal heritage.
>
> However, protecting English or French, Irish or Italian heritage is not the issue. While all of these cultures deserve to be preserved and respected, they are not being subjected to social and economic genocide within their homelands. It is the aboriginal languages, institutions, culture and populations of Canada that are threatened by external laws, policies and prejudices. Opening the community to receive the children of different nations or those with mixed blood is perhaps just another example of the aboriginal way of life.[178]

In fact, race-based claims to priority were all the more complicated at the end of the twentieth century. Youngsters increasingly reflected the diverse origins of Canadians as a whole. Such was the case with one small boy, born of a status mother from Manitoba, who had been adopted by white Americans, and a Black American father. In response to claims by both his maternal birth grandfather and adoptive grandparents, the judge of the BC Supreme Court concluded that the child's African ancestry was also important and 'equally deserving of preservation and nurturing'.[179]

The 1990s also produced two important federal investigations that spoke directly to ongoing debates. The Royal Commission on New Reproductive Technologies concluded that adoption of Native children, as well as of others, constituted no solution to mainstream Canadians' search for sons and daughters. The Royal Commission on Aboriginal Peoples (RCAP) summed up Native perspectives. Volume 3, *Gathering Strength,* reviewed the harsh history of child welfare. It reminded readers of the essential strength of the First Nations: 'When the number of Aboriginal children in care is considered as a proportion of all Aboriginal children, the percentage of children in care ranged from a low of 1.8 per cent in the Northwest Territories to a high of 5.9 per cent in British Columbia.' The sting lay in the comparison. Across Canada, on average, 4.6 per cent of Aboriginal children were in agency care in 1980–2, compared to just over 1 per cent of the general Canadian child population.[180]

As the RCAP understood full well, Aboriginal peoples had many perspectives and opinions on child transfer. As the 2005 obituary for Terance 'Duke' Across the Mountain/Hairy Bull Naistaohkomi demonstrated, many customs thrived into the twenty-first century. This well-loved and well-educated member of Alberta's Blood Reserve had been raised by his maternal grandparents. Without 'children of his own', and as an 'eligible bachelor', he adopted '3 nieces and 2 nephews as his own'. 'He loved and took care of them from the time they were babies until they grew up, even then he babied them.'[181] Not everyone was so lucky. In response to growing demands on their resources, a product of quickly expanding populations and federal policy shifts that offered Native women greater equality in inheritance, many late-twentieth-century bands began to institute citizenship and blood quantum rules to exclude claimants, including some adopted children, who might otherwise be eligible for collective benefits. Such was the case for a Jewish-Black Mohawk, adopted in 1955 and a lifelong resident of Kahnawake, who found himself and his Mohawk-'blood' wife suddenly denied band membership.[182] There were no easy answers to the dilemma of balancing rights and resources, but the RCAP emphasized that recognition of Aboriginal title to land and of long-standing racism on the part of mainstream authorities and agencies was the place to start.

Canadians in general continued to debate passionately what exactly constituted the best interest of youngsters. In May 1998, the popular magazine *Chatelaine,* in the course of an extended discussion of transracial adoption, invited readers to respond to an on-line poll that asked 'Should we permit non-Caucasian kids to be adopted by white families?' The results were firmly in favour, hardly surprising in light of the magazine's mainstream readership.[183] Progressive-minded adopters, such as Pierre Berton and Marie Adam, who firmly believed they had acted out of the best of humanitarian and liberal motives, were increasingly upset and confused as they found themselves confronting charges of racism and genocide.[184] They found unwanted company in reactionaries who insisted that youngsters' 'best interests' were being sacrificed on the altar of 'political correctness'.[185]

Some Aboriginal adoptees came forward with happy stories. Such was the case with a Métis man, adopted in the early 1950s, who reckoned his adoption at age four as 'exceedingly lucky' and confessed feeling 'that I have perhaps been given the tools to help other native kids who don't, or won't, have the opportunities that were given to me through adoption. . . . I am very aware of the fact that I was chosen. In the blackest moments of my life, that realization will always provide warmth and comfort.'[186] The 'Lives Lived' obituaries in the *Globe and Mail* told the story of another son, born in 1931, of an Ojibwa mother, who was raised by a loving white working-class couple and educated in philosophy and theology at the University of Toronto. He quit school to work as a probation officer in order to help his sister care for his foster mother. Eventually he studied for a graduate degree in clinical psychology and decided to 'serve the poor on the streets of Toronto' with the aid of his friends. At his funeral in 1998, he was 'eulogized as a "spiritual giant."'[187] An equally remarkable story came from the daughter of a Mohawk mother and an English airman. She remembered years of abuse in foster care homes secured by an Ontario CAS. Fortunately, 'warm and loving parents', who proved better than the system, rescued her. 'Thanks to my foster parents, the education they encouraged me towards is paying off. Today I work as a nurse in the penitentiary service, where I encounter Natives on a daily basis. My background helps me better relate to them.'[188] Deeply flawed as the conditions that produced them, interracial adoptions could work well.

At the end of the twentieth century, stories whether bad or good, were appraised within the context of disturbing discoveries. FASD, first clinically identified in 1973 and quickly coming to stigmatize Natives, deterred many adopters, just as it documented the extent of community and individual distress.[189] The discovery of long-standing histories of sexual abuse scarring both Aboriginal and non-Aboriginal households similarly compromised optimism. The visibility of such problems reinforced conclusions such as those from social work scholar Chris Bagley that Native adoptions were 'significantly' more likely than other transracial exchanges to fail[190] and confirmed the bankruptcy of old models of proceeding. Ultimately, natural and adoptive families, child welfare agencies, and Aboriginal communities needed far more resources if vulnerable youngsters were to be lovingly cared for. In the meantime, many prospective adopters, who might in the 1960s and 1970s have chosen Aboriginal sons and daughters, took their needs to the international stage.

The transfer of Native children beyond their birth families has been indelibly affected by contact. In fact, the shift from emphasis on residential schools to fostering and adoption captured much of the overall evolution of Native–European relations from the late nineteenth to the twentieth century. Determined efforts at the erasure of Aboriginal identity were succeeded by uncertain support for retention. 'Racial essentialism' on the part of settler society ebbed in face of liberal espousal of 'colour-blindness' and, eventually, some embrace of 'race cognizance'.[191] By the 1990s, Aboriginal adoptees, like the First Nations of Canada in general, found themselves cautiously encouraged to retain their histories into a common present. Just as unprecedented space became available at some federal-provincial summits for the Assembly of First Nations, although rarely for the Native Women's Association of Canada, Aboriginal children more often found acknowledgement of their claims to their past and to fair treatment. The resolution of one of the dominion's abiding dilemmas—the reconciliation of First Nations and settler communities—has thus been acted out on familial as well as national stages. As we shall see in the next chapter, international relations are similarly domestically embodied.

Foreign Affairs

With the notable exception of many First Nations who claim their origins in North America itself, Canadians commonly recognize cultural and genetic connections to other places in the world. They have also been both donors and recipients of migrant children. Just as family origins in the former Soviet Union helped inspire some Canadians' search for offspring in Russian orphanages at the end of the twentieth century, a sense of ties, real or imagined, with diverse geographies and cultures has shaped much intercountry adoption (ICA). As with much else in the transfer of youngsters, ICA has rarely been straightforward. Issues of class, religion, region, race, ethnicity, age, gender, and ability have regularly made youngsters more or less agreeable to prospective parents. Provincial and territorial boundaries have sometimes been seen as significant as national frontiers. The rescue theme that touches all adoption stories is especially pervasive in international encounters. Yet, promises of salvation never obscure the clear presence of more self-serving motives.

Cross-border adoption has a long history in the northern half of North America. The first section of this chapter briefly considers the persistent temptation of Canadians to see themselves as heroes of the story, as the rescuers of youngsters not properly cared for by less responsible or less lucky adults and communities. Whatever they may have thought, Canadians pursued adoption strategies in the context of global exchanges that were inextricably tied to relations of power among empires, states, and peoples. The second part examines the long period up to the end of the First World War, when legal adoptions were highly unusual and introduction of youngsters into new households was characterized by much commonplace custom and practice. In the course of their early contact with newcomers to the continent, indigenous peoples continued long-standing traditions of integrating strangers into domestic communities. On establishing permanent settlements, Europeans and others maintained their own habits of child transfer. In the imperial, border-crossing world of which Canada has always been part, the migration of youngsters to new homes was taken for granted and largely unregulated. The third section examines shifts in practices and attitudes from the 1920s to the 1960s, after which it was generally recognized that demand for girls and boys, especially healthy infants, was greater, often by far, than the domestic supply. These years also introduced unprecedented provincial, national, and international efforts to regulate the traffic in young lives. The last part of the chapter turns to Canadians' widening search for offspring in countries such as Vietnam, Romania, Russia, and China, which varied in many ways but shared the predicament of widespread child poverty and adult desperation. The story that unfolds in all periods testifies to the value placed on different groups of youngsters and the adult relations of power that precipitated exchanges.

Rescue across Borders

Canada has regularly appeared as a beacon of hope to regions wracked by economic and political tragedies. Many Canadians have assumed that children disadvantaged elsewhere would find better times in their part of the world. Growing acceptance in Canada of a sentimental ideology that conflated proper childhood with dependence, protection, segregation, and delayed responsibilities provided the measure of childcare at home and abroad.[1] When communities could not or would not meet such standards, apprehension was readily justified as in the interests of youngsters and not merely self-serving on the part of adults.

The response to girls and boys from elsewhere has often appeared an extension of local preferences. Outsiders most favoured as offspring have been healthy, young, often female, and from culturally related communities. Just as at home, top choices have never been as available as adopters would have liked. Indeed the turn to increasingly global searches was often a second or third choice in itself. For the most part, Canadians have looked abroad only when fertility and domestic options proved unavailing. Not surprisingly then, so long as relatively large numbers of potential progeny were available at home, Canadians were frequently casual about or indifferent to children elsewhere. The frequent brutal treatment of early child migrants was one result. Only as alternatives dried up, were some would-be parents willing to pass critical class, racial, and other checkpoints that marked kids as unacceptable or at least inferior additions to the domestic landscape.

The hierarchy of adoption preference has drawn heavily on English Canada's powerful heritage of Christian and European imperialism. Assumptions of cultural superiority and entitlement have regularly infected relations with other jurisdictions, just as they did with Aboriginal nations in Canada. Adopters have nevertheless frequently fancied that their personal hopes somehow operated innocently outside of history. Self-serving assumptions have been aided and abetted by the popular predilection for romanticizing child rescue. Newspapers and magazines in both the nineteenth and twentieth centuries readily championed white Canada's claim to the progeny of others. The result, as Laura Briggs has suggested of similar American efforts, has diverted 'attention away from structural explanations for poverty, famine and other disasters, including international, political, military and economic causes.'[2] When history is ignored, Canadians have been happy to masquerade as innocents abroad. As Claudia Castaneda has further argued, would-be saviours of girls and boys have tended to treat racial identities as 'entirely individualized' and defend their actions as promising 'racial harmony'.[3] Such assumptions take for granted what Castaneda has termed 'distributive maternity', whereby races and classes of women have been differently positioned to benefit from various reproductive technologies, among which she would include international adoption.[4]

For all the ideology of self-help and private initiative that has pervaded so much discussion of international adoption, acquiring children from elsewhere has meant participation in a particular version of what might be termed 'foreign policy by other means'. Long-standing Canadian support for UNICEF, Foster Parents Plan, Save the Children, and a variety of non-governmental organizations (NGOs) that laboured hard to mobilize 'pity and ideologies of rescue' in order 'to position some people as legitimately within a circle of care and deserving of resources' has often been correspondingly naive.[5] Too often participation in movements for international child welfare, whether individual or collective, has readily taken for granted global hierarchies, thus easily exonerating beneficiaries.

In the nineteenth and twentieth centuries, migrant children, even from related cultural communities, were readily exploited. Removal from the 'old world' was sometimes considered good luck enough. Their future welfare largely escaped attention unless major tragedy such as murder or suicide was involved. In the years after the Second World War, many North Americans, including Canadians, were still inclined to regard adoption as a benefit conferred by, and sometimes owed by, the powerful on the less fortunate. Major Coldwell, the leader of the Co-operative Commonwealth Federation (CCF) spoke for the liberal left in 1954, when he assessed the advantages of sending monthly sums to maintain European war orphans. Much preferable, he believed, was to 'bring a child into this country, and place that child in a good Canadian home, because there are homes that are seeking children for adoption. The child could be brought up in a Canadian home, in a Canadian environment and then would become a first class citizen of our country.'[6] More than three decades later, this prairie socialist found a counterpart in Reginald Stackhouse, the Conservative member of Parliament from Scarborough, Ontario, a PhD in historical theology, and a future chair of the Commons' Standing Committee on Human Rights, delegate to the UN Human Rights and Refugee Committee, and member of the Ontario Human Rights Commission. His question to the minister of state for immigration about support for the 'large number of Canadians' seeking foreign progeny captured the mix of supposed moral innocence and political pragmatism that typified much adoption border-crossing: 'In other parts of the world extraordinary numbers of helpless and homeless children would welcome the great privilege of being taken into a Canadian family.' Such transfers were, he argued, 'obviously humanitarian in nature and potentially advantageous to Canada.'[7] For much of Canada's history, individual child rescue has thus been readily aligned with the national good. Canadians with more progressive or even radical assessments of global politics confronted hard realities when they attempted to do good in a troubled world.

As It Was in the Beginning

Integrating children from other places into households may be properly said to begin with Native peoples who adopted war captives, both young and old, to replace deceased tribal members. The arrival of newcomers to North America presented many opportunities for boundary-crossing, as the monumental eleven-volume *Garland Library of North American Indian Captivities* aptly demonstrates.[8] Captive narratives have not generally been linked to other adoption stories. This is unfortunate, as there are marked similarities. *The Garland Library* narratives set forth outcomes that resemble those of adoptees in general. Some narrators identified firmly with new families; others rested uneasily, torn between two worlds; some reported abuse and sought escape. As newcomers came to dominate the continent, they assumed their own superiority and that no one would prefer, or be better served by, Aboriginal kin. While occasional stories of Native acceptance of white youngsters as family members surfaced in the nineteenth and twentieth centuries, they were rare. At the same time, with the exception of some early French experiments, Aboriginal girls and boys, like those of African origin, were regarded as beyond the pale, except for possible servitude, in respectable settler households. As chapter 6 has explained, youngsters with known Aboriginal origins were unlikely to be integrated into white households much before the 1960s.

Whatever the opportunities presented by its own desperate children, Canada loomed large not only for adults seeking escape from harsher settings but also in the eyes of authorities who sought to rescue and reshape youngsters judged excess to their birthplace. Dickensian hardship and poverty in the United Kingdom made the settler colonies and dominions appealing to philanthropists in the nineteenth and twentieth centuries. Men and women like Thomas Barnardo, William Quarrier, and Annie Macpherson hoped to transport Britain's surplus children to more salubrious settings. Just as Scottish child welfare authorities shifted children to the margins of their nation and Canadian social workers later moved charges around North America in search of more promising surroundings, British child-savers looked to Canada. It might have been an ocean away, but it was also readily perceived as an extension of home, not so very different from far-flung locations in the United Kingdom.

Champions of imperial emigration assumed that colonies of white settlement might offer a better return for child labour than a British homeland where it was brutally cheap. Given the depths of deprivation in the motherland, it was easy enough to believe that life might be better elsewhere. This assumption was fuelled when emigration entailed critical distancing from relatives readily evaluated as poor influences or present dangers. Newcomers, like those Canadians placed by J.J. Kelso, were to become effectively 'deodorized' by removal from the interference and 'wrong doing' of kin.[9]

Nearly a hundred years of migrating British children, most of whom had at least one living parent, produced at best a mixed record. Marilla Cuthbert's relief when Anne of Green Gables proved respectably Canadian-born, rather than a pauper boy from Britain, communicated widespread reservations. Positive popular accounts were rare until the end of the twentieth century. Inspired by her own fostering of an adopted grand-niece and grand-nephew and her great-grandparents' engagement of a Barnardo boy, prize-winning children's author Jean Little offered a reconsideration in *The Belonging Place* (1997) and *Orphan at My Door: The Home Child Diary of Victoria Cope* (2001). *The Belonging Place*, dedicated to adopted children 'everywhere', supplied a first-person testimonial from Scottish-born Elspet

Mary Iveson, who emigrated with relatives after her parents died. For her and other orphans in the story, Canada became 'our belonging place'.[10] *Orphan at My Door* featured twelve- and eight-year-old 'home children', Marianna and Jasper Wilson, dispatched by a Barnardo Home. Marianna entered Ontario as a household help while her brother arrived as a farm labourer. Their small sister disappeared entirely when 'adopted' by Canadians. The older siblings ultimately overcame prejudice, including physical abuse, to win favour. As in *Anne of Green Gables*, Little's upbeat endings celebrate the orphan—but this time one born elsewhere—as catalyst. She, more rarely he, transformed new households by demonstrating superior virtues. Such stories reminded readers that rescue might very well be two-sided. Canadians were as likely as newcomers to be beneficiaries.

Early news from Britain's Canadian outposts foreshadowed Little's essential optimism. Even backwoods Ontario's commonly cynical 'genteel pioneer' Susanna Moodie claimed to find that

> many an orphan child, who would be cast utterly friendless upon the world, finds a comfortable home with some good neighbour, and is treated with more consideration, and enjoys greater privileges, than if his own parents had lived. No difference is made between the adopted children and the young ones of the family; it is clothed, boarded, and educated with the same care, and a stranger would find it difficult to determine which was the real, which the transplanted scion of the house.[11]

High expectations fostered the illusion of safety, so that the Anglican *Dominion Churchman* in the 1870s could seem perfectly content with the half-time supervision, by a well-intentioned lieutenant-colonel, of more than three hundred Scottish children dispersed throughout Nova Scotia.[12]

But integration in the New World turned out to be hard. Even admirers acknowledged, 'we do not take angels to Canada, but very human little boys and girls with every variety of temper and character, and sometimes hereditary disadvantage which it is hard to battle with. But patient forbearance and gentle treatment and time do so much for them.'[13] More threatening was the prejudice that regularly awaited newcomers. Instead of offering a family-like welcome, an Ontario county moved a resolution protesting 'vicious youths', 'weeds and poisonous growth', who could become only 'pestilential additions to our population.'[14]

Dr Barnardo and others tried to offset calumny by insisting that their missions were solidly based and that 'every individual child sent out has, without exception, done well.'[15] Such arguments were occasionally echoed in Canada. In 1894, the first report under Ontario's Children's Protection Act 'concluded that benefits far outweighed disadvantages. Young immigrants did well in rural areas, offsetting the outmigration of the Canadian-born. The report nevertheless recognized corrosive prejudice: 'It must be remembered too that those who succeed in life are not anxious that their antecedents should be publicly known, and their benefactors are thus deprived of incontrovertible testimony as to the good work accomplished.'[16]

In fact, British immigrant children, both boys and girls, were desired chiefly for labour. Canadian farmers saw their own children drift away to cities or to their own farms and were understandably 'desirous of adopting children who would prove of great help as they grew older.' Newcomers might well become no more than hired men or maids of all work, ranking near the bottom of Canada's social and economic hierarchy.[17] Indifferent monitoring of their well-being, as with the youngsters sent to the Ango-Irish Coombe Home in Hespeler, Ontario, often spelled disaster.[18] The Anglican and imperially minded *Canadian Churchman* might have advertised for farmers to 'adopt' girls from Dr Barnardo's, but indenture was more common than kinship.[19]

The faith that racial bonds might protect children from exploitation nonetheless continued in some quarters. In 1914, G. Bogue Smart, chief inspector of British immigrant children and receiving homes in Canada was determined to give 'the children', and, more accurately, their adult employers, 'a chance'. His survey of 2,204 emigrants, aged three to seventeen, observed that even 'the poorest home' was 'palatial compared with that from which they have been brought.'[20] First World War losses through battle and disease reinvigorated nationalist worries lest Canada become the 'dumping-ground for undesirables', but it also sparked continued hope that the motherland might offer 'her best', to be 'welcomed with all heartiness as among the most valuable elements of our future moral and economic welfare.'[21] What seems clear, however, is that even cultural kin were not readily taken in as family members. Class, accents, disabilities, age, and other factors kept many, probably most, home children on the margins of new households.

British migrant children were centre stage when it came to Canadians' early consideration of youngsters from elsewhere, but they were not entirely alone. Signs of future interests were also evident. In particular, the missionary societies of the Protestant churches provided regular reminders of the possibilities of a worldwide Christian kinship. Rosemary Gagan and Ruth Compton Brouwer have pointed to the preoccupation of Methodist and Presbyterian women missionaries with Asian youngsters.[22] From the early nineteenth century, Sunday school and church attendance introduced parishioners to child rescue the world over. In 1883, the story 'The Dying Orphan' in the Anglican *Dominion Churchman* offered a typical tale of poor youngsters, in this case in Indian orphanages, who pulled at hearts and wallets.[23] The modern sentimentalization of childhood, though it provided little immediate succour to child migrants, increasingly informed many liberal- and imperial-minded Canadians as they looked beyond their own borders.

Half a Century of Rescue and Suspicion, 1920s to 1960s

After 1920, adoption seemed all the more in the air. The child welfare movement was increasingly international in scope. As Karen Balcom has convincingly demonstrated, social work professionals developed extensive networks in NGOs, the League of Nations, and, after 1945, the United Nations. Canadians such as the Canadian Council on Child Welfare's Charlotte Whitton readily assumed the superiority of the imperial West as they contributed to formulating international standards.[24]

Nationwide struggles to balance the rights of birth parents with the protection of children and the desires of adopters were echoed in the Geneva Declaration of the Rights of the Child approved by the League of Nations in 1924 and the Declaration of the Rights of the Child set out by the UN in 1959.[25] Canadians also watched as notables such as Queen Mary endorsed adoption. In 1926, readers of the *Toronto Star* learned that she had sponsored a boy to be educated at her expense at the Royal Infant Orphanage at Wanstead; several years later, they saw her select a little girl under the adoption program of the Princess Mary Village Homes.[26]

Early on, the twentieth century offered prospective adopters wider vistas to explore. As illegitimacy and adoption in general remained stigmatizing, would-be parents had obvious incentives to move beyond the ken of knowing neighbours. As a journalist in *Chatelaine* noted in 1932, many offspring knew nothing of their ancestry because 'a good deal of trouble and expense' had been taken to 'cover up the fact'. He cited, rather approvingly, several examples, including the case of a woman who told friends of a European jaunt. Absent for some months, she returned with 'a little baby supposedly born to her in England.' In fact the prize had been picked up in another Canadian city. His new parents had been aided and abetted by a 'social service agency which entered into the spirit of the thing, and even close relatives of this couple have no idea of the fraud worked off on them.'[27] Influential Canadians such as leading internationalist Mary McGeachy, much like Mazo de la Roche before her, might be particularly well-situated to acquire offspring. In the 1950s, she presented the daughter and son of a bereaved English family from Swaziland as biological kin.[28] Americans who picked offspring from Nova Scotia's Ideal Maternity Home showed similar entrepreneurship.

Other private arrangements on the part of 'donor' families, as well as public agencies, testified to the permeability of national borders. In 1923, an English nine-year-old, orphaned by the death of her father in the First World War and later her mother, travelled by steamship and train to Vancouver to live with aunts.[29] American orphanages, especially those in northern states such as Illinois, where the Loyal Order of the Moose maintained 'Mooseheart', might well include the Canadian-born. Canadian social workers regularly observed private cross-border arrangements. In 1929, experts reviewing New Brunswick practice described the sad case of eight-year-old John. His unwed mother placed him with an 'old woman of doubtful reputation' and without home or means. Then at age six he was sent 'to a far distant western province', but that experiment failed with charges of ill treatment. He had become no one's responsibility, but 'no one seemed to care'.[30] At much the same time, the Vancouver Children's Aid Society (CAS) rather typically sent a motherless eight-year-old, deserted by her father, off to a brother and grandfather in Scotland, a young boy to an aunt in another province, a girl to a grandfather in Finland and another to Montreal relatives, and a brother and sister to Swiss kin. As an observer reflected, 'distances are naught in the modern world, and modern social work must look upon the nations of two continents as one great community, and knit together the broken threads that lead across international boundaries.'[31]

Still more visible after the First World War were long-standing controversies about emigrating British children. Parliamentarians reactivated commonplace polarized debates about such youngsters. In 1922, the Liberal minister of immigration and colonization saluted prior child migration and proposed to subsidize still more when faced with stiff postwar competition from Australia and South Africa: 'I am rather keen on the question of securing for Canada all the child immigration that it is possible for us to obtain.'[32] Canada's first female MP, Agnes Macphail, a schoolteacher and daughter of Ontario farmers, cut through these platitudes to point out that Britain's urban refugees hardly suited Canadian needs and that they fled quickly to cities, as few had the funds and skills for successful farm ownership.[33] The protests of another Progressive spokesman, this time from Alberta, summed up the opposition's mix of humanitarian concern and outright chauvinism:

> I do not think it is fair to Canada, nor do I think it is fair to the children themselves who are coming over here. I would like to ask any member of this House how he would like to see his children hired out to unknown persons in an unknown country. To be frank with the committee I think such a policy amounts to brutality. Taken to farms where there are already children, and I am afraid that in the majority of cases the grossest discrimination will be displayed against the unfortunate immigrant child. . . . What type of immigrants must these children be? Probably they come from orphan homes, or from the home of degenerate families. Nobody but degenerate parents would want to part with children to send them away to work in a distant country. How are you going to obtain the family history of children coming from such homes? You will be able to ascertain little or nothing about them. Therefore, I say child immigration is wrong.[34]

Still another Albertan asked, 'Would it not be more beneficial to Canada if we looked after our own children . . . before bringing to Canada children from the poorer homes in the cities of another country? I think we are making a mistake to-day in this country—probably in other countries it is the same—because we are possibly laying too much stress on the value and the sacredness of the almighty dollar.'[35]

Such criticism left the Liberal minister seemingly unfazed. He later hailed Barnardo's, pointing out that in the 'wild rose province' alone

> there are always more applications for children than we are able to satisfy. Indeed, the only children in the hands of the government to-day, or a year ago, so far as I know, were those who were slightly mentally deficient. The robust, physically fit child was adopted into a foster home as soon as he was able to go there. There is in Ontario and eastern Canada a great field for this work, and there are in the Old Country children of deceased soldiers by the thousands, children of respectable parents by the thousands, who will make splendid settlers and citizens of Canada if we can bring them here.[36]

To emphasize their importance, he supplied the House with an estimate of close to 80,000 arrivals since 1868 (see Table 7.1). Such faith prompted his inclusion of

Table 7.1   Groups supporting child emigration and numbers emigrated, 1868–1922

Group	Year	Children immigrating
Miss Macpherson and Mrs Birt, London and Liverpool, (Canadian headquarters), Marchmont Homes, Belleville, Ont.	1868–1921	13,976
Miss Rye and Church of England, Niagara-on-Lake, Ont., and Sherbrooke, Que.	1868–1921	3,766
Mr (now Sir) J.T. Middlemore, Fairview, Halifax, NS	1873–1921	4,915
The National Children's Home and Orphanage (formerly Dr T. Bowman Stephenson), Hamilton, Ont.	1874–1921	2,761
Mrs Bilbrough-Wallace (Marchmont Home), Belleville, Ont.	1878–1915	5,529
Cardinal Manning (Ottawa and Montreal)	1880–1888	1,403
Dr Barnardo, Toronto, Peterborough, and Winnipeg	1882–1922	25,456
Mr J.W.C. Fegan, Toronto	1884–1922	2,798
Mr Wm. Quarrier, Brockville, Ont.	1890–1922	4,074
The Catholic Emigration Association and amalgamated Societies, St George's Home, Ottawa	1897–1922	5,998
The Salvation Army	1905–22	820
Minor Agencies	1897–1922	4,920
Total		76,416

SOURCE: Canada, House of Commons, *Debates*, 23 March 1923, 1470 (C.A. Stewart).

youthful migrants in the Imperial Settlement Agreement negotiated with Britain in 1923.

Also in the early 1920s, Canada's superintendent of juvenile immigration mounted a spirited defence before the Canadian Council on Child Welfare. He dramatized good outcomes, assuring his audience that girls and boys below age nine or ten were adopted and did 'not work but are educated and brought up as members of the family.' They were properly supervised because they represented a substantial investment, 'the bone and sinew of the daughter nation, and to take rank with the useful, true and loyal citizens.'[37] At about the same time and before the same group, the chief migration officer for the Barnardo Homes emphasized empire-building and thorough monitoring. His defence centred on the claim that 'Canada is not a foreign country.'[38] In Ottawa, the Liberal minister continued to argue that children were carefully selected and supervised, although admittedly not all were adopted. In 1926, a Conservative MP cited modern child welfare principles: migration offered an alternative to institutionalization, something that permanently disadvantaged children. Instead the newcomers would grow up as 'normal' Canadians.[39]

Such optimism was increasingly challenged on both sides of the Atlantic. In 1924, a fact-finding report by British Labour MP Margaret Bondfield bluntly catalogued abuse, and a year later her government banned the emigration of unaccompanied minors under fourteen.[40] At much the same time, an influential woman activist from Toronto decried the treatment of immigrants, who rarely became 'actual members of the family' or received 'a share in the family's resource'. First and foremost, they were workers, and this was not satisfactory as 'Canada has subscribed to certain standards for her own children and she cannot recognize child labour for children brought into our territory.'[41] A representative from the Canadian Trades and Labour Congress observed that exploitation was common by 'those who have no children of their own, by those who use them to save their own.' More particularly, he suggested that Canadian-born youngsters in need of homes were rejected in favour of immigrants who were more readily abused.[42]

In 1928, the Canadian Council on Child Welfare published an analysis of juvenile immigrants brought to Canada in 1910 and 1920 by British emigration societies. It cited suicides and deaths as proof positive that something was badly wrong. The author chided British agencies for ignoring 'unpleasant' truths about their lack of supervision and the children's longing for their birth families. She found serious problems among the 311 children she sampled:

> In no case was a child legally adopted. In 8 cases there was evidence of the wish and intention on the part of the foster parents to bring the child up as their own but three of these children were later returned to the Society as unsatisfactory.
>
> ... It is a mistake to suppose that the employers in applying for the children are actuated by altruistic motives. There is no more reason why this should be expected of them than of the business man who applies for an office boy. ...
>
> This system then resolves itself almost entirely into a labour question and should be treated as such from a business standpoint. It is nevertheless from a human standpoint a very acute child protection problem and should be surrounded by all the safeguards known to child-caring organizations.[43]

The council's slightly more positive assessment in 1928 of the New Brunswick Cossiar farm experiment with Scottish boys nevertheless similarly concluded that modern child welfare protection was largely absent.[44]

Ironically enough given the anti-institutional preference of most British agencies, one experiment in child migration that began in 1934 and continued until 1951 was carried out in an institutional setting. The Fairbridge Farm School in Cowichan, British Columbia, combined imperial sentiment and elite sponsorship to maintain a project that social workers condemned as 'reminiscent of an orphanage in the last century'.[45] While it aided a mere three hundred or so British youngsters, the experiment incorporated pervasive problems.[46] Wanted by few British Columbians except for their labour, Fairbridge children only reluctantly surrendered earlier associations. When faced with starting near the bottom of Canada's British hierarchy, many longed for home.

As is often the case with adoption, the saddest tales regularly surfaced, some in the *Globe and Mail*'s long-running 'Lives Lived' column. There was George Miles, who retired as 'Canada's oldest barber' at age ninety-three in 1994. He and his brothers and sisters had arrived in Ontario as Barnardo children in 1909. One sister disappeared entirely. He toiled hard on a farm and was not told of his birth mother's mailing of 'letters and locks of her hair'. His dentist son summed up the results of his trauma: his dad never overcame fear of giving offence.[47] Another home child, Roy Edward Henley, who also arrived in 1890, enthusiastically deserted his 'foster-parents' in 1914 to go overseas, where he won the French Croix de Guerre for bravery.[48] A later arrival, Robert (Steve) Brodie, an 'influenza orphan' in care of the Salvation Army, was farmed out as a rural labourer in 1919. Looking around, this soon-to-be lay preacher concluded that 'capitalism made miserable the many for the benefit of the few,' joined the Communist Party, and took part in the 1938 'Bloody Sunday' battle with the RCMP in Vancouver.[49] In 1922, John T. Lake and his sister were dispatched, the first to New Brunswick and the other to Nova Scotia, only to reunite many years later. He never got past Grade 3, but 'you could not beat John at arithmetic.' For years, he saved to go home but a 'well-hitched' marriage at long last transformed Canada into home.[50] Such stories testify to many things but very clearly to the fact that British children were not readily accepted as one of the family.

In the midst of such histories of border-crossing after 1920, modern social workers diversified networks and resources. Charlotte Whitton was in some ways typical, at various times cooperating with the US Children's Bureau and the League of Nations. Her leadership in the Canadian Welfare Council helped citizens keep up to date on global developments. A typical article, entitled '"No Man's" Child Seeks Justice from the World', on the changing status of illegitimate children in 1936, signalled widespread thinking about placement of such youngsters.[51] Whitton, like the Saskatchewan, Ontario, and Quebec experts who, in the early 1950s, joined a UN committee to propose 'desirable practices and standards' in adoption, acted as self-conscious members of a worldwide professional community.[52]

When options such as orphanages and residential schools were increasingly discredited and drives to attract more foster and adoptive homes domestically regularly faltered, Canadian authorities acted much like their British counterparts and contemplated placement beyond their borders. The fact that so many Canadians had connections elsewhere meant that frontiers often seemed less important than a hoped-for welcome or even matching religion, ethnicity, and race in more dis-

tant homes. When they tried to address the seemingly poor fit between local supply and demand, especially for certain groups of children, child welfare workers
had good reason to search more widely. Ironically, long-standing criticism of the
placement of 'home children' rarely appeared to inform the behaviour of Canada
as a 'donor' of children.

Because Canadians' own cross-border contributions focused on state wards who
found few offers at home, they disproportionately involved racialized and other
minority youngsters. Western provinces in particular readily participated in the
export of Aboriginal clients. Champions of such solutions sometimes noted that
Native children might well find parents with their ancestry in the United States or
sympathy that they more rarely found in home provinces. The situation for African-
Canadian children was similar. In 1955, the CAS of Nova Scotia's Sunbury County
reported a shortage of applicants for such youngsters and noted that 'we have to go
outside our boundaries for homes for these children.'[53] When birth families were
considered unworthy, the benefits of dispersing offspring appeared all the clearer.
Like the 'orphan trains' that transported American children from supposedly dangerous Eastern cities and families to respectable households in the Midwest,[54] border-crossing appeared to promise solutions to a multitude of difficulties.

Opportunities to link strangers varied across the country. During the Second
World War, the presence of a major American military base in Newfoundland's
Avalon Peninsula, like similar installations elsewhere in the world, contributed
both to the production of additional offspring and to their subsequent export. The
number of putative fathers and unwed mothers, if never precisely known, was
always reckoned high. The overall uncertainty was conveyed by the musing of officials in the Division of Child Welfare in the colony, as it then was, about depart-
ing servicemen's adopting children who may have been their biological offspring.[55] Only slightly later, Alberta's Royal Commission on Child Welfare recognized that temporarily resident American military personnel also adopted children
upon their departure.[56] Persisting outmigration from Newfoundland generated
other worries. How, wondered provincial bureaucrats in 1949, were they to handle 'an increasing number of unmarried Newfoundland girls who have become
expectant mothers in Canada'? Who was responsible for advising and assisting
them? Which jurisdiction was responsible for the babies?[57] In the same year, BC
authorities described frustration in monitoring kin placements from the United
Kingdom. A British teenager with 'serious behaviour disorders' was sent to 'well-
intentioned relatives' in the province but was eventually deported.[58] In 1956, the
province presented the case of a couple who cross-border shopped for offspring
denied in their home state. Settling briefly in British Columbia, these Americans
advertised for and obtained a baby and slipped back over the forty-ninth parallel,
declaring the child their own. When, a few years later, the couple divorced, with
the father ending up in a penitentiary, a seven-year-old stood in limbo, not a US
citizen and ignorant of her birthplace.[59]

Relations among child welfare ministries might be taxed by arguments over
duties. During the Second World War, BC authorities became aware that a publicly unnamed province, presumably Alberta, was placing wards in the Peace River

region and completing adoptions in its own courts. That was problem enough, but further questions were raised when investigation and supervision appeared lacking.[60] Although modern social workers prided themselves on casework and supervision during a probationary period, they were especially hard-pressed when different jurisdictions were involved. In 1944, Nova Scotia's Royal Commission on Provincial Development and Rehabilitation assessed the failure to legislate the probationary protection was typical of other provinces. Pointing to the abuses associated with institutions such the Ideal Maternity Home, it strenuously argued against 'adoption on an "over-the-counter"' basis, whereby non-residents made hurried visits, selected babies from commercial creches, rushed through legalities, and swiftly departed only 'to face a lifetime of responsibility for the care of a child about which they knew little or nothing.'[61] Going unmentioned was the equal or greater threat to children's well-being.

News of girls and boys sent to foreign climes sometimes generated moral panics.[62] After the Second World War, Charlotte Whitton, supported by the Imperial Order Daughters of the Empire (IODE), condemned Alberta for sending unprotected Canadian-born children south to the dominion's old foe.[63] In 1947, the *Vancouver Sun* reported a 'rising export trade in Canadian babies' who moved from Montreal to Vermont, from Windsor to Detroit, and from Halifax to New England and points south. Racketeers were also believed to traffic Johnny and Janey Canucks into South America.[64] In 1948, Ottawa MPs raised questions about lost infants and in both 1953 and 1954 voiced apprehension about the 'international baby export racket' and the 'sale of babies'.[65] The 1960s renewed such fears. The *Victoria Colonist* pointed to concerns about Catholic wards sent off to other provinces and to Alaska.[66] Across the strait, a writer in the *Vancouver Sun* categorized such practices as a 'grave disservice to this country and to adopted children', arguing that such youngsters should not forfeit citizenship.[67] Several years later, the *Toronto Telegram*'s Washington Bureau announced that US senators had reported that 'baby salesmen' were at work in Montreal. Black marketeers were portrayed dealing infants just as they had in the early 1950s, when a New York policewoman revealed that she had purchased a baby for $3,000.[68] Much worse was reported when Native victims of the 'sixties scoop' began to provide their own tales of abuse in American homes.

Fears of a national baby drain prompted jurisdictions such as New Brunswick to insist that cross-boundary placements be tightly monitored. Despite the obvious shortfall of resources to meet even local demands for supervision, the province claimed to have 'carefully checked' its wards with the appropriate authorities in other provinces and US states and only placed children with their American blood kin.[69] A few years later, the director of the Vancouver Catholic CAS provided a commonplace justification: 'We believe the advantages of being raised in a good American home far outweigh the advantages of being raised a Canadian in an orphanage.'[70] A short time later, British Columbia's minister of social welfare implied that by sending four non-Indian babies to Yukon, the province was merely helping to rectify a national imbalance in supply and demand.[71]

Whatever their reservations, hard-pressed social work experts readily worked on a continent-wide basis. They might prefer keeping children with birth families, but they also took pride in the promise of modern casework. In 1938, BC child welfare authorities claimed to receive

> many applications for children from outside British Columbia, and are quite candidly told by adopting parents from the United States and from other provinces that they wish to get a child in British Columbia because they have heard that proper investigations of the child's background are made and that one may be reasonably sure of getting a satisfactory child. When it is in the interests of a child to be placed outside the province—particularly an older child, we are glad to take advantage of superior homes offered as long as we are able to obtain co-operation in investigation and supervision from recognized social agencies.[72]

Typically, Canadians and American experts at a 1954 'lively morning meeting on Adoption Placements Across the International Boundary between Canada and the United States' concluded that a foreign home was better than none.[73]

By the end of the 1950s, the BC Division of Child Welfare was experienced in negotiating with departments elsewhere. One mixed-race youngster went to Ontario, another with 'special needs' to Manitoba, and another to Yukon. It also encouraged the Vancouver Catholic CAS to investigate placements in Oregon, where Roman Catholic parents waited, as 'it is right and human that the two be brought together.' Whatever the importance of citizenship, it was 'second to a good stable family life.'[74] Later in the decade, Manitoba was similarly sanguine as it described a program that placed 25 of 797 wards in Ontario, Minnesota, North Dakota, and Oregon. Because homes for 'minority race' wards were usually 'located far from the children who need them,' such children were, for the most part, partly Native and older.[75] In the 1950s and 1960s, Saskatchewan began using regional placement conferences to the same end, encouraging workers 'to be constantly aware of problems outside their borders.'[76] On the east coast in the 1970s, the Atlantic Adoption Exchange allowed for similar opportunities. Sensitive to critics, Nova Scotia also pledged to place 'children within Canada whenever possible.'[77]

Canadian children nevertheless continued to go south. As the director of the Catholic Social Welfare Bureau in Charlottetown pointed out in 1973, she had been making American placements for 'close to half a century'.[78] For many years, Alberta's child welfare authorities prided themselves on assistance to Americans seeking Catholic, often Aboriginal, children. In 1947, the charges put forward by the IODE investigation, with which the minister of public welfare had refused to cooperate, were damning. The entire provincial system was condemned as unprofessional and retrogressive. Adoption, the report concluded, was simply an excuse to reduce state expenditures.[79] Girls and boys became mere 'commodities', to the point that unrelated youngsters were marketed as twins and passports rushed through to expedite 'expatriation to another land, sovereignty and new parenthood.'[80] The report was especially scathing in its assessment of the province's child welfare leadership. The fact that the long-time director of child welfare was an honorary consul for Costa Rica suggested possible conflict of interest.

Table 7.2   Illegitimate births and cross-border placements in Alberta, 1934–47

Year	Total illegitimate births	Cross-border placements
1934	589	1*
1935	614	0
1936	607	1
1937	626	2
1938	683	1
1939	617	7
1940	681	3
1941	720	14
1942	777	12
1943	866	21
1944	849	42
1945	1050	52
1946	1218	61
1947	1121	26
Total	11018	243

* Said to be the first such placement.

SOURCE: Alberta, Royal Commission on Child Welfare, *Report* (1948), 33.

Such criticisms provoked the immediate appointment of the Alberta Royal Commission on Child Welfare. While it admitted many concerns, it concluded that the issue around young exports had been blown out of proportion. Its table on illegitimate births and cross-border placement reported very small numbers (see Table 7.2). The stigma such youngsters regularly encountered, however, made them obvious candidates to be parcelled off to twenty-four American states and Alaska, Costa Rica, Guatemala, and El Salvador. And despite reassuring replies from the cross-border adopters it surveyed, the commission acknowledged substantive objections, including 'national interest', the loss of protection for wards, and the fact that some children were left 'virtually stateless'.[81] Despite its recommendation that they be discontinued, trans-border placements persisted, as Table 7.3 indicates.

In the face of rising numbers in care, the Child Welfare Branch remained happy to off-load responsibilities: 'In the past there have always been a considerable number of American adopting parents coming back to Alberta to adopt their second and third child but they are now able to adopt these children in their own State.'[82] Late in 1964, its US adoption program staggered when a district court judge in

Table 7.3   Adoption placements in and beyond Alberta, 1957–66

	In	Beyond	Total
1957	768	45	813
1958	843	44	887
1959	825	40	865
1960	755	27	782
1961	777	43	820
1962	988	25	1,013
1963	1,136	17	1,153
1964	1,203	15	1,218
1965	1,361	3	1,364
1966	1,336	11	1,347

SOURCE: Alberta, Department of Public Welfare, Child Welfare Branch, *23rd Annual Report* (1966–7), 13.

northern Alberta insisted that the probationary period could not be waived. Such setbacks proved little initial deterrent. The Calgary CAS remained typically upbeat when a representative testified before the provincial commission investigating adoption in 1965. In response to queries about the export of Métis youngsters to Latin America, he responded:

> As is well known there is Spanish-Indian culture in that part of the world. I think that everyone at that time . . . [was] of the opinion that this was a good thing and these adoptions worked out very well indeed. It was shortly after the war and some of these adoptions, some of these children had been placed for adoption into families of officers who were attached to military commands in Alberta at that time, who had something to do with the Alaska Highway and so on, and they worked out very well and there certainly had not been repercussions of any kind. So, I say, place a child in a home no matter where the home is.[83]

Commission member Marjorie Bowker, who filed a supplementary report, drew on her own experience to arrive at similarly positive conclusions. She cited an Idaho couple who accepted a part Japanese Catholic infant 'for whom there was no hope of adoption in Alberta.' The father had served with the American forces in the Pacific and married a 'Japanese girl'. As far as Bowker was concerned, such surrenders were even better when transfer occurred directly from the hospital.[84] Provincial authorities nevertheless remained self-conscious. In 1968, Alberta's Child Welfare Commission argued 'there is nothing illegal or "black market" about our American adoption program. We are very proud of the exceptionally fine homes we have been able to provide for our children in the United States. We work very closely with the American state-approved adoption agencies, securing in every instance their help and co-operation in doing a home study and following normal adoption procedures.'[85]

As these examples testify, children have often been in transit among sites that promised more or less salvation. Custom and evolving professional practice regularly took for granted that internal and foreign borders were permeable. The experience of the home children had demonstrated the problems attendant on distant placements, but surrenders of Canadians across frontiers tended to become controversial only when they involved donations to the Americans, especially of Aboriginal youngsters, as we have seen in the previous chapter. Exported offspring rarely appeared to have regularly embarrassed Canadian donors.

While remaining a donor nation in the case of so-called special needs children between 1920 and 1970, Canada also extended its role as a recipient in the global exchange of children. Well-meaning citizens were regularly swayed by the plight of youngsters abroad. NGOs, often associated with the League of Nations and the UN, combined with long-standing interests represented by missionary societies and the churches in general, to generate enthusiasm. Despite its pre-eminent interest in British youngsters, the Church of England in Canada endorsed the Save-the-Children Fund in Greece and the 'Armenian Orphanage' in Georgetown, Ontario, in 1924.[86] The plight of girls and boys in Europe after the First World War encouraged the dominion's institutions and schools to sponsor youngsters in ways that became familiar. In 1919, the *Globe and Mail* pointed proudly to three schools each of which had 'adopted' French war orphans.[87]

The Depression of the 1930s precluded much enthusiasm for international duties, but the return of war overseas renewed attention. Canadians turned to consider the plight of child refugees and in particular those whom Madame Chiang Kai-shek dubbed 'warphans'.[88] In 1938, the Canadian National Committee on Refugees (CNCR) pleaded with Ottawa to make special provision for children and joined with the Canadian Friends Service Committee to challenge the racism and thrift of policy-makers as well as the resistance of child welfare experts who protested that native-born youngsters already waited in line for assistance and adoption.[89] By 1940, matters had become far more urgent. Representatives from provincial governments joined those from the CNCR and the Canadian Welfare Council to assess what could be done about 'the barbarous situation and the cruel plight of children' in Europe. Experts confronting wartime confusion and determined to protect hard-won standards—even if these were honoured more in theory than practice—were unsure how to proceed, contemplating no more than the rescue of some hundred children aged three to thirteen. Battle-hardened practitioners rightly wondered whether the 'emotional appeal' could be 'effective very long'.[90] During six long years, the European conflict generated considerable sympathy, and the popular press issued regular pleas like that in the headline 'Save the Children Now, Before It Is Too Late,' but few actually reaped any benefits. Even then the experience of British evacuees and Jewish refugees during and immediately after the Second World War demonstrated that the early concerns were quite realistic.[91]

Despite its at best mixed history with the home children, English-speaking

Canadians rallied quickly to rescuing the motherland's offspring from the Blitz and the threat of German invasion.[92] Canada's only mass-circulation women's magazine welcomed the arrivals with moving fictional portrayals of respectability and heroism.[93] The 'guest children' or evacuees, some of whom arrived with their mothers, often drew on kin and other personal networks in their escape, but Canada and Britain soon arranged an official program. Migration was also distinguished by the removal to the dominion of some British private schools. One Canadian journalist in the high-tone *Saturday Night* magazine hailed the British students 'as valuable a type of human beings as can be selected' and hoped that many would settle permanently.[94] Such youngsters were welcomed by Canada's independent schools as well as by the Canadian elite more generally.[95] Even as the nation was poised to rescue the 'pathetic cargoes' sent from the old 'homeland', experienced observers understood that even preferred newcomers needed protection. As one journalist put it 'in past decades the improperly supervised migration of British children to Canada has been a nightmare to responsible placing agencies.' Children's Aid Societies and their counterparts took charge across the country.[96]

Canada's promise to take up to 100,000 British youngsters, so enthusiastically and naively embraced in the early days of conflict, sparked ongoing debate in the House of Commons. In July 1940, the Social Credit member for Red Deer, Alberta, invoked memories of earlier discussions about home children. Although he agreed that youngsters should be rescued, he pointed out that Canadians were also in need. He inquired, 'If we can provide all these things for the children who are brought here from abroad, why did we not a year or so ago make these very same things available for the thousands of starving children in our own country? ... [They were] fleeing before another type of monster, the economic depression. Our children are a national asset, the best and most lasting asset which we have, and since they are a national asset they are of extreme concern.'[97] Some MPs asked practical questions about tax implications for extra household members, especially because, as the leader of the CCF pointed out, unmarried mothers were taxed as single persons.[98] By the end of the war, such critics helped convince Ottawa to allow tax credits for all dependants under eighteen, including illegitimate and guest children. The insistence from governments that private homes be provided free, however, raised the prospect of the recurrence of previous problems.[99]

Social workers were soon overwhelmed even by the limited numbers who arrived before the program was halted in 1940 by the torpedoing of the ocean liner *The City of Benares,* with its cargo of youngsters. A social work thesis investigating 150 evacuees in Nova Scotia offered familiar observations. While that province was 'honoured' as the first to accept such youngsters, it encountered immediate difficulty in meeting social work standards. Supervision was irregular at best, all the more so as local CASs lacked additional funds. Ultimately, only eight of the twenty-five foster children closely studied by the researcher were judged as having made 'excellent adjustment'.[100] Shortcomings existed across the country; only this observer's bluntness was unusual. In 1948, Alberta's Royal Commission on Child Welfare concluded cheerfully that British refugees 'received excellent handling, up to a standard not excelled in any other province.'[101] If so, they were better treated

Table 7.4 Ages of Jewish refugee
children admitted to
Canada, ca 1947–9

Age	Number of refugees
Under 5	0
5–7	6
8–10	31
11–13	69
14–16	386
17+	610
Age not given	24

SOURCE: Ben W. Lappin, *The Redeemed
Children: The Story of the Rescue of War
Orphans by the Jewish Community of
Canada* (Toronto: University of
Toronto Press, 1963), 371.

by far than the majority of the province's children in care. In Manitoba, some male guest children ended up in the Knowles Home for Boys, along side other youngsters consigned by the juvenile court.[102] Most guest children returned to Britain by the close of hostilities. A few stayed to be adopted. In 1947, BC's Social Welfare Branch reported that five children under eighteen remained: 'Three of these will continue to live with the foster-parents, one will remain with a relative, and one is to be adopted legally by her foster-parents.' Such permanency directly contradicted initial agreements but, as social workers recognized, 'circumstances have developed within the five children's own families making it inadvisable for them to return.'[103]

Jewish survivors of the Holocaust supplied another significant group of youngsters to enter the dominion as a result of the Second World War. The Canadian Jewish Congress (CJC) and the CNCR began trying to persuade Ottawa to undertake rescue in the 1930s, but anti-Semitism that held that 'none is too many' barred them until 1947.[104] When some thousand were finally admitted, their costs and supervision were completely covered by the CJC, which also cooperated with local CASs to maintain standards. High hopes accompanied their reception but, like the British guest children, Jewish youngsters had to accept the role of free boarders.[105] A flurry of offers initially came from Canadian Jewish families. But couples for the most part put in familiar requests for little girls. In fact, 352 girls and 764 boys were on offer. And, as table 7.4 suggests, nearly 80 per cent were aged between fifteen and eighteen. Girls and younger children had been less likely than older boys to survive the hell of the Second World War. Thus Canadians found themselves confronting male adolescents, a group they had regularly spurned. Some requests for girls also proved problematic, little more than familiar schemes for cheap household help.[106] These were not the only problems. Since Holocaust survivors commonly arrived 'with well-defined values by which they often judged and found local communities wanting,' problems came early. In time 'most of the free home placements broke down.'[107]

Jewish youngsters were distributed across the country. An initial contingent of fifteen boys and eight girls, all thirteen and older, went to Vancouver. The city's CAS worked with the local religious community to supervise placements. It summed up apprehensions in 1948: 'We learned a great deal about the difficulties inherent in "sight unseen" placements during the war when the British evacuee group came to Canada and we are presently aware of these same difficulties in our work with Jewish overseas children.'[108] A year later, it had become sufficiently optimistic to report of the group, by then numbering forty-six, that 'considering the devastating experiences these children had known in Europe during the war years, they are making a remarkably good adjustment to Canadian life.'[109] As the executive director of Toronto's Jewish Family and Child Service noted in 1950, however, adjustment could easily be compromised by survivor guilt.[110] Not surprisingly, one journalist reported that 92 of 137 Winnipeg placements required more than one foster home and 28 more than four.[111] While some such traumatized young people went on to worldly success, they were never typical children or adoptees. Indeed in 1955, British Columbia reported of one bright sixteen-year-old with 'plans to continue her education' that she was being 'legally' adopted by her foster parents, 'the only instance in this group of children where this plan seemed feasible.'[112]

Whatever the special problems represented by the global recovery of children, Canadians grew increasingly enthusiastic in the years after the Second World War. In 1950, BC's Social Welfare Branch received applications for forty-six children from other nations, four from Yugoslavia, three from Poland, one from France, four from Italy, one from Greece, two from Germany, eleven from England, three from Scotland, six from Ireland, three from Iceland, and eight from the United States. Social workers again described commonplace difficulties: 'The weak point in planning for a child who is in another country and coming to other than his parents is the difficulty of preparing him for placement with people he does not know. Distance keeps him from becoming more than a "picture child" until he arrives— both to the prospective foster-parents and to the agency. . . . This kind of placement will continue to be difficult and hazardous for the child.'[113] While the vast majority of new arrivals came from European countries, including former enemy states, matching was not inevitable. In 1948, CCF MP Gladys Strum told the House of Commons about constituents, a Scottish doctor and his wife, who 'ask now for a Polish child because they say that the Polish people suffered more than any others.'[114] This was certainly the spirit embraced by the *Canadian Churchman,* when it published a half-page collage of children's pictures advertising international refugees and celebrated the reception of 58,000 'DPs', or displaced persons.[115] The Canadian Welfare Council also grew more positive, concluding that, for all the very real problems associated with migrating children, they weren't insurmountable.[116]

National self-interest also surfaced as Canadians surveyed potential offspring in war-torn Europe. In 1946, a Manitoba CCF MP argued for taking a full 'share of refugees', including perhaps 10,000 children. They would grow up 'in the spirit of Canadianism, and will have grown up under our laws and will be perhaps the most grateful type of Canadian . . . because they will realize that we have come to their help when they needed it most. Those who go back would also be a great help to us, because they will be ambassadors of good will of the very best type. . . . Back in Europe they can preach the gospel of friendship to Canada.'[117] Some eight years later, a BC Liberal MP saluted a migration plan proposed for homeless youngsters from the United Kingdom. He argued that importing kids made good economic sense and urged Ottawa bureaucrats to be helpful: 'I can think of no finer way of helping Canada with many of her difficulties, and also in the matter of employment and the sale of our goods, than by adding to the small population of Canada.

Let us add not only workers to population; let us let in every orphan in the world who wants to come and live here, and who has an assured home here. We need these people. If we can get them while they are young they will make top-notch citizens later.'[118] Even such enthusiasm proved insufficient, however, when it came to proposals from Ukrainian and Latvian Canadians to admit displaced youngsters from their European homelands. Postwar agreements required their repatriation to their country of origin.

After the war, enthusiasm largely died down, but the progressive-minded, often the would-be colour-blind liberals referred to in earlier chapters, kept an eye on global child welfare. In 1954, Adelaide Sinclair, whose credentials included stints as assistant to the deputy minister of welfare and as Canadian representative to UNICEF in 1946, became a deputy director of UNICEF.[119] Other citizens grew accustomed to sending funds to NGOs, including the Unitarian Service Committee Foster Parents Plan for 'shelter, care, and security' for global orphans.[120] The 1956 Hungarian Revolution provided new opportunities, and the *Globe and Mail* responded by urging relaxed procedures for adoption.[121] By 1958, British Columbia reported thirty-six Hungarian youngsters in care. Like other displaced children, many did not prove easy clients. Even though most were younger than eighteen, they 'had long since finished with childhood interests and seemed experienced and disillusioned far beyond their years.' Refugee camp life had, according to social workers, 'left them ill equipped emotionally and morally for successful adjustment in any community.' Not surprisingly, they, like other international travellers, didn't settle in easily.[122]

Visions of rescue nevertheless continued to dance in many heads. Media attention such as a 1964 article in the *Toronto Telegram* that described a foreign child as '4, Cute—and Doomed' fed fantasies.[123] *Maclean's* magazine did much the same in featuring an ad for the Christian Fund of Canada headlined, 'This year—give a child for Christmas' and provide 'a thrill for your family of friends.'[124] A variety of post–Second World War foster parent programs encouraged extending sympathies and firmly connected child salvation to individual acts of good will. While such initiatives often very much aimed to maintain birth families, as emphasized in League of Nations and UN declarations, they commonly succumbed to the temptation to isolate youngsters in their advertising. Like the domestic products arrayed in popular newspaper columns such as 'Today's Child' and 'Tuesday's Child', individual youngsters appeared, for the most part, to stand alone, bereft of responsible adults. Canadian easily slipped into familiar paternalistic or maternalistic habits that paid little attention to the global relations that left some countries ill-equipped to care for so many of their young. Some too were simply overwhelmed by the magnitude of the world's problems and determined to make a personal contribution to human happiness. Foster parents' plans also embodied more progressive and even radical possibilities, allowing for the sharing of duties with other parents. The educational convenor of Toronto's Save the Children Fund, who, like more than 1,200 other Canadian members, '"adopted" a needy child', shared that youngster. In return for critical support that enabled her birth family to keep the young girl, the Torontonian received the news and photos that, ironically enough, birth parents in later open adoptions would also be offered.[125]

Some Canadians were well satisfied with such contributions. Although the Foster Parents Plan remained in many ways an American agency until 1968, by that year the 3,130 Canadian members represented nearly one-quarter of North Americans registered.[126] Heavy American involvement in Asia, notably during the Korean War, generated other opportunities for that country's citizens to rescue children. As the numbers of available white infants dropped in the United States, intercountry adoption, embraced by personalities such as Pearl S. Buck, increasingly involved youngsters from Asia. In 1952, the US government made special provision for military and government personnel stationed in Korea to adopt.[127] Canadians lacked such immediate inspiration. Only in 1962 did the Conservative government of John Diefenbaker, encouraged by the Canadian Welfare Council, introduce policies for the adoption of individual youngsters from abroad. These had to be full orphans and to have refugee status. Equally limiting, and, in response to rising levels of domestic children in care, prospective adopters had to demonstrate that no suitable Canadian candidate was available. Not surprisingly, interest was limited. Not until 1968 did the *Toronto Star* introduce the first Korean orphan to be adopted by Canadians.[128] By the end of the decade, only an estimated sixty-seven adoptees had arrived from Hong Kong, with still smaller numbers from Korea.[129] Small as the group was, long-standing imperial linkages were also clear. Canadians appeared more likely to seek youngsters from the British protectorate than from the nation where their contribution to the United Nations forces was dwarfed by the Americans', with their particular resolve to counter communism in Asia.

Such limited initiatives left some citizens restive. Pleas for greater involvement were sometimes tied to more general concerns about Canadian policies. In 1956, the *United Church Observer* described the plight of 4,000 Japanese 'war babies', of whom 1,000 had been adopted in the United States but only two in Canada. It linked the shortfall to the general failure of immigration policy to welcome diverse peoples, a theme it would return to many times.[130] Other connections were also made, as when in 1960 the front page of the *Globe and Mail* portrayed Prime Minister Diefenbaker wondering whether Canadian children in care could also benefit from enlarged sympathies.[131] Whether such connections were typical was unclear, but, some three months later, the same newspaper reported that Canada had received only six inquiries and no firm applicants for refugees.[132] Supposedly the first arrival, but in fact preceding the official policy, was a three-year-old girl from Hong Kong. She settled in with Montreal parents of the same origin. Later in the decade, the *United Church Observer* portrayed two Canadian families hoping for Hong Kong orphans. Eventually one was sufficiently discouraged by red tape and self-conscious of unmet domestic need that it selected a First Nations child.[133]

By the 1960s, especially after World Refugee Year in 1960, the International Social Service (ISS), with origins working with refugees in post-First World War Europe, emerged as the global arm of the Canadian Welfare Council. It anchored Canadians all the more in the professional networks addressing migration. Child protection and placement were central to this mission. Its representatives began accompanying Hong Kong children to meet new Canadian families. One escort communicated the general philosophy of ISS initiatives, when she hoped that such adoptions would deepen 'understanding of other peoples and their willingness to help them.'[134] Canadians also worked individually in the British protectorate, applying to agencies for children. In British Columbia, the ISS had helped find both Asian and Caucasian homes for at least eleven Hong Kong girls and boys by 1967.[135] The same decade also inaugurated interest in young victims of the struggle between local nationalists in Vietnam and the French and then the Americans, but real enthusiasm coincided with the collapse of the southern regime in the mid-1970s.[136] That rescue would also have to contend with provincial bureaucracies that prioritized the needs of hard-to-place youngsters on their own rolls.[137] At least as important in restricting arrivals was the traditional preference for babies and the relative indifference towards 'children over 13 with personalities of their own and attachments to families still living in Vietnam.'[138]

While support for Asian offspring surfaced intermittently in the years after the Second World War, the near absence of interest in youngsters of African origin was notable. Even the tragedy of the Nigeria civil war in the 1960s could not generate more than a tiny handful of prospective takers for Biafran orphans. As Prime Minister Pierre Elliott Trudeau noted, citizens seemed little interested in that tragedy: only one responded to his invitation to adopt.[139] Racial integration in mainstream families, as in the state itself, had real limits.

As these examples suggest, the poor fit between the desires of would-be rescuers and the needs of foreign youngsters was frequently evident. In 1949, the editors of *International Child Welfare* explained the situation quite clearly, pointing out that 'the number of children that have not found any family connections since the end of the war is really very small, and in general they are older children, perhaps adolescents who do not in any way fulfill the conditions desirable in an adoption, which implies complete integration in the new family environment.' Like their counterparts among provincial child welfare workers, they insisted that poverty was never a sufficient reason for apprehension. They also stressed the pull of blood ties. Even kin in dreadful circumstances rarely readily released youngsters, who often represented 'the only precious thing left to them. Furthermore, the countries who have suffered the most and lost the flower of their youth are not at all anxious to let their physically and mentally most robust children go abroad, as obviously it is from this group of children that adopters desire to make their choice.'[140] In 1961, a UN seminar formulated the Leysin principles for ICA. It asserted the paramount needs of the child. ICA should be employed only when all domestic options had been fully explored. International audiences were reminded once again that girls and boys flourished best in their own families, cultures, and surroundings. Ten years later, a World Conference on Adoption and Foster Care in Milan, Italy, recognized the need to improve international regulations to safeguard the interests of adopted children and signalled an acceleration of the global transfer of youngsters.[141]

In Canada, the 1970s began with hopeful speculation. British Columbian authorities foresaw heightened demand for international adoptions, springing from improved birth control options, including abortion. They looked forward to fewer youngsters on offer within Canada and the prospects of 'an exciting challenge for the next decade in bringing cultures and races of the world closer together.'[142] That confidence was to be tested.

Canvassing the World: Saving Ourselves and Others, 1970s to 1990s

In the last decades of the twentieth century, prospective adopters found themselves confronting new roadblocks at home and abroad. Falling fertility, decreased stigma about illegitimacy, and Aboriginal protest removed many candidates; offspring-in-waiting were more likely than ever to be male, older, and bearing the weight of seeming mental and physical disabilities. While new reproductive technologies were increasingly explored, some would-be parents chose to look beyond their communities, especially if that provided the prospect of healthy female infants. Beginning in the 1970s, sharp differences distinguished domestic and international adoptions. There was, as one scholar has pointed out, 'a double standard' in operation: 'ethnic identity for child nationals available for adoption was an issue, but ethnic identity for children migrating for adoption was not.'[143] For a time it appeared that international adopters might escape the cultural issues that increasingly dominated discussions of Native adoptions in particular.

Expanding demand for ICA nevertheless occurred in the midst of rising collective sensitivity to oppression and discrimination. Domestic liberation movements, redress campaigns by Asian Canadians, and the Charter of Rights and Freedoms readily spotlighted fertility and parenting as contentious matters involving issues of social justice. Although charges of abduction and 'stolen generations' emerged first from First Nations critics, it was easy enough to make international connections. When donor nations such as Vietnam and Russia shut their doors, for shorter or longer periods, to foreign surrenders, the message became all the more clear: adopters had to pay attention to racial and cultural differences and to global inequalities more generally.

As before, and despite the occasional optimism of child welfare authorities, experienced social workers with heavy Canadian caseloads were rarely leading exponents of ICA. When they catalogued the unmet needs of their charges, they had good reason for scepticism. Better than most, they understood the dangers of border-crossing. One advocate of foreign adoption found opposition commonplace in her 1986 survey of Alberta child welfare workers: they preferred that children be maintained in natal families and that scant welfare resources be devoted to the Canadian needy. That province's welfare workers also resented bullying from ICA adopters, most of whom were middle-class or better, unaccustomed to frustrated desires, and skilled in campaigning for children.[144]

Canadian authorities remained hard pressed to supervise adoptions even within North America, and they were loath to direct scarce resources to ICA. They preferred to focus their attention on children like the fourteen youngsters whom

British Columbia placed in the United States in cooperation with ARENA and the seven allocated to other provinces in 1972. A decade or more later, across the continent, Prince Edward Island social workers similarly had their hands full in attempting to supervise out-of-province transfers, included thirteen children in 1984–5, sixteen in 1985–6, twelve in 1986–7, four in 1987–8, and five in 1988–9.[145] In the 1970s, Newfoundland had to employ a special worker to deal 'exclusively' with its out-of-province transfers through four agencies—the Sister Mary Eugene Foundation of New Jersey, the New York Foundling Hospital, the CAS of Ontario, and the Massachusetts Adoption Resource Exchange.[146] Many such exported youngsters were older and with 'special needs'. By the 1980s, the province was using relations with other agencies, including Ottawa's National Adoption Desk (NAD), to find 'native, black, and Asian origin' progeny within Canada for Newfoundland adopters.[147] Such work was exhausting. For many adoption workers, there was simply no time for ICA.

Canadian social workers also rightly worried about the impact of ICA on newcomers and their countries of origin. In 1972, the executive secretary of the Canadian Branch of ISS recommended caution. It was not fair to expect a child to deal with racial prejudice in the course of educating his new home in tolerance. Removing youngsters might also well mean a child would be 'irrevocably cut off' from some sense of his true identity.'[148] At much the same time, another expert, who had struggled to develop services for unmarried mothers in Seoul, South Korea, pointed out that foreign apprehensions might let foreign authorities off the hook for home-grown solutions.[149] For all such continuing cautions, ICA grew in Canada, as in the West, more generally. Even Canadian social workers were not insensitive to its appeal. As one noted, 'there is a growing world social consciousness' among couples who wish to share 'the richness and good life in Canada' with a child 'who has nothing'.[150]

All provinces except Quebec, which completed more ICAs than any other throughout the last decades of the twentieth century, chose to cooperate with the NAD, which began to negotiate agreements with surrendering countries in 1975. This was a slow process. While some donor nations ignored negative Canadian home studies on prospective adopters, as the director of the NAD acknowledged, strong lobbying for ICA made it very difficult to cut off any source of supply. Negotiation of international agreements nevertheless always seemed cumbersome and slow to those demanding immediate access to children. Critics of the NAD sometimes suggested that policy development remained highly dependent on individual commitment. This might vanish as quickly as it appeared. This was said to be the problem in 1983 when Immigration Minister Lloyd Axworthy returned from a tour of Salvadorean refugee camps to advocate an orphan adoption program. He appointed an activist from Families for Children, an especially vocal group, to organize arrangements, but a few months later he moved on to another ministry and the initiative faltered.[151] The NAD was even accused of conflict of interest. Its preoccupation with thrift and domestic caseloads meant, some argued, that it prioritized domestic alternatives rather than acting to improve ICA.[152]

Nor, ultimately, did the NAD handle all arrangements abroad. Federal budgets and initiatives remained limited. Canadian efforts were always diverse. In 1990, in response to demands from residents with Romanian ancestry, Saskatchewan dispatched its own adoption coordinator to Romania.[153] Private efforts on the part of both individuals and groups were widespread. But since even basic record-keeping remained limited, one expert has suggested that ICA calculations were even more unreliable than those at home.[154] Estimates of the number of youngsters acquired from outside Canada's borders do, nevertheless, convey a sense of the relative importance of various sources (see Table 7.5).

A 2002 study suggested that data, with the exception of those on children adopted abroad who entered as family class immigrants, were increasingly reliable from 1993. Numbers averaged about 2,000 a year for the 1990s, with a high of 2,223 in 1998 and a low of 1,738 in 1993. From 1993 to 2002, Canadians adopted 19,576 foreign youngsters. The ranking of surrendering nations sometimes shifted quickly in response to legislative or procedural changes or panics about corruption or health (see Table 7.6). The Chinese contribution (some 98 per cent female) ensured that the majority of foreign adoptees were girls, some 68 per cent in these years. Without the Chinese adoptions, the proportion would have been 54 per cent female, 46 per cent male. Most arrivals were younger than four years of age.

In 1991, Canada ratified the 1989 UN Convention on the Rights of the Child, the most rapidly accepted treaty in the history of human rights. That convention approved ICA only when youngsters could not be cared for in birth families or otherwise suitably, including in foster or institutional care, in their countries of origin. It required states to combat the world traffic in children. For most Westerners, including Canadians, however, institutions were unacceptable childcare alternatives. Their criticism and rising demand helped bring a sharp change in 1993. In that year, The Hague Convention on Protection of Children and Co-operation in Respect of Intercountry Adoptions (HCIA) stressed the benefits of permanent families, first nationally and then internationally, over all other arrangements. In 1994, Canada became a signatory to what has been revealingly dubbed the 'GATT for kids'.[155] The HCIA came into force in Canada three years later with the Child, Family and Community Division of Human Resources Development Canada designated the responsible agency. By 2004, all provinces and territories had passed enabling legislation.

Not all 'source' countries ratified the HCIA, providing still ample opportunity for 'the black market in babies'. In 1999, the UN Commission on Human Rights nominated a special rapporteur on the 'Sale of Children, Child Prostitution and Child Pornography.' As Canadian scholar Annalee Lepp has concluded, this well-intentioned initiative failed to appreciate the 'survival strategies' of poor mothers. Just as disadvantaged Canadian parents had consigned offspring to orphanages hoping for the best, their international counterparts confronted limited options. Their willingness to surrender children is not best understood as 'a transgression of motherhood/parenthood, a decline in spiritual and family values, or a function of greed.' Such a damning perspective has nonetheless too often informed the HCIA and the approach of the rapporteur to the UN.[156]

International agreements also highlighted Canada's frequent failure to eliminate

Table 7.5   Prospective adoptive children entering Canada by area of last permanent residence, 1978–88

Area	1978	1979	1980	1981	1982	1983	1984	1985	1986	1987	1988	1978–88, N (% of total)
Europe	7	6	4	5	10	11	2	7	3	10	4	69 (2.6)
Africa	1	2	1	4	0	2	3	2	4	2	4	25 (0.9)
Asia	108	106	113	114	132	149	151	183	175	224	250	1,705 (64.5)
North and Central America	7	10	7	12	23	8	17	11	14	15	10	134 (5.1)
Caribbean	10	29	33	18	39	48	16	16	30	22	19	280 (10.6)
South America	8	25	41	34	38	41	43	40	56	54	45	425 (16.1)
Other★	0	0	0	1	1	1	0	0	0	0	1	4 (0.2)
Total	141	178	199	188	243	260	323	259	282	327	333	2,642 (100)

★ Includes Australasia, Oceania, and other islands.

SOURCE: Katherine McDade, 'International Adoption in Canada: Public Policy Issues', discussion paper 91.B.1, *Studies in Social Policy* (Ottawa, April 1991), 25, table 3.

Table 7.6   International adoptions within Canada by country of last permanent residence, 1993–2002

Country of last permanent residence	1993	1994	1995	1996	1997	1998	1999	2000	2001	2002	1993–2002
China	320	466	665	682	519	901	687	603	602	800	6,245
India	255	366	203	180	232	179	136	79	112	126	1,868
Russia	105	128	73	125	164	160	208	147	142	146	1,398
Haiti	135	131	160	151	119	156	138	124	160	98	1,372
Philippines	224	206	116	64	30	80	75	81	65	43	984
United States	47	84	94	95	91	78	102	78	64	53	786
Jamaica	94	64	77	89	90	85	82	53	42	37	713
Vietnam	16	39	64	71	50	79	87	76	131	84	697
Romania	32	55	95	147	104	91	70	59	25	15	693
Guatemala	83	88	75	68	78	70	74	68	22	14	640
Thailand	15	39	21	27	28	47	57	49	35	38	356
Korea	1	2	1	9	15	8	15	64	90	98	303
Other	411	377	377	356	279	289	289	385	385	373	3,521
Total	1,738	2,045	2,021	2,064	1,799	2,223	2,020	1,866	1,875	1,925	19,576

SOURCE: 'International Adoptions', Citizenship and Immigration Canada, *Monitor* (fall 2003), available at http://www.cic.gc.ca/english/monitor/issue03/06-feature.html (accessed 22 December 2005).

Table 7.7 International adoptions by province, 1993–2002

	1993	1994	1995	1996	1997	1998	1999	2000	2001	2002	Total
Newfoundland	5	n/a	6	5	6	4	13	8	11	6	64
Prince Edward Island	n/a	n/a	0	0	n/a	n/a	n/a	n/a	n/a	n/a	0
Nova Scotia	9	11	11	19	14	22	35	34	47	40	242
New Brunswick	6	16	14	10	9	18	19	12	21	23	248
Quebec	694	831	977	954	700	918	809	722	714	791	8,110
Ontario	517	557	596	609	651	823	725	712	704	679	6,573
Manitoba	109	85	38	32	47	28	29	47	31	44	490
Saskatchewan	21	16	22	28	27	41	35	16	26	17	249
Alberta	62	117	72	94	65	89	80	96	95	85	855
British Columbia	313	402	279	310	278	278	273	215	220	238	2,806
Territories and not stated	n/a	7	6	3	n/a	n/a	n/a	n/a	n/a	n/a	28

SOURCE: 'International Adoptions', Citizenship and Immigration Canada, *Monitor* (fall 2003), available at http://www.cic.gc.ca/english/monitor/issue03/06-feature.html (accessed 22 December 2005).

distinctions between children adopted at home and abroad. In the 1990s the House of Commons saw many exchanges over the question of citizenship. In 1993, one Liberal MP, pressed by anxious constituents with a daughter from the People's Republic of China, asked why youngsters didn't automatically receive Canadian citizenship upon adoption, only to receive a weak assurance from the minister of multiculturalism and citizenship that procedures were under consideration.[157] In 1999, the minister of citizenship and immigration presented a new citizenship bill to address a 'rapidly evolving world'. She suggested that 'in keeping with our tradition of justice and fairness, we propose changes to ensure greater equity between the natural born and adopted child.'Whereas foreign adoptees had been treated as immigrants, they would now be 'granted citizenship' without going through the immigration process.[158] The bill did not pass. Despite the Charter of Rights and Freedoms, distinctions between children born abroad or adopted abroad by Canadians survived into the twenty-first century.[159] In July 2001, Ottawa implemented an 'interim' measure by which Canadians abroad could apply for a special grant of citizenship for their adopted offspring. This was still in effect in 2005.

The last decades of the twentieth century produced a profusion of ICA activists. Groups such as Canadadopt, AWARE (Awareness to World Adoption and Responsibility to Everyone), Families for Children (FFC), and a host of imitators offered a variety of services, sometimes specializing in particular regions. FFC, which operated in India and El Salvador, collaborated with the NAD, which referred all applications for youngsters from these nations. Unlike many competitors, it also promised ongoing supervision of adoptees. ICA businesses or philanthropies—a distinction often difficult to make—sometimes had checkered histories. L'Arc en Ciel, which handled Mexican arrangements, went bankrupt in September 1988, leaving many clients in the lurch.[160] Not surprisingly, some provinces experimented with regulating the private adoption industry in these years.

The typical arguments of ICA lobbyists were set out before the Parliamentary Committee on International Adoption in 1974. A representative from Enfants du Monde/Children of the World, argued that ICA was one way to share the world's riches.[161] Another from FFC insisted that adoption was often a 'matter of life and death' and that governments should not interfere: 'a couple has almost an inherent right to adopt any child that would fit well into their family—from whatever country.' Cultural differences were dismissed as over-rated; in any case many adopters did their homework on surrendering nations. Thus, 'to put up roadblocks to international adoption because of a child facing "culture shock" in Canada is very shortsighted—indeed cruel. A child's life is at stake.'[162] The sense of grievance among ICA advocates was palatable. One Ottawa doctor and supporter of the JMJ Children's Fund argued that it took 'special qualities to accept with equanimity the slights, rebuffs, irrational demands and interminable delays presently imposed on Canadian families wanting to adopt a child from another country.' While his organization supported Children's Villages—essentially a modern form of orphanage—and birth families in potential donor nations, he insisted that sometimes ICA was entirely the right way to proceed.[163]

Another doctor and his wife, Robert and Helke Ferrie, from Burlington, Ontario, spoke on behalf of the Kuan-Yin Foundation, named after the Chinese Buddhist goddess who hears cries of anguish. They emphasized the misery of the poor in Southeast Asia and the dangers of orphanages. Their foundation required that adopters be 'totally flexible' regarding age and sex, as 'children are not posses- sions that are tailored to specifications' and 'the whole point of adoption is to put yourself in the service of the child who is in need.' They also rejected the com- monplace objection: 'Our experience has been that the emphasis on culture is nowadays one of the most convenient ways to hide one's racial prejudices by attributing tremendous value to something that is irrelevant to survival.' The com- ments of Helke Ferrie suggested an insider's knowledge of Asia: 'Do we really want to keep up the myth of the extended family system when that extended family system in all of the thousands of years of Asian history never extended itself to the aid of illegitimate children, and to orphaned children only if they were male, or came from a very high society family. . . . What exactly is so bad about Western culture than an orphan should not grow up in it?' For many disadvan- taged boys and girls, Canada was simply best. Nor were benefits one-sided, for 'to have a Chinese face, a black face or a brown face with almond shaped eyes smile at one and say "I am a Canadian" is perhaps the greatest compliment that can be paid to our country.'[164]

The president of Ottawa's Open Door Society (ODS) voiced similar sentiments, adding that 'holiday visits back' to native lands 'were becoming almost routine.' He suggested that opponents of 'international adoptions should ask themselves if they are not just practicing racism. To advocate barring such immigrants betrays a cal- lous indifference to human needs. For many of us, our forefathers came to North America to escape economic, religious or political hardship, and they were cer- tainly alien to the local scene.'[165] ICA champions employed such arguments throughout the last decades of the twentieth century. In the process, they often firmly linked their cause to the multicultural and, sometimes, anti-racist politics of modern Canada.

In the 1970s a series of international crises, ranging from the Pakistani civil war that created Bangladesh to the continuing conflict in Vietnam, energized ICA. In 1972, Helke Ferrie went on a hunger strike to dramatize the plight of Bangladeshi orphans.[166] She soon found herself nose-to-nose with Ontario's welfare author- ities, who prioritized the needs of the province's line up of Native wards.[167] She stood, however, with the rising tide of public opinion. Within a few months, all provinces faced demands to open doors to Vietnamese 'orphans'. According to a British Columbia report, April and May 1975 brought 'a tremendous surge of interest', with some 2,000 telephone offers. Yet ultimately, for all such hullabaloo, the province's Department of Human Resources reported placing only fourteen children from South Vietnam.[168]

As the Americans retreated from Saigon in 1975, Canadians demanded emer- gency airlifts, and some thousand Torontonians requested young refugees.[169] So- called mercy flights were hailed as a test of the country's 'ultimate humanity'.[170] In the House of Commons, MPs such as Toronto Conservative Otto Jelinek demanded that immigration be fast-tracked. Another Conservative, Douglas Roche from Edmonton, was more cautious, warning lest Canadians be overwhelmed by guilt about the Vietnam conflict. He also emphasized the dangers of rescue.[171] Just as they would be told after the December 2004 tsunami disaster in Asia, Canadians were reminded that local people could well regard foreign adoptions as abduction and that not all youngsters were in fact orphans.[172] The crash of an American Air Force jet with some 234 'war children' bound for Canada and the United States revealed still other dangers.[173] Eventually it was estimated that Canadians adopted approximately seven hundred children from Vietnam between 1963 and 1976.[174]

In the following years, Canadians readily resonated to global catastrophes, such as the Italian earthquake in 1980.[175] The fall of the Romanian dictator Nicolae Ceausescu and the collapse of the Union of Soviet Socialist Republics renewed the rush for progeny. In the 1980s and 1990s, horrific tales of abuse in Romanian and Russian orphanages documented by Human Rights Watch and other NGOs, journalists, and western observers in general appeared once again to justify Canadian saviours.[176] The evident social and economic power of many ICA adopters made their commitment to the familiar rescue plot all the harder to deny.

The arrival of Romanian girls and boys represented the first mass movement since the war in Vietnam. Some 663 entered Canada between 1989 and 1991 in what has been termed the 'Romanian free-for-all'.[177] In 1990, a federal visa officer was posted to Bucharest 'primarily' to expedite visas.[178] By the end of 1991, over a thousand had been issued, more than half for young inmates of orphanages and hospitals.[179] Canadian and other western adopters soon found themselves mired in scandal as corruption dogged transactions in a cash-poor and politically fragile nation. The Romanian government quickly grew self-conscious about the condition and fate of its nationals and began to restrict their export. Far worse was to come. By the mid-1990s, Canadian developmental psychologist Dr Elinor Ames was documenting, although not without hope, the terrible consequences of early deprivation.[180] While voices reminded Canadians that 'joys and satisfactions' were present and that Romanian newcomers were much like many home-grown counterparts,[181] continuing bad news gave many adopters pause.

While would-be parents went worldwide for their candidates, many initially turned to Russia, where there also appeared to be a surplus of adoptable children in the 1990s. Very much environmentalists, optimistic Canadians trusted that rescued progeny would escape the life of criminality and abuse predicted for many orphanage inmates. Canadians also supported non-profit groups such as the Canadian Commonwealth of Independent States Friendship Exchange Society that promised to send medicine and clothing to Russian orphanages.[182] Soon, however, despite the supposed 'amazing good luck—the privilege of growing up as the children of well-educated, affluent and loving Canadian parents', former Soviet bloc newcomers became associated with a 'minefield of hidden health problems, corruption and even baby-selling.' In sharp contrast, would-be parents were regularly portrayed as well-intentioned victims. Such was the press treatment of one BC couple whose adoptees, diagnosed with alcohol-related problems, were seized by provincial welfare authorities.[183] The desperation of an Ontario public schoolteacher in her late forties who turned to Ukrainian suppliers went largely unquestioned. Like many others, she had 'her heart set on adopting a baby girl stranded in an orphanage.' After paying an estimated $46,000 she found herself offered only boys or youngsters with disabilities and returned empty-handed.[184]

If eastern Europe supplied disturbing accounts at the end of the twentieth and beginning of the next century, Canadians were reported as discovering better outcomes in Latin America and the People's Republic of China. While the former frequently received publicity that evoked comparisons with the disorganized, often corrupt, options Canadians had found in the former Soviet Union, China offered a 'well-organized international program that carries a relatively low price tag (about $20,000).' These advantages, when combined with strong post-adoption networks and the appeal of healthy 'abandoned' children in problematic institutions, regularly trumped youngsters from eastern Europe and Latin America.[185] China's one-child policy also appeared to deliver the healthy female infants most in demand. Agencies such as Children of the World found themselves busy as Canadian couples were estimated in March 1991 to have paid 'almost $2 million to adopt Chinese baby girls in the last 19 months.' Those leery of charges of baby-selling were reassured that such 'contributions' went directly to improve institutions.[186] Just as with the Romanian and Russian child-rushes, initiatives sometimes generated a strong sense of community, as in 1999 when eleven 'Canadian bundles of joy', all from the same orphanage, were collectively sworn in as new citizens in Oshawa, Ontario.[187]

Applicants who were older, commonly above forty, single, and lesbian or gay were often prime candidates for global searches. Although they had sometimes been permitted to adopt domestically, such would-be parents had often found access limited to youngsters least in demand. In 1978, the *Globe and Mail* featured two single women who exemplified common options. A nurse and teacher, they could afford single parenthood. The director of nursing adopted a female Korean toddler, while the teacher acquired two older daughters in Canada, one diagnosed with cerebral palsy and the other as emotionally disturbed and further singled out by a harelip.[188] Such long-stigmatized youngsters and mothers were both in effect 'special needs' when younger heterosexual couples stood at the front of line for supposedly perfect infants. As one Alberta investigator noted, if domestic applicants were able to get their 'first choice child (healthy and white) they will not pursue with the international adoption.'[189] Abroad, domestically challenged candidates might well hope to better their chances in the adoption sweepstakes. As one single female physiotherapist, who discovered a boy and a girl in a Guatemala orphanage, confessed: 'It turned out a lot better than if I'd waited to adopt a Canadian child. Now you can only adopt special needs kids—they're usually mentally or physically handicapped. I've ended up with two that seem to be very smart and perfectly normal in every way.'[190]

The publicity given ICA sometimes prompted self-consciousness. One Canadian who adopted a Chinese daughter in 1998 admitted her reservations about acquiring a child available because of discrimination against women. Like many others, she tried to make personal and, ultimately, collective sense of her actions by concluding, 'if I give up on adopting from China, what will change? I've decided I'm going to find an organization that works with women and children in China and give them my support. That makes me feel better.' She promised to make her new daughter knowledgeable and proud of her Chinese heritage since 'differences can be wonderful.' She also hoped, especially after the massacre at Tiananmen Square in 1989, that her child would treasure 'all the benefits and privileges of being a Canadian.'[191] An adoptive father, who discovered a new career writing the 'Autumn Jade Mystery Stories' for young readers claimed, despite his European background, a stronger affinity with China than Russia or South America and looked forward to a lifelong affair with the East.[192] However heartfelt, such tales did not always escape a sense of the exotic that often accompanied Asian adoptions. Such youngsters also benefited from their commonplace association with intelligence and good behaviour more generally. Unlike their proliferation of sad Russian and Romanian stories, the media readily profiled good outcomes with youngsters from across the Pacific.[193]

In sharp contrast to Asia and Europe, and even Latin America, one regularly disaster-struck continent, Africa, supplied few adoption stories to the media at any time during twentieth century. The Rwandan civil war in the 1990s, like the earlier Nigeria conflict, generated minimal interest in progeny. Only a handful of francophone girls and boys were airlifted from the 'killing fields' to Quebec.[194] African-ancestry youngsters from the Caribbean seeking to join blood relatives were also likely to receive a cold shoulder from Canadian authorities.[195] In contrast, children brought in from the United States might well be the black. They might be effectively 'surplus' in the southern market, but white Canadian adopters sometimes appeared more receptive. The handful of white adopters of youngsters with African roots could be popularly applauded. Such appeared the case with a gay couple from British Columbia's Lower Mainland who adopted a son from Chicago's ghetto. They understood that their new family member would need assistance in settling into a region whose population counted few of his background. They planned to celebrate Kwanza in honour of his African American heritage and to join the Afro-Canadian Adoption Network for 'friends, mentors, and role models'.[196] Not for their son, however, the near delirious media welcome that so often accompanied the appearance of China's little girls.

As demand for ICA grew, so did global fears about the international traffic in children. By the 1980s, charges of prostitution and organ harvesting were beginning to appear in Canadian publications.[197] Once subject to close scrutiny, the motives and behaviour of some international adopters sometimes failed critical moral tests. This was certainly the case with an Ontario woman who adopted a Mexican five-year-old in order to acquire his four-year-old sister. Not surprisingly, things went wrong, and she turned him, as an eight-year-old, over to Toronto's Catholic CAS. She then barred him from seeing his sister, with whom she eventually left the country. The boy's predicament eventually included juvenile offences and arrest. Since no arrangement had been made to secure him Canadian citizenship, the teenager was subject to deportation.[198] The situation was equally suspicious in 1998 in the case of a BC couple. They attempted to acquire a Nepalese daughter whose birth mother resisted their claim. That such tragedies were far from unusual was suggested when Nepal's former home minister was charged at much the same time with accepting bribes to speed up foreign adoptions.[199] In 2005, Canadians were once again awakened to the abuses in their midst by the story of a nine-year-old Romanian girl, Alexandra, adopted by an Ancaster, Ontario, doctor and his wife in 1991 and summarily dispatched on her own to her birthplace a few months later. Her impoverished birth family could offer little help as the so-called Canadian was denied educational and other benefits by the Romanian state. Not until Canadian filmmaker Mary Anne Alton took up the cause of the young woman with the equivalent of a Grade 3 education in *Return to Sender* was there any hope of redress.[200] Such stories are reminiscent of the abuses associated many decades earlier with the home children.

In Canada, foreign youngsters were closely linked, as they had been in the past, to immigration in general. On the one hand, governments continued intermittently to contemplate the demographic benefits for an aging native-born population.[201] One long-standing policy adviser mused in 2004: 'The rescue of children from deprivation and despair is one of the most appealing of causes.'[202] On the other hand, lingering suspicions of 'foreigners' and 'illegal entry' remained. In 1976, BC officials publicly noted an increase in the number of applications for adoption of overseas nieces and nephews who otherwise would not meet immigration requirements. Although this was not spelled out, such instances were probably Asian.[203] ICA sometimes offered opportunities to bypass immigration restrictions. Such seemed the case with one landed immigrant's effort to adopt a younger brother in 1978.[204] In the next decade, Alberta courts, upon the advice of the provincial superintendent of child welfare, rejected the application of Indo-Canadians to adopt the child of family friends from the subcontinent who were reckoned 'too poor to provide education and employment opportunities.'[205] The same courts refused to accept the petition of an Alberta couple to adopt the twelve-year-old daughter of the wife's brother, both of whom lived in India.[206] Such refusals were always complicated, inevitably invoking Canada's racist history of objections to the reunification of Asian families.

The course of international adoption since the nineteenth century presented a mixed history for adoptees and families. Tragic stories have been highly visible. By the end of the twentieth century, Britain was subsidizing visits 'home' by elderly 'home children' and Barnardo Aftercare UK had officially apologized. Happy, if less newsworthy, stories also surfaced. In the early 1990s, Canadian social work scholars Anne Westhues and Joyce C. Cohen interviewed 126 families in British Columbia, Ontario, and Quebec who were involved in ICA. While more than 80 per cent of ICA kids experienced racial discrimination, the majority did well in school and reported high self-esteem.[207] In 2004, Vancouver's *Georgia Strait* held out hope for its readers, whom one suspects supplied a demographic sympathetic to ICA. It described a thirty-year-old who had been airlifted out of Saigon to grow up in Burlington, Ontario. Supported by parents who 'left the door open for him to explore his Vietnamese background,' he never did so but married and studied, evidently with success. Vancouver's Chinatown was portrayed as welcoming an early adoptee from the People's Republic of China. Now an adolescent, that little girl had benefited from a Chinese Canadian housekeeper and had studied the pipa or Chinese lute. She and her mother, a single middle-class professional, conveyed a reassuring image of healthy multicultural normality.[208] One author of a Canadian manual on ICA, himself the father of a daughter from China concluded that, although abuses had been 'awful', they were exceptional. More common was 'win–win situations for children, parents, and all the others.' Such results could be obtained if Canadians behaved responsibly in the context of a 'world of much suffering and want.' To this end, he supplied 'An Ethics Test for International Adoption.'[209]

While girls and boys themselves sometimes seemed almost invisible in transactions, ICA has been regularly defended as in the 'best interests of children'. What benefits do they receive through migration? How important is the loss in part or in whole of original families and cultures? Such questions and their answers ultimately differed little from those raised about domestic exchanges. As provincial adoption practices evolved to offer more protection, international exchanges sometimes provided opportunities to bypass evolving safeguards. Children might well be victims of adult agendas in both impoverished and richer nations. As the BC Panel to Review Adoption Legislation understood in 1994, ICA generally severed contact with birth families: 'In fact, international adoptions create the same conditions widely criticized in domestic adoption: a child in need is taken from his or her family and regarded "as if born to" another family. Exceptions to this lack of openness in international adoption are rare.'[210] As one Canadian adopter of four children abroad insisted in the course of the bitter 2005 debates over Ontario's proposed bill to grant full access to information: 'We adopted abroad so that we can be a family with no meddling and confusion in the lives of our children. They know we love them and care for them. They are not being leased to us. . . . We will never adopt from Canada because we do not want intrusion into our family.'[211] This father fondly imagined that his youngsters would have no interest in exploring their past and would accept unquestioningly the good things they were offered. Improvements in material circumstances and the love of new parents were to wipe out the history of loss. In stark contrast was the busy two-way traffic, testified to so regularly on the World Wide Web, that had developed between original homelands and Canada. Some adopters and their sons and daughters have always committed themselves to sustaining ties to and sometimes support for older worlds that had been forced to surrender progeny.

Like its domestic counterpart, ICA confronts critical questions about the relationship of past and present. How is it possible to integrate difference into households without succumbing to the persisting temptation to ignore historically oppressive relations? Canadians, like Americans, whose response to transnational adoption has recently been much studied, find themselves facing the dilemma of 'constructing a cultural identity' for the newcomer that goes beyond the celebratory to confront the politics that has positioned some people's offspring to be rescued by others.[212] Honest self-consciousness would require acknowledgement of what the international program manager for International Social Services characterized as a 'pernicious philosophy', the widespread assumption of 'a right to a child'. Canadian 'acts of selfishness', like those in the rest of the West, have only too easily aided and abetted the trafficking in children.[213] The elevation of Western middle-class norms as universals when it comes to children has justified, as Derek Kirton, another international scholar of ICA, has observed, imperial apprehensions. For 'beneath the child-centred language lies a hegemonic view that the children of other countries are "our children". . . . The partiality of the liberal view becomes clear when it is realized that they are only "our children" when "we" want to adopt them.' This distinction similarly surfaces in the 'differential treatment meted out to white intercountry adopters' in the United Kingdom, as in Canada, and the resistance to efforts of minority groups to reunite globally dispersed families.[214]

As yet, the ideology of rescue overwhelmingly permeates discussion of intercountry adoption. In December 2004 and January 2004, many Canadians only too readily rushed to propose the adoption of Asian youngsters presumably orphaned in the wake of a devastating tsunami. Their remedy did not go unchallenged by thoughtful observers. Authorities in Canada, including the Adoption Council of Canada, joined those in the stricken countries themselves to remind would-be adopters that few youngsters had no families to claim them and that the great majority would be better served by fostering and home services. Canadians reading the accounts of Barnardo and other home children found in the *Globe and Mail's* 'Lives Lived' in the course of the previous decade should appreciate the merits of that advice.[215]

Ultimately, any assessment of the evolution of ICA in Canada has to confront motives that run the gambit from the crassly economic to the deeply humanitarian. As one aspect of immigration policy, it also necessarily reflects judgment about what is good for Canada and its citizens as a whole. Do child immigrants bring the cultural, moral, and physical inheritance that will shore up the preferred vision of Canada? As Kirsten Lovelock has observed in her study of Canada, New Zealand, and the United States, acts of individual adopters 'seldom stand in stark opposition to national interests, indeed there is a considerable degree of convergence. The actions of individuals (nationals) have often served national ends.'[216] Just as would-be parents have increasingly sought abroad for youngsters when healthy Caucasian infants became largely unavailable at home, Canadian immigration policy has considered younger newcomers assets in the context of aging native-born population.[217] Governments have been hard put to resist the desires of middle-class citizens, whether for adult servants in every decade, child labourers in the nineteenth and early twentieth centuries, and, later on, for acceptable progeny from elsewhere. Canada and the other 'importing' nations 'prioritized the needs of their own citizens and domestic/international/political concerns over the needs and well being of the child migrant for adoption.'[218] Happily, needs sometimes coincided.

Origins and Destinations: Connecting Individuals and Communities

As the continuing literary appeal of adoptions confirms, origins have intrigued Canadians. Observers have, however, found it more difficult to engage with the hard realities behind surrenders or the personal puzzles they leave behind. Anne Shirley, the creation of Lucy Maud Montgomery, embodied early romanticization. Rather like Cabbage Patch dolls, the Christmas 1983 fad, she appeared to have no past that could compromise her assimilation as the cherished daughter of Marilla and Mathew Cuthbert. Not until the third volume in Montgomery's series, *Anne of the Island* (1915), did the red-headed heroine display any real interest in her biological parents, and this is largely unpremeditated and without significant consequence.[1] Unlike so many real-life counterparts, Anne never pined for a birth mother and father or searched for other kin. This lively orphan was credited with the silenced but agreeable class and ethnic antecedents that many would-be parents sought. By the close of the twentieth century, the complications of adoption were much more the fictional order of the day. In her novel *Sundogs* (1992), Métis writer Lee Maracle introduced Monique, who has 'no family of her own' and does not know her Native band. She calls her white adopters 'Mom' and 'Dad', but they can't erase her poignant sense of loss.[2] Award-winning writer Elyse Gasco similarly recounted an intricate story of pain involving a daughter and her adoptive and birth mothers. In her *Can You Wave Bye Bye, Baby?* (1999), modern readers learned again that the past is not readily discarded.

Adopted children and adults have been regularly pressed to assimilate, relinquishing previous life texts as irregular, ultimately disposable, preliminaries to the real thing. Throughout the nineteenth and twentieth centuries, many daughters and sons of the less powerful nevertheless resisted their appropriation. First-person accounts from the apprehended tell of recurring efforts to claim older narratives and connect the disjointed chapters of their lives. Many birth mothers and, more occasionally, birth fathers and other kin, similarly attempted to counter injunctions to be silent. As chapter 1 pointed out, biological families and communities at home and abroad were often loath to give up all associations. Adopters, in contrast, were more likely to be enthusiastic about forgetfulness. As H. David Kirk understood, many wished to pretend that their households matched biological families. Whether they hoped to hide infertility, avoid prejudice, rid themselves of suspect, even dangerous, predecessors, or free themselves and their new offspring to commit unconditionally to new relationships, such parents have generally preferred rivals to be out of the picture. They have regularly put their faith in socialization and tried to sidestep heredity. Distance has been especially attractive when surrendering families were strangers, but kin groups did not escape such inclinations. Decades of lawsuits for custody among family members testify convincingly to suspicion, dislike, and jealousy. While 'open adoption' gained fans in the last decades of the twentieth century, sharing youngsters, like maintaining loyalties to more than one 'home' land, has frequently proved difficult.

This chapter takes up the complex story of efforts to renew and understand original relations. It begins with a discussion of efforts prior to the 1970s—the first year of that decade being Canada's peak year for legal domestic adoptions—when searches and reunions attracted relatively little attention and were conducted overwhelmingly on an individual basis. Only at the end of this period were confidentiality and secrecy for the most part legislatively upheld, although it was always assumed that privacy meant in the first instance protection from the public gaze rather than ignorance within the adoptive circle itself. The second section considers the emergence of the mainstream searching movement, which originated in the United States after the Second World War but quickly found Canadian counterparts in groups such as Parent Finders. Such searchers were overwhelmingly white and middle class. Most were adoptees, but they were also birth mothers and other members of the adoption circle. They were effective enough to transform, albeit insufficiently from their perspective, legislation that by the 1970s began uncertainly to provide for reunions and registries. Such searchers are readily distinguishable from advocates of Aboriginal repatriation, who are considered in the next section. Like other searchers, Canadian First Nations communities demanded opportunities for reconnection within the context of the Canadian Charter of Rights and Freedoms and post–Second World War liberation movements. Their campaigns for reconnection with lost youngsters were also, however, a fundamental part of larger efforts to demand a fair deal from settler society. And where much of the initiative for mainstream searchers came from adoptees, Native inspiration came too from surrendering communities. In closing, this chapter considers the late-twentieth-century debates about openness that once again highlighted history, both individual and collective, as a source of contention for Canadians.

Keeping in Touch: The Early Days

From the inauguration of adoption legislation, record-keeping regarding the transfer of children has been notoriously uncertain. No effort at reconnection can be understood without recognizing the recurring shortcomings of data. At the end of the twentieth century, adoptees from jurisdictions such as China and Russia often arrived with little information about their origins, but Canadians had long experienced such lacunae. For those adopted much before the 1950s, case records were typically far from adequate. Both surrendering and adoptive parents frequently considered it in their own best interest and that of their offspring to obscure and even destroy proof of other ties. Private arrangements, long organized by doctors, lawyers, and variously intentioned traffickers in children, rarely left much of a trail.

The poor, whose offspring were those commonly transferred to other families, might live relatively near to adopters, but they were also more likely to be itinerant and vulnerable to illness and earlier death. They might well soon become invisible. In the course of both private and public transactions, documents have also been readily massaged to reflect preferred stories. Searchers commonly had good reason to be frustrated and angry.

On the other hand, right from the beginning, not all formally or informally adopted Canadians and their birth kin have been prepared to demand rights over the past. Not everyone has wished to initiate contact or to reclaim knowledge. Some participants in the adoption circle imbibed the culture of shame often attached to adoption in the early years, especially but not only if illegitimacy was involved. Some were too disoriented by difficult lives or by traumatic separations to seek remedy. Some simply hoped for the best. Adoptees might fear hurting adoptive parents if they checked into their pasts while these parents were alive. In other cases, adoptees might suspect nothing of their history. Some adoptees preferred to rely on what they had rather than to follow up potentially dangerous or indifferent earlier associations. Others have been upset and alienated by what they might interpret as abandonment by first families. Before the Second World War and long afterwards, there was also the 'chosen baby' story. This did little to encourage curiosity about antecedents and the situations that led to surrender. Nevertheless, for all such disincentives, which continued into the twenty-first century, searching emerged as a fact of life for many Canadians well before the modern movement arose. This has been especially true for women, who were so often the central characters in adoption stories.

Whether emigrated from Great Britain or plucked from the dominion's own impoverished urban, rural, and frontier districts and populations, children given to others were expected to reject pasts that critics judged unsatisfactory or sometimes dismissed as savage and pre-modern. Forgetting was always easier recommended than embraced. Recurring prejudice and suspicion might make amnesia difficult even for those who wished, sometimes desperately, to leave the past behind. Whether it was taunts about stigmatized origins from schoolmates or some other unsettling inspiration, many did not forget the preliminaries to adoption. Whatever their shortcomings, including the worse kinds of abuse, blood ties readily surfaced to disturb the promise of the future.

Contradictory forces were always at work. Public and private welfare agencies regularly hoped to separate offspring from problematic parents. Lingering attachments compromised hopes for fresh starts. Early and late advocates of adoption devoutly wished that youngsters escape the shackles of class, religious, and racial prejudice. They regularly suggested, as did J.J. Kelso, Ontario's superintendent of dependent and neglected children in 1899, that transferred girls and boys promised to become 'bright and interested' instead of 'gaping and stunted mental dwarfs'. Citing Friedrich Froebel, the world-renown Swiss authority on early childhood, Kelso proclaimed: 'In every child the possibility of a perfect man.'[3] One apparition who appeared in his office captured the benefit of renouncing the past. Here was 'a young lady, very tastefully dressed and apparently well brought up' who 'explained that she herself had been adopted when very young from one of the public institutions, and had been kindly and affectionately reared and educated by a worthy couple, whom she looked upon as her parents in the truest sense.'[4] A Canadian novel from 1897, featuring a woman doctor, made much the same case. The author described adoption as one solution to poverty and crime. Despite, as the main character admitted, the attachment of the poor for their offspring, 'the absolute success of the experiment would depend upon the child being kept in total ignorance that it had any ties except those which bound it to you.'[5] It was very much in this vein that Mary Ellen Smith, the first woman elected to the BC legislature, urged an amendment to the provincial adoption act in 1926 that would 'make it impossible for relatives of children to interfere with foster parents after their legal adoption.'[6] Advocates of legal transfer, like champions of heightened immigration, hoped for bright results undiminished by links to questionable origins.

Reformers' plans early on ran straight into the hopes of those unfortunate enough to require their services. Poor families in Britain and in Canada had long used philanthropic supports, from orphanages to emigration societies, to tide them through bad times, far more rarely to sever ties. The director of Toronto's Children's Aid Society (CAS) and a consultant to the League of Nations on child welfare was mindful of long-standing experience when he urged caution in 1939. Adoption was not to be undertaken quickly or without investigation. As he reminded readers, 'Parents who have given up their children frequently want them back again.' Nor, he suggested, was return necessarily a bad option. Whatever the promise of new arrangements, they did not match the 'happy dénouement' of a rehabilitated birth family. 'Parents', he further warned, 'are not interchangeable.'[7] A year later, before the supporters of the Boys' Home in Hamilton, Ontario, he again emphasized the dilemma facing everyone involved in child welfare. Friends and relatives stood not far off for most youngsters in care even when those individuals were a

> 'blessed nuisance' to those who are chiefly interested in running the institution. The job for them would be very much easier if parents would be wiped out of the picture entirely. However, to those primarily interested in the children themselves, parents and relatives are of the greatest importance. If modern psychology has taught us anything worthwhile, it certainly has taught the importance of a sense of security; and the feeling of really 'belonging' in a family group is, without doubt, the greatest possible contributor to that fundamental 'security'.[8]

Not surprisingly, this expert, and others like him, most often preferred arrangements that helped potentially worthy families over tough patches and offered inducements to behaviour that better matched dominant expectations of normalcy.

Over time, social security, beginning with mothers' pensions and allowances during the First World War, combined with falling maternal mortality rates and generally rising life expectancy to eliminate many candidates for adoption and to keep original families intact. In the twentieth century, unwed mothers supplied the outstanding source of youngsters free for adoption. Even then, as many would-be adopters discovered to their distress, these women could not be counted on to step aside for their supposed betters. Whatever hardship single mothers faced, they too, especially when they lacked resources of class and race that promised redemption and a good life if they left 'mistakes' behind, regularly proved reluctant to surrender offspring. When they did acquiesce, many found it difficult to forget what they had lost. In the 1960s, one judge of Edmonton's family and juvenile court recalled a correspondent, 'to outward appearances happy', who, despite a later marriage and other offspring, every day recalled a baby she had given up twenty years earlier. Similarly, a woman in another province was described as asking Alberta child welfare authorities about the fate of an infant she had surrendered in 1938. That mother had married the father, and both continued to worry about their firstborn. Such requests trickled in along side a still larger number from adopted adolescents and adults. The judge reported that all inquiries were treated 'sympathetically and with understanding, divulging what information they can, without revealing identity.' Very much in keeping with the opinion of her day, she believed that such communications nevertheless often indicated 'an unsatisfactory relation or lack of communication with the adoptive parents.'[9] While sympathetic to individual concerns, she remained sure that moving on was best for all concerned.

Whether emigrated from abroad or homegrown, youngsters were from the beginning entangled in contradictory impulses about their future. Much to the chagrin of would-be rescuers, some 16 per cent of the Barnardo orphans returned home permanently to Britain.[10] They were not alone. One boy dispatched from Scotland to New Brunswick described a not uncommon situation: 'My mother is anxious for me to go back home to Glasgow and she wrote and asked me to apply to your department to repatriate me.'[11] A major survey of juvenile immigrants brought to Canada in 1910 and 1920 confirmed that many girls and boys left anxious families in the United Kingdom and pointed to 'recurring evidence of the longing of the children for their own people. Frequent and pathetic appeals were made by the children to the inspectors for news and addresses of their brothers and sisters.'[12] In 1932, the executive secretary of Montreal's Ladies' Benevolent Society described the throng of clients returning to learn of 'relatives, lost to them forty, fifty years ago, even brothers and sisters who were with them in the institution but who were allowed to slip away into the outside world without a trace.' Many had turned out well but they were resentful and frustrated. She described a man who came all the way from the western United States and who protested: 'I wrote and got an answer that you had no information, but I just refused to believe it, and I have been saving for years to make this trip. I had a mother, and four brothers and sisters, and you let me be adopted out. I have a lad now myself, just reaching manhood, and he needs some background to tie up to.' Clearly, such appeals educated many workers. This observer also credited the contemporary 'mental hygiene movement', with its interest in child psychology, for making her agency more aware of the significance of family ties.[13]

A quarter of a century later, the CAS of New Brunswick's Westmorland County grappled with much the same distress. Whatever the apparent shortcomings of birth parents, children were upset at separation and resentful about apprehension. Once they reached eighteen years of age and were under their own authority, most endeavoured to renew original ties.[14] Cape Breton authorities confirmed such observations.[15] No wonder such child welfare authorities, like earlier investigators of child migrants, concluded that it was generally preferable to find ways to keep natal families intact.[16]

Siblings could be as desperately desired as parents. After six years' experience as a servant in Canadian homes, one British teenager explained, 'I have a brother and sister and I want to see tham [*sic*] very badly. . . . My brother and sister have been wanting me to go home for some time.'[17] Another woman recalled: 'I had been in Canada five years, never hearing a word about my sister, when all of a sudden Mr Neil of Barnardo's told me that she was coming to Canada. What joy! Finally when I got married to a Canadian boy we returned to England and had a wonderful family reunion with my family. We had so much to talk about.'[18] Her sentiments were echoed everywhere. In 1939, one BC observer described a four-year-old, the youngest of eight children of deceased parents. Even when her brothers agreed that she should take 'the extra advantages of an adoption home,' she failed to settle in and 'talked about them constantly.' Several months later, she was returned, when the adopters had to admit that 'she would never really belong to them.' Upon reunion, 'the child's joy in seeing her own little brothers again was pathetic as she would keep touching them as if to reassure herself that they were really there.'[19]

Many cases involved searches for blood relatives of any sort. At the end of the 1960s, a fifty-one-year-old man from Fort St John in British Columbia wrote the Vancouver CAS requesting information about his birth parents. He had been placed some half-century earlier with 'wonderful parents'. They had, however, refused him any information about his past. They were now dead and he was 'completely alone'. Hardly any records survived, but eventually the CAS found a name written on the back of the file cover, in faint pencil from 1919. From this meager piece of evidence, the original birth certificate was traced, and a brother, sister, and, eventually, mother recovered. The Fort St John resident thanked the agency workers, writing, 'I now have a family of my own! Many thanks.'[20] Even youngsters who expressed some gratitude to those who had dispatched them to other homes admitted regrets about 'the breaking up of family ties.'[21]

The recurrence of such sentiments forced Barnardo's to begin winter excursions to Britain in 1896 and eventually, at the end of the twentieth century, the British government to finance trips back to the motherland for home children.[22] Canadian children's aid societies and ministries of child welfare acknowledged similar desires in the course of their growing insistence on the collection of case histories. At the beginning of the twentieth century, J.J. Kelso, Ontario's superintendent of neglected and dependent children censured the carelessness of private agencies. Too often their poor practices allowed guardians to move without forwarding addresses, or even to trade youngsters to neighbours. As a result, many 'were lost sight of, and relatives, who made enquiries about these children a few years later were fortunate if they could obtain any trace at all.' While he agreed that 'there are some children so cursed with degraded relatives and friends that the only hope of their doing well is to place hundreds of miles between them and their former friends,' this did not obviate the need for records.[23] Thus later, when children 'in years of maturity' were 'anxious to know something of their early history,' which 'under certain conditions, it may be desirable that they should know,' the information would be properly available.[24] There was also the practical consideration that 'fullest possible particulars' ensured that children in care did not lose opportunities to inherit from birth kin.[25] Such early sentiments would be echoed by social workers engaged in international adoptions after the Second World War. A veteran of International Social Services, which handled many such exchanges, concluded, 'it is also in the child's best interests that some background about him be obtained before he is adopted out: there is a danger that in removing a child from his native land he will be irrevocably cut off from some sense of his true identity.'[26]

Fears about problematic or brutal beginnings—including evidence of rape and incest—that might compromise fresh starts never disappeared. They helped justify efforts at secrecy on the part of child welfare authorities and deterred some searchers. Kelso acknowledged the difficulties associated with complete histories. When information was 'not favourable', as with the case of a 'clever young man' whose 'dissolute' mother had given birth in prison, authorities would have to 'put the young people off with vague uncertainties.' In any case, it was important that records survive so decisions could be made.[27]

From the nineteenth century on, child welfare workers nevertheless publicly emphasized the importance of telling youngsters of some of the circumstances of their arrival in new households. Most believed the truth would emerge at some point, whether on the playground, in a family gathering, or upon the death of adopters, and it was best to control the telling. Determination to find homes for as many youngsters as possible sometimes edited information to be delivered. In 1952, an adoption expert told Canadians that 'adoption authorities don't think it's a sensible idea' to tell adopters 'the true but "bad" things' about the child's history; they feared that 'parents may have a tendency to blame the child's undesirable traits on his background rather than on environmental causes in the adoptive parents' own personality and home.' Underage adoptees should be similarly protected from injurious details. New parents were nevertheless repeatedly reminded that children might well be curious and even that it might be best for them to examine records and visit their first parents after they were twenty-one. The same expert noted that 'adoptive parents who can do this successfully show rare wisdom and understanding. They have done something no natural parent is ever asked to do—share their child with another set of parents. They have performed one of the most inspiring acts of human selflessness.[28]

As such reports suggest, authorities often understood that adoption established somewhat unique family arrangements that needed to be directly addressed. Almost without exception, too, they observed that new parents found 'telling' painful. In 1948, one social work student, noting that the Toronto CAS was grappling increasingly with demands from adult adoptees and birth parents for information, tried to make sense of communication within adoptive families. She found that some parents believed that good homes meant that 'their children never think about being adopted.' Adopters themselves commonly preferred to know little or nothing about earlier parents. One mother went so far as to 'cut out that part of the [adoption] papers where the [original] name appeared.' When faced with having to explain why children had been given up, many said that birth parents had died or that they were too poor to rear them. Once adopters told offspring they were adopted, they tried to forget and hoped children would too.[29] They were also likely to be uncomfortable about illegitimacy, especially when rearing a daughter. How, they wondered, could they simultaneously not appear to approve of out-of-wedlock sex while not condemning the birth mother?[30] Some also expressed gratitude to their predecessors. 'Mrs T.', a middle-class mother of two adopted daughters, thought of their birth mothers on birthdays. She had saved 'the little dress, bonnet, and booties' that one mother had made and intended to show them to her daughter when she was older.[31] The investigator believed that later dilemmas sometimes originated with social workers' temptation to emphasize 'sameness', the similarity of birth and adoptive families, in order to ease the transition. Like H. David Kirk at much the same time, she suggested that anxiety over 'telling' often stemmed from fears about discussion of sexuality and from adopters' difficulty with infertility. She urged post-adoption support so that new parents could work out these problems. She further noted that adoptees themselves reacted in a variety of ways. Most seemingly accepted the news calmly. Typically, they showed some interest in birth mothers but none in genetic fathers, and desired not to share the information outside the family. None of sample, however, had yet entered adolescence, when anger and grief were most likely to surface. She concluded that the 'best-adjusted children' were those whose parents could accept their complete histories.[32]

Another post–Second World War Canadian expert suggested that there was too much stress on the 'chosen' baby. After all, to be chosen implied previous rejection.[33] In a CBC broadcast, Dr Juanita Chambers, the senior psychologist at Montreal's Children's Hospital, argued it would be better not to treasure a 'prettied-up picture of deliberate choice and preference, but rather the bond between three people who had had a rather tough break though no fault of their own, and are trying to do something to mend it.'[34] As social work pioneer Winona Armitage discovered in her remedial efforts with BC's Fairbridge Farm children in the 1940s, lack of truth bred fantasies and contributed to later difficulties in coming to terms with original separation.[35] Yet, progress on telling always remained uncertain. As late as 2000, a Canadian survey reported that some 20 per cent of respondents thought youngsters should be told only in some circumstances and 2 per cent felt they should never know. Seemingly less worried and more confident about socially constructed relations, women were significantly more inclined than men to favour the truth.[36]

By the 1960s, unprecedented public confessions confirmed long-standing official observation of desires for reconnection. Canada's most popular illustrated magazine, the *Star Weekly*, profiled a variety of liberal causes in the decade, from desegregation in the American South to anti-apartheid politics in South Africa. In keeping with its coverage of controversial subjects, it printed stories about adoption and the desire for roots. In 1962, one adoptive mother outlined difficulties. Her daughter had at first treasured her status as 'chosen', but with adolescence came another story: this 'good student' insisted that she had been 'adopted into the wrong family.' Her parent clearly empathized as she wrote:

> We accepted as cliché knowledge that we come into the world alone, and that alone we must leave it. But the adopted child undergoes a third experience of aloneness when he faces the ordinary, banal and overwhelming realization that he entered the world an unwanted being—for reasons of poverty, illegitimacy, disease or other tragedy. . . . It is this surrender of himself and his unknown heredity that constitutes the core of the ordeal. Only he himself can resolve the conflicting concessions he must make, alone, little by little, differing with each child and situation, with no signposts to guide him.[37]

Some four years later, the *Star Weekly*'s readers heard again about the challenge of adjustment. Two letters to the editor presented rather different views. 'Mrs M.J.W.' of Nova Scotia, the mother of an adopted daughter, insisted that 'nothing you can do or say can fill the gap in this child's life. Some children are a bit proud and it's something they just can't live with. She feels she is a disgrace and often says she wishes she were dead. When the law enforces every mother to keep and provide for her own child there will not be these nervous, disordered children.' Much more positive was the recent 'Adopted Mother' from Saskatchewan. She wanted birth mothers to understand how much their babies were loved and she intended to tell 'our daughter her mother loved her very much but felt that a child should have two parents to care for her.' This telling would help give her daughter the necessary psychological resources to cope with the fact of surrender.[38] In 1966, an unwed mother added her own reflections. As a pregnant Grade 12 student, she had been deserted by a 'graduate engineer'. Fortunately, her family stood by her as she went into a maternity home and labour. She spoke of her 'quicksand of guilt' and the choice of adoption as 'a profoundly unselfish act'. She hoped that when her daughter was 'married with children of her own, she may come to know of me. Then I can meet her and talk to her of all the many things I shall have saved for just such a time.'[39] In the course of such conversations with the Canadian public in the 1960s, the *Star Weekly* both illuminated long-standing desires for connection and helped usher in unprecedented openness among all members of the adoption circle. It is also clear that many commentators believed that the facts of adoption should not be publicly available but that participants in the exchange might well claim knowledge when all were adults. There was little indication that anyone assumed that ignorance was permanent.

Not all Canadians were equally receptive. When 'telling' proved frequently so difficult, adopters right from the onset often resisted contact with, and even information about, surrendering households. It was significant that the vast majority of candidates advertised by Canadian newspapers and children's aid societies in the 1960s were portrayed as standing alone. No crowd of relatives or any community stood close to compromise future assimilation. Stripped of prior associations, the *Toronto Telegram*'s 'Today's Child' and others in newspapers from one part of the country to another were effectively rendered orphans and emerged as prime candidates for redemption. Rescuers did not have to confront the problems that brought youngsters to their attention or consider the possibility of shared parenting.

Alberta's committee examining adoption in the 1960s encountered the hostility and fear that had long been common across the nation. One representative of the Presbyterian Church told Calgary hearings how he had adopted a boy at Christmas 1961. He found support for his anger about foster parents visiting with a seasonal gift and he demanded the Welfare Department stop all such contact. As he added about the birth parents, 'We certainly would not go to the trouble or want to become involved in finding out anything about them and that is why I say that the names are quite superfluous not only quite superfluous, but they definitely should not be given to the adoptive parents.' He insisted that adopters preferred not to learn details about the past lest it lead to the 'problem of the children as they grow up, prying for information once they know they are adopted.'[40] Judge H.S. Patterson, the chairman of the Alberta investigation, believed that such resistance was widespread. He pointed to the results of a questionnaire his inquiry had circulated among the province's adopters:

> a common complaint, we wish we had never learned the name of the natural mother or the name that the natural mother gave the child. This business of identification with the child's previous situation is something that they wish they never did learn about. One woman complained about that when they went to the Crèche, or wherever they went to pick the child up, there was a medicine bottle that had the child's name on the medicine bottle that they couldn't help seeing and this bothered them.[41]

By the 1950s and 1960s, child welfare workers had for the most part recognized adoption's complex emotions, even as, in the face of growing numbers of youngsters in care, they remained deeply attracted by its potential for happy endings. Many understood that surrendering mothers were frequently deeply conflicted. They also appreciated challenges facing new parents, all the more so when adoption increasingly emerged as a possibility for children previously judged unsuitable by reason of race or supposed ability and in the past commonly directed to institutional care. The steady stream of adoptees inquiring about the past also continued to raise questions about reconnection. By the mid-twentieth century, even as legal adoption flourished as never before, social workers readily appreciated the need for post-adoption services that would address long-standing issues that showed no signs of disappearing.

Searching's Rising Tide

In the 1970s, annual reports from provincial child welfare authorities across Canada started to comment regularly on surging numbers of requests for information and reunions. In 1971, the responsible BC ministry first mentioned searchers and a registry and noted that many applications involved 'health and social information' but that they also dealt with the 'settlement of estates'. As requests were judged a 'natural desire', the province was contemplating a central registry.[42] Within four years, British Columbia's newly minted Department of Human Resources, with its slogan 'services for people', announced a 'considerable' jump in requests despite its policy of giving only non-identifying social information and no assistance. It pointed to the spur of 'civil rights groups' and the publicity generated by the Royal Commission on Family and Children's Law with its early sympathy for an adoption registry for adult adoptees.[43] In 1976, Ontario's Committee on Records Disclosure recommended the creation of a reunion registry; two years later, after a 37–36 vote, the province adopted a bill establishing a three-party disclosure registry that gave adopters a veto.[44] Because of its limits on access, notably the veto, that initiative provoked continuing protest. The progressive journalist June Callwood offered a typically outspoken endorsement of openness in *Chatelaine*. As she pointed out, there was plenty of precedent. For example, the well-known Browndale homes for troubled children had made it a practice 'for many years to locate biological parents of their patients.' Indeed she went so far as to propose that adopters consider 'adopt[ing] the mother too'.[45] The outcry was sufficient that Queen's Park ultimately appointed the University of Toronto's dean of social work, Ralph Garber, to investigate. He recommended giving adult adoptees unqualified access to original birth registration and creating a fully active Adoption Disclosure Register. Subsequent legislation, including the Adoption Disclosure Statute Law Amendment Act (1987), reflected some of his recommendations, such as no longer requiring consent of adoptive parents and providing for counselling, but the register did not provide access to original birth certificates.[46] In 1987, the province's CASs received more than 4,500 requests for information, a year later, 6,900, and maintained a waiting list of over 5,400.[47]

Similar news came from other jurisdictions. In 1977–8, the *Annual Report* of Saskatchewan's Department of Social Services for the first time acknowledged inquiries from adult adoptees, some 342 over twelve months.[48] In September 1978, British Columbia established a division of Post-Adoption Services to respond to demands that had jumped from about six per month in the mid-1960s to some thirty a decade later. In 1980, the Supreme Court of the province, in *Kelly v. Superintendent of Child Welfare,* heard the first application from a Canadian who wanted his adoption file opened. The plaintiff argued that his 'lack of identity' and 'fear of abandonment' had damaged his marriage and that his lack of a medical history raised questions about his occupation as a diver and whether he should have children. None of this was reckoned 'good cause' by the judge, who denied the petition.[49] That same year, Manitoba courts came to a similar determination regarding a female petitioner with 'an identity crisis' in *Re Adoption of A. (B.).*[50] In *Tyler v. Ontario District Court*, a birth mother's claims that social pressures on the unwed and lack of counselling had forced the surrender of her baby and that this, in turn, led to her nervous breakdown were rejected as sufficient to justify access.[51] In 1987, denial greeted an adult biological sibling who wished to require

Table 8.1   Inquirers and their relationship to adoptees, British Columbia, 1979–82

| | Fiscal year | | |
Inquirer	1981–2	1980–1	1979–80
Adoptee him/herself	360	321	278
Adoptee's biological mother	206	131	122
Adoptee's biological father	17	20	18
Adoptee's siblings or half-siblings	36	33	27
Other relatives of adoptee	11	12	8
Other than adoptee or member of his/her biological family★	421	426	337

★ Includes adopting parents, Ministry of Human Resources district offices, other provinces' child welfare departments, doctors, lawyers, and the federal Department of Indian Affairs.

SOURCE: BC Ministry of Human Resources, *Annual Report* (1980–1), 41, table 47; ibid. (1981–2), 37, table 43.

Manitoba's director of child welfare to contact an adoptee and inform him of his right to join the post-adoptive registry. The fact that adoptive parents had informed the province's child welfare authorities in 1955 that their child did not know he was adopted and that they did not wish contact with his sibling was more influential.[52] In 1985, in contrast, a Maritime adult adoptee prevailed in *Ross v. Prince Edward Island (Registrar of the Supreme Court, Family Division)*. When she had been adopted, provincial law had not required non-disclosure of documents. This loophole was closed in the 1988 PEI Adoption Act, which that made non-disclosure retroactive.[53] That initiative contradicted a more pervasive sea change, however. As Ontario's Ralph Garber noted, 'the trend in legislation in both Canada and the US is towards openness.' As he also observed more generally, 'judicial opinion, however, has been much more restrictive.'[54] Suits of every kind nevertheless continued to wind their way through the courts.

As the number of applicants in just one province suggests (see Table 8.1), judicial petitions represented only the tip of the proverbial iceberg. While there was a large undifferentiated group of petitioners, adoptees stood out, as did biological mothers. In contrast, biological fathers filed fewer requests than did birth siblings, a pattern that was repeated across the country. The majority of all applicants were women. In Ontario, Canada's first registry to coordinate reunions discovered, typically, that 356 female and 127 male adoptees applied in the first year.[55]

On the East Coast, Newfoundland's Department of Social Services found it necessary to establish Post Adoption Services, with a part-time coordinator, in 1983. Little more than a year later, it reported receiving 170 new inquiries and reopening 60 cases, a considerable jump from the mere 24 requests received in 1980.[56] In 1984, Nova Scotia responded to demands by establishing a passive reg-

Table 8.2   Provision of search and reunion registries in Canada

Province	Passive	Semi-active	Active
Alberta	1985	1995	1996
British Columbia	1991	n/a	1991
Manitoba	1981	1986	1999
New Brunswick	1981	1989	2000
Newfoundland and Labrador	1983	1990	1999
Northwest Territories[a]	1998	n/a	1998
Nova Scotia	1984	n/a	1997
Nunavut[b]	1999	n/a	1999
Ontario	1979	1987	n/a
Prince Edward Island	1993	1993	n/a
Quebec[c]			
Saskatchewan	1982	1985	1995
Yukon	1985	n/a	1997

[a] In the Northwest Territories, unofficial active and passive registries existed between 1989 and 1998, when official legislation was passed.

[b] The Nunavut Adoption Act was drafted in 1999 but had yet to be passed in the legislature in 2002. Statutes of Nunavut are not currently available after 2002. In the instance that legislation has not been passed, the statutes of the Northwest Territories apply with regard to adoption.

[c] There is no central registry in Quebec. Local adoption agencies are mandated to carry out searches and reunions for the adoptions that they facilitated. The Quebec director of Child and Family Services offers non-identifying background information only.

istry, in which contact was not initiated unless both parties applied. Some 789 individuals were registered in the fiscal year 1983–4.[57] In 1989–90, the annual report of the responsible department in Prince Edward Island described inquiries, citing over 300 'recorded requests', and it transferred adoption records from the Protestant Family Service bureau to the Department of Health and Social Services 'in the hopes that there will be an official centralized disclosure service in the future.'[58] Like other jurisdictions, it soon reported a waiting time for services, first estimated at sixteen months and then dropping to twelve by 1997–8.[59] The evolution across the country commonly saw first a 'passive register' that permitted exchange of information when two parties made unsolicited requests for union. Next might come a 'semi-active' register. Adult adoptees, but not birth parents, could initiate a search. The next stage was an 'active registry' that allowed both adoptees and birth parents to request searches to see if the other wished contact or disclosure (see Table 8.2).[60]

Rising pressure for disclosure reflected the emergence of an organized searching movement. Women were always most visible, although, as Canadian sociologist Karen March has pointed out, 'searchers represent all age cohorts, socioeconomic status positions, educational levels, and degrees of satisfaction with the
adoption outcome.'[61] In 1974, Joan Vanstone, together with two other searchers,
one male, one female, initiated the non-profit group Parent Finders after a meeting for adult adoptees sponsored by a Vancouver social worker. By 1976, Parent
Finders had grown nationwide, determined to reunite adoptees with birth families, lobby governments for change, and, if necessary, operate its own registries.
Although it had imitators, such as the Canadian Adoption Reunion Register
Search and Support Group, formed in 1987, it quickly emerged as the strongest
expression of the Canadian movement. The middle-aged Vanstone, who was
inspired by Jean Paton, the influential American founder of the searching group
Orphan Voyage and the author of *The Adopted Break Silence*,[62] reckoned that
reunion had brought her 'a new inner peace'. Eager recruits hoped for the same.[63]

    In terms of publications, Clare Marcus emerged as something of a Canadian
Paton. Her *Adopted? A Canadian Guide for Adopted Adults in Search of Their Origins*
(1981) and *Who Is My Mother?* (1979) voiced similar longings and the same palatable sense of injustice. Marcus, born in Winnipeg in 1924 to an unwed mother,
was privately adopted from a maternity hospital with the assistance of the presiding doctor. Like many others, the exchange involved the signing of indenture
papers, a relic from the past that obligated the adopters to 'maintain, board, lodge,
clothe and educate me in a manner suitable to their station, "as if" I were their
own child until I reached the age twenty-one or until I married.'[64] Working as a
journalist for the *Winnipeg Free Press* and the *Star Weekly*, Marcus learned the benefits of publicizing a cause. By the time she moved to Vancouver in the 1960s to
become a full-time searcher and member of Parent Finders, she was enraged by 'a
system that denies basic human rights.'[65] As she further explained, 'knowing where
we came from helps us to understand who we are today.'[66]

    Members of the adoption circle have described their response to their pasts in
a variety of sometimes contradictory ways.[67] An essentialist position, emphasizing
blood ties and embracing a genetic determinism that would have horrified early
advocates of adoption, has commonly surfaced.[68] That point of view, uncritically
presented by American pop psychologist Nancy Verrier's *The Primal Wound:
Understanding the Adopted Child*,[69] credited adoption with an over-riding impact on
all subsequent experience. The popularity of this interpretation prompted experienced Australian social work scholar-practitioners to observe that Verrier's 'apparently global application of the concept carries with it the stigmatizing implication
that all adoptees are to a greater or lesser degree walking wounded,' with 'worrying overtones of predestination or self-fulfilling prophecy given the great multi-
plicity of factors which may impact on the happiness or otherwise of the adopted
child and his or family. It is not supported by the results of more rigorously
research studies of the effects of early trauma and deprivation.'[70]

    The diagnosis of an enduring injury pervaded Canadian Michelle McColm's
Adoption Reunions: A Book for Adoptees, Birth Parents and Adoptive Families. Adopted

at four months of age in 1959, McColm met her birth mother in 1987 and her birth father a year later. She ascribed lifelong depression, like that of 'many other adoptees', and a heightened need for mental health care to the fact of primal loss. Deprivation of blood kin over-rode other influences. Despite acknowledgement of good adoptive parents, she believed she had always mourned 'my birth family, my identity and my heritage.'[71] She drew on a studies pursued by Dr P.A. Vernon, a psychologist at the University of Western Ontario, an institution sometimes distinguished by the ideology that biology is destiny,[72] to insist that heredity largely trumped environment.[73] Citing her adoptive father as reflecting that 'we thought then that bloodline was 5 per cent and the rest of it was 95 per cent,' she concluded, 'today we know that genetic endowment has a much greater influence than was previously assumed.'[74] Differences existed at the most fundamental physiological level. As McColm put it, 'My adolescence was also marked by "smelling" different from my adoptive family. The "chemical attraction" we hear about that leads lovers to fall madly for each other backfired in my case; my adoptive mother was repelled by my emerging adolescent bouquet.'[75] Essentialism continued when she elevated searching to 'a deep, primal yearning'.[76] More pragmatically, she argued that even unpleasant histories required recovery. Otherwise, adoptees would continue to be infantilized and disempowered. Retrieving birth names or recombining them with the new offered opportunities to gain control, in much the same way that many modern women retain their own names upon marriage.[77] McColm also placed the searching movement within a wider political context as part of a larger agenda 'in healing ourselves, each other and our planet.'[78]

The essentialism that seemed central to McColm's narrative has been recurrent in the searching movement, but environments and socialization always had firm advocates. In her *Reunion: The Search for My Birth Family*, Madelene Allen told superficially the same story but with a significantly different emphasis. Associated, like McColm, with Parent Finders, Allen agreed that 'adult adoptees are living in a personal historical void. . . . The quandary in which we find ourselves stems not from a wish to choose between parents but from a wish to know our background, our heritage.'[79] Like other searchers, she pointed to the Charter of Rights and Freedoms, with its guarantee of equal treatment. Adoption laws continued past injustices. She also acknowledged 'dearly loved' adopters, who, like many, had been older when she arrived in their lives:

> My parents gave me a warm and caring home, a love of good books and music, a private school education, summer camp; they gave me gifts from the heart, not the least of which was their time (how can I ever forget the hours my mother spent drilling me in spelling, and in French verbs?). She gave me my love of classical music. . . . Most importantly, they gave me their love and support through my tempestuous growing-up years, and later as I branched out to make my own life.

In contrast to McColm, Allen ascribed adolescent and other difficulties not so much to biology as to the 'values and attitudes' of older parents that differed significantly from those of her friends' mothers and fathers.[80] While she sometimes experienced 'discomfort and confusion' and felt she had to prove that she 'was everything' her parents had hoped for, Allen concluded that 'search for identity is all part of growing up.' Unfortunately, her father had destroyed all the adoption papers before his death. She was nevertheless ultimately successful, affirming 'I am part of that family but no less a part of my adoptive family.'[81] *Reunion* also featured an 'Open Letter' directed to adoptees. In many ways, its humane and sensible reflection on avoiding hurt to both birth and adoptive families captured the preferences of the mainstream searching movement:

> If you are searching for a replacement family, or a 'better' family, or to punish your adoptive parents, please, stop *now* and save yourself and others profound heartache and distress. No one will replace them, and no one should. It's not fair to expect this of your birth family should you meet them. If you are looking for replacements, you are setting the scene for disaster. . . . Proportionately, there are just as many sensitive, caring adoptees as there are among the population of non-adoptees. . . . Why must the past rule the present?[82]

Unlike essentialist accounts, Allen articulated a vision that was not handcuffed to the past.

By the turn of the twenty-first century, female adoptees were highly visible in broadcasting stories for wide distribution. Marie Klassen worked with documentary filmmaker Beverly Shaffer on *To My Birthmother*[83] to portray a search sparked by the birth of her two children. Like McColm and Allen, she appeared solidly middle class, well equipped to demand results. She discovered parents and an older sister. Unlike McColm and Allen, the younger Klassen had been given at eighteen all the documents in possession of her adoptive parents. Her second family also included other adopted children: 'It was always a special and celebrated thing to be adopted in my family.' In contrast, Klassen's birth sister, also adopted, was raised as an only child. She too appeared happy and successful but expressed no interest in tracking origins: 'Because this woman had sex twice, you should be important to me. I don't get it.' Once identified, the birth mother wanted to keep the relationship secret and evidently felt overwhelmed by contact. In all these encounters Klassen, like McColm and Allen, concentrated on the female actors. Men, in contrast, stand very much to the side.

Vancouver journalist Rick Ouston supplied a rare example of the reflections of a male searcher.[84] In *Finding Family: A Journalist's Search for the Mother Who Left Him in an Orphanage at Birth*, he began his story with another, that of his adopted sister, an unwed Catholic mother at seventeen, who gave up her baby in 1967. Ouston had been adopted ten years previously. He believed that the three adopted siblings in his family were treated differently by their 'nana', who 'had more candies for our cousins than she had for us. She'd give them extra when she knew we weren't looking but we were looking anyway and I think she knew. It wasn't a big deal, really. . . . That's the way things are.' As far as he was concerned, however, his working-class parents loved all their kids. They made adoption papers available and never disparaged their predecessors. The sister, who surrendered the baby, initiated Ouston's search by taking him to Parent Finders, 'a sort of adoption underground, with meetings in living rooms and community halls.' He discovered that his mother was born in Newfoundland in 1934 and that he had a sister born a year earlier. Inaccurate records led him on a wild goose chase for his birth father. He found his mother in the United States, where she feared acknowledging him. He soon pitied her but didn't much like someone he judged naive and reactionary.[85] His Newfoundland grandmother refused to accept him. Not surprisingly, as this liberal journalist reviewed his genetic material, he appeared much more the advocate of socialization than heredity.

What all these voices shared was a conviction about the injustice of adoption laws. Unlike other adults, adoptees were barred from records with critical information about their social and medical antecedents. They agreed that 'amnesia is what it feels like being adopted and knowing nothing about your biological background.'[86] The sixty reunited Canadians interviewed by sociologist Karen March communicated much the same sense of alienation from a society that regularly prioritized blood ties and genealogies. One thirty-six-year-old woman pointed out that 'not knowing things about yourself makes it so you don't belong. Like, my nationality. Everybody has a background. They're Italian, English, Jewish or whatever. I couldn't say what mine was. If anyone mentioned my nationality, they would start to guess. Because I didn't know it became a real topic of conversation. A guessing game. Sometimes it would last and last. It wouldn't go away. I wished I knew just so it would stop.'[87] As March concluded, 'by denying adoptees access to both the genetic and genealogical information possessed by the majority of their society, secrecy distinguishes them as a separate category of people with suspect family membership and questionable social identity.'[88]

While searchers have occasionally hoped for close emotional ties to those they have lost, more often they concentrated on the details to anchor their own lives. They employed modern analogies and professional jargon to explain preoccupations with identity: 'I see now that my natural mother, in a way, was my computer bank. She had all the information in her head that I needed to know. So I had to find her.'[89] Another thirty-five-year-old-man man explained, 'It's like coming in out of the closet.'[90] Despite their up-to-date expression, observations from late-twentieth-century adoptees differed little from earlier sentiments expressed for many years by migrants and Canadians separated from birth families.

In the 1970s and beyond, there remained adoptees whose memories of previous families were sufficiently horrendous and precise to discourage interest in reunion or who found no sufficient reason to search. Some were older when they secured second families, and they continued to prize their good fortune in escaping abuse and brutality.[91] One woman explained to *Chatelaine* readers that she had always known she was adopted and never felt any need to search: 'I had always accepted my adoption the same way other kids accepted their origins in their own mothers' wombs. I had a real tangible family who loved me. What else was there to know?' She didn't need another beginning. Unlike adoptees preoccupied with genealogy, her response was deeply anti-essentialist:

When you search for a preface, you're implying that something's missing—a page torn out. Yet, I don't need another beginning. I'm happy with the one I had. . . . I've learned that ancestry is who is in your life right now. It's about the people who've believed in you and supported you, whether or not they share your DNA. . . . There are some forms best left blank. My name may have been Stacey Lynn for a few weeks, but it's been Beth for as long as I can remember. I understand why other adoptees search but I tell myself I'm not like them.[92]

While such reluctance was never deemed as newsworthy, it has always existed along side active searching.

Birth mothers who went public in the last decades of the twentieth century have not been as numerous as adoptees, but their accounts have also been powerful.[93] Many, probably most, have been young unwed mothers, who supplied the majority of available babies for many years.[94] For obvious reasons, women who lost children because of perceived neglect or abuse have appeared less likely to line up for contact. Studies of relinquishing single mothers emphasize their continuing sense of connection, and those who surfaced clearly found themselves unable to let go. Mothers were often told they would forget. This was clearly rarely true. Paul Sachdev's important Canadian study, *Unlocking the Adoption Files,* provided ample evidence that many women continued to harbour 'loss, pain, and grief till the day they met their child.'[95] For some, reunion, or at least information about offspring, offered opportunities to resolve some part of their distress. Perhaps this was the case with the ninety-year-old birth mother who made her hopeful application in the first year of Ontario's reunion registry.[96]

Birth mothers, like teenaged 'Mary Smith' in the *Canadian Nurse* in 1975, have spoken of terrible initial pain.[97] In *Gone to an Aunt's,* journalist Anne Petrie later remembered similar feelings as a university student in 1960s Vancouver and contributed other tales of young women across the country.[98] Petrie, like the mothers interviewed in Ben Wicks's *Yesterday They Took My Baby,* for the most part stressed powerlessness and victimization. Many women, especially those who had babies while still quite young, claimed permanent trauma and blamed parents, birth fathers, social workers, and society generally. As one survivor put it, 'I was coerced into giving up my beautiful baby. . . . I became quite neurotic. . . . In short, I believe my life was ruined by being forced to give away my precious offspring, although I have forgiven those who forced the issue.'[99]

A University of Calgary psychology study conducted with eight members of the Canadian Council of Natural Mothers (CCNM, until 2002 the Canadian Council of Birth Mothers) was typical in judging all surrenders 'extremely negative' for the mothers.[100] Like much work in this discipline, it largely ignored the social construction of gender and embraced an essentialist perspective. Maternal feelings were taken for granted as natural and all-powerful. In this scenario, the love of adoptive mothers seemed to come off second-best, just as many of them feared: 'Many people don't understand how you could love a child that is not your own. . . . They seem to think that the blood tie has some sort of magical effect on parents. It induces instant love for the child and that this doesn't work in the case of adoptive parents.'[101]

In fact, prolonged grief and pain do not have to be ascribed to biology. Such emotions seemed hardly surprisingly when female fertility and maternal feelings have regularly been viewed as the epitome of normality. Women cannot readily escape reminders that they have seemingly failed at one of the major tests of their sex. It would take considerable bravery to admit publicly that maternal sentiments were limited or non-existent. As Barbara Melosh has observed of American mothers, such women faced a dilemma. As they attempted to shed the 'stigma of unwed motherhood', they took on 'the shame and guilt of relinquishment'. Not surprisingly, most insisted that they were 'pressured' and 'brainwashed' and ultimately blameless. Yet 'the more they proclaim the power of nature, the more vulnerable they become to the censure of others ready to regard them as "unnatural" mothers for relinquishing their children.'[102] Feelings could be further complicated for Native women. Their grief over lost children might be accentuated by fears that the future of Aboriginal communities was compromised.

Some birth mothers have nevertheless concluded that their sacrifice had made sense. 'Second Chance Cora', the daughter of a poor family, got pregnant when her husband was overseas during the Second World War. Giving her baby to Nova Scotia's Ideal Maternity Home was 'the only option available at the time' and 'a godsend for a lot of us.'[103] One nineteen-year-old, forced to leave a bad marriage with a two-year-old, defended her choice: 'I was having a very hard time coping, both financially and emotionally.' She loved her daughter but she was 'going to go crazy with worry, fear, guilt (because I found myself resenting the fact that my life seemed to be over before it had even started) and very afraid that sooner or later I was going to take it out on my daughter.' She listened to social workers and a minister but she took responsibility for what happened: 'it was ultimately my decision, and I let her go. . . . Yet in many ways it saved my life. Giving up my daughter was really a sacrifice in order to save my own life, to get my own life back. I went back to school, traveled, went to university and now own my own business. . . . In many respects I probably made the right choice. My biggest fear is wondering how her life has turned out.'[104] For reassurance, she had only to look around Canada to see how impoverished and stigmatized motherhood regularly jeopardized the well-being of both parents and children.

Many Canadians believed as well that maternal sacrifice could be a good thing. Charlene Miall and Karen March's 2000 survey of Canadians' views of adoption found that 80 per cent of female respondents believed that surrender was a responsible act; 72 per cent of male respondents agreed. Ultimately, interpretation depended very much on what was perceived to have happened subsequently in the lives of mothers and children. The discovery by 'Pat Tyler' that her son's 'situation was less than perfect' encouraged her to see her loss as basically an abduction.[105] In contrast, one woman who traced the alcoholic mother who had surrendered her and three siblings concluded, 'I was given up to a great set of parents and she did do the right thing by allowing me to be adopted rather than keeping me and trying to raise me herself. What a scary prospect that might have been.'[106]

Women who believed they made the right decision have been largely left out of many discussions regarding birth mothers.[107] Such individuals may contribute to the resistance to being located that Richard Sullivan and David Groden uncovered in their assessment of BC's Adoption Reunion Registry: of the 11 per cent of search subjects who refused contact, an overwhelming 84 per cent were birth parents.[108] Such rejection also emerged in Nova Scotia when an adoptee used an amended (1975) Vital Statistics Act to access his original birth certificate. When he found his birth mother, she was married. She had told neither husband nor subsequent children, and her son's return 'had the effect of shattering her family and life and causing the woman great trauma.' As a result, Nova Scotia provided that adoption records could be opened only with ministerial or judicial approval. In 1999, its Conservative government backed off promises when opposition to more openness again erupted.[109] While the majority of opposition to open records seems to come from adopters, some birth mothers have not wanted to revisit their past. That possible perspective needs to be remembered along side the pain and loss of rights appropriately emphasized by activist birth mothers in the CCNM, associated with Parent Finders, and more local groups such as Our Darlings Counselling and Registry from Prince Edward Island.[110]

Birth fathers have surfaced far more rarely for public assessment. Sachdev's otherwise comprehensive study of Newfoundland captured their lack of visibility. He entirely excluded such fathers, as birth mothers normally took the initial decision, agency records were 'highly deficient', and searchers for the most part looked first, and sometimes only, for mothers.[111] This omission has nevertheless been challenged. An American writer of popular psychology, Mary Martin Mason, signalled new attention in *Out of the Shadows: Birth Fathers' Stories*, as did groups with scholarly credentials such as the Father Involvement Research Alliance based at the University of Guelph.[112] Here again, essentialism can loom large, all the more so when some enthusiasm is associated with a North American fathers' rights movement that is often deeply anti-feminist and invested in the restoration of patriarchal authority. There is, nonetheless, a caring story to tell. A few birth fathers have always sought to do more than punish previous partners or blackmail them in order to decrease financial obligations. Meaningful relationships with offspring have sometimes been important. In the 1980s and 1990s, some Canadian unmarried fathers challenged long-standing laws that gave them no rights to custody and access.[113] A handful became searchers, despite prospects that one legal authority summed up with the statement 'the road to unwed fatherhood is all but impassable.'[114] Jurisdictions began to listen as when British Columbia established a birth fathers' registry in 1995.

Two rare Canadian accounts from birth fathers have conveyed concern for lost offspring. British Columbian Barrie Clark discovered much later in life that his girlfriend from university days had surrendered a baby at Toronto's Presbyterian Home for Unwed Mothers. He pleaded for reform in access to information.[115] Randy Shore, a journalist from the same province, also took his search public. In 2003, he told how two teens had given up a baby twenty-three years before. Shore and the young mother chose a couple, a Mountie and a nurse, to parent their daughter but maintained no contact. Years afterwards, the birth mother began to look and Shore joined her. They found a daughter who recounted a happy tale of life with her second family.[116] While clearly delighted at the outcome, Shore did not present the original decision, in which he participated, to give up his first-born as determining the rest of his life. While something was lost, he nonetheless moved on. His account did not indicate whether this was equally true of his former girl-friend. In any case, both fathers were clearly at some greater emotional distance from the fact of loss than were birth mothers who have chosen to tell their tales.

By the end of the twentieth century, searchers had placed their disadvantage on the Canadian human rights agenda. Ralph Garber described the 'storm of protest' that greeted the demand of Ontario's 1978 Child Welfare Act for adopters' consent to disclosures. Briefs and letters flew into Tory government offices, but Queen's Park insisted on restrictions in the Child and Family Services Act, passed in December 1984. Before its proclamation and in light of a coming election, the minister of community and social services buckled. As we have seen, Ralph Garber was commissioned to extinguish the firestorm. He received over 300 letters and a petition with over 2,000 signatures. Only four writers opposed improved access. On 31 October 1985, viewers of TV Ontario's *Speaking Out* called in nine to one in support of greater openness.[117] Such opinions confirmed Garber's assessment that the time had come to move beyond secrecy.

Yet, into the twenty-first century, provinces and territories faced a dilemma and regularly allowed vetoes on full disclosure and access. On the one hand, there has been a significant constituency of opponents to openness. In 1974, BC's Royal Commission on Family and Children's Law discovered strenuous resistance to any reunion registry. Adopters judged this a betrayal of the 'as if born to' promise they had been given.[118] They created the Organization to Save the Adopted Family and an uproar that intimidated the government.[119] The presence of adopters in provincial cabinets sometimes encouraged legislative foot-dragging. In the mid-1980s, some observers believed that Ontario's minister of community and social services, Frank Drea, the adoptive father of an eighteen-year-old searcher, stood behind the Conservative government's efforts to restrict access. On a CBC broadcast, he insisted, 'It's no one's damn business to find out private and confidential information about adopted children! The Cabinet has accepted this, and it's going to be the law!'[120] As late as 1979, one social worker acknowledged, 'it would certainly be the ideal situation for these parents if the past could be washed away and life would go on as though there were no birth mother or birth father other than themselves.'[121] As Sachdev observed of his Newfoundland sample, adopters commonly trailed in support for searching and regularly harboured 'underlying apprehension and reservation'.[122]

Governments tried to balance obligations under the Charter of Rights and Freedoms with those mandated by the Freedom of Information and Privacy Act. Although jurisdictions remained extremely nervous about promises of confidentiality, they also increasingly included grandparents, blood and adoptive siblings, and birth fathers among those with rights to information. Canadian social workers frequently supported searchers, '"leaking" out information to an adoptee who is desperately seeking a birth parent.'[123] From the 1980s, legislative trends crept towards openness. In 1995, Sullivan and Groden's evaluation of BC's Adoption Reunion Registry discovered that nearly half of adoptive parents had anticipated reunion and 38 per cent suggested they would have appreciated reunion as an option when they adopted.[124] In 2000, Miall and March heard 46 per cent of a telephone sample of Canadians 'strongly' approve and another 45 per cent 'somewhat' approve of reunions. Less than 10 per cent disapproved, either somewhat or strongly. Eighty-four per cent supported adoptees' discovering the identity of their biological parents without the approval of adopters, and 77 per cent agreed that adult adoptees should not need permission from biological parents. Another 55 per cent supported release of information to birth parents without the permission of adopters. The poll indicated that women were always more supportive of disclosure and reunion than men.[125]

Conversions owed much to growing recognition of the damage of secrecy and the increased acceptance of civil rights in the late twentieth century. The inspiration has not, however, been entirely liberal in nature. As Australian social work scholars Audrey Marshall and Margaret McDonald have observed, there has been 'a return to the belief in the overriding importance of the blood tie, echoing the views of those in the 1920s [who] strongly opposed the legalizing of adoption because of its breaking the blood tie.'[126] Such a perspective might discourage adoptions of some children for whom such outcomes are far and away their best hope of love and commitment. American historian of adoption Barbara Melosh has also noted that few reunion and searching stories reach past the first encounter to assess the overall experience. She has suggested that 'one likely reason is that such endings sustain a fantasy of ideal kinship that is seldom realized in actual reunion aftermaths (or, for that matter, in family life more generally). . . . Exploring the aftermath of reunion also subtly undercuts the political agenda of adoption rights activists, since the occasional bad reunion and the more common anticlimactic aftermath might seem to diminish the value of the search.'[127] From Melosh's standpoint, searching supplied just one more variant on the sentimentalization of family life that discourages hard examination of actual practice.

Other conclusions have been more positive. The psychiatric consultant to BC's Berger Commission, who studied twelve reunions, five conducted with the permission of the attorney general and the rest 'accomplished with non-identifying information in some cases, aided in several others by memories of the birth parent's name by adoptees who were not adopted by birth,' suggested that most brought some peace and well-being.[128] The weight of evidence overall strongly suggested that the need to know is normal and not restricted to unhappy adoptees.[129] As one Canadian appreciated, 'adoption is a life-long process requiring continuing adaptation and integration for both the adoptee and his family.'[130]

In her recent studies, sociologist Karen March has profitably summed up common results of renewed contact:

> Following reunion, adoptees have verifiable answers for others' questions about their biological background and the reasons for the adoption. By

removing the constrains of secrecy, they have gained more power over their presentation of self and over negative assumptions that others might make about their biological history and the reasons for their adoption. The adoptees' ability to integrate their biological background as a part of their adoptive identity also gives them power by removing any doubts that may emerge over the source of particular traits and characteristics.[131]

One searcher put it most simply in her grateful letter to the *United Church Observer*: 'I now feel like a real person with roots and history.'[132]

Repatriation

The terms 'repatriation' and 'searching' conjure up somewhat different realities. As the *Short Oxford English Dictionary* puts it, the former involves 'return or restoration to one's own country.' Such a definition effectively designates First Nations and Métis youngsters, whether adopted within or outside of Canada, as subjects of interstate politics, in some ways not unlike children acquired from beyond the dominion's borders. Repatriation also holds connotations of 'property', a metaphor that frequently haunts exchanges of children. Finally, the term further invokes a colonial history of oppression and dispossession that has left Aboriginal peoples vulnerable first to the residential schools and then to the child welfare 'scoop' of the 1960s and later. Unlike searching, repatriation also holds the implicit promise of a place of return, some geographical location that may be truly called home. As one 1999 Ontario study outlined, repatriation might take several forms:

- periodic visits by adoptees/foster children to the birth community (if arranged with the adoptive parents) so the family and the community become regular parts of their lives;
- [adoptees/foster children] moving back to the Reserve [or home] on a temporary basis, without establishing permanent residence in the community;
- [adoptees/foster children] moving back to the Reserve [or home] permanently.[133]

Whatever its precise form, repatriation is very much part of the ongoing struggle of First Nations peoples to be recognized as founding peoples and to reclaim territory. The distinction between searching and repatriation remains fundamental for adoption circles involving Aboriginal youngsters. It is, however, also the case that efforts at reconnection share much with the mainstream searching movement.

As chapter 6 discussed in detail, First Nations girls and boys were conspicuous victims of well-intentioned, although often effectively racist, colour-blind liberalism, especially in the decades from the 1950s to the 1970s. Child welfare authorities and progressive white Canadians trusted that 'love' was enough and that 'red' was just one more shade in the national mosaic. Youngsters snatched from parents and communities devastated by contact and economic marginalization were to integrate seamlessly into the emerging 'just society'. Their heritage might be incorporated in new families by way of occasional visits and preservation of a few rituals, but for the most part it would pass away, a relic of pre-modern times. Such optimistic environmentalism failed to take account of its own ethnocentrism, Canadians' continuing prejudice, the damage done to Aboriginal communities by the loss of the next generation, injuries inflicted as a result of substance abuse, and Aboriginal revitalization in the last quarter of the twentieth century.

Within a comparatively short time, liberal mainstream attitudes to Native adoptions underwent something of a sea change. By the 1980s, adoption and fostering by European Canadians were no longer hailed as signs of an inclusive new world but suspect as proof of ongoing colonialism. Tragic tales, including those of Manitobans Cameron Kerley, who killed his abusive American adopter, and Carla Williams, who was taken to Holland to be tormented by an adoptive father, were widely circulated. And then there were commonly discussed tragedies such as Prime Minister Jean Chrétien's Native son. Early optimism faltered before reports that Aboriginal adoptions had a higher than average failure rate and news of rising opposition.[134] In Canada, the story of First Nations adoptions contributed substantially to what one American historian has characterized as the return of 'the language of risk' to adoption in the 1980s.[135]

Happier outcomes were nevertheless also present, perhaps especially when adoptive parents embraced Native culture and ensured that the adoptees were exposed to their culture and history. Significant numbers of adopters endeavoured to do just that, as with a United Church minister and teacher in Prince Rupert, British Columbia, in the 1960s. When their adopted daughter was very young, they lived in communities with significant Aboriginal populations among which they had friends. As she grew older, they encouraged her to learn more about Native culture and to seek her birth parents. Ultimately she was able to integrate her two families.[136] Such adopters found counterparts across the country. In the early 1980s, Project Opikihiwawin in Manitoba assisted parents with adoptees to connect with their Aboriginal origins.[137] Yet, Native voices testifying to individual success never enjoyed the attention given tragedies.[138] As sociologist Anne-Marie Ambert observed, 'accusations of genocide and racism have come to rest on the shoulders of adoptive parents and have filled them with feelings of guilt and isolation. Although the children they adopted were those apparently unwanted by anyone else, the parents learned that the very native groups they thought would have supported them in their efforts were now against them.'[139] Not surprisingly, demoralization has been widespread, and increasingly only the hardy, often it seemed armed by religious evangelism, pursued Native adoptions by the end of the twentieth century.[140]

Bad news was largely confirmed in a series of public investigations beginning in the 1970s. In 1975, Thomas Berger set out typical concerns in the report of the BC Royal Commission on Family and Children's Law. In response to rising levels of Natives in care and protest that had produced a moratorium on such adoptions in 1973, Berger recommended that 'the highest possible priority must be given to finding native homes for native children.' To the same end, he urged recognition of custom adoption, permission for adoption by common-law couples, and subsidies. When they could not be avoided, non-Aboriginal adopters were to take an orientation program designed by Native communities and should not be allowed to adopt unless they formally agreed to 'familiarize the child with his Native heritage.' BC's superintendent of child welfare should also be obligated to inform adoptees at age twenty-one of their status under the Indian Act. Berger endorsed the recommendation of Chief Andy Paul, research director of the Union of BC Indian Chiefs, for legislation to protect the legal rights of status children. He also encountered a problem that would perplex subsequent inquiries: the conflict between individual and collective rights. On the one hand, he found that 'the majority of Indian people with whom we have discussed this matter believe the band should always be notified of the birth of a child to any of its members; that the rights of the band supersede those of the individual.' On the other, he believed that the right to confidentiality and 'self-determination' of birth mothers should be respected, just as with other women.[141]

Some ten years later, Manitoba judge Edwin Kimelman toured Metis settlements and Indian communities, as well as receiving submissions to his Committee on Indian and Métis Adoptions and Placements. As we have seen, his *No Quiet Place* diagnosed 'cultural genocide' at the heart of the 'scoop' and urged efforts to increase Native adopters and to protect Native inheritance. In Ontario, Ralph Garber's 1985 report extended the condemnation. He too voiced the dilemma of the conflict between individual and collective rights. Birth mothers should not be stripped of the capacity to determine the future of their offspring. Their permission should be required before bands were notified of births or transfers of children. 'My contention in respect of Indian rights, adoptive or birth parents' collective rights, or any religious or other group's rights is that the individual's rights are paramount.' This recommendation was somewhat less powerful than it appeared. The majority of Ontario's Native children in care, like many elsewhere in the country, were Crown wards. Their parents had already lost custody and thus the government was free to notify bands.[142]

In the 1990s, government investigations found Native communities all the more determined to claim rights over planning for Aboriginal youngsters. In 1994, two years after another provincial moratorium on non-Native adoptions, BC's Panel to Review Adoption Legislation heard firm rejections of any further non-Native adoptions.[143] It recommended that the moratorium be extended to include the growing number of private adoptions and that efforts be strengthened to recruit Native adopters, including the use of subsidies. More radical was the suggestion that Canada create a separate Native Child Welfare Law and that a federal-provincial agency be establish to assist 'reunification'. In order to curb losses, the panel recommended that birth families be given resources to retain offspring. Despite some opposition from the non-Native community, the panel concluded that 'the child's connectedness to its aboriginal family *is* in the best interests of the child, the family and the community.' This was the case even with youngsters 'whose physical characteristics are not obviously aboriginal, such as children with light-colored skin and blue eyes.'[144] The panel insisted that Aboriginality was more than a question of mere 'blood quantum' and that only Aboriginal peoples should

decide who properly belonged. European and other heritages did not need equivalent protection. And as the panel concluded, 'mixed blood is perhaps just another
example of the aboriginal way of life.'[145] Once again, Native observers were not
unanimous. Adoptees with positive experiences and birth mothers who wished to
retain the right to choose rejected prioritizing the claims of bands.[146]

Two years later, the federal Royal Commission on Aboriginal Peoples confirmed
the diagnosis of widespread racism and abuse in adoption. It too admitted that birth
mothers might not wish to submit to community directives. Many Aboriginal
women witnesses rejected silence about abuse and discrimination as a condition of
loyalty. Some, such as the Aboriginal Women's Unity Coalition, believed that male
leadership had poorly served many vulnerable community members. Rosemary
Kuptana presented this point of view in *No More Secrets: Acknowledging the Problem
of Child Sexual Abuse in Inuit Communities—The First Step Towards Healing.*[147] For her
and many indigenous women, taking responsibility for child welfare meant healing
from male violence and indifference as well as confronting racism.

All these investigations worked in a context of highly visible Native protest in
the last decades of the twentieth century. In 1981, BC's Spallumcheen Band inaugurated the repatriation movement with its successful campaign for return of
youngsters. Two years later, Grand Chief David Ahenakew of the Assembly of First
Nations (AFN) announced 'a plan to ask provincial Attorneys-General and social
services departments to contact adoptees and tell them of their status' and suggested the AFN would seek to 'erode the confidentiality of social services' by challenging the right of confidentiality under the *Charter of Rights and Freedoms*.' In the
same decade, Alberta's Yellowhead Tribal Council, representing five bands, searched
government institutions, foster homes, and adoptive homes for its members who,
if they did not learn of their status, would be deprived of oil and gas royalties.[148]
At much the same time, Manitoba began to formulate policies for restoring apprehended girls and boys to tribal communities, and Ontario anticipated reunions by
beginning reviews of Native case files.[149] In 1992, the agencies and bands of the
Manitoba First Nations Child and Family Services developed the Southern
Manitoba First Nations Repatriation Program to deal with 'displaced persons', a
telling phrase that placed adoption firmly within a global politics of disadvantage.[150] Alberta initiated several agreements respecting return with Indian agencies,
but a study observed that Natives were generally to the forefront of such efforts in
many provinces.[151] In the 1980s, the Ojibway Child Welfare Agency in Dryden,
Ontario, reunited forty-one children, most between thirteen and eighteen years of
age, with their birth families. In Manitoba, Anishinaabe Child and Family Services
assisted in some hundred reunifications. In Regina, Saskatchewan, the Peyakowak
agency worked to support returnees.[152]

As with the Spallumcheen in British Columbia, where former foster child Chief
Wayne Christian helped to develop Canada's first band child welfare bylaw, inspiration often came from returnees. After a showdown with the provincial government, Christian was instrumental in winning recognition that, should adoption
break down, children would be returned to the community. The United Native
Nations Reconnection Program, started in 1988, acted to assist 'off-Reserve

Aboriginal adoptees and foster care persons in British Columbia with birth family searches, First Nations status re-instatement and advocacy.'[153] By the 1990s, BC's Gitksan First Nation deliberately set out to locate lost youngsters in order 'to help strengthen their community and help heal the wounds from the past.'[154] In Manitoba the First Nations Repatriation Program operated, and in Ontario various Native Child Welfare authorities and Friendship Centres provided ad hoc services. Southern Ontario also produced the Native Children's Support Group, operated by non-Aboriginal volunteers, which supported Niagara Peninsula adoptees in retaining their culture.[155]

Right from the beginning, reconnection was hindered by pervasive anger and grief. A psychologist working with the Anishinaabe Child and Family Services observed that most adoptees came from middle-class homes in large cities and found isolated northern reserves next to impossible to accept. While none of the children he encountered had been hospitalized or imprisoned, 'by the time the child has been reunified with his or her family of origin the child is often feeling a triple load of rejection: rejection from the birth family/home, rejection from the adoptive home as adoption breaks down, and rejection from birth home (again) if family is not as loving and accepting as fantasized.' While many returnees benefited from continuing contact with the adoptive parents, relations sometimes floundered on anger and misunderstanding.[156] Problems were compounded when there was no provision for costs or re-adoption by natural parents. Questions of citizenship for those surrendered to Americans further complicated matters.[157]

Repatriation efforts have been further handicapped by limited resources and mixed feelings about those long absent from First Nations communities. An Ontario study has noted that violence and 'severe culture shock' have frequently caused repatriated band members to leave communities of 'which they so much wanted to be a part.'[158] Native groups devastated by poverty and substance abuse have not been well situated to address the needs of newcomers, all the more when they sometimes assessed them as essentially foreign and privileged. It was easy to resent sharing scant resources. Kin themselves often experienced a heavy burden of guilt and shame and could not always offer help. Many had died over the intervening years.

Perhaps not surprisingly, Ontario First Nations communities largely failed to answer a questionnaire sponsored by Toronto's Native Child and Family Services regarding repatriation in 1999: only 6 of 135 First Nations communities and 9 of 26 Friendship Centres replied.[159] The unwillingness of many Aboriginal leaders to prioritize repatriation stood in stark contrast to the preoccupation with residential schools. This may have something to do with the generation in power in the AFN, formerly the well-named National Indian Brotherhood, and elsewhere. At the end of the twentieth century, many Aboriginal leaders still had a direct experience of the earlier residential system. Native women have also criticized male-dominated groups for their lack of substantive commitment to issues, such as domestic abuse, that might precipitate apprehension. Revealing its priorities, the AFN waited until 2004 to appoint a Women's Council, to which it allocated one vote on the executive.[160]

Many difficulties encountered in the course of repatriation resembled those identified by searchers. The Gitxsan Reconnection Program discovered that 84 per cent of the searchers were being conducted on behalf of adoptees/foster children.'[161] Ontario's Native child and family agencies reported that many more adult adoptees than birth parents and more women than men exhibited interest in reunions. The Manitoba First Nations Repatriation Program observed that many clients were inspired to search when they contemplated starting their own families. Everywhere, Aboriginal adoptees sought their birth mothers first and foremost.[162] As with other efforts at reunion, results have been mixed. High hopes have often proved unrealistic. Few of the repatriated stayed in Aboriginal communities. For the most part, their futures have been other than with blood kin. Nevertheless, first returns on repatriation suggest that, even when expectations were not entirely met, returning adoptees, especially those supported by their adoptive families, have been helped. A young Manitoban adopted in the United States in the 1970s and reconnected with his community in the 1990s through the province's Repatriation Program typically reported discovering 'a measure of peace'.[163] His reflection would not have seemed foreign to the majority of searchers.

Unfortunately, even more than other searching, repatriation has frequently generated particularly negative press. The publicity surrounding two little girls, daughters of a drug-addicted member of the Squamish Nation but fostered with Ontario white families who wished to adopt them, appeared representative. Both the *Globe and Mail* and the *National Post* devoted much space to editorials and columns determined to condemn 'reverse racism'. While the facts of the case were complicated, as with all such matters, the absence of more than token acknowledgement of the bad history of such adoptions was striking.[164] Native efforts at repatriation here and elsewhere elicited a self-righteousness that was conspicuously ahistorical in its condemnation of Aboriginal efforts to regain control of community children.

Open Connections

In the last decades of the twentieth century, efforts at searching and repatriation demonstrated that adoption could not guarantee the autonomy and independence of adoptive families. Other developments further confirmed the reminder that pasts were not readily jettisoned. The emerging recognition of the benefits of continued state support in the case of 'special needs' children and the inauguration of subsidies placed adoptive families clearly within broader networks of interdependence. Many modern foster parents also committed themselves to long-term placements for provincial wards who were not free for adoption, thus helping to diminish the distinction among different groups of mothers and fathers. As Canadian social work scholar Heather Whiteford has correctly pointed out, the requirements of hard-to-place youngsters challenged 'the traditional definition of the parental role as an "all-or-nothing" one with sole responsibility for the day-to-day care of the child.' Duties had to be shared.[165] Challenges to the supposed anonymity of donor insemination—commonly AI, or artificial insemination—a procedure used since at least the nineteenth century, also increasingly entered the spotlight, again to call into question unfettered individualism. In a foretaste of future claims, a University of British Columbia student at the beginning of the twenty-first century set out to locate an AI father who had been a medical intern at Vancouver General Hospital. As she explained, 'My mom may have signed away her rights, but I didn't.' Canadian filmmaker Barry Stevens presented his successful search for a donor and half-siblings in *Offspring: One Man's Search for Identity*. Once again, the acquisition of children was clearly embedded in multiple relations that could no longer be ignored.[166]

The continuing quest for connection, the recognition that adoptive, like other, families might well need on-going assistance, all contributed to growing interest in 'open' adoptions in the last decades of the twentieth century. Like customary adoptions, which had won significant legislative acknowledgement, openness arrangements recalled more traditional exchanges of children in which givers and receivers might well know each other. Although their purpose was often to expedite the transfer of babies to prospective parents rather than to forge relations between past and future, private adoptions, commonplace in many jurisdictions, had long sidestepped much confidentiality and secrecy.[167] Sometimes birth mothers participated in such arrangements in order to be more confident about outcomes. Such appeared to be the hopes of a pregnant forty-year-old mother of two sons in the 1980s. The birth of the baby with Down's syndrome effectively ended her initial plans and captured the inevitable uncertainty of such negotiations.[168] Another mother, who described feeling overwhelmed by responsibilities for two sons, aged one and five, in her *From We to Just Me: A Birth Mother's Journey,* similarly undertook her own discussions with replacement parents.[169] For such women, openness within private arrangements offered some promise of continued contact and control.

As in the past, not everyone in the adoption circle has been equally enthusiastic about enduring relations. Fears stalked adopters in particular. One Canadian outlined common reservations:

> The idea that your child will have other parents, however you qualify the term, may initially make you feel ill. Suggesting you might want to meet them or have ongoing communication probably seems intolerable. You don't want to have anything to do with them. You don't even want to think about them; never mind have any kind of relationship with them. You simply want them to go away.
>
> However, no matter how you adopt, what you know about them and them about you, they will continue to exist. . . . An open relationship might happen in that liberal enclave to the south, California, but not here, not with me.
>
> Well, by the time we talked to the birth mother of our son, six months after we began searching, I had changed my mind. I was not only willing to meet her; I wanted to meet her. I was terrified, but I had come to realize that it would relieve her concerns about us and our concerns about us. . . . The meeting was wonderful. It created a trust that continues to this day.[170]

In 1999, another adopter recalled her own early optimism, but she had to tackle her male partner's 'terror about the birthmother's involvement.' To avoid such entanglement, he preferred an international adoption. Eventually however, he was persuaded to meet a fifteen-year-old birth mother, herself an adopted child, and they decided to go ahead with the adoption.[171] Modern openness arrangements might involve more than babies. In 2002, the *Globe and Mail* published an account of an evangelical Canadian couple participating in the 'cross-border adoption of a human embryo' and hoping for 'the prospect of a continuing relationship' with the American recipients.[172] This evolution of thinking and practice spoke volumes about the possibilities of growth and generosity in the sharing of children.

While connections between new and old families had become more visible to the public eye, they were far from unprecedented. What was new at the end of the twentieth century was legislative recognition. In 1994, the BC Panel to Review Adoption Legislation recommended provision for open adoption. After hearing from BC's Lower Mainland Fetal Alcohol Syndrome/Effect Support Group and others, it also admitted that 'open adoptions are not necessarily for everyone. They require preparedness and a degree of emotional maturity and security on the part of all the parents.'[173] In 1995, the province allowed for 'openness agreements', becoming the first Canadian jurisdiction to reverse the 'prevailing presumption of disclosure and confidentiality' in its Adoption Act.[174] In 1997, Manitoba's Adoption and Consequential Amendments Act revealed the breadth of possible relations. Agreements could occur between adopters and any of birth parents, extended birth family, or indeed 'any other person who has established a meaningful relationship with the child,' or the prospective adoptive or actual adoptive parent of a sibling, or a member of a Native band of which the child was entitled to be a member.[175]

Such affirmation of connections promised to transform adoption. It need no longer seek to match the ideal nuclear family but might emerge as a distinctive model explicitly and formally rooted in a wider network of relations. Champions, like American anthropologist Judith S. Modell in *Kinship with Strangers*, have emphasized the subversive potential of open adoptions. By shared parenting, connecting donors and takers of children, and trusting birth parents, they demonstrated 'what kinship is supposed to do.'[176] H. David Kirk made a similar claim years earlier in his vision of the 'utopian potential . . . of families joined by choice not by blood.'[177] That radical possibility both inspired and intimidated. Not surprisingly, Canadians remained nervous, as was obvious in British Columbia's provision that 'failure to comply with an openness agreement is not grounds for the court to revoke consent to adoption.'[178] At the beginning of a new century, the public was far from completely on board. A 2003 editorial from the conservative *National Post* applauded an Alberta court ruling against a birth mother who wished 'regular updates'. Openness might be the 'fashion among sociologists and family counselors,' but the *Post* argued that the 'best interests' doctrine should be invoked to protect adopters and children from interference from suspect kin and community. In this particular case, the child was identified as a possible victim of fetal alcohol syndrome disorders.[179]

A commitment to openness meant forging relations with individuals and groups from whom modern adopters in particular had commonly shied away. Contact meant that they could not entirely ignore the pain and the tragedy that made children available. Native and non-Native birth parents also have their own feelings of distress, anger, and responsibility to work out in the course of negotiating the conditions of surrender. In the maelstrom of such emotions, (mis)understandings are very possible. If not handled carefully, and even then, they can endanger the future of children and adults. As in the history of adoption more generally, not all parties are equally vulnerable. Historian Barbara Melosh has painted a worrying portrait in *Strangers and Kin*. Openness can sometimes mean little more than private negotiations between individual parties. In such exchanges, birth mothers commonly possess the low cards. That is not the only issue. Open adoption could only too readily 'embody and reinforce another troubling assumption: that children are property, belonging to their parents by right of ownership. . . . It is bad social policy and poor ethical practice to rely on a laissez-faire system of adoption that, in practice, becomes modeled on the market place.'[180]

Open adoptions readily lend themselves to scenarios of both hope and foreboding. The initial assessments of reunions, while far from complete, notably for First Nations participants, give cause for optimism.[181] However, the temptation of some Canadians to turn to artificial insemination and international adoption at least in part to avoid entanglement with other claimants to children lends support to Melosh's overall pessimism.[182] Some youngsters will lose better futures because fewer prospective parents will take the risk of encountering prior relations. Given the recurring evidence that silence, confidentiality, and isolation do not meet the needs of so many in the adoption circle, backtracking to embrace the 'like our very own' philosophy is, however, not a real option. By the end of the twentieth century, adoption required rethinking old assumptions about how children could be reared with reference to all the communities of which they were a part.

In recovering the past and confronting its various meanings for everyone concerned, end-of-the-twentieth-century adoption appears very much in keeping with its times. Canadians, like others in the world, live in an age of apology and restitution, where groups seek to know their histories and to win acknowledgement of trauma and loss. Unhealed memories of Irish famine migration, head taxes on Chinese immigrants, Native residential schools, Armenian massacres in Turkey during the First World War, the European Holocaust, the internment of Japanese Canadians during the Second World War, and the abuse of children by the Christian Brothers and Catholic priests, among other traumas, have all prompted demands for contrition, reparation, and redress. Canadians have been told that an equitable future, for the nation, as for the adoptive circle, depends ultimately on both addressing history and not perpetuating its errors into the present. In both cases, it is a message that has yet to be fully accepted.

Conclusion

Canada has hosted many exchanges of peoples. Adoption is one part of that larger tale. *Finding Families, Finding Ourselves* has explored how matters commonly deemed private have intersected at multiple points with a nation's public struggle to make sense of itself in the modern world. Like evolving citizenship and immigration regimes, adoption raises questions about what recruits are available, and why, and how their movement is to be understood and managed, both as part of the collective imaginary and in day-to-day practices. How are matters of class, gender, religion, ethnicity, race, indigeneity, and foreignness in general to be interpreted and negotiated? How is the past to merge with the present and the future? And what place do equality and justice have in encounters? Ultimately, discussions about appropriate relations between birth and adoptive families, as between 'old' and 'new' Canadians, raise universal questions about how diverse groups of human beings can live together more equitably. And as *Finding Families, Finding Ourselves* has suggested, answers are diverse and none are easy.

This volume extends to adoption Eva Mackey's important recognition of pluralism's uncertain purchase on the hearts and minds of Canadians.[1] Surrendering and receiving families have acted out personal relations that invoke the politics of multi-group coexistence that have so often disturbed the dominion. Just as Mackey observed with regard to the nation-state, identities constructed in the course of the transfer of children have attempted both to use and to discard history. Pasts have been treated as more or less disposable. Results have never, however, been predictable or necessarily enduring. Canadians came to adoption with many views on how to live with others.

The history of adoption, like that of immigration and citizenship more generally, repeatedly demonstrates that border-crossing does not necessarily confer equality or end abuse. As Himani Bannerji so effectively reminds us in *The Dark Side of Nation*, enduring racism has left many migrants and the First Nations vulnerable to permanent marking as somehow less worthy.[2] Class and supposed ability have proved equally injurious. Potential recruits for new worlds have found no assurance of fairness in the here and now or in the future. Not all individuals have been equally positioned to exert influence over stories or outcomes. Some Canadians have always held high cards. Guests of every sort have frequently been expected to surrender that part of themselves that connects to alternate beginnings. As Peter Schuck has suggested of 'original nationality'—the equivalent of birth families—in his evocatively titled *Citizens, Strangers, and In-Betweens*, preceding identities are readily regarded as threats.[3] In their persisting efforts to match the classical family of western nostalgia or the normative ideal imagined by twentieth-century experts, many adopting parents trusted that different environments would transform progeny into pliable subjects of new realms. Recurring resistance to linking birth and adoptive histories rested on a flourishing faith that active adults could rescript the chosen few and that past lives were better forgotten or well edited.

Adopters, like the nation itself, have often feared that arrivals might be pulled back into older tales and loyalties. From the point of view of opponents of openness and reunions, as from contemporary critics of multiculturalism such as writer Neil Bissoondath, the renunciation of problematic pasts is a good and necessary step. Families and Canada are presumed to be far better off without potentially divisive distinctions from abandoned worlds.[4] In 1994, persisting misgivings spurred Canada's Standing Committee on Citizenship and Immigration to hope that 'dual' and 'naturalized' citizens 'accord primacy' to their Canadian nationality.[5] In much the same spirit, the governor general designate, Michaëlle Jean, was applauded in September 2005 when she gave up her French nationality. Advocates of closed adoption have often made just this demand for closure. The past should indeed be a foreign country and one to which no repatriation or reconnection is really possible. Indeed to return or to be sent back supplies an emotional equivalent to desertion or deportation. Offenders appear unworthy of grafts to happier worlds. That looming condemnation regularly troubles adoptees and immigrants alike.

As adoption's human currency, youngsters have found their value recognized, inflated, or debased over the years by what they are believed to embody. Since adoption was first legislated in 1873, the gold standard for mainstream English-Canadian families has frequently been healthy white female babies. Welcome for boys, like class and racialized strangers and those assumed to possess disabilities of any sort, has always been at least somewhat uncertain. Their reception nevertheless improved over the course of the twentieth century, when hopes flourished for socialization and inclusion and when prized candidates for new homes became harder to find. Even as an ultimately inadequate social security system evolved to shelter some disadvantaged populations from the loss of youngsters, the mounting devastation of many Aboriginal communities and worldwide tragedies produced a variety of child casualties. Their rescue, with its frequent embrace of colour-blind liberalism and sometimes a more progressive anti-racist politics, transformed adoption in the last decades of the twentieth century. As sociologist H. David Kirk, author of the classic *Shared Fate* and other studies, pointed out, adoption promised second chances to those who were prepared to understand the suffering of others. An enlarged imagination provided the surest foundation for living together. Changes in national life in the 1960s and 1970s allowed the unprecedented embrace of the utopian possibilities he highlighted. One white adoptive mother of a Black daughter in these years summed up the optimistic perspective: 'The multicultural family, as the multicultural nation, must be the model upon which we pin our hopes and direct our actions.'[6]

At the beginning of the twenty-first century, such hope still mobilizes much support for adoption of every kind. Yet, much has changed. Canada's searching and repatriation rights-seekers increasingly demand that adoption's links to the past be exposed and extend Kirk's recognition of loss to include birth families and communities. Their efforts form part of the various movements of historical redress—targeting, among others, the Chinese head tax, the internment of Japanese and Ukrainian Canadians, Native residential schools, the destruction of Africville—that emerged even as the nation experimented with multiculturalism. This wide-ranging assault on national amnesia has challenged the power of the mainstream to dictate relations and to ignore the bad news on which the present has so frequently been constructed. It provided, as Canadian political scientist Matt James has suggested, unprecedented opportunities for 'forging a new discursive context in which the beneficiaries and the victims of historical injustice can begin meaningfully to discuss their joint histories and future.'[7] That conversation has been overdue in adoption, as in much else. While some Canadians preferred the promise of new reproductive technologies, those in search of offspring had to confront as never before their dependence on domestic and global inequalities. Their sober reflections on their own and their nation's role in the trade in children may herald happier prospects for the future than the history so often documented by *Finding Families, Finding Ourselves.*

Relations between hosts and newcomers—whether First Nation and non–North American, Canadian-born and immigrant, or birth and adoptive kin—have been complex and multi-dimensional. In the course of intimate relations, alliances and sympathies or conflict and antipathy are all possibilities. Domestic relations, like those on grander stages, have had many scripts. Canadian families, like the nation they inhabit, have been flexible, evolving creations, products of both effort and inattention. The transfer of youngsters confirms both malleability and permeability. Losers as well as winners in the high-stakes game of finding families have contributed to ongoing diversity in Canadian households, as in much else. By the closing years of the twentieth century, the growing significance of single or same-sex adopters and interracial families locates adoption close to the leading edge of domestic pluralism. It is also revealing that lesbians and gays were winning unprecedented opportunities to immigrate and marry just as they gained adoption rights from provinces. More than ever, diverse family forms are visible in anchoring and defining the national community. In households, as in nations, encounters with sometime strangers have proved catalysts that enlarge minds and the community in general.

It is also worth remembering that blood ties and origins offer no guarantee of happiness or security; kith and kin can cripple and kill at least as well as strangers.[8] History is not an easy friend. Women and children need to be especially sceptical of the romantic essentialization that has often accompanied discussions of domestic or national roots and origins. Their best interests have regularly been sacrificed on the altar of tradition, concocted and otherwise. Adoptees with little or no information about the past may find it tempting to 'make up fantasies about their birth parents',[9] but nostalgia can disable the future. New beginnings in families or

Canada itself can sometimes be a very good thing, offering hope in place of despair and death.[10] Second chances do indeed occur—we need only think of a remarkable trio of Canadian-born artists Buffy Sainte-Marie, Renée Rosnes, and Sarah McLachlan.

Today, adoption, much like citizenship regimes, is in flux. Both were once regarded as relatively straightforward, as conveying, at least to the chosen, important benefits and legitimate demands for renunciation. While such desires persist in some quarters, they increasingly falter. Director Karin Lee's documentary film *Made in China: The Story of Adopted Children from China* (2000) captures the growing realization that understanding the past promises the surest means of constructing shared futures that all can accept. The 77 per cent of Canadians who at much the same time supported release of confidential information to adoptees without permission of adopters or birth parents appear to agree.[11]

Other signs also suggest that mainstream Canadians might be willing to open themselves to unprecedented possibilities. Michaëlle Jean's Haitian origins, much like the Chinese background of her predecessor, Adrienne Clarkson, were widely celebrated as an advantage in a modern nation. The fact that Jean's daughter, Marie-Eden, is adopted from the birthplace of the new representative of the queen met similar approval. Even the conservative political columnist for 'Canada's national newspaper' fell under the spell, writing, 'here is this beautiful young Canadian of Haitian birth, with a smile that makes you catch your breath, with a bemused older husband by her side, and a daughter who literally personifies our future, and you look at them and you think: Yes, this is our great achievement, this is the Canada that Canada wants to be.' Unfortunately, more than its aura of self-congratulation spoiled this welcome. The columnist's next words invoked familiar denials. The history of contestation and truth-telling that has permitted Canada to mature sufficiently to choose a black, female, immigrant head of state who was also an adoptive mother was tossed into the dustbin: 'And suddenly, the arguments of the nationalists and the sovereigntists and the fire-wallists, of the alienated and resentful and estranged, are so tired, so *yesterday*, that you just don't want to have to listen to them any more.'[12] Unobservant readers might well have thought that Jean and the Canada she embodied were the creation of conservatives rather than their long-time nightmare. When it required accountability, history, it seemed, no longer mattered.

Ultimately, however, this journalistic sleight of hand should not detract from the achievement glimpsed at the investiture of the dominion's twenty-seventh governor general. In 2005, the reality was that a different kind of family inhabited Rideau Hall. The highest office in the land embraced a history that identified adoption, as well as questions of immigration and citizenship, as central to the Canadian story. Such an outcome could hardly have been envisaged when Anne of Green Gables first found her way into the popular imagination. Ultimately, however, both the irrepressible redhead and the daughter of the vice-regal couple in 2005 reminded Canadians that families, like the nation itself, could be constructed so as to accord respect and fair play to all their members. *Finding Families, Finding Ourselves* has told part of the story of just how that came to be.

Notes

Introduction

1. Ipsos-Reid, *Adoption in Canada: A Report on Public Opinion* (August 2004).
2. Patricia Hill Collins, 'Producing the Mothers of the Nation: Race, Class and Contemporary US Population Policies', in *Women, Citizenship and Difference*, ed. Nira Yuval-Davis and Pnina Werbner (London and New York: Zed Books, 1999): 118–19.
3. H. David Kirk, *Shared Fate: A Theory and Method of Adoptive Relationships* (Port Angeles, WA and Brentwood Bay, BC: Ben-Simon Publications 1984). The assessment comes from June Callwood, 'Adoption Not All Hearts and Flowers', *Chatelaine* (April 1976), 108.
4. H. David Kirk, as quoted in Ralph Garber, *Disclosure of Adoption Information*, Report of the Special Commissioner to the Honourable John Sweeney, Minister of Community and Social Services (Government of Ontario, November 1985), 25.
5. Kirk, *Shared Fate*, 13.
6. Eva Mackey, *The House of Difference: Cultural Politics and National Identity in Canada* (Toronto: University of Toronto Press, 2002), 5. See also Michel Foucault, 'Disciplinary Power and Subjection', in *Power*, ed. Steven Lukes (London: Basil Blackwell, 1992), 229–42, and 'Governmentality', in *The Foucault Effect*, ed. Grahm Burchell, Colin Gordon, and Peter Miller (London: Harvester Wheatsheaf, 1991), 87–104.
7. Mackey, *House of Difference*, 14.
8. On the conventional rescue plot in adoption see Julie Berebitsky, *Like Our Very Own: Adoption and the Changing Culture of Motherhood, 1851–1950* (Lawrence: University Press of Kansas, 2000), 3, 59, 76, and Laura Briggs, 'Mother, Child, Race, Nation: The Visual Iconography of Rescue and the Politics of Transnational and Transracial Adoption', *Gender and History* 15, no. 2 (2003): 179–200.
9. Mackey, *House of Difference*, 148 (emphasis in original).
10. Pauline Gardiner Barber, 'Citizenship and Attachment across Borders? A Transnational and Anthropological Research Agenda', *Canadian Diversity/é Canadienne* 2, no. 1 (2003): 45.
11. On Quebec see, *inter alia*, Marie-Paule Malouin, ed., *L'Univers des enfants en difficulté au Québec entre 1940 et 1960* (Quebec: Editions Bellarmin, 1996); Françoise Romaine Ouellette and Joanne Séguin, *Adoption et redéfinition contemporain de l'enfant, de la famille et de la filiation* (Quebec: Institute québécoise de recherche sur la culture, 1994), and Denyse Baillargeon, 'Orphans in Quebec: On the Margins of Which Family?' in

Mapping the Margins: The Family and Social Discipline in Canada, 1700–1975, ed. Nancy Christie and Michael Gauvreau (Montreal and Kingston: McGill-Queen's University Press, 2004), 305–26.

12. Arguments stressing heredity revived in the last decades of the twentieth century. See Audrey Marshall and Margaret McDonald, *Many Sided Triangle: Adoption in Australia* (Carlton South, Victoria: Melbourne University Press, 2001), esp. 2.

13. For the coining of this invaluable phrase see William J. Goode, *World Revolution and Family Patterns* (New York: Free Press; London: Collier-Macmillan, 1963).

14. On mythologies and realities regarding children see Veronica Strong-Boag, 'Long Time Coming: The Century of the Canadian Child?' *Journal of Canadian Studies* 35, no. 1 (2000): 124–37, and her 'The Spotlight on Children', *Canadian Bulletin of Medical History* 19, no. 1 (2002): 5–16.

15. On the invention of tradition see the classic volume, Eric J. Hobsbawm and Terence O. Ranger, *The Invention of Tradition* (Cambridge: Cambridge University Press, 1983).

16. See Veronica Strong-Boag and Carole Gerson, *Paddling Her Own Canoe: The Times and Texts of E. Pauline Johnson* (Tekahionwake) (Toronto: University of Toronto Press, 2000), esp. ch. 5.

17. Lucy Maud Montgomery, *Anne of the Island* (London, ON: Gatefold Books, 1982), 73.

18. For an introduction, see Leslie McCall, 'The Complexity of Intersectionality', *Signs* 30, no. 3 (2003): 1772–1800.

19. Rickie Solinger, *Beggars and Choosers: How the Politics of Choice Shapes Adoption, Abortion and Welfare in the United States* (New York: Hill and Wang, 2001).

Chapter 1

1. *Re Davis* (1909), cited in *The Canadian Abridgment: A Digest of Decisions of the Provincial and Dominion Courts, Including Appeals therefrom to the Privy Council, but Excluding Decisions based on the Quebec Civil Code. From the Earliest Times to the End of 1935,* ed. William Renwick Riddell and Frederick Clyde Auld (Toronto: Burroughs and Company, 1940), 22: 654.

2. Neil Sutherland, *Growing Up: Childhood in English Canada from the Great War to the Age of Television* (Toronto: University of Toronto Press, 1997), esp. ch. 5.

3. The literature on family devastation is abundant. For a beginning, see Robin F. Badgley, *Sexual Offences against Children: Report of the Committee on Sexual Offences against Children and Youths* (Ottawa: Minister of Justice and Attorney General of Canada and the Minister of National Health and Welfare, 1984); S.H.S. Hughes, *Report of the Royal Commission of Inquiry into the Response of the Newfoundland Criminal Justice System to Complaints* (St John's: the Commission, 1991); M.E. Wright, 'Unnatural Mothers: Infanticide in Halifax, 1850–1875', *Nova Scotia Historical Review* 7, no. 2 (1987): 13–29.

4. William Goode, *World Revolution and Family Patterns* (New York: Free Press of Glencoe, 1963). See also John R. Gillis, *A World of Their Own Making: A History of Myth and Ritual in Family Life* (Oxford: Oxford University Press, 1997).

5. See Susan McDaniel and Robert Lewis, 'Did They or Didn't They? Intergenerational Supports in Families Past: A Case Study of Brigus, Newfoundland, 1920–1945', in

Family Matters: Papers in Post-Confederation Family History, ed. L. Chambers and E.-A. Montigny (Toronto: Canadian Scholars' Press, 1998), 475–97.

6. See Mona Gleason, *Normalizing the Ideal: Psychology, Schooling, and the Family in Post-War Canada* (Toronto: University of Toronto Press, 1999). On the use by conservatives of familial ideologies, see Veronica Strong-Boag, 'Independent Women, Problematic Men: First and Second Wave Anti-Feminism in Canada from Goldwin Smith to Betty Steele', *Histoire sociale/Social History* 57 (May 1996): 1–22.

7. On the role of health professionals in particular see Cynthia R. Comacchio, *'Nations Are Built of Babies': Saving Ontario's Mothers and Children, 1900–1940* (Montreal and Kingston: McGill-Queen's University Press, 1993).

8. See also the claims in E.C. Kimelman, *Transcripts and Briefs: Public Hearings, Special Hearings, Briefs. Review Committee on Indian and Métis Adoptions and Placements* (Winnipeg: Manitoba Community Services, 1985), and Lavina White and Eva Jacobs, comps, *Liberating Our Children, Liberating Our Nations: Report of the Aboriginal Committee, Community Panel, Family and Children's Services Legislation Review in British Columbia* (Victoria: The Committee, 1992): 10.

9. See Patricia Rooke and Rudy Schnell, *Discarding the Asylum: From Child Rescue to the Welfare State in English Canada, 1800–1950* (Lanham, MD: University Press of America, 1983).

10. L. Ashby, *Endangering Children: Dependence, Neglect, and Abuse in American History* (New York: Prentice Hall, 1997), 181.

11. Margrit Eichler, *Families in Canada Today: Recent Changes and Their Consequences*, 2nd ed. (Toronto: Gage Educational Publishing Co., 1988), esp. chs 1–4.

12. 'A Vicar Goes to Prison', *Toronto Star*, 22 October 1898.

13. See Paul Walton, 'Tooshley Appeals May Have Lapsed', *Cowichan Valley Citizen*, 13 October 2002, 12; 'Aboriginal Heritage Won't Be Considered', *Alberni Valley Times*, 18 October 2001, A2.

14. H.D. Kirk, *Shared Fate: A Theory and Method of Adoptive Relationships*, 2nd ed. (Port Angeles, WA: Ben-Simon Publications, 1984), xiv.

15. For various efforts to estimate, see E.W. Carp, *Family Matters: Secrecy and Disclosure in the History of Adoption* (Cambridge: Harvard University Press, 1998); A. Douglas and T. Philpot, eds, *Adoption: Changing Families, Changing Times* (London and New York: Routledge, 2003); H.P. Hepworth, *Foster Care and Adoption in Canada* (Ottawa: Canadian Council on Social Development, 1980), 169.

16. G.C. Emery, *Facts of Life: The Social Construction of Vital Statistics, Ontario 1869–1959* (Montreal and Kingston: McGill-Queen's University Press, 1993), 96.

17. J.B. Wisdom, 'Adoption as a Preparation for Life', *Proceedings of the First Annual Meetings of the Canadian Conference on Social Work* 1 (1928): 82.

18. *Report of the New Brunswick Child Welfare Committee* (Saint John: Kiwanis Club of Saint John City, 1929), 30.

19. S. McLean, *Report of the Superintendent* (St John's: Child Welfare Association of St John's, 1931), 11.

20. J.S. Robertson, 'Births and Stillbirths', *Nova Scotia Medical Bulletin* 34, no. 2 (1954): 115–16.

21. Nora Fox, 'New Policies in Child Welfare', *Canadian Welfare* 32, no. 2 (1956): 63.

22. K.J. Daly and M.P. Sobol, *Adoption in Canada* (Guelph, ON: University of Guelph, May 1993), 42.

23. Hepworth, *Foster Care and Adoption in Canada*, 3.

24. Carol Smart, 'Stories of Family Life: Cohabitation, Marriage and Social Change', *Canadian Journal of Family Law* (hereafter *CJFL*) 17, no. 1 (2000): 22.

25. For a beginning of the Canadian story see Nic Clarke, 'Sacred Daemons: Exploring British Columbian Society's Perceptions of "Mentally Deficient" Children, 1870–1930', *BC Studies* no. 144 (winter 2004/5): 61–90.

26. See Michele Stairs, 'Matthews and Marillas: Bachelors and Spinsters in Prince Edward Island in 1881', in *Mapping the Margins: The Family and Social Discipline in Canada, 1700–1975*, ed. Nancy Christie and Michael Gauvreau (Montreal and Kingston: McGill-Queen's University Press, 2004), esp. 255, which points to the number of adult siblings raising both related and unrelated children.

27. Marshall Saunders, *The House of Armour* (Philadelphia: A.J. Rowland, 1897), 528.

28. G.L. Hogg, 'The Legal Rights of Masters, Mistresses and Domestic Servants in Montreal, 1816–1929' (MA thesis, McGill University, 1989), 48.

29. Bettina Bradbury, 'Surviving as a Widow in Nineteenth Century Montreal', *Urban History Review* 17, no. 3 (1989): 148–60. See also her forthcoming *Wife to Widow: Lives, Laws and Politics*.

30. C.S. Fish, 'Images and Reality of Fatherhood: A Case Study of Montreal's Protestant Middle Class, 1870–1924' (Ph.D. thesis, McGill University, 1991), 129–30.

31. 'Parents on Kids: How Do Fathers Bring Up Children Single-handed?' *Star Weekly*, 24 May 1969, 6.

32. Public Archives of Alberta (hereafter PAA), Agreement for Adoption, Saskatchewan, access no. 76.272 SE, 5 January 1925, p. 3.

33. On the possibility of acceptance by family and community see Peter Ward, 'Unwed Motherhood in Nineteenth-Century English Canada', Canadian Historical Association *Historical Papers* (1981), esp. 46–8.

34. See the important reminder by Suzanne Morton, 'Nova Scotia and Its Unmarried Mothers', in Christie and Gauvreau, *Mapping the Margins*, 328–9.

35. For typical observations see the Nova Scotia Department of Social Welfare and Rehabilitation, Director Child Welfare Branch, *Annual Report* (1959–60), 23.

36. Ollivier Hubert, 'The Invention of the Margin as an Invention of the Family: The Case of Rural Quebec in the Eighteenth and Nineteenth Centuries', in Christie and Gauvreau, *Mapping the Margins*, 188–90.

37. Newfoundland Department of Public Health and Welfare, Division of Child Welfare, *Third Annual Report* (ending 31 March 1948), 21.

38. Robert Hartlen, *Butterbox Survivors: Life after the Ideal Maternity Home* (Halifax: Nimbus, 1999), 63

39. See Suzanne Morton, 'Managing the Unmarried Mother "Problem": Halifax Maternity Homes,' in *Mothers of the Municipality: Women, Work, and Social Policy in Post-1945 Halifax*, ed. Judith Fingard and Janet Guildford (Toronto: University of Toronto Press, 2005).

40. Miss Kathleen Sutherton, 'The Relationship between Maternity Homes and Children's Aid Societies', Armagh Annual Meeting, 10 March 1959 (Toronto: Unmarried

Parent Department Children's Aid Society of Metropolitan Toronto, 1959), 7 (Koener Library, UBC, vertical file).

41. Nova Scotia, Director of Child Welfare, Pictou County Children's Aid Society, *34th Annual Report* (for the fiscal year ending 30 November 1946), 2.

42. Morton, 'Nova Scotia and Its Unmarried Mothers', 330–1.

43. Harry MacKay and Catherine Austin, *Single Adolescent Mothers in Ontario: A Report of 87 Single Adolescent Mothers' Experiences, Their Situation, Needs and Use of Community Services* (Ottawa: Canadian Council on Social Development, 1983), ix.

44. Roberta G. Aggas, 'Social Class Influences in Illegitimacy: A Study of the Effects of Social Class Affiliation, Corresponding Patterns of Socialization and Their Relationship to Illegitimacy' (MSW thesis, Maritime School of Social Work and University of King's College, 1967).

45. Marcel Arseneau, 'A Study of Ninety Wards in Child Caring Institutions in Halifax: An Analysis of the Personal Characteristics, Family Background and Placement Experience of Wards of Child Welfare Agencies who were in Child Caring Institutions during the Year 1958' (MSW thesis, Maritime School of Social Work, 1960), 44

46. Gillis, *A World of Their Own Making,* 11.

47. Ibid., 15.

48. Vera [aka Kate Madeline Barry Bottomley], *Honor Edgeworth, or, Ottawa's Present Tense* (Ottawa: A. Woodburn, 1882), 9.

49. On the distinctive response of the Catholic Church, see the very helpful analysis of Denyse Baillargeon, 'Orphans in Quebec: On the Margin of Which Family?' in Christie and Gauvreau, *Mapping the Margins,* 304–26. As she notes too, the Roman Catholic Church was divided on this matter. Some nuns on the front lines of child welfare supported foster families. See her 322n34 and Soeur Allaire, *L'entrée à l'orphélinat* (Montreal: École sociale populaire, 1930).

50. See David Gagan, *Hopeful Travellers: Families, Land, and Social Change in Mid-Victorian Peel County, Canada West* (Toronto: University of Toronto Press, 1981); Michael B. Katz, *The People of Hamilton, Canada West: Family and Class in a Mid-Nineteenth-Century City* (Cambridge: Harvard University Press, 1975). See also Cynthia R. Comacchio, *The Infinite Bonds of Family: Domesticity in Canada, 1850–1940* (Toronto: University of Toronto Press, 1999).

51. See the reminder in Françoise Noël, *Family Life and Sociability in Upper and Lower Canada: A View from Diaries and Family Correspondence* (Montreal and Kingston: McGill-Queen's University Press, 2003), 192.

52. Susanna Moodie, *Life in the Clearings versus the Bush* (London: R. Bentley, 1853), 161.

53. Dorothy W. Rungeling, *Life and Works of Ethelwyn Wetherald, 1857–1940, Canadian Poet-Journalist* (n.p., 2004), 68.

54. Canada, Royal Commission on New Reproductive Technologies, *Proceed with Care: Final Report of the Royal Commission on New Reproductive Technologies* (Ottawa: Canada Communications Group, 1993): 1: 189–92.

55. Ibid., 1: 171.

56. See Elaine Tyler May, *Barren in the Promised Land: Childless Americans and the Pursuit of Happiness* (New York: Basic Books, 1995).

57. John Strachan, as cited in *The Town of York, 1815–1834: Further Collections of Documents of Early Toronto*, ed. Edith G. Firth (Toronto: Champlain Society, 1966), 255.

58. Catherine Laura Johnstone, *Winter and Summer Excursions in Canada* (London: Digby, Long, 1894), 164–6.

59. Charlotte Whitton, *Welfare in Alberta: The Report of a Study* (Edmonton: Douglas Printing, 1947), 99.

60. The literature on child immigrants is extensive, but see especially Joy Parr, *Labouring Children: British Emigrant Apprentices to Canada, 1869–1924* (Toronto: University of Toronto Press, 1994); Frederick J. McEvoy, '"These Treasures of the Church of God": Catholic Child Immigration to Canada', Canadian Catholic Historical Association, *Historical Studies* 65 (1999): 50–70; Mrs J. Breckenridge McGregor, *Several Years After: An Analysis of the Histories of a Selected Group of Juvenile Immigrants brought to Canada in 1910, and in 1920, by British Emigration Societies* (Ottawa: Canadian Council on Child Welfare, 1928); and Geoffrey Sherington and Chris Jeffery, *Fairbridge: Empire and Child Migration* (London and Portland, OR: Woburn Press, 1998).

61. See, *inter alia*, Rebecca L. Hegar, 'The Cultural Roots of Kinship Care', in *Kinship Foster Care: Policy, Practice and Research*, ed. Rebecca L. Hegar and Maria Scannagpieco (New York: Oxford University Press, 1999), 23.

62. See Alastair Bissett-Johnson, 'Protecting Children in the North', *CJFL* 4 (1985): 419.

63. Rebecca L. Hegar and Maria Scannagpieco, 'Kinship Foster Care in Context', in Hegar and Scannagpieco, *Kinship Foster Care*, 3.

64. Roger Greeff, ed., *Fostering Kinship: An International Perspective on Kinship Foster Care* (Aldershot, UK: Ashgate Arena, 1999), 1.

65. Margaret Jane H. Little, '*No Car, No Radio, No Liquor Permit': The Moral Regulation of Single Mothers in Ontario, 1920–1997* (Toronto: Oxford University Press, 1998), 57, tables 3.2; 132, table 5.4.

66. Roger Greeff, Suzette Waterhouse, and Edwina Brocklesby, 'Kinship Fostering: Research, Policy and Practice in English', in Greeff, *Fostering Kinship*, 36.

67. Prince Edward Island, Department of Health and Social Services, Social Services Branch, Field Services Division, *Annual Report* (1982–3), 38.

68. Newfoundland and Labrador, Department of Social Services, *Annual Report* (1985–6), 25.

69. Hegar, 'Kinship Foster Care: The New Child Placement Paradigm', in Hegar and Scannagpieco, *Kinship Foster Care*, 235; and also Greeff, 'Introduction', *Fostering Kinship*, 3.

70. 'Minni Sheila Audrey (nee Walker)', *Vancouver Sun*, 21 June 2003, B8.

71. Canada, House of Commons, *Debates*, 22 November 1976, 1249 (Crawford Douglas).

72. See Christie, 'A "Painful Dependence": Female Begging Letters and the Familial Economy of Obligation', in Christie and Gauvreau, *Mapping the Margins*, 76.

73. *Latimer v. Hill* (1916), 26 D.L.R. 800 (Ont. S.C.).

74. *Brown v. Patridge et al.*, [1925] 1 D.L.R. 761 (Sask. C.A.).

75. *Re McAvena*, [1952] 4 D.L.R. 204 (Sask. C.A.).

76. *C v. K.* (1960), 22 D.L.R. 81 (Sask. C.A.).

77. See *L.(A.) v. M. (B.A.)* (14 May 1993), Doc. No. Kenora 59/93 (Ontario General Division)' in *Adoption Law in Canada: Practice and Procedure,* ed. Douglas.W. Phillips, R.J. Raphael, D.J. Manning, J.A.Turnbull (Toronto: Carswell Thomson Professional Publishing, 1995), 7-4-41.

78. Victor Malarek, *Hey Malarek! The True Story of a Kid Who Made It* (Halifax: Formac, 1984), 2.

79. 'Christina's New Home?' *Vancouver Province,* 12 July 1957, 1.

80. R. Crowder, 'James Albert (Al) Crowder', *Globe and Mail,* 20 November 2002; S.A. Cook, 'Harriet Ethel (Fry) Killins', ibid., 9 July 2003; E. (Woodward) Henry, 'Reta Ellen Woodward', ibid., 20 November 2003; D. Crawford, 'Isabel Strickland', ibid., 21 April 2003.

81. British Columbia, Superintendent of Neglected Children, *Annual Report* (for the year ending 31 March 1938), 3; *Annual Report* (for the year ending 31 March 1941), 71.

82. Mary Brechin, 'Danger: Child Growing Up', *Maclean's,* 15 August 1943, 48.

83. See 'Parents Seeking Giveaway Child', *Vancouver Sun,* 26 October 1960, 1, and 'Judge Can Please Only One Mother', ibid., 2 December 1960, 2.

84. *Re Moores and Feldstein* (1973), 34 D.L.R. 449 (Ont. H.C.).

85. Newfoundland, Department of Public Health and Welfare, Division of Child Welfare, *3rd Annual Report* (for the year ending 31 March 1948), 33.

86. Saskatchewan, Department of Social Welfare, Director of Child Welfare, *Annual Report* (1947–8), 19.

87. Peter Gossage, 'Tangled Webs: Remarriage and Family Conflict in Nineteenth Century Quebec', in Chambers and Montigny, *Family Matters,* 355–76; and his 'Marginal by Definition? Stepchildren in Quebec, 1866–1920', in Christie and Gauvreau, *Mapping the Margins,* 141–70.

88. Alastair Bissett-Johnson, 'Adoption within the Family', in *Adoption: Current Issues and Trends,* ed. Paul Sachdev (Toronto: Butterworths, 1983), 217.

89. 'Mommie, Come Get Me!' in Hartlen, *Butterbox Survivors,* 69–71.

90. Newfoundland Provincial Archives, Box S6-1-8, Public Health and Welfare, General Administration, Folder 5, Division of Child Welfare 1944–47, Report of Period 1 January to 31 March 1946, p. 7.

91. See E.J. Dickson-Gilmore, '"More Mohawk Than My Blood": Citizenship, Membership and the Struggle over Identity in Kahanawake', *Canadian Issues* 21 (1999): 44–62; S. Holt, 'Poor Little White Girl', *Star Weekly,* 4 February 1967, 2–7.

92. Joan B. Silk, 'Adoption among the Inuit', *Ethos* 15, no. 3 (1987): 325.

93. Marjorie Lismer, 'Adoption Practices of the Blood Indians of Alberta, Canada', *Plains Anthropologist* 19, no. 63 (1974): 27, 29.

94. Ann McElroy, 'Arctic Modernization and Change in Inuit Family Organization', in *Marriage, Family, and Society: Canadian Perspectives,* ed. S. Parvez Wakil and F.A. Wakil (Toronto: Butterworths, 1975), 388–9. See also Jérôme Rousseau, *L'Adoption chez les Esquimaux tununermiut* (Quebec : Université Laval, 1970), and Morton I. Teicher, 'Adoption Practices among Eskimos on Southampton Island', *Canadian Welfare* 29, no. 2 (1953): 32–7.

95. Ann W. Acheson, 'The Kutchin Family: Past and Present', in *Canadian Families: Ethnic*

Variations, ed. K. Ishwaran (Toronto: McGraw-Hill Ryerson, 1980), 241–65.

96. Claudia Lewis, *Indian Families on the Northwest Coast* (Chicago: University of Chicago Press, 1970), 4.

97. Bill Lomax, 'Hlugwit'y, Hluuxw'y—My Family, My Child: The Survival of Customary Adoption in British Columbia', *CJFL* 14, no. 2 (1997): 209.

98. Lynn Kettler Penrod, *Adoption in Canada,* Master of Law thesis, University of Alberta, (1986): 233.

99. Ibid., 234.

100. Anna Davin, *Growing Up Poor: Home, School and Street in London, 1870–1914* (London: Rivers Oram Press, 1996), 18, 20, 40. On London see also Ellen Ross, *Love and Toil: Motherhood in Outcast London, 1870–1918* (New York: Oxford University Press, 1993).

101. Lynn Abrams, *The Orphan Country: Children of Scotland's Broken Homes from 1845 to the Present Day* (Edinburgh: John Donald Publishers, 1998), 23.

102. James Overton, 'Self-Help, Charity, and Individual Responsibility: The Political Economy of Social Policy in Newfoundland in the 1920s', in *Twentieth Century Newfoundland: Explorations,* ed. James Hiller and Peter Neary (St John's: Breakwater, 1994), 90.

103. Douglas J. McCann, 'Apprenticeship in Nova Scotia' (MA thesis, Dalhousie University, 1982), 2.

104. Martha J. Bailey, 'Servant Girls and Masters: The Tort of Seduction and the Support of Bastards', *CJFL* 10, no. 1 (1991): 144.

105. See announcement in *Canada Lancet* 15, no. 4 (1882): 127. The variety is emphasized in Nurith Zmora, *Orphanages Reconsidered: Child Care Institutions in Progressive Era Baltimore* (Philadelphia: Temple University Press, 1994), and Timothy A. Hacsi, *Second Home: Orphan Asylums and Poor Families in America* (Cambridge: Harvard University Press, 1997).

106. Rooke and Schnell, *Discarding the Asylum,* 81.

107. See John Bullen, 'J.J. Kelso and the New Child-Savers: The Genesis of the Children's Aid Movement in Ontario', *Ontario History* 72 (1990): 107–28.

108. See also Margaret Stevenson, 'Some Emotional Problems of Orphanage Children', *Canadian Journal of Psychiatry* 6, no. 4 (1952): 179–82.

109. See, for example Paul Langan, *Hespeler's Hidden Secret: The Coombe Orphanage, 1905–1947* (n.p., 2000); Canada Law Commission, *Restoring Dignity: Responding to Child Abuse in Canadian Institutions* (Ottawa: Queen's Printer, 2000).

110. Bettina Bradbury, 'The Fragmented Family: Family Strategies in the Face of Death, Illness, and Poverty, Montreal, 1860–1885', in *Childhood and Family in Canadian History,* ed. Joy Parr (Toronto: McClelland and Stewart, 1982).

111. See the arguments of Janice Harvey, 'The Protestant Orphan Asylum and the Montreal Ladies Benevolent Society: A Case Study in Protestant Child Charity in Montreal, 1822–1900' (Ph.D. diss., McGill University, 2001), 5.

112. Sara Posen, 'Examining Policy from the "Bottom Up": The Relationship between Parents, Children and Managers of the Toronto Boys' Home, 1859–1920', in Christie and Gauvreau, *Family Matters,* 3–18.

113. Diane Purvey, 'Alexandra Orphanage and Families in Crisis in Vancouver,

1892–1938', in *Dimensions of Childhood: Essays on the History of Children and Youth in Canada,* ed. Russell Smandych, Gordon Dodds, and Alvin Esau (Winnipeg: Legal Research Institute of the University of Manitoba, 1990).

114. Heidi Macdonald, 'Doing More with Less: The Sisters of St. Martha (PEI) Diminish the Impact of the Great Depression', *Acadiensis* 33, no. 1 (2003): 37.

115. George Caldwell, *Child Welfare Services in New Brunswick: Report to the Honourable W.R. Duffie, Minister of Youth and Welfare, Province of New Brunswick* (Fredericton: Office of the Minister of Youth and Welfare, 1965), 10.

116. See Charles R. Saunders, *Share and Care: The Story of the Nova Scotia Home for Colored Children* (Halifax: Nimbus Publishing, 1994).

117. See Reuben Slonim, *Grand to Be an Orphan* (Toronto: Clarke Irwin, 1983), Judy Gordon, *'Four Hundred Brothers and Sisters': Two Jewish Orphanages in Montreal, Quebec, 1909–1942* (Toronto: Lugus, 2002), and Stephen A. Speisman, *The Jews of Toronto: A History to 1937* (Toronto: McClelland and Stewart, 1979). On one Jewish orphanage in the United States, see Howard Goldstein, *The Home on Gorham Street and the Voices of Its Children* (Tuscaloosa: University of Alabama Press, 1996).

118. See William and Jeannette Raynsford, *Silent Casualties: Veterans' Families in the Aftermath of the Great War* (Madoc, ON: Merribrae Press, 1986).

119. 'Society for the Relief of Widows and Orphans', *Christian Guardian,* 5 September 1832, 171.

120. Stuart J. Coleman, 'Children for Adoption,' *Canadian Churchman,* 8 July 1897, 433.

121. 'For Adoption', *Canadian Churchman,* 1 May 1913, 281; 'Boy to Adopt', ibid., 5 February 1914, 82; ibid., 1 February 1917, 64.

122. 'Wanted to Adopt', *Canadian Churchman,* 4 February 1909, 67; 'Wanted', ibid., 2 December 1920, 792.

123. The Orange Order, one of the most powerful of Canada's fraternal bodies, operated a number of orphanages, including institutions in New Westminster, British Columbia; Indian Head, Saskatchewan; and St Charles, Manitoba.

124. See 'The Formal Opening of the I.O.F. Orphans' Home by Its Great Founder,' *Toronto Star,* 29 August 1904.

125. Ethel M. Chapman, 'An Orphanage That Is a Home,' *Maclean's,* 15 July 1920, 71.

126. 'Canadians Find Haven in "City of Orphans"', *Star Weekly,* 1 November 1958, 16–17, 18, 20.

127. For the largely positive assessment see David T. Beito, *From Mutual Aid to the Welfare State: Fraternal Societies and Social Services, 1890–1967* (Chapel Hill: University of North Carolina Press, 2000), 86.

128. Kenneth Cmiel, *A Home of Another Kind: One Chicago Orphanage and the Tangle of Child Welfare* (Chicago: University of Chicago Press, 1995), 96.

129. See Tamara Myers, 'Qui t'a debauchée? Family Adolescent Sexuality and the Juvenile Delinquents' Court in Early Twentieth-Century Montreal', in Christie and Gauvreau, *Family Matters,* 377–94, and Joan Sangster, *Girl Trouble: Female Delinquency in English Canada* (Toronto: Between the Lines, 2002).

130. See John Sheridan Milloy, *National Crime: The Canadian Government and the Residential School System, 1879 to 1986* (Winnipeg: University of Manitoba Press, 1999).

131. Patrick Johnston, *Native Children and the Child Welfare System* (Ottawa: Canadian

Council on Social Development, 1983), 2.

132. Jessa Chupik-Hall, "Good Families Do Not Just Happen": Indigenous People and Child Welfare Services in Canada, 1950–1965' (MA thesis, Trent University, 2001), 39.

133. H.B. Hawthorn, et al. eds., *A Survey of the Contemporary Indians of Canada: A Report on Economic, Political, Educational Needs and Policies* (Ottawa: Indian Affairs and Northern Development, Indian Affairs Branch, October 1966), 1: 327.

134. Richard A. King, *The School at Mopass: A Problem of Identity* (New York: Holt, Rinehart and Winston, 1967), 52.

135. See the uncritical story told by Vernon J. Story, Henry Kennedy, and Terry Worobetz, *The Home: Orphans' Home to Family Centre, 1873 to 1998* (Victoria, BC: Cridge Centre for the Family, 1999).

136. See Hacsi, *Second Home.*

137. Ontario, Sessional Papers No. 97 (1894), *First Report under the Children's Protection Act* (1893), 44, 45, 47.

138. On the significance of this development of a 'respectable working class' for fostering, see Robert Van Krieken, *Children and the State: Social Control and the Formation of Australian Child Welfare* (Sydney, NSW: Allen and Unwin, 1991), esp. 75.

Chapter 2

1. Honourable Mr Justice John D. Bracco, Court of Appeal of Alberta, in *Adoption Law in Canada: Practice and Procedure*, ed. Douglas W. Phillips, Ruth J. Raphael, Douglas J. Manning, Julia A. Turnbull (Toronto: Thomson Professional Publishing, 1995), v.

2. *Report of the New Brunswick Child Welfare Survey, 1928–29* (Saint John: Kiwanis Club, 1929), 24, 141.

3. *Statutes of New Brunswick, 1971–74*, 82–4.

4. Adoption of Children, *New Brunswick Revised Statutes, 1903*, 70–1.

5. *Halifax Morning Chronicle*, 31 January 1896, 8. On Wickwire, see S.B. Elliott, *The Legislative Assembly of Nova Scotia, 1758–1983: A Biographical Directory* (Halifax: Public Archives of Nova Scotia, 1983), 33.

6. 'Provincial Legislation', *Halifax Morning Chronicle*, 10 January 1896, 4.

7. An Act Respecting the Adoption of Children, *Nova Scotia Laws, 1895–96*, 29–32.

8. An Act to Amend Chapter 122, of the Revised Statutes, 'Of the Adoption of Children', *Nova Scotia Statutes, 1901*, 78.

9. An Act Respecting Apprentices and Minors, *Statutes of Manitoba, 1877*, 16. See also An Act Respecting Infants and Apprentices, *Revised Statutes of Manitoba, 1892*, where the situation remained much the same.

10. Infants' Act, *Statutes of Manitoba, 1897*, 167.

11. An Act Regarding the Adoption of Children, *Statutes of Prince Edward Island, 1916*, 10.

12. Suzanne Morton, 'Nova Scotia and Its Unmarried Mothers', in *Mapping the Margins: The Family and Social Discipline in Canada, 1700–1975*, ed. Nancy Christie and Michael Gauvreau (Montreal and Kingston: McGill-Queen's University Press, 2004), 327–48.

13. On this legislation see Margaret Little, *'No Car, No Radio, No Liquor Permit': The*

Moral Regulation of Single Mothers in Ontario, 1920–1997 (Toronto: Oxford University Press, 1998).

14. An Act Respecting the Welfare of Children, *Statutes of Saskatchewan, 1927*, 373.

15. See Angus McLaren, *Our Own Master Race: Eugenics in Canada, 1885–1945* (Toronto: McClelland and Stewart, 1990).

16. See Veronica Strong-Boag, 'Intruders in the Nursery: Childcare Professionals Reshape the Years One to Five, 1920–1940', in *Childhood and Family in Canadian History*, ed. Joy Parr (Toronto McClelland and Stewart, 1982), 160–78.

17. For a discussion see Frederick Read, 'The Legal Position of the Child of Unmarried Parents', *Canadian Bar Review* (hereafter *CBR*) 9, no. 9 (1931): 609–18; and ibid., no. 10 (1931): 729–36.

18. An Act to Amend Chapter 122, Revised Statutes, 1900, 'Of the Adoption of Children', *Statutes of Nova Scotia, 1921*, 420.

19. Health and Public Welfare Act, *Acts of Newfoundland, 1931*, 20.

20. An Act Respecting the Welfare of Children, *Statutes of Manitoba, 1922*, 33; An Act to Amend the Child Welfare Act, *Statutes of Manitoba, 1926*, 14.

21. An Act Relating to Domestic Relations, *Statutes of Alberta, 1927*, 32.

22. An Act Respecting the Adoption of Children, *Statutes of Ontario*, 1921, 1925, 1926, and 1927. For an important discussion of the evolution of this doctrine in Canada see Susan B. Boyd, *Child Custody, Law, and Women's Work* (Toronto: Oxford University Press, 2003).

23. *Re Grafasso* (1916), 30 D.L.R. 595 (Ont. S.C., Appellate Division), and *Brown v. Partridge et al.*, [1925] 1 D.L.R. (N.S.) 761 (Sask. C.A.).

24. Joyce M. Schlosser, 'Third Party Child-Centred Disputes: Parental Rights v. Best Interest of the Child', *Alberta Law Review* 12, no. 3 (1984): 410–11.

25. See Wayne Carp, *Family Matters: Secrecy and Disclosure in the History of Adoption* (Cambridge: Cambridge University Press, 1998) for his recognition that early legislation did not intend so much to hide the details of adoption from participants as from the greedy eye of the public.

26. Judith P. Ryan, 'The Overlapping Custody Jurisdiction: Co-existence or Chaos', *Canadian Journal of Family Law* (hereafter *CJFL*) 3 (1980): 116.

27. The Transfer of Guardianship Act, *Acts of Prince Edward Island, 1930*, 122.

28. An Act Respecting the Welfare of Children, *Statutes of Saskatchewan, 1927*, 348.

29. Health and Public Welfare Act, *Acts of Newfoundland, 1931*, 359–60.

30. An Act Respecting the Welfare of Children, *Statutes of Manitoba, 1936*, 38.

31. The Children's Act, *Statutes of Prince Edward Island, 1940*, 190.

32. An Act to Amend The Domestic Relations Act of 1927, *Statutes of Alberta, 1941*, 466.

33. An Act to Amend The Child Welfare Act, *Statutes of Manitoba, 1948*, 6.

34. The Children's Act, *Statutes of Prince Edward Island, 1940*, 190.

35. Nova Scotia, Royal Commission on Provincial Development and Rehabilitation, vol. 4, *Report on Public Welfare Services* (Halifax: King's Printer, 1944), 62. See also An Act to Amend Chapter 139 of the Revised Statutes, 1923, on the Adoption of Children, *Statutes of Nova Scotia, 1943*.

36. An Act Respecting the Welfare of Children, *Statutes of Alberta, 1944*, 96.

37. Welfare of Children Act, Part V, The Adoption of Children, *Newfoundland Acts, 1944*,

354.

38. See An Act Respecting the Welfare of Children, *Statutes of Saskatchewan, 1927,* 359.

39. An Act Respecting Maternity Boarding Houses, *Statutes of Nova Scotia, 1940,* 225–7. See also the excellent discussion by Karen Balcom, 'The Traffic in Babies: Cross-Border Adoption, Baby-Selling and the Development of Child Welfare Systems in the United States and Canada' (PhD diss., Rutgers University, 2002) and her 'Scandal and Social Policy: the Ideal Maternity Home and the Evolution of Social Policy in Nova Scotia, 1940–51', *Acadiensis* 31, no. 2 (2002): 3–37.

40. Julie Berebitsky, *Like Our Very Own: Adoption and the Changing Culture of Motherhood, 1851–1950* (Lawrence: University Press of Kansas, 2000).

41. Adoption Act, *Statutes of New Brunswick, 1946,* 173, 181, 184.

42. An Act to Amend the Adoption Act, *Statutes of New Brunswick, 1957,* 115.

43. 'An Act to Authorize and Make Legal the Adoption and Change of Name of Norma Frances Scott and Marjorie Agnes Scott, *Statutes of New Brunswick, 1948,* 607.

44. An Act to Validate Certain Adoptions of Children Formerly under the Care and Control of What Is Now 'New Brunswick Protestant Orphans' Home', *Statutes of New Brunswick, 1953,* 84.

45. An Act to Amend the Child Welfare Act of 1954, *Statutes of Manitoba, 1956,* 24.

46. Jack Sissons, *Judge of the Far North. The Memoirs of Jack Sissons* (Toronto: McClelland and Stewart, 1968), 143–4. See also the decision in *Re Katie's Adoption Petition* (1961) in Phillips et al., *Adoption Law in Canada,* 5–38.

47. Aboriginal Custom Adoption Recognition Act, *Statutes of the Northwest Territories, 1994,* 343–5.

48. Jo-Anne Fiske, 'The Supreme Law and the Grand Law: Changing Significance of Customary Law for Aboriginal Women of British Columbia', *BC Studies* nos. 105/6 (spring/summer 1995): 194. See also Jo-Anne Fiske and Claudien Herlihey, 'Courting Customs: Taking Customary Law to the BC Supreme Court', *International Journal of Race and Ethnicity* 1, no. 11 (1994): 49–65. See also *Casimel v. Insurance Corporation of British Columbia* (1991), 106 D.L.R. (4th) 720 (B.C. C.A.). My thanks to Jo-Anne Fiske for drawing these arguments to my attention.

49. An Act to Amend the Child Welfare Act, *Statutes of Alberta, 1958,* 1: 54.

50. See also C.P. Daniels, 'Case and Comment. Adoption—Consent of Natural Parent—Revocation,' *CBR* 35 (1957): 838.

51. An Act to Amend the Adoption Act, *Statutes of British Columbia, 1961,* 1.

52. An Act Relating to Child Welfare, Part IV, Adoption, *Statutes of Ontario, 1958,* 47.

53. An Ordinance to Provide for the Welfare of Children, *Ordinances of the Northwest Territories, 1961,* 32. See also Ordinances for 1966 and 1969.

54. An Act Respecting the Welfare of Children, *Statutes of Saskatchewan, 1946,* 776.

55. The Adoption Act, *Statutes of Prince Edward Island, 1950,* 7

56. Adoption Act, *Revised Statutes of Nova Scotia 1954,* 24–5.

57. An Act to Amend Chapter 4 of the Revised Statutes, 1954, The Adoption Act, *Statutes of Nova Scotia, 1959,* 59; and, Adoption Act, *Revised Statutes of Nova Scotia, 1967,* 6.

58. An Act Relating to the Adoption of Children, *Statutes of Newfoundland, 1964,* 97, 101.

59. An Act Respecting Child Welfare, *Statutes of Alberta, 1966,* 82.
60. *Price v. Cargin and Cargin* (1956), 4 D.L.R. (2d) 652 (Ont. C.A.).
61. *Re Wells* (1962), 33 D.L.R. (2d) 243 (B.C. C.A.).
62. *Re Duffell: Martin v. Duffell* (1950), 4 D.L.R. 1 694 (S.C.C.); *Hepton and Hepton v. Maat and Maat* (1957), 10 D.L.R. (2nd) 1 (S.C.C.); and *Re Roebuck* (1966), 58 D.L.R. 716 (B.C. S.C.).
63. F.M. Fraser, 'Children in Need of Protection', in *Studies in Canadian Family Law*, ed. D. Mendes Da Costa (Toronto: Butterworths, 1972), 1: 96.
64. Lynn Kettler Penrod, 'Adoption in Canada' (Master of Laws thesis, University of Alberta, 1986), 405–7.
65. Ibid., 123.
66. An Act to Amend the Child Welfare Act, *Statutes of Manitoba, 1966–67,* 8.
67. Penrod, 'Adoption in Canada', 155.
68. An Act Respecting the Welfare of Children, *Statutes of Saskatchewan, 1946,* 776–7.
69. An Act to Consolidate and Revise The Children's Protection Act, The Children of Unmarried Parents Act and The Adoption Act, *Statutes of Ontario, 1954,* 62.
70. Gilbert D. Kennedy, letter to the editor *CBR* 34 (1956): 363.
71. An Act to Amend the Child Welfare Act, *Statutes of Ontario, 1958,* 49; An Act to Amend The Child Welfare Act, *Statutes of Alberta, 1958,* 52.
72. *Bland v. Agnew,* [1993] 2 D.L.R. 545, 46 B.C.R. 491 (C.A.), leave to appeal to S.C.C. refused [1993] S.C.R. 345, [1933] 3 D.L.R. 639, in Phillips et al., *Adoption Law in Canada,* 1–7.
73. *Re Lamb,* [1961] O.W.N. 356 (Dist. Ct.), in Phillips et al., *Adoption Law in Canada,* 1–30.
74. An Act Respecting Child Welfare, *Statutes of Alberta, 1966,* 71.
75. An Act to Amend The Child Welfare Act, *Revised Statutes of Saskatchewan, 1968,* 4: 55.
76. An Act to Amend the Child Welfare Act, *Statutes of Manitoba, 1970,* 102.
77. Dorothy Lipovenko, 'Charter May Undercut Faith as Adoption Factor', *Globe and Mail,* 31 May 1985, 1. See also Lipovenko, 'Present Adoption Rules May Not Pass Charter, Ontario CASs Warned', ibid., 29 May 1985, 1–2.
78. An Act Respecting the Welfare of Children, *Statutes of Saskatchewan, 1946,* 773–5.
79. See Veronica Strong-Boag, '"Today's Child": Creating the Just Society One Family at a Time in 1960s Canada', *Canadian Historical Review* 86, no. 3 (2005): 673–99.
80. The Child Welfare Act, *Statutes of Ontario, 1965,* 2.
81. An Act to Amend the Adoption Act, *Statutes of New Brunswick, 1972,* 203.
82. Child and Family Services and Family Relations Act, *Statutes of New Brunswick, 1980,* 1.
83. The Child and Family Services Act (Bill 12), *Statutes of Manitoba, 1985–86,* 1: 761 and 765.
84. Adoption Act, *Acts of Prince Edward Island, 1992,* 3.
85. Child and Family Services Act, *Statutes of Northwest Territories, 1997,* 98.
86. An Ordinance to Provide for the Welfare of Children', *Yukon Ordinances, 1970,* 51.
87. 'Child and Family Services and Family Relations Act, *Statutes of New Brunswick, 1980,* 55.

88. An Act to Amend Chapter 8 of the Acts of 1976, The Children's Services Act, *Statutes of Nova Scotia, 1979,* 299.

89. An Act Respecting Adoption, *Statutes of Saskatchewan, 1989–90,* 5.

90. Adoption Act, *Statutes of the Northwest Territories, 1998,* 74.

91. The Child Welfare Act, *Statutes of Ontario, 1978,* 773.

92. Children's Act, *Statutes of Yukon, 1984,* 61.

93. An Act Respecting Adoption, *Statutes of Saskatchewan, 1989–90,* 14–15.

94. See *DIS v. MFC* (19 January 1982) Thunder Bay (Ont. Dist. Ct.), in Phillips et al., *Adoption Law in Canada,* 7–37. See also the unsuccessful suit waged by grandmother in *D. v. F.* (1985), 8 F.L.R.R. 43 (Ont. C.A.), in ibid., 7–37.

95. *S. (C.) v. T. (G.),* [1985] N.W.T.R. 269 (S.C.), in ibid., 6–37

96. See *Re MacVicar and Superintendent of Family and Child Services et al.* (1986), 34 D.L.R. (4th) 488 (B.C.S.C.), and see also Phillips, et al., *Adoption Law in Canada,* 4–9.

97. On court cases see *B.(D.) v. F. (D.)* (1988), 68 Nfld. & P.E.I.R. 261, 209 A.P.R. 261 (Nfld. T.D.), in ibid., 6–79.

98. See *Re Lorena Jacqueline K. (No. 2)* (19 February 1992) (Ont. Prov. Ct.), in ibid., 6–43.

99. On court cases see *Silk v. Silk* (1985), 46 R.F.L. (2d) 290 (Man. Q.B.), in ibid., 7–20. See also *Z. (G.M.) v. B. (T.F.S.)* (1981), 115 D.L.R. (3d) 706, 4 Man. R. (2d) 390 (C.A.), in ibid., 7–17.

100. The Act Respecting Services to Children and their Families, the Protection of Children and Adoption, *Statutes of Nova Scotia, 1990,* 99.

101. See *Re F. (J.R.)* (25 October 1990), Doc. No. A32/89 (Ont. Prov. Ct.), in Phillips et al., *Adoption Law in Canada,* 6–44.

102. Emily F. Carasco, 'Canadian Native Children: Have Child Welfare Laws Broken the Circle?' *CJFL* 5, no. 1 (1986): 112.

103. *Natural Parents v. Superintendent of Child Welfare et al.* (1975), 60 D.L.R. (3d) 148.

104. Carasco, 'Canadian Native Children', 125.

105. *N. (M.L) v. Superintendent of Family and Child Service* (11 July 1990), Vancouver No. A391209 (B.C. S.C.), Oppal J., summarized at [1990] W.D.F.L. 993, and in Phillips et al., in *Adoption Law in Canada,* 1–11.

106. British Columbia Royal Commission on Family and Children's Law (chair, Justice Thomas Berger), *Report* (Vancouver: Family and Children's Law Commission, 1975); Manitoba, Review Committee on Indian and Métis Adoptions and Placements (chair, Assoc. Chief Judge Edwin Kimelman), *No Quiet Place: Final Report to the Honourable Muriel Smith, Minister of Community Services* (Winnipeg: Manitoba Community Services, 1985); and Ralph Garber, *Disclosure of Adoption Information: Report of the Special Commission to the Honourable John Sweeney, Minister of Community and Social Services, Ontario* (Toronto: Ministry of Community and Social Services, November, 1985).

107. An Act to Amend the Adoption Act, *Statutes of British Columbia, 1973,* 1.

108. An Act Respecting the Protection and Well-Being of Children and Their Families, Part VII Adoption, *Statutes of Ontario, 1984,* 704.

109. Carasco, 'Canadian Native Children', 135.

110. Adoption Act, *Statutes of British Columbia, 1995,* 558.

111. Children's Act, *Revised Statutes of Yukon, 1986,* 57.

112. Jo Cain, 'Urban Native Child Welfare in BC: A Proposal for Matching Services with Client Needs' (MSW thesis, University of British Columbia, 1985), 21

113. On the slow beginnings see G. Galley, 'Interracial Adoptions', *Canadian Welfare* 39 (1963): 248–50.

114. See Karen Dubinsky, '"We Adopted a Negro": Interracial Adoption and the Hybrid Baby in 1960s Canada', in *Canada's 'trente glorieuses': Readings on Family, Community and Nation, 1945–1975,* ed. M. Fahrni and R. Rutherdale (Vancouver: UBC Press, 2006).

115. Ferguson Colm O'Donnell, 'The Four-Sided Triangle: A Comparative Study of the Confidentiality of Adoption Records', *University of Western Ontario Law Review* 21, no. 1 (1983): 135.

116. See Child and Family Services and Family Relations Act, *Statutes of New Brunswick, 1980,* 65.

117. Children's Act, *Statutes of Yukon, 1984,* 56. See also A. Bissett-Johnson 'Protecting Children in the North', *CJFL* 4 (1985): 413–35.

118. See 'On Second Thoughts' (editorial), *Globe and Mail,* 27 May 1985, 6; June Callwood, 'Adopted People May Never Know', ibid., 3 May 1985, L2; Doris Anderson, 'Adoption Law Will Leave Parents, Kids in Limbo', *Toronto Star,* 13 April 1985, L1; Janice Dineen, 'New Adoption Law "Retrogressive"', ibid., 20 May 1985, C1; see also Rev. Grace and Rev. Alan Craig, letter to the editor, ibid., 4 May 1985, B3, and Patricia Cohen et al., 'Have Your Say', *Sunday Star,* 12 May 1985, D3, and ibid., 26 May 1985, D3.

119. Act to Amend the Child and Family Services Act, 1984, and Certain Other Acts in Relation to Adoption Disclosure, *Statutes of Ontario, 1987,* 20.

120. Adoption Act, *Acts of Prince Edward Island, 1992,* 2–3.

121. Ibid., 4.

122. The Adoption and Consequential Amendments Act, *Statutes of Manitoba, 1997,* 528.

123. Adoption Act, *Statutes of British Columbia, 1995,* 564.

124. Penrod, 'Adoption in Canada', 217.

125. An Act Respecting Adoption, *Statutes of Saskatchewan, 1989–90,* 30.

126. See *Kelly v. Superintendent of Child Welfare* (1980), 23 B.C.L.R. 299 (S.C.), in Phillips et al., *Adoption Law in Canada,* 9–4; *Phelps v. Director of Child and Family Services (Manitoba)* (1987), 51 Man. R. (2d) 64 (Q.B.), in ibid., 9-6-7; *Tyler v. Ontario District Court* (1986) 1 R.F.L. (3d) 139 (Ont. Dist. Ct.), in ibid., 9–15; *Ross v. Prince Edward Island (Registrar of the Supreme Court, Family Division)* (1985), 50 R.F.L. (2d) 283, 56 Nfld. & P.E.I.R. 248 (P.E.I. S.C.), in ibid., 9–17; *Ferguson v. Director of Child Welfare of Ontario* (1983), 40 O.R. (2d) 294, 142 D.L.R. (3d) 609 (Co. Ct.), in ibid., 9–14 and 9–15; *Re Adoption of A (B.)* (1980), 17 R.F.L. (2d) 140 (Man. Co. Ct.), in ibid., 9–7.

127. An Act Respecting Family Services, *Statutes of Saskatchewan, 1973,* 147.

128. An Act Respecting the Protection and Well-Being of Children and Their Families, Part VII, Adoption, *Statutes of Ontario, 1984,* 719.

129. Children's Act, *Statutes of Yukon, 1984,* 12.

130. Susan Boyd, 'The Impact of the Charter of Rights and Freedoms on Canadian Family Law', *CJFL* 17, no. 2 (2000): 293–332.

131. An Act Respecting Family Services, *Statutes of Saskatchewan, 1973,* 16.
132. Children's Act, *Revised Statutes of Yukon, 1986,* 57.
133. See Child Welfare Amendment Act, *Statutes of Alberta, 1988,* 632.
134. H. Whiteford, 'Special Needs Adoption: Perspectives on Policy and Practice' (MSW thesis, University of British Columbia, 1988).
135. See for example *Re Government of Punjab, India, Birth Registration No.* 77 (1978), 9 B.C.L.R. 184 (S.C.), in Phillips et al., *Adoption Law in Canada,* 1–8; *Re K. (K.M.)* (31 May 1984), Peel No. A268/83 (Ont. Prov. Ct), Karswick Prov. J., summarized at [1984] W.D.F.L. 902, in ibid., 1–34; *Re L. (H.K.)* (1988), 17 R.F.L. (3d) 451, 63 Alta. L.R. (2d) 36 (Q.B.), in ibid., 1–3; *M. (C.) v. H. (H.),* [1990] W.D.F.L. 1141 (Alta. Q.B.), ibid., 6–59.
136. Kerry J. Daly and Michael P. Sobol, 'Public and Private Adoption', *Family Relations* 43, no. 1 (1994): 86. See also K. Shirley Senoff, 'Open Adoptions in Ontario and the Need for Legislative Reform', *CJFL*15, no. 1 (1998): 189.
137. Vorna Butler, 'Private Adoption in British Columbia', *Social Worker / Le travailleur social* 54, no. 4 (1986): 156, 158.
138. J.P. Hornick, R.J. Thomlison, L.E. Nesbitt, *Policy Recommendations for Private Adoption Practices and Procedures in Alberta* (Edmonton: Alberta Social Services and Community Health, 1986), 1.
139. The best place for keeping track of federal government initiatives is the website of the Adoption Council of Canada: http://www.adoption.ca/
140. Daly and Sobol, 'Public and Private Adoption', 87. 'Looking for a "Forever Family"', in *Profiling Canada's Families III* (Ottawa: Vanier Institute of the Family, 2004), 60.

Chapter 3

1. BC Department of Social Welfare, Child Welfare Division, *Annual Report* (for the year ending 31 March 1963), 39.
2. Amal Treacher, 'Narrative and Fantasy in Adoption: Towards a Different Theoretical Understanding', in *The Dynamics of Adoption: Social and Personal Perspectives,* ed. Amal Treacher and Ilan Katz (London and Philadelphia: Jessica Kingsley Publishers, 2000), 23.
3. On this see Gillian Creese, *Contracting Masculinity: Gender, Class, and Race in a White-Collar Union, 1944–1994* (Toronto: Oxford University Press, 1999), and Nancy Fraser, 'After the Family Wage: Gender Equity and the Welfare State', in *Gender and Citizenship in Transition,* ed. Barbara Hobson (London: Macmillan, 2000), 1–32.
4. Thomas C. Haliburton, *The Clockmaker, or, The Sayings and Doings of Sam Slick, of Slicksville* (Halifax: J. Howe, 1836), 177 (italics in original).
5. Jo Cain, 'Urban Native Child Welfare in BC: A Proposal for Matching Services with Client Needs' (MSW thesis, University of British Columbia, 1985), 18.
6. See Veronica Strong-Boag, 'Getting to Now: Children in Distress in Canada's Past', in *Community Work in Child Welfare,* ed. Brian Wharf (Toronto: Broadview, 2002), 29–46.
7. Ian Adams, W. Cameron, B. Hill and Peter Penz, *The Real Poverty Report* (Edmonton: Hurtig, 1971), xi.
8. Ontario, Superintendent of Neglected and Dependent Children and Provincial

Officer . . . the Adoption Act, *35th Annual Report for 1928, Sessional Papers* (1929), 16.

9. Jane Pulkingham and Gordon Ternowetsky, 'The Changing Context of Child and Family Policies', in *Child and Family Policies: Struggles, Strategies and Options*, ed. Jane Pulkingham and Gordon Ternowetsky (Halifax: Fernwood Publishing, 1997), 16.

10. On this motif see Laura Briggs, 'Mother, Child, Race, Nation: The Visual Iconography of Rescue and the Politics of Transnational and Transracial Adoption', *Gender and History* 15, no. 2 (2003): 179–200.

11. Ashby LeRoy, *Endangered Children: Dependence, Neglect, and Abuse in American History* (New York: Prentice-Hall, 1997), 2.

12. See, *inter alia*, Michel Foucault, *Discipline and Punish: The Birth of the Prison* (New York: Vintage Books, 1995).

13. *Re Grafasso* (1916), 30 D.L.R. 30 595 (Ont. S.C.).

14. *Re D'Andrea* (1916), 31 D.L.R. 751 (Ont. S.C.).

15. *Re Pipke* (1922), 63 D.L.R. 430 (Alta. S.C.).

16. *Re Fex*, [1948] 3 D.L.R. 757 (Ont. C.A.).

17. See June Callwood, 'Adopted People May Never Know', *Globe and Mail*, 2 May 1985, L12.

18. *Re Mailman*, [1927] 2 D.L.R. 529 (N.S. S.C.).

19. *Re Maat and Maat* (1957), 7 D.L.R. 488 (Ont. C.A.).

20. *Re Roebuck* (1966), 58 D.L.R. 716 (B.C. S.C.).

21. Florence Marryat, *'No Intentions': A Novel* (New York: D. Appleton; Halifax: M.A. Buckley, 1875), 86.

22. E.P. Johnson, 'The Barnardo Boy', *Boys' World*, 13 August 1910, 1, 8.

23. Nora Tynan, 'The Christmas Baby', *Canadian Magazine* 30 (1907–8): 164–8.

24. J.T. Stirrett, 'A Tale of Two Families', *Maclean's*, March 1911, 55.

25. Stan Fitzner, 'The Development of Social Welfare in Nova Scotia: A History' (a Centennial Project for the Department of Public Welfare, 1 December 1967), 11–13 (typescript).

26. Nova Scotia, *Journal and Proceedings of the House of Assembly of the Province of Nova Scotia*, Session 1917, Part 1, Appendix No. 3D, Report of the Inspector of Humane Institutions (1915–16), 6.

27. Jean Grant, 'A Charity Family', *Saturday Night*, 1 January 1898, 7.

28. Joy Parr, *Labouring Children: British Immigrant Apprentices to Canada, 1869–1924* (London: Croom Helm, 1980); Gail H. Corbett, *Barnardo Children in Canada* (Peterborough, ON: Woodland Publishing, 1981).

29. Rev. John Macpherson, 'Introduction' to Clara Lowe, *God's Answers: A Record of Miss Annie Macpherson's Work at the Home of Industry, Spitalfields, London, and in Canada* (London: James Nisbet, 1982), ix.

30. 'Importing Waifs', *Saturday Night*, 11 June 1882, 6.

31. Percy Roberts, 'Barnardo's Contribution to Ontario', *5th Annual Canadian Conference on Child Welfare* (Ottawa, 1925), 183.

32. Canada, House of Commons, *Debates*, 16 June 1922, 3063 (Edward J. Garland).

33. Mrs Adelaide Plumptre, 'Barnardo's Contribution to Ontario', *5th Annual Canadian Conference on Child Welfare* (Ottawa, 1925), 184, and Tom Moore, ibid., 192.

34. Vic Satzewich and Terry Wotherspoon, *First Nations: Race, Class and Gender Relations* (Winnipeg and Saskatoon: Canadian Plains Research Center, 2000), 50.

35. Elizabeth Graham, *The Mush Hole: Life at Two Indian Residential Schools* (Waterloo, ON: Heffle Publishing, 1997), 439.

36. Ibid., 17.

37. John S. Milloy, *'A National Crime': The Canadian Government and the Residential School System, 1879 to 1986* (Winnipeg: University of Manitoba Press, 1999), 214. See also James R. Miller, *Shingwauk's Vision: A History of Native Residential Schools* (Toronto: University of Toronto Press, 1995).

38. 'Toronto Infants' Home and Infirmary', *Dominion Churchman,* 11 December 1879, 590.

39. Wilma M. Gibson, 'The Social Worker in Adoption Practice: An Exploratory Study of 23 Adopted Children Who Were Referred Privately to the Vancouver Child Guidance Clinic, 1953–55' (MSW thesis, University of British Columbia, 1955), 75.

40. Newfoundland, Department of Public Welfare, *Annual Report* (1970), 127.

41. As told to Marie LaCoste, 'I Gave My Baby Away', *Star Weekly,* 21 May 1966, 24. On illegitimate pregnancies among middle-class girls in general in this period, see also Michelle Landsberg, 'Illegitimacy: Finding the Truth behind Reassuring Statistics', *Globe and Mail,* 12 September 1963.

42. See Roberta G. Aggas, 'Social Class Influences in Illegitimacy: A Study of the Effects of Social Class Affiliation, Corresponding Patterns of Socialization and Their Relationship to Illegitimacy' (MSW thesis, Maritime School of Social Work and the University of King's College, 1967).

43. Martha J. Bailey, 'Servant Girls and Masters: The Tort of Seduction and the Support of Bastards', *Canadian Journal of Family Law* (hereafter *CJFL*) 10, no. 1 (1991): 144.

44. See the Honourable Thomas J. Gove, *Report of a Commission of Inquiry into the Adequacy of the Services, Policies and Practices of the Ministry of Social Services as They Relate to the Apparent Neglect, Abuse and Death of Matthew John Vaudreuil* (Victoria: The Inquiry, 1995).

45. See W. Ward Allen, *Judicial Inquiry into the Care of Kim Anne Popen by the Children's Aid Society of Sarnia and the County of Lambton* (Toronto: Queen's Printer, 1982), and Cyril Greenland, *Preventing Child Abuse and Neglect Deaths: The Identification and Management of High Risk Cases* (Ottawa: Health Canada, National Clearinghouse on Family Violence, Family Violence Prevention Division, 1986).

46. Christie Blatchford, 'A Child Whose Interests Have Finally Been Served', *Globe and Mail,* 28 October 2004, A15.

47. See Terry Chapman, 'Sex Crimes in the West, 1890–1920: An Overview', in *Papers Presented at the 1987 Canadian Law in History Conference* (Ottawa: Jurisprudence Centre, Carleton University, 1987), 1–46.

48. 'Anti-Poverty Society', *Canadian Churchman,* 17 July 1890, 452.

49. Thomas F. Maunders, 'A Casework Study of Parents Requesting the Adoption Placement of Legitimate Children: A Study of Cases from Greater Vancouver Social Agencies, 1951' (MSW thesis, University of British Columbia, 1953), 41, 45.

50. 'The Real Poor in Canada: And Why We Don't Know Who They Are', *Maclean's,* January 1971, cited in Adams et al., *The Real Poverty Report,* 24.

51. *Re Chiemelewski,* [1928] 2 D.L.R. 49 (Ont. S.C.).

52. See Victor Malarek, *Hey Malarek! The True Story of a Kid Who Made It* (Halifax: Formac, 1984).

53. Jo-Anne Fiske, e-mail communication to the author, August 2005.

54. Mark Lowey, 'Placenta Barrier to Cocaine, Study Finds', *Calgary Herald,* 11 June 1994, and an open letter to the media demanding they stop perpetuating the 'Crack Baby Myth' by leading North American doctors. 25 February 2004. Canadian signatories were Peter Fried, PhD, Department of Psychology, Carleton, and Gideon Koren, MD, FRCPC, Professor of Pediatrics, Pharmacology, Pharmacy, Medicine, and Medicine Genetics, University of Toronto; available at http://www.jointogether.org/sa/files/pdf/sciencenotstigma.pdf (accessed 19 December 2005).

55. Fred R. MacKinnon, 'Foster Home Care and Group Care of Children and Children Pending Adoption: A Study for the Canadian Conference on Children' (2–6 October 1960), 1.

56. Public Archives of Alberta (hereafter PAA), ACC 73.51, Legislative Assembly Sessional Papers etc. Box. 24, Alberta Child Welfare Commission Submission to the 'Adoption Study Committee' (folder 896), February 1968; SP 275/68 in answer to request by Len Werry, MLA, 16 April 1968, 3.

57. Philip H. Hepworth, *Foster Care and Adoption in Canada* (Ottawa: Canadian Council for Social Development, 1980), 262.

58. PAA, ACC 73.51, Legislative Assembly Sessional Papers etc. Box. 24, Executive Committee of the Council of Social Agencies, Report of the Provincial Committee on Child Welfare, Edmonton (16 August 1943), 8.

59. Ontario, *Report under Children's Protection Act* (1893), 26.

60. Ontario, Superintendent of Neglected and Dependent Children, *36th Annual Report* (1929), 8.

61. Miss J.V. Moberly, 'A Thousand Babies a Year and Never an Institutional Bed', *Canadian Child and Family Welfare* (hereafter *CCFW*) 10, no. 4 (1934): 6.

62. Ethel M. Chapman, 'Could You Adopt a Baby?' *Maclean's,* December 1919, 116.

63. See BC Ministry of Human Resources, *Annual Report* (1980–1), 36.

64. Alberta, Department of Public Welfare, *1st Annual Report* (1944–5), Superintendent of Child Welfare, *Report,* 26.

65. Charlotte Whitton, *Welfare in Alberta: The Report of a Study* (Edmonton: Douglas Printing, 1947), 74, 81, 90. For a confirmation of the problems in Alberta see Alberta, Royal Commission on Child Welfare, *Report of the Child Welfare Branch* (Edmonton: n.p., 1948). See also Maurice Norbert Coté, 'The Children's Aid Society of the Catholic Archdiocese of Vancouver: Its Origins and Development, 1905 to 1953' (MSW thesis, University of British Columbia, 1953), 8.

66. Constance M. Harrison, 'Foster Homefinding: A Study of Effective Ways of Increasing the Number of Foster Homes Available for Children' (MSW thesis, University of Toronto, 1948), 83.

67. See the important study by Teresa Toguchi Swartz, 'Mothering for the State: Fostering Parenting and the Challenges of Government-Contracted Carework', *Gender and Society* 18, no. 5 (2004): 567–87.

68. Deborah Shapiro, 'Fostering and Adoption: Converging Roles for Substitute

Parents', in *Adoption: Current Issues and Trends*, ed. Paul Sachdev (Toronto: Butterworths, 1983), 274. See also Hepworth, *Foster Care and Adoption in Canada*, and Heather Whiteford, 'Special Needs Adoption: Perspectives on Policy and Practice' (MSW thesis, University of British Columbia, 1988), 19.

69. Grace Hill, 'Wanted: Boarding Homes for Babies', *Canadian Welfare* 20, no. 5 (1944): 24.

70. Marjorie M. Bowker, *Supplementary Report on Adoption in Alberta* (Edmonton: n.p., July 1965), 173.

71. Herbert B. Ames, *'The City Below the Hill': A Sociological Study of a Portion of the City of Montreal, Canada* (1897; rpt., Toronto: University of Toronto Press, 1972).

72. Harrison, 'Foster Homefinding', 14, 41.

73. John McCullagh, *A Legacy of Caring: A History of the Children's Aid Society of Toronto* (Toronto: Dundurn, 2002), 251.

74. See Jill Duerr Berrick, 'When Children Cannot Remain Home: Foster Family Care and Kinship Care', *Future of Children* 8, no. 1 (1998): 72–87.

75. See Annette Wigod, 'Let's Ask the Middle Class', *Canadian Welfare* 44, no. 6 (1968): 14–5, 18–9.

76. Robert Van Krieken, *Children and the State: Social Control and the Formation of Australian Child Welfare* (North Sydney, NSW: Allen and Unwin, 1991), 24.

77. Ibid., 107.

77. Anna Geneviève Singleton, 'Child Welfare Administration under Protection Acts in British Columbia: Its History and Development 1901–1949' (MSW thesis, University of British Columbia, 1950), 45.

78. Darnell Consulting Inc., *Residential Care Research Project: The Future of Foster Care* (prepared for the Ontario Association of Children's Aid Societies) (Toronto: OACAS, January 1988), 207.

79. K. Phyllis Burns, 'Institutional Resources in Canada for Dependent Children', *Canadian Welfare* 18, no. 5 (1952): 31–4.

80. See Judy Krysik, 'Canada', in *The World of Foster Care: An International Sourcebook on Foster Family Care Systems,* ed. Matthew Colton and Margaret Williams (Aldershot, UK: Ashgate, 1997).

81. BC Superintendent of Neglected Children, *Annual Report* (for the year ending 31 March 1939), 24.

82. Ibid. (for the year ending 31 March 1942), 23–4.

83. BC Social Welfare Branch of the Department of Health and Welfare, *Annual Report* (for the year ending 31 March 1949), 42–3.

84. BC Provincial Advisory Committee on Indian Affairs, *6th Annual Report* (1955), 11.

85. BC Provincial Advisory Committee on Indian Affairs, *9th Annual Report* (1958), 9.

86. BC Provincial Advisory Committee on Indian Affairs, *11th Annual Report* (1960), 9.

87. BC Department of Human Resources, *Annual Report* (with fiscal addendum 1 April 1973 to 31 March 1974), 46.

88. Miss Kathleen Gorrie, 'Placement Opportunities for the Exceptional and Problem Child', *CCFW* 13, no. 3 (1937): 22.

89. Hepworth, *Foster Care and Adoption in Canada*, 99.

90. Krysik, 'Canada', 47.

91. 'The Horrors of Abuse', *Maclean's*, 19 May 1997, 33.
92. 'Foster Care Gone Berserk', *Canadian Welfare* 44, no. 3 (1963): 16.
93. See, *inter alia*, Margaret Wente, 'The Best Interests of the Child?' *Globe and Mail*, 22 February 2004, A15
94. Chris Wood, 'Trouble on the Ranch', *Maclean's*, 12 April 1999, 27.
95. Richard Clark, 'Hard-Sell Adoption' and 'Leaving the Doors Open', *Maclean's*, 26 July and 16 August 2004, 8.
96. Whiteford, 'Special Needs Adoption', 14. See also BC Department of Social Welfare, *Annual Report* (for the year ending 31 March 1962), 29.
97. Alberta, Committee on Adoption in Alberta, *Final Report* (15 July 1965), 37.
98. BC Department of Rehabilitation and Social Improvement, *Annual Report* (for the year ending 31 March 1971), 31.
99. See Shapiro, 'Fostering and Adoption, 267. On the limits of subsidies, see the excellent study by Whiteford, 'Special Needs Adoption,' 62–71.
100. Patricia Hill Collins, 'Producing the Mothers of the Nation: Race, Class and Contemporary US Population Policies', in *Women, Citizenship and Difference*, ed. N. Yuval-Davis and Pnina Werbner (London and New York: Zed Books, 1999), 121.
101. Karl Bernhardt, 'The Case for Taking Children Away from Their Parents', *Maclean's*, 16 June 1962, 18.
102. Ontario, *4th Report of Work under the Children's Protection Act* (1896), xxxiv.
103. Ontario, Annual Report of the Superintendent of Neglected and Dependent Children, *18th Report* (1910), 10.
104. Victoria, Children's Aid Society, *Annual Report* (1945), 8.
105. Alberta, Department of Public Welfare, Child Welfare Commission, *14th Annual Report* (1957–8), 28.
106. Ontario, Ministry of Public Welfare, Superintendent of Children's Aid Branch, *Annual Report* (1931), 13.
107. Ethel M. Chapman, 'Could You Adopt a Baby?' *Maclean's*, December 1919, 116.
108. Jessie M. Burt, 'Adopted', *Chatelaine*, April 1933, 14–15, 36–8.
109. James Wedgwood Drawbell, 'Experiment in Adoption', *Chatelaine*, January 1935, 6.
110. Anonymous, 'Adapting to an Older Adopted Child', *Toronto Telegram*, 7 April 1965, 47.
111. *New Families for Young Canadians: The History and Current Practice of Adoption in British Columbia* (Victoria: Department of Social Welfare, 1967), 3.
112. BC Services for People, Ministry of Human Resources, *Annual Report* (with fiscal addendum 1 April 1975 to 31 March 1976), 48.
113. Helen Levine, 'Group Work with Adopters', *Ontario Association of Children's Aid Societies Journal* (February 1971), 1.
114. Alberta, Committee on Adoption in Alberta, *Final Report* (15 July 1965), 35.
115. J.V. Moberly, 'We Want a Child', *Maclean's*, 15 September 1938, 50–1.
116. See cases of 'Riva', 'Rita', 'Marilyn', and others in Robert Hartlen, *Butterbox Survivors: Life after the Ideal Maternity Home* (Halifax: Nimbus Publishing, 1999).
117. Adrienne MacLeod, 'Telling a Child about His Adoption', *Canadian Welfare* 35, no. 3 (1959): 100–4.
118. Margaret and Don Henshaw, 'Our Adopted Children', *Canadian Welfare* 31 (1

February 1956): 282, and June Callwood, 'The Cooneys and Their Seven Adopted Children', *Maclean's*, 12 November 1955, 112.

119. Robert Walker, 'Is Our System of Child Adoption Good Enough?' *Maclean's*, 26 September 1959, 15–17, 71–74.

120. Whiteford, 'Special Needs Adoption', 13–14.

121. Mrs Brisbin, testimony before the Committee on Adoption in Alberta, in *The Child Welfare Act, In the Matter of the Child Welfare Act, Being Chapter 39 of the Revised Statutes of Alberta* (Edmonton: n.p., 1965), 1: 3.

122. Ibid.

123. Mr Bishop, ibid., 1: 15.

124. Mrs Bowker, ibid., 1: 16.

125. Judge Patterson, ibid., 1: 20.

126. Mr Bishop. ibid., 1: 23.

127. Judge Patterson, ibid., 1: 23.

128. Mr H.S. Coulter, ibid., 3: 649.

129. Dr Hamilton, ibid., 1: 103.

130. Mr Bowker, ibid., 3: 651.

131. Kerry J. Daly and Michael P. Sobol, 'Public and Private Adoption', *Family Relations* 43, no. 1 (1994): 86.

132. Ibid.

133. Children's Fund of Canada, 'This Year-Give a Child for Christmas', *Maclean's*, 2 December 1964, 48.

134. Roberta Avery, 'Orphan Pulled from Gutter', *Toronto Star*, 10 September 1997, A01, A28.

135. Ann Anagnost, 'Scenes of Misrecognition: Maternal Citizenship in the Age of Transnational Adoption', *Positions* 8, no. 2 (2000): 414.

136. *Report of the Committee on International Adoptions/Rapport du Comité sur les adoptions internationales* (Ottawa: n.p., October 1974), Appendix F: Submissions from Private Groups, 'Families for Children' to Miss Monique Perron, 7 March 1974, 2, in the Social Services and Community Health Library, Alberta.

137. Jane Covernton, 'Bringing Renaldo Home', *Saturday Night*, September 1989, 56. The press has remained fascinated by the phenomenon, especially when it involves celebrities. See for example, Rae Corelli, 'Where the Boys Are Rare', *Maclean's*, 21 August 1995, 34–8, on the adoption of a boy in China by a Canadian actress and her producer husband.

138. E. Kaye Fulton and Sharon Doyle Driedger, 'Bringing Baby Home', *Maclean's*, 21 August 1995, 34.

139. Ontario, 'Re Legal Adoptions', *Canadian Child Welfare News* 1, no. 4 (1925): 22.

140. Christopher Bagley, 'Adoption Research Update', *Ontario Association of Children's Aid Societies Journal* 28 (September 1984): 8.

141. David Howe, *Patterns of Adoption: Nature, Nurture and Psychosocial Development* (London: Blackwell Science, 1998), 119.

142. John Porter, *The Vertical Mosaic: An Analysis of Social Class and Power in Canada* (Toronto: University of Toronto Press, 1965).

Chapter 4

1. Patricia Baird, *Proceed with Care: Final Report of the Royal Commission on New Reproductive Technologies* (Ottawa: Ministry of Government Services Canada, 1993), 171.

2. On this commonplace emphasis rather than efforts to curtail fertility see Angus McLaren, *Reproductive Rituals* (London and New York: Methuen, 1984). Perhaps not surprisingly, Angus McLaren served as a historical consultant for the Royal Commission on New Reproductive Technologies.

3. Darlene Ryan, *A Mother's Adoption Journey* (Toronto: Second Story Press, 2001), 26.

4. Lee Maracle, *Daughters Are Forever* (Vancouver: Polestar, 2002), 286.

5. Quoted in 'Guatemala Frees Four Quebec Women', *Globe and Mail*, 24 December 1981, 10.

6. See Angus McLaren, *Our Own Master Race: Eugenics in Canada, 1885–1945* (Toronto: McClelland and Stewart, 1990).

7. Patricia Hill Collins, 'Producing the Mothers of the Nation: Race, Class and Contemporary US Population Policies', in *Women, Citizenship and Difference*, ed. Nira Yuval-Davis and Pnina Werbner (London and New York: Zed Books, 1999), 119.

8. Elaine Tyler May, *Barren in the Promised Land: Childless Americans and the Pursuit of Happiness* (New York: Basic Books, 1995).

9. See Margaret Jane Hillyard Little, *'No Car, No Radio, No Liquor Permit': The Moral Regulation of Single Mothers in Ontario, 1920–1997* (Toronto: University of Toronto Press, 1998).

10. See Nancy Christie, *Engendering the State: Family, Work and Welfare in Canada* (Toronto: University of Toronto Press, 2000).

11. Baird, *Proceed with Care*, 189–92.

12. Janet Morris, 'A Son of Their Own at Last', *Vancouver Sun,* 7 December 1968, 40.

13. Claudia Nelson, *Little Strangers: Portrayals of Adoption and Foster Care in America, 1850–1929* (Bloomington and Indianapolis: Indiana University Press, 2003), 115.

14. See Karen Dubinsky, *Improper Advances: Rape and Heterosexual Conflict in Ontario, 1880–1929* (Chicago: University of Chicago Press, 1993), and Arlene McLaren and Angus McLaren, *The Bedroom and the State: The Changing Practices and Politics of Birth Control and Abortion in Canada, 1880–1980* (Toronto: McClelland and Stewart, 1986).

15. Andrée Levesque, *Making and Breaking the Rules: Women in Quebec, 1919–1939* (Toronto: McClelland and Stewart, 1994).

16. Miss Kathleen Sutherton, 'The Relationship between Maternity Homes and Children's Aid Societies', Armagh Annual Meeting, 10 March 1959 (Toronto: Unmarried Parent Department Children's Aid Society of Metropolitan Toronto, 1959), 31 (Koener Library, UBC, vertical file).

17. Alberta, Provincial Legislature, *Debates*, 23 February 1923.

18. Quoted in 'Charges Girl of 17 Forced into Asylum Was "Perfectly Sane"', *Toronto Star,* 21 December 1933, 7.

19. Saskatchewan, Department of Social Welfare, *Annual Report,* Report of the Director of Child Welfare (1945–6), 23.

20. McGill University Archives (hereafter MUA), Montreal Council of Social Agencies,

Report of the Committee on Unmarried Parenthood (March 1949), 8 (typescript).

21. Newfoundland, Division of Child Welfare, Department of Public Health and Welfare, *Third Annual Report* (ending 31 March 1948), 14.

22. Dr N.W. Philpott and Mrs Goodwin James, 'Care of the Unmarried Mother and Her Child', *Canadian Mental Health Journal,* September 1946, 11.

23. MUA, Montreal Council of Social Agencies, Report on the Committee on Unmarried Parenthood (March 1949), 8.

24. Sutherton, 'The Relationship between Maternity Homes', 4.

25. MUA, Welfare Council of Greater Winnipeg, 'Study of Services to Unmarried Parents in Manitoba', 1 September 1960, 8.

26. New Brunswick, Department of Youth and Welfare, Report of the Children's Aid Society of Fredericton, *Annual Report* (for the fiscal year ending 31 March 1964), 75–6.

27. Simma Holt, *Sex and the Teen-Age Revolution* (Toronto: McClelland and Stewart, 1967), 15, 41.

28. B. Kredentser, 'The Unmarried Mother and Her Doctor', *Alberta Medical Journal* 28, no. 2 (1963): 116. On a similar situation in Australia see Shurlee Swain, with Renate Howe, *Single Mothers and Their Children: Disposal, Punishment and Survival in Australia* (Cambridge: Cambridge University Press, 1996), 140–1.

29. Josie Svanhuit, 'The American Caricature of the Unmarried Mother', *Canadian Welfare* 31, no. 5 (1955): 248–9.

30. Kathleen Sutherton, 'Another View', *Canadian Welfare* 31, no. 5 (1955): 249–52.

31. Rickie Solinger, *Wake Up Little Susie* (New York and London: Routledge, 2000), 15.

32. See Carole Gerson and Veronica Strong-Boag, 'Pauline Johnson Rejects the Squaw', in *Embodied Contact: Women in Canada's Colonial Past,* ed. Katie Pickles and Myra Rutherdale (Vancouver: UBC Press, 2005).

33. Marlee Kline, 'Complicating the Ideology of Motherhood: Child Welfare Law and First Nation Women', *Queen's Law Journal* 18 (1993): 306–42.

34. L.E. Lowman, 'Mail-Order Babies', *Chatelaine,* April 1932, 26.

35. Peter Bruton, 'Young Hearts Break but Baby Gets Chance', *Victoria Colonist,* 29 June 1957, 1.

36. 'Empty Stocking Hung Up Again: Baby Mary Asks Your Help', *Vancouver Province,* 24 November 1962.

37. Winona Armitage, 'The Unmarried Mother and Adoption', *Proceedings of the 9th Canadian Conference on Social Work* (Winnipeg: n.p., June 1944), 79–85.

38. Public Archives of Alberta (hereafter PAA), ACC 73.51, Legislative Assembly Sessional Papers etc. Box. 24, Alberta Child Welfare Commission Submission to the 'Adoption Study Committee' (folder 896) February 1968; SP 275/68 in answer to request by Len Werry, MLA (16 April 1968), 9.

39. Sheila Kieran, 'Motherhood and the Single Girl', *Star Weekly,* 20 July 1970, 28.

40. Sutherton, 'The Relationship between Maternity Homes', 7.

41. Erica Bell, *One-Parent Family in Edmonton* (n.p., 1975), 12.

42. Chairman of Durham Region's Welfare Committee, cited in Harry MacKay and Catherine Austin, *Single Adolescent Mothers in Ontario: A Report of 87 Single Adolescent Mothers' Experiences. Their Situation, Needs, and Use of Community Services* (Ottawa:

CCSD, 1983), 1.

43. PAA, ACC 73.51, Legislative Assembly Sessional Papers etc., Box 24, Alberta Child Welfare Commission Submission to the 'Adoption Study Committee' (folder 896) February 1968, SP 275/68 in answer to request by Len Werry, MLA (16 April 1968), 9.

44. See Sylvia Bashevkin, *Welfare Hot Buttons: Women, Work and Social Policy Reform* (Toronto: University of Toronto Press, 2002), esp. ch. 2.

45. Canada, House of Commons, *Debates,* 13 February 1987, 3437 (Rob Nicholson).

46. Ibid., 26 July 1988, 17995 (Alain Tardif).

47. Ibid., 26 July 1988, 17995 (Ross Belsher).

48. This soon expanded into other Canadian provinces, set up shop in the United States in 1972, and by the late 1970s operated in South Africa. See Jeff Koloze, 'Academic Perceptions of Abortion: A Review of Humanities Scholarship Produced within the Academy', available at http://uffl.org/vol12/koloze12.pdf.

49. Fr John Dietzen, 'Baptism of an Adopted Child', *B.C. Catholic* 58, no. 44 (1988): 12. See also 'Adoption, Not Abortion', ibid. 62, no. 12 (1992): 12, and Sr Roma De Robertis, 'Adoption, the Loving Option', ibid. 64, no. 28 (1994): 13.

50. The CCNM was earlier known as the Canadian Council of Birth Mothers. See the website http://www.originscanada.org (accessed 10 April 2003).

51. Karen Lynn, 'Adoption in Whose Best Interests?' available at www.exiledmothers.com/articles/adoption_in_canada.html (accessed 10 April 2003).

52. Maracle, *Daughters Are Forever,* 55.

53. See, for example, the arguments of Patricia Monture-Angus, *Journeying Forward: Dreaming First Nations' Independence* (Halifax: Fernwood Publishing, 1999).

54. Madame Louise DeKiriline, 'Mother Love and the Quints', *Chatelaine,* May 1936, 11.

55. See Julie Berebitsky, *Like Our Very Own: Adoption and the Changing Culture of Motherhood, 1851–1950* (Lawrence: University Press of Kansas, 2000).

56. E. Kaye Fulton, with Sharon Doyle Driedger and Christina Wolaniuk, 'I Knew He Was My Son', *Maclean's,* 21 August 1995, 34.

57. See Berebitsky, *Like Our Very Own,* 77.

58. H. David Kirk, *Shared Fate: A Theory of Adoption and Mental Health* (London: Free Press of Glencoe, 1964), 19.

59. Ontario, Superintendent of Neglected and Dependent Children, *8th Report* (for the year 1900) (1901), 22. James J. Montague, 'The Wicked Little Babies', as cited in the *8th Report,* p. 35, and Rose Turnbull, 'Nobody's Child', Ontario, Superintendent of Neglected and Dependent Children, *18th Report* (1911), 40.

60. Sheila M. Russell, 'The Boy Nobody Wanted', *Chatelaine,* August 1965, 24.

61. Elyse Gasco, *Can You Wave Bye Bye, Baby?* (Toronto: McClelland and Stewart, 1999), 219. In November 2004, this story became a play performed in Montreal. Its complicated politics of adopter, adoptee, and birth mother evoked a spirited exchange on the electronic news group of the Adoption Council of Canada. Contributors to the discussion ranged widely but they appeared to agree that Gasco, an adoptee herself, provoked strong feelings among all members of the adoption circle.

62. Newfoundland, Department of Public Health and Welfare, Division of Child

Welfare, 'Report of the Regional Welfare Office for the West Coast Area.' *Annual Report* (for the year ending 31 March 1950), 49.

63. Alberta, Committee on Adoption in Alberta, *Report* (Edmonton, 15 July 1965), 35.

64. Bessie Marchant, *Daughters of the Dominion: A Story of the Canadian Frontier* (Toronto: Musson Book Company, 1909), 271.

65. Rose Barton, 'The Child Who Adopted Me', *Chatelaine,* September 1958, 102, 103, 105.

66. Joan Givener, *Mazo De La Roche: The Hidden Life* (Toronto: Oxford University Press, 1989), 158–9.

67. See Maggie de Vries, *Missing Sarah: A Vancouver Woman Remembers Her Vanished Sister* (Toronto: Penguin, 2004).

68. Dorothy Rungeling, *Life and Works of Ethelwyn Wetherald, 1857–1940, Canadian Poet-Journalist* (n.p., 2004), 75. My thanks to Carole Gerson for bringing this case to my attention.

69. Dorothy W. Rungeling, *It's Fun to Grow Old* (n.p., 2002), 19.

70. Dorothy W. Rumpling, *The Road to Home: Tales of Rural Life in the Early 1900s* (n.p., 2001), 8. For an example of a Toronto orphan, adopted by a single woman professor from Wellesley College, in the United States, see Ekbert Faas with Maria Trombacco, *Robert Creeley: A Biography* (Montreal: McGill-Queen's University Press, 2001). This includes excerpts from the memoirs and 1944 diary of Creeley's first wife, poet and adoptee Ann MacKinnon.

71. Phoebe Knight, 'Demand for Babies Exceeds Supply', *Victoria Times,* 12 March 1938, 1.

72. 'Single Women Not Encouraged Here as Mothers by "Adoption"', *Vancouver Province,* 9 November 1943, 12.

73. Olive Skene Johnson, 'The Case History of a Single Woman and Her Happy Adopted Child', *Star Weekly,* 23 March 1968, 22.

74. Isabel Stevenson and David MacDonald, 'I Am a Bachelor Mother', *United Church Observer,* 15 November 1968, 20–4, 46.

75. Jacqueline Brewer, 'Mother Is a Minister—and She's Not Married', *Star Weekly,* 16 October 1971, 3.

76. 'A Single Parent Better Than None for Orphan', *Globe and Mail,* 25 November 1971.

77. 'Single Women Who Adopted Children Don't Regret the Decision', *Globe and Mail,* 27 April 1978.

78. Vivian Bright, 'Single Parent Adoption' (master's project, Maritime School of Social Work, 1985), 31, 34, 35, 39.

79. Alberta, Committee on Adoption in Alberta, *Report,* 35.

80. Alberta, Social Services and Community Health, *Child Welfare Programs* (Edmonton: Social Services and Community Health, April 1982), 247.

81. Johnson, 'The Case History of a Single Woman', 22, 27.

82. Berebitsky, *Like Our Very Own,* 126, 103.

83. Ontario, Superintendent of Dependent and Neglected Children, *35th Annual Report* (1928), 16.

84. Daniel Cappon, 'Medical Counselling in the Family Setting', *Academy of Medicine*

Toronto Bulletin 28, no. 11 (1955): 232–s7.

85. Carl Tupper and R.J.Weil, 'Psychotherapy in Habitual Abortions', *MD of Canada* 17, no. 10 (1962): 96.

86. Robert E. Mills, 'The Placing of Children in Families', *Canadian Child and Family Welfare* 14, no.1 (1938): 53. See also 'A Family—by Adoption: A Discussion Series of Five Weekly Meetings', Post Adoption Discussion Series, Children's Aid Society of Vancouver, Summary of Discussions, Discussion Record (19 October–16 November 1965), 1 (mimeograph).

87. See Karen Balcom, 'The Traffic in Babies: Cross-border Adoption, Baby-Selling and the Development of Child Welfare Systems in the United States in Canada, 1930–1960' (Ph.D. diss., Rutgers University, 2002).

88. Benjamin Schlesinger, 'Single Parent Adoptions: A Review', *Ontario Association of Children's Aid Societies Journal* 21, no. 2 (1978): 5.

89. Gay and lesbian parents soon discovered the conflicts that had always characterized their heterosexual counterparts. See Allison Hanes, 'Toddler Centre of Custody War among Lesbian Moms and Donor', *Vancouver Sun,* 27 November 2004.

90. REAL Women of BC, 'British Columbia Adoption Act Bill 51. Submission to the Honorable Penny Priddy, Minister for Children and Families', September 1996, available at http://www.realwomen.bc.ca/index.cfm/page/24/mid/8/home.htm (accessed 26 July 2005). See also Cindy Wooden, 'Good of Children Must Come First in Adoptions', *B.C. Catholic* 64, no. 133 (1994): 31.

91. Minda M. Posen, 'A Study of Adopted Children' (MSW thesis, University of Toronto, 1948), 35.

92. Marie Adams, *Our Son, A Stranger: Adoption Breakdown and Its Effects on Parents* (Montreal and Kingston: McGill-Queen's University Press, 2002), 114–15.

93. Kathryn Cole, *Double Take* (Toronto: Stoddart, 1995), 83.

94. Bridget Moran, *A Little Rebellion* (Vancouver: Arsenal Pulp Press, 1992), 11.

95. 'Children's Aid Society', *Canadian Churchman* (10 December 1896).

96. Robert Adamosky, 'The Child–The Citizen–The Nation: The Rhetoric and Experience of Wardship in Early Twentieth-Century British Columbia', in *Contesting Canadian Citizenship: Historical Readings*, ed. Robert Adamoski, Dorothy E. Chunn, and Robert Menzies, (Peterborough, ON: Broadview Press, 2002), 326.

97. Ontario, Superintendent of Neglected and Dependent Children, *14th Annual Report* (1906), *Sessional Papers* 34 (1907), 8.

98. See the theses that reject David Kirk on this preference: Judith A. Simms, 'Attitudes Affecting the Adoption Process: A Study of Sex Preference in Adoption and Its Possible Relationship to Tradition-oriented Kinship Groups' (MSW thesis, Maritime School of Social Work and the University of King's College, 1966); Monica McMullen, 'Differential Sex Preference in Adoption: A Study of the Relationship between Traditional Kinship Sentiments and Sex Preference Expressed by Non-fecund Adopting Couples' (MSW thesis, Maritime School of Social Work and St Francis Xavier University, 1968); and Linda O'Neill, 'Sex Preference Patterns in Adoption: A Study of Sex Preference Patterns of Adopting Parents Who Made Application to the Home of the Guardian Angel, the Nova Scotia Department of Public Welfare Regional Office, Halifax, and the Halifax Children's Aid Society dur-

ing the Calendar Year 1962' (MSW thesis, Maritime School of Social Work and Mt Allison University, 1966).

99. See Barbara Melosh, *Strangers and Kin: The American Way of Adoption* (Cambridge: Harvard University Press, 2002), 54.

100. Philip H. Hepworth, *Foster Care and Adoption in Canada* (Ottawa: Canadian Council on Social Development 1980), 156.

101. 'Good Homes for Soldiers' Orphans', *Toronto Star,* 24 June 1921.

102. Kirk, *Shared Fate*, 144.

103. Posen, 'A Study of Adopted Children', 54.

104. Protestant Orphan's Home (Halifax), *5th Annual Report* (1862), 5.

105. Ontario, Department of Neglected and Dependent Children, *7th Annual Report* (for the year ending 15 December 1899), 43.

106. 'Boy vs Girl Babies in Foster Homes', *Globe and Mail,* 7 March 1951.

107. Cole, *Double Take*, 24.

108. 'Plight of the Unwanted: Newspapers Help to Find Children Homes', *Globe and Mail,* 9 September 1957, 8.

109. 'Chinese Child First of Refugee Adoptions', *Globe and Mail,* 27 May 1961.

110. Steve Whan, 'The Story behind the Stories', *Rice Paper* (Fall 2003): 36–7.

111. BC Department of Health and Welfare, Social Welfare Branch, *Annual Report* (for the year ending 31 March 1955), 54.

112. Helen Allen, '2,500 in Ontario Want to Be Adopted', *Toronto Telegram,* 6 June 1964.

113. PAA, ACC 73.51, box 24, Marjorie M. Bowker, 'Supplementary Report on Adoption in Alberta' (Edmonton, July 1965), 97, 110.

114. On this sorry tale, see Ben Lappin, *The Redeemed Children: The Story of the Rescue of War Orphans by the Jewish Community of Canada* (Toronto: University of Toronto Press, 1963).

115. See H.B. Murphy, 'Natural Family Pointers to Foster Care Outcomes', *Mental Hygiene* 48, no. 3 (1964): 383.

116. See, *inter alia,* Hepworth, *Foster Care and Adoption,* 156; Kirk, *Shared Fate,* 124–40; Melosh, *Strangers and Kin,* 54, 62; Nelson, *Little Strangers,* 43; United Nations Department of Social Affairs, *Study on Adoption of Children* (New York: United Nations, 1953), 35, and BC Department of Social Welfare, *Annual Report* (for the year ending 31 March 1961), 42.

117. See 'Judge Allows Hearing on Orphan's Bid for Right to See Sister', *Globe and Mail,* 23 February 1995.

118. 'He's Canada's Champion Baby', *Star Weekly,* 13 December 1958, 14–15.

119. Janice Harvey, 'The Protestant Orphan Asylum and the Montreal Ladies Benevolent Society: A Case Study in Protestant Child Charity in Montreal, 1822–1900' (PhD diss., McGill University, 2001), 203.

120. Lappin, *The Redeemed Children,* 53–4.

121. Ontario, Superintendent of Neglected and Dependent Children, *Annual Report* (1906), 8.

122. See H.B. Murphy, 'Natural Family Pointers to Foster Care Outcomes', *Mental Hygiene,* July 1964, 380–95, and Murphy, 'Foster Home Variables and Adult Outcomes', ibid., October 1964, 587–99, and Christopher Bagley, 'Adoption Research

Update', *Ontario Association of Children's Aid Societies' Journal* 28 (September 1984): 1–9. See also R.J. Cadoret and C. Cain, 'Sex Differences in Predictors of Antisocial Behaviour in Adoptees', *Archives of General Psychiatry* 37 (1980): 1171–5. Observations of somewhat lesser injury to girls appear in part similar to conclusions scholars have sometimes drawn from studies of girls and boys in Native residential schools and orphans. See, for example the study by Richard King, *The School at Mopass: A Problem of Identity* (New York: Holt, Rinehart and Winston, 1967), Jo-Ann Fiske, 'Carrier Women and the Politics of Mothering', in *Rethinking Canada: The Promise of Women's History*, 4th edn, ed. Veronica Strong-Boag, Mona Gleason, and Adele Perry, (Toronto: Oxford University Press, 2002), 235–48, James Roger Miller, *Shingwauk's Vision: History of Native Residential Schools* (Toronto: University of Toronto Press, 1996), and Charles R. Saunders, *Share and Care: The Story of the Nova Scotia Home for Colored Children* (Halifax: Nimbus Publishing, 1994), 60.

123. Sally E. Palmer, 'Children in Long-Term Care: Their Experiences and Progress' (study financed by the Welfare Grants Directorate of the Department of Health and Welfare as Project 55-36-4, MSW thesis, University of British Columbia, August 1976), 54 (typescript).

124. Ontario, *Sessional Papers* (1896) 'Third Report of Work under the Children's Protection Act of Ontario' (1895), 7.

125. Alberta, Royal Commission on Child Welfare, *Report* (Edmonton, 1948), 37.

126. L.E. Lowman, 'Mail-Order Babies', *Chatelaine,* April 1932, 26.

127. 'Today's Child', *Toronto Telegram,* 8 June 1964, 25; 9 June 1964, 27; 10 June 1964, 37; and 12 June 1964, 25.

128. 'Today's Child', ibid., 30 June 1966, 64.

129. Allen, 'Among Today's Children: Three Young Brothers Want to Stay Together', ibid., 29 May 1965, 57.

130. 'Little Scottie Wins Hearts with His Tiny World of Fun', *Vancouver Sun,* 10 February 1968, 7.

131. The Children Aid Society of Brant County, 'Have You Room in Your Heart for This Boy?' *United Church Observer,* 1 March 1969, 35.

132. Alberta, Committee on Adoption in Alberta, *Report*, 29.

133. Judith A. Simms, 'Attitudes Affecting the Adoption Process: A Study of Sex Preference in Adoption and Its Possible Relationship to Tradition-Oriented Kinship Groups' (MSW thesis, Maritime School of Social Work and the University of King's College, May 1966), 51.

134. Janet Morris, 'A Son of Their Own at Last', *Vancouver Sun,* 7 December 1968, 40.

135. Colin Thomas, 'Babies without Borders: International Adoption Comes with Risks, Not to Mention Big Bills. So Why Is It So Popular?' *Georgia Straight* (22–9 January 2004), 22. See also Margaret Philip, 'Gaybaby Boom', *Globe and Mail,* 3 May 2003, F4–5.

136. See Rick Ouston, *Finding Family: A Journalist's Search for the Mother Who Left Him in an Orphanage at Birth* (Vancouver: New Star, 1994); Susan McClelland, 'Who's My Birth Father', *Maclean's,* 20 May 2002, 20–5.

137. For a typical lament about the lack of research on birth fathers, see Marjorie M. Bowker, 'Supplementary Report on Adoption in Alberta' (July 1965), 188.

138. Cynthia Comacchio, 'Bringing Up Father: Defining a Modern Canadian Fatherhood, 1900–1940', in *Family Matters: Papers in Post-Confederation Canadian Family History*, ed. Lori Chambers and Edgar-André Montigny (Toronto: Canadian Scholars' Press, 1998), 304. See also Laura Johnson and Rona Abramovitch, 'Between Jobs': Paternal Unemployment and Family Life* (Toronto: Social Planning Council of Metropolitan Toronto, 1986).

139. For the case of a rapist, see *Re Lorena Jacqueline K. (No. 2)* (19 February 1992) (Ontario Provincial Court), in *Adoption Law in Canada: Practice and Procedure*, ed. Douglas W. Phillips, Ruth J. Raphael, Douglas J. Manning, Julia A. Turnbull (Toronto: Carswell Thomson Professional Publishing, 1995), 6–43. See also *Re Lorena Jacqueline K. (No. 1)* (8 October 1991) (Ont. Prov. Ct.), in ibid., 6–43.

140. On the legal situation prior to the abolition of distinctions between the children of married and unmarried relationships see A.L. Foote, 'Family Organization and the Illegitimate Child', in *Studies in Canadian Family Law*, vol. 1, ed. D. Mendes Da Costa (Toronto: Butterworths, 1972), 45–66.

141. See Lori Chambers, '"You Have No Rights, Only Obligations": Putative Fathers and the Children of Unmarried Parents Act', in Chambers and Montigny, *Family Matters*, 115–33.

142. Saskatchewan, Department of Social Welfare, Director of the Child Welfare Division, *Report* (1951–2), 16.

143. *Re Lorena Jacqueline K. (No. 2)*. On the role of the Charter in family law see Susan Boyd, 'The Impact of the Charter of Rights and Freedoms on Canadian Family Law', *Canadian Journal of Family Law* (hereafter *CJFL*) 17, no. 2 (2000): 293–332.

144. On some of the implications of military bases, see Saundra P. Sturdevant and Brenda Stoltzfus, *Let the Good Times Roll: Prostitution and the U.S. Military in Asia* (New York: New Press, 1992).

145. Newfoundland Provincial Archives, Files GN38 Secretary of the Commission of Government, GN38, S6-1-7, Folder 10, 'Child Welfare Act 1944' (report of period 1 January to 31 March 1946), 4.

146. Lori Chambers and John Weaver, '"The Story of Her Wrongs": Abuse and Desertion in Hamilton, 1859–1922', *Ontario History* 92, no. 2 (2001): 107–26. On the failure of many fathers to pay maintenance orders, see Andy Wachtel and Brian E. Burtch, *Excuses: An Analysis of Court Interactions to Show Cause Enforcement of Maintenance Orders* (Vancouver: Social Planning and Research, United Way of the Lower Mainland, 1981).

147. Paul Sachdev, *Unlocking the Adoption Files* (Lexington, MA: Lexington Books, 1989), 147, 159.

148. Elizabeth S. Cole, 'Societal Influences on Adoption Practice', in *Adoption: Current Issues and Practices*, ed. P. Sachdev (Toronto: Butterworth, 1983), 18–19.

149. See *Re S*, [1927] 2 D.L.R. 9193, in *Digest of British Columbia Case Law* (Vancouver: Wrigley Printing Company, 1953), 376, and Re Lemon and Director, Child Welfare Act (1981), 124 D.L.R. (3d) 318 (N.B.Q.B.).

150. See BC Department of Rehabilitation and Social Improvement, *Annual Report* (for the year ending 31 March 1971), 28.

151. BC Royal Commission on Family and Children's Law, *Fifth Report* (March 1975),

90.

152. Margaret Lord, *Final Report to the Minister of Social Services of the Panel to Review Adoption Legislation in British Columbia* (Victoria: Ministry of Social Services, 1994), 57–8.

153. An Act Respecting Adoptions, *Statutes of Newfoundland, 1999,* c. A-2.1, p. 215.

154. Audrey Marshall and Margaret McDonald, *Many Sided Triangle: Adoption in Australia* (Carlton South, Victoria: Melbourne University Press, 2001), 87.

155. *O'Driscoll v. McLeod* (1986), 10 B.C.L.R. (2d) 108 (S.C.), in Phillips et al., *Adoption Law in Canada,* 4–9, and *Re MacVicar and Superintendent of Family and Child Services et al.* (1986), 34 D.L.R. (4th) 488 (B.C.S.C.).

156. Kerry J. Daly and Michael P. Sobol, *Adoption in Canada* (Guelph, ON: University of Guelph, May 1993), 81–2; *Re S. (C.E.). v. Children's Aid Society of Metropolitan Toronto* (1988), 49 D.L.R. (4th) 469 (Ont. Div. Ct). For another negative decision see the case of *Hobbs (Buck) v. Coradazzo* (1984), 40 R.F.L. (2d) 113, 54 B.C.L.R. 303 (B.C.C.A), in Phillips et al., *Adoption Law in Canada,* 4–8.

157. See *Waddell v. Hunter* (1993), 48 R.F.L. (3d) 203, 84 B.C.L.R. (2d) 104 (S.C.), in Phillips et al., *Adoption Law in Canada,* 4–10.

158. See Barbara Hobson, *Making Men into Fathers: Men, Masculinities and the Social Politics of Fatherhood* (London and New York: Cambridge University Press, 2002). For Canada, see the advocacy of father's rights in Edward Kruk, *Divorce and Disengagement: Patterns of Fatherhood within and beyond Marriage* (Halifax: Fernwood, 1993).

159. See Boyd, *Child Custody, Law, and Women's Work,* esp. ch. 6.

160. Melosh, *Strangers and Kin,* 245. See also Gary Coles, *Ever After: Fathers and the Impact of Adoption* (Christie's Beach, South Australia: Clova Publications, 2004) for its unhappy story that includes a long-lost son who has imposed a veto on revealing his identity to Coles.

161. Barrie Clark, *My Search for Catherine Anne: One Man's Story of an Adoption Reunion* (Toronto: Lorimer, 1989).

162. Randy Shore, 'The First Supper', *Vancouver Sun,* 27 October 2003, C1, C3.

163. Michelle McColm, *Adoption Reunions: A Book for Adoptees, Birth Parents and Adoptive Families* (Toronto: Second Story Press, 1993), 60.

164. Nathan Dreskin, 'Why Fathers Are the Hardest to Adopt', *Star Weekly Magazine,* 11 February 1961, 3.

165. See Nancy J. Cohen, James Duvall, James C. Coyne, *Characteristics of Post-Adoptive Families Presenting for Mental Health Service: Final Report* (Newmarket, ON: Children's Aid of York Region, January 1994), iv.

166. See Cynthia S. Fish, 'Images and Reality of Fatherhood: A Case Study of Montreal's Protestant Middle Class, 1870–1914' (PhD diss., McGill University, 1991); J.I. Little, 'Introduction' to *Love Strong as Death: Lucy Peel's Canadian Journal, 1833–1836* (Waterloo, ON: Wilfrid Laurier University Press, 2001), and Robert Rutherdale, 'Fatherhood and Masculine Domesticity during the Baby Boom: Consumption and Leisure in Advertising and Life Stories', in Chambers and Montigny, *Family Matters,* 309–33.

167. See BC, Superintendent of Neglected Children, *Annual Report* (for the year ending 31 March 1940), 2.

168. Nora Tynan, 'The Christmas Baby', *Canadian Magazine* 30 (1907–8), 168.
169. *Kerr v. McWhannel* (1974), 16 R.F.L. 185, 46 D.L.R. (3d) 624 (B.C.C.A.), in Phillips et al., *Adoption Law in Canada*, 7-8-9.
170. Whan, 'The Story behind the Stories', 36–7.
171. Abigail B. Bakan and Daiva Stasiulis, eds., *Not One of the Family: Foreign Domestic Workers in Canada* (Toronto: University of Toronto Press, 1997).

Chapter 5

1. Frances Henry, Carol Tator, Winston Mattis, and Tim Rees, *The Colour of Democracy: Racism in Canadian Society* (Toronto: Harcourt Brace, 1995), 99.
2. BC Superintendent of Neglected Children, *Annual Report* (for the year ending 31 March 1939), 3–5.
3. Robert E. Mills, 'The Placing of Children in Families', *Canadian Child and Family Welfare* 14, no. 1 (July 1938): 54.
4. This fifteen-minute documentary was narrated by early television personality Fred Davis, who visited the Montreal agency to learn of the procedure for adopting and matching. It was directed by Bernard Devlin.
5. Gordon Donaldson, 'Baby Salesmen 'Busy in Montreal', *Toronto Telegram,* 16 June 1964, 1.
6. H.L.O. Shapiro, cited in Audrey R. Taylor, 'Adoption Information for the Adopted Child: A Descriptive Study of Relationships between Adoptive Parents and Adopted Children between the Age of Six and Ten, Based on Children's Aid Society of Vancouver Cases, 1947–1957' (MSW thesis, UBC, 1957), 5. On developments in transracial adoption in Britain and the United States, see Ivor Gaber and Jane Aldridge, eds., *In the Best Interests of the Child: Culture, Identity and Transracial Adoption* (London: Free Association Books, 1994).
7. Ruth Frankenberg, *White Woman, Race Matters: The Social Construction of Whiteness* (Minneapolis: University of Minnesota Press, 1993), 14.
8. Yasmeen Abu-Laban and Christina Gabriel, *Selling Diversity: Immigration, Multiculturalism, Employment Equity, and Globalization* (Peterborough, ON: Broadview, 2002), 109.
9. See Himani Bannerji, *The Dark Side of Nation: Essays on Multiculturalism, Nationalism and Gender* (Toronto: Canadian Scholars' Press, 2000).
10. Frankenberg, *White Woman, Race Matters*, 14–15.
11. See Anna Gupta, 'Adoption, Race and Identity', in *Adoption: Changing Families, Changing Times*, ed. Anthony Douglas and Terry Philpot (London and New York: Routledge, 2003), 208–14.
12. 'Woman's Department: A New Scheme of Mission Work', *Toronto Star,* 14 March 1900.
13. 'Little Rock Could Learn a Lot', *Star Weekly,* 7 December 1957, 28, 30, 31.
14. *Toronto Telegram,* 30 December 1965, 9.
15. See Betty M. Flint, Jean G. Partridge, Elizabeth G. Stark, eds., *Pathways to Maturity: Insights from a Thirty-Year Study of Deprived Children* (Toronto: University of Toronto Press, 1996). See also Betty M. Flint, *Security of Infants* (Toronto: University of Toronto Press, 1956), and her *The Child and the Institution: A Study of Deprivation and*

Recovery (Toronto: University of Toronto Press, 1966).

16. Adoption Conference, Victoria, 8, 9, 10 December 1967, 2 (typescript). See also Patrick Jamieson, *In the Avant Garde: The Prophetic Catholicism of Remi De Roo and Politics within the Catholic Church* (Victoria: Ekstasis Publications, 2002).

17. Thirza M. Lee, 'How We Adopted an Interracial Family', *Chatelaine*, December 1966, 33, 70. See also her 'There's Always Room for One More', *United Church Observer* (15 May 1967): 16–18, 40.

18. Rosalyn Haynes, 'We Adopted a Part-Negro Child', *United Church Observer*, 1 November 1963, 25, 36.

19. P.A. Nowlan, 'Big, Happy and Varied: One Sackville Family's Story', *Star Weekly*, 10 March 1973, 6.

20. D.B. Knight, 'Transracial Adoption', *Ontario Association of Children's Aid Societies Journal*, February 1974, 5–8.

21. *New Families for Young Canadians: The History and Current Practice of Adoption* (Victoria: Department of Social Welfare, 1967), 3

22. Pierre Berton, *My Times: Living with History, 1947–1995* (Toronto: Doubleday Canada, 1995), 269.

23. See Margaret Philip, 'The Battle over Native Adoption', *Toronto Star*, 23 February 1999, and Linda Frum, *Barbara Frum: A Daughter's Memoir* (Toronto: Random House, 1996).

24. Paul Grescoe, 'A Daughter—or a Symbol', *Star Weekly*, 10 May 1969, 2–4.

25. Eleanor Lemon, 'Achieving Adoption through Publicity', *Canadian Welfare* 32, no. 3 (1956): 124.

26. Karen Balcom, 'The Traffic in Babies: Cross-Border Adoption, Baby-Selling and the Development of Child Welfare Systems in the United States and Canada' (Ph.D. diss., Rutgers University, 2002), ch. 5.

27. Marjorie M. Bowker, *Supplementary Report on Adoption in Alberta* (Edmonton, July 1965), 95–6.

28. *Saturday Night*, 7 February 1914, 2.

29. *Re Grafasso* (1916), 30 D.L.R. 595 (Ont. C.A.); *Re Taggart* (1917), 39 D.L.R. 559 (Ont. S.C.); *Cullen v. Kemp*, [1925] 4 D.L.R. 579 (Ont. S.C.); *Bland v. Agnew*, [1933] 2 D.L.R. 545 (B.C. C.A.); *Re Ward Dill v. Children's Aid Society of Catholic Archdiocese of Vancouver*, [1933] 3 D.L.R. 467 (B.C. C.A.).

30. Frank P. McKernan, letter, *Globe and Mail*, 23 November 1961, 6.

31. 'Rabbi Says Jewish Children Are "Spiritually Kidnapped"', *Globe and Mail*, 26 June 1945, 11.

32. See Ellen Herman, 'The Difference Difference Makes: Justine Wise Polier and Religious Matching in Twentieth-Century Child Adoption', *Religion and American Culture* 10 (winter 2000): 57–98.

33. Jack Harrison Pollack, 'A Close Look at Interfaith Marriage', *Star Weekly*, 1 February 1958, 26.

34. Robert Walker, 'Is Our System of Child Adoption Good Enough?' *Maclean's*, 26 September 1959, 71.

35. Joan Mackenzie, letter, 'Adoption and Religion', *Globe and Mail*, 23 November 1961, 6. See also 'Judgment Sets Ontario Precedent: Allows Couple to Adopt Child

of Another Faith. Protestants Awarded Catholic Boy', ibid., 17 November 1961, 1, 8, and 'Catholic Bishop Calls for Change in Adoption Act', ibid., 18 November 1961, 1 and passim during all of November 1961. For the decision, see *Re Lamb,* [1961] O.W.N. 356 (Dist. Ct.) in *Adoption Law in Canada: Practice and Procedure,* ed. Douglas W. Phillips, Ruth J. Raphael, Douglas J. Manning, Julia A. Turnbull (Toronto: Carswell Thomson Professional Publishing, 1995), 1–30.

36. 'The Dark Ages Are Over', *Star Weekly,* 31 August 1963, 19.

37. Gunther W. Plaut, 'The Child's Rights in the Adoptive Process', *Osgoode Hall Law Journal* 3, no. 14 (1964): 35 (italics in original).

38. Darren L. Michael, 'The Religious Factor in Adoptions', ibid., 16.

39. W. Ward Markle, 'Catholic Adoptions in Ontario', ibid., 31.

40. Ontario, Advisory Committee on Child Welfare to the Minister of Public Welfare, *Report* (May 1964), 50.

41. Mr Nolan, Committee on Adoption in Alberta, *Report* (Edmonton, 15 July 1965), 1: 65.

42. Mrs Brisbin, ibid., 3: 65.

43. Rev. David Cline, ibid., 3: 574.

44. Ibid., 1: 14–15.

45. Alberta, Department of Public Welfare, Child Welfare Branch, *23rd Annual Report* (1966–7), 10.

46. BC Royal Commission on Family and Children's Law, *5th Report* (March 1975), 30.

47. See, for example, *Re Lee et al. and Children's Aid Society of the County of Ontario* (1971), 15 D.L.R. 656 (Ont. High Ct.); *Re LeBlanc* (1971), 13 D.L.R. 225 (N.S.S.C.); *Re F. and F. and D.* (1965), 51 D.L.R. 36 (Man. C.A.).

48. Today's Child', *Toronto Telegram,* 23 June 1964.

49. Helen Allen, 'Pretty Sisters Are Bilingual', ibid., 15 May 1965, 10.

50. Today's Child', ibid., 31 December 1964, 34.

51. Ibid., 6 February 1965, 5.

52. Ibid., 12 April 1965, 39.

53. Ibid., 10 June 1965, 49.

54. Ibid., 21 June 1965, 33.

55. Ontario, *Sessional Papers,* 1896, *3rd Report of Work under the Children's Protection Act of Ontario,* Report of the Guelph Humane Society (1895), 47.

56. 'Children for Adoption', *Canadian Churchman,* 8 July 1897, 433.

57. Ontario, Superintendent of Neglected and Dependent Children, *37th Annual Report* (1931), 11–12.

58. Tanya L. Gogan, 'Surviving as a Widow in Late Nineteenth-Century Halifax' (MA thesis, Dalhousie University, 1994), 138.

59. Roberta G. Aggas, 'Social Class Influences in Illegitimacy: A Study of the Effects of Social Class Affiliation, Corresponding Patterns of Socialization and Their Relationship to Illegitimacy' (MSW thesis, Maritime School of Social Work and University of King's College, 1967), 55.

60. Marcel Arseneau, 'A Study of Ninety Wards in Child Caring Institutions in Halifax: An Analysis of the Personal Characteristics, Family Background and Placement Experience of Wards of Child Welfare Agencies Who Were in Child Caring

Institutions during the Year 1958' (research project for MSW, Maritime School of Social Work, May 1960), 63.

61. See Charles R. Saunders, *Share and Care: The Story of the Nova Scotia Home for Colored Children* (Halifax: Nimbus Publishing, 1994), and Renée N. Lafferty, '"To Assure That We Compare Favourably": The Nova Scotia Home for Colored Children and Institutional Care in Nova Scotia, 1900–1930' (paper presented to the Annual Meeting of the Canadian Historical Association, Halifax, 2003).

62. Canada, House of Commons, *Debates,* 26 June 1954, 6797 (J. Coldwell).

63. 'The Color Problem: A Moral Issue', *Star Weekly,* 11 October 1958, 59.

64. Bridget Moran, *Little Rebellion* (Vancouver: Arsenal Press, 1992).

65. BC Department of Health and Welfare, Social Welfare Branch, *Annual Report* (for the year ending 31 March 1951), 53.

66. Ibid. (for the year ending 31 March 1954), 55.

67. Ibid.

68. Ibid. (for the year ending 31 March 1956), 51.

69. BC Department of Social Welfare, *Annual Report* (for the year ending 31 March 1960), 42.

70. BC Department of Health and Welfare, Social Welfare Branch, *Annual Report* (for the year ending 31 March 1956), 51.

71. BC Department of Social Welfare, *Annual Report* (for the year ending 31 March 1959), 46.

72. Ibid. (for the year ending 31 March 1962), 41.

73. Bowker, *Supplementary Report on Adoption in Alberta,* 101.

74. See K. Dubinsky, '"We Adopted a Negro": Interracial Adoption and the Hybrid Baby in 1960s Canada', in *Canada's 'trente glorieuses': Readings on Family, Community, and Nation, 1945–1975,* ed. M. Fahrni and R. Rutherdale (Vancouver: UBC Press, 2006).

75. The connection is implicit, rather than explicit, in some of the official reports. See, for example, Newfoundland, Department of Public Welfare, *Annual Report* (1960).

76. Eva Bassett, 'Our Negro Children: A Venture in Understanding', *Newsletter* (Child Welfare Division, Canadian Welfare Council) 6, no. 2 (1958): 2 (mimeograph).

77. Margaret Edgar, 'Mixed Blood Canadians', *United Church Observer,* 15 September 1960, 2.

78. Miss Gallay, 'Interracial Adoptions', *Canadian Welfare* 39 (November–December 1963): 248.

79. *The Adoption of Negro Children: A Community-wide Approach* (n.p., July 1966), 3.

80. Ibid., 1.

81. 'Project on Adoption of Negro Children', *Canadian Welfare* 38, no. 4 (1962): 187

82. Quoted in *Concerning Families and Children* 10, no. 2 (1962): 3.

83. In 1962, the committee included Mrs Wilson Brooks (chair), Mrs A.D. Margison, (past chair); Mr Bernard Berger, Mrs Pierre Berton, Mr George E. Carter, Mr Charles P. Connolly; Mrs Charles P. Connolly; Mrs F. Des Tombe, Mr R.G. Fitzpatrick; Mrs H. Goldenson, Mr Henry G. Goodman; Mr Stanley G. Grizzle, Dr Daniel Hill; Mrs D.F. Kent; Mr Kenric R. Marshall; Mrs J.J. Matthews; Mrs E.F. McNamara; Dr Richard R. Medhurst and Dr Norma Ford Walker. *The Adoption of*

Negro Children, 25. On Ford Walker, see the revealingly entitled article by Fiona Miller, 'The Importance of Being Marginal: Norma Ford Walker and a Canadian School of Medical Genetics', *American Journal of Medical Genetics* 115, no. 2 (2002): 102–10. Lawrence Hill's autobiography, *Black Berry, Sweet Juice: On Being Black and White in Canada* (Toronto: HarperFlamingo Canada, 2001), touches variously and lovingly on the interracial marriage of his parents

84.   *The Adoption of Negro Children*, 20.
85.   Ibid.
86.   Ibid., 5, 14, 16–17
87.   'Today's Child', *Toronto Telegram*, 11 February 1965, 49.
88.   Ibid., 13 November 1964, 25.
89.   Sheri Craig, 'New Hope for Negro Children', ibid., 6 October 1964, 29.
90.   Helen Allen, 'Offers for Orphans Pour In', ibid., 13 June 1964, 3.
91.   Maggie de Vries, *Missing Sarah: A Vancouver Woman Remembers Her Vanished Sister* (Toronto: Penguin Canada, 2003), 1.
92.   *The Adoption of Negro Children*, 53–9.
93.   Shirley J. Morrison, 'An Examination of the Adoption Placement of Black Children with White Families in the Metropolitan Area of Nova Scotia' (MSW thesis, Dalhousie University, 1987).
94.   Ibid., 40, 98, 116.
95.   Saunders, *Share and Care*, 138.
96.   Ibid., 142.
97.   Wayne MacKay, *The Halifax Loyalist*, 6 November 1977, 139, citing a 1963 study by Edith Roskie in Saunders, *Share and Care*, 139.
98.   Study by Diane Smaggus and Blair Blakeney for Savannah Williams, cited in Saunders, *Share and Care*, 140.
99.   See, for example, Arnold R. Silverman, 'Outcomes of Transracial Adoption', *Future of Children* 3, no. 1 (1993): 104–18. See also Harriet Fancott, ed., *Raising Healthy Multiracial Adoptive Families: A Question and Answer Guide for Adoptive Parents* (Surrey, BC: Adoptive Families Association of British Columbia, 1999).
100.   Adoption Council of Ontario, 13 September 2005, available at http://www.adoption.on.ca/acomain.html
101.   Deborah Jones, 'Canada's Real Adoption Crisis', *Chatelaine*, May 1998, 44.
102.   Charles Taylor, *Multiculturalism and the 'Politics of Recognition': An Essay* (Princeton, NJ: Princeton University Press, 1992). See also Ian Angus, *A Border Within: National Identity, Cultural Plurality and Wilderness* (Montreal and Kingston: McGill-Queen's University Press, 1997).
103.   David B. Knight, 'Transracial Adoption', *Ontario Association of Children's Aid Societies Journal* (February 1974): 6, 7–8.

Chapter 6

1.   Thanks to Jo Fiske for reminding me of the various purposes served by adoption. See Antonia C. Mills, *Eagle Down Is Our Law: The Witsuwit'en Law, Feasts, and Land Claims* (Vancouver: UBC Press, 1994) and Jo-Anne Fiske, with the assistance of Betty Patrick, *Cis dideen kat – When the Plumes Rise: The Way of the Lake Babine Nation*

(Vancouver: UBC Press, 2000).

2. Vic Satzewich and Terry Wotherspoon, *First Nation: Race, Class, and Gender Relations* (Saskatoon: Canadian Plains Research Center, 2000), 51.

3. Harry B. Hawthorn, Cyril S. Belshaw, and Stuart M. Jamieson, *The Indians of British Columbia: A Study of Contemporary Social Adjustment* (Toronto: University of Toronto Press and UBC Press, 1960), 141, 107.

4. Ibid., 189.

5. William Stanbury, *Success and Failure: Indians in Urban Society* (Vancouver: UBC Press, 1975), 167. In 1971, 32 per cent of his sample—not including the unemployed—were union members; if the latter were counted 40 per cent were unionized. This compared with about 42 per cent of the total BC labour force (284n4).

6. See ibid., table 10-6, 'Measures of Cultural Identity in Relation to a Number of Variables, BC Indians Living Off Reserves, 1971', 393.

7. On Six Nations see Veronica Strong-Boag and Carole Gerson, *Paddling Her Own Canoe: The Times and Texts of E. Pauline Johnson (Tekahionwake)* (Toronto: University of Toronto Press, 2000), ch. 1, and Jean Usher, *William Duncan of Metlakatla: A Victorian Missionary in British Columbia* (Ottawa: National Museums of Canada, 1974).

8. As Jo-Anne Fiske and Claudien Herlihey have reminded us, paternal lineages can have an important role even in matrilineal societies in providing for Native children. The clans of maternal grandfathers may well adopt youngsters whose fathers do not belong to those communities. Yet, when so many mixed-race children have white fathers or even grandfathers, they remain additionally vulnerable. See their 'Courting Customs: Taking Customary Law to the BC Supreme Court', *International Journal of Race and Ethnicity Studies* 1, no. 11 (1994): 59.

9. This assessment is based on a reading of www.coverage, and that in the *Globe and Mail*, the *Toronto Star*, the *National Post*, and the Vancouver *Sun*. See, for example, Siri Agrell, 'BC Band Halts Battle to Take Children Away from Non-Native Foster Parents', CanWest News Service, 20 July 2004; Siri Agrell, 'Families Win Right to Adopt Aboriginal Girls 3 1/2-Year Legal Battle', *National Post*, 24 July 2004; M. Mandel, 'Their 2 Little Girls Are Home for Good', *Toronto Sun*, 25 July 2004, and 'Finally, Love Trumps Race', *National Post*, 26 July 2004. While no author appears to sympathize with the Squamish, these limited facts seem clear. The 3,323 (2001) members of the Squamish Nation live in eight villages stretching from British Columbia's Sunshine Coast to Burrard Inlet. Such small numbers obviously offer little margin for coping with additional, often troubled, youngsters.

10. See John A. MacDonald, 'The Spallumcheen Indian Band By-Law and Its Potential Impact on Native Indian Child Welfare Policy in British Columbia', *Canadian Journal of Family Law* (hereafter *CJFL*) 4 (July 1983): 75–95. Note that Hawthorn, Belshaw, and Jamieson characterized the Spallumcheen band as 'economically unsuccessful', in *The Indians of British Columbia*, 141.

11. See Judith Fingard, *The Dark Side of Life in Victorian Halifax* (Halifax: Pottersfield Press, 1989), 16, for the general distinction. Her discussion of rough Halifax suggests that its parade of violent men, prostituted women, and abused children might match the disarray and violence sometimes observed in First Nations communities.

12. Mary Lawrence, *My People, Myself* (Prince George, BC: Caitlin Press, 1996), 16.

13. Jo Cain, 'Urban Native Child Welfare in BC: A Proposal for Matching Services with Client Needs' (MSW thesis, University of British Columbia, 1985), 3 (emphasis in original).

14. See Fiske and Herlihey, 'Courting Customs', 63.

15. See, *inter alia*, the observations of the Indian Homemakers of BC in Charlene Mignacco, 'Towards Native Control of Child Welfare: The Nuu-Chah-Nulth Tribal Council "A Case in Point"' (MSW thesis, University of British Columbia, 1984), 12; Community Panel Family and Children's Services Legislation Review in British Columbia, Aboriginal Committee, *Liberating Our Children, Liberating Our Nations* (Victoria: Government of British Columbia, 1992), 9–10.

16. Jean Barman, 'Taming Aboriginal Sexuality: Gender, Power, and Race in British Columbia, 1850–1900', *BC Studies* 115/116 (autumn/winter 1997/8): 237–66.

17. J.R. Miller, *Shingwauk's Vision: A History of Native Residential Schools* (Toronto: University of Toronto Press, 1997), 141–2.

18. Stanbury, *Success and Failure*, 385, table 9–10.

19. See http://www12.statcan.ca/english/census01/products/analytic/companion/abor/tables/total/agegroups.cfm (accessed 6 January 2005).

20. Patrick Johnston, *Native Children and the Child Welfare System* (Ottawa: Canadian Council on Social Development, 1983), 70.

21. Anna Davin, *Growing Up Poor: Home, School and Street in London, 1870–1914* (London: Rivers Oram Press, 1996), and Lynn Abrams, *The Orphan Country: Children of Scotland's Broken Homes from 1845 to the Present Day* (Edinburgh: John Donald Publishers, 1998).

22. Wendie Redmon and Sherry Sleighholm, *Once Removed: Voices from Inside the Adoption Triangle* (Toronto: McGraw-Hill Ryerson, 1982), 27.

23. Simma Holt, 'Poor Little White Girl', *Star Weekly*, 4 February 1967, 2, 4. See also the story of a white baby given to an Indian family by an unwed teenager in the short story by Eleanor Brass, *Medicine Boy and Other Cree Tales* (1978), quoted in *Our Bit of Truth: An Anthology of Canadian Native Literature,* ed. Agnes Grant (Winnipeg: Pemmican Publishing , 1990), 229–30.

24. Shurlee Swain, 'Child Rescue: The Emigration of an Idea', in *Child Welfare and Social Action in the Nineteenth and Twentieth Centuries: International Perspectives,* ed. Jon Lawrence and Pat Starkey (Liverpool: Liverpool University Press, 2001), 115. She also makes this argument specifically with regard to the treatment of Aboriginal children in Australia, noting that preoccupation with difference 'rests upon an imagined contrast with a qualified professional child welfare service, which did not exist in Australia until the 1960s and even then paid little regard to parents' rights' (110).

25. See Johnston, *Native Children and the Child Welfare System*, 2.

26. Robert Adamoski, 'The Child–The Citizen–The Nation: The Rhetoric and Experience of Wardship in Early Twentieth-Century British Columbia', in *Contesting Canadian Citizenship: Historical Readings,* ed. Robert Adamoski, D.E. Chunn, and R. Menzies (Peterborough, ON: Broadview Press, 2002), 319.

27. See the case of the light-skinned illegitimate daughter of a prostitute mother in C.J. South to Superintendent of Indian Affairs, 20 September 1905, cited in Renisa

Mawani, 'In Between and Out of Place: Mixed-Race Identity, Liquor and the Law in British Columbia, 1850–1913', in *Race, Space, and the Law: Unmapping a White Settler Society,* ed. Sherene Razack (Toronto: Between the Lines, 2002), 68.

28. Jessa Chupick-Hall, '"Good Families Do Not Just Happen": Indigenous People and Child Welfare Services in Canada, 1950–1965' (MA thesis, Trent University, 2001), 39.

29. H.B. Hawthorn, ed., *A Survey of the Contemporary Indians of Canada: A Report on Economic, Political, Educational Needs and Policies* (Ottawa: Indian Affairs Branch, October 1966), 1: 327.

30. Elizabeth Graham, *The Mush Hole: Life at Two Indian Residential Schools* (Waterloo, ON: Heffle Publishing, 1997), 10.

31. Miller, *Shingwauk's Vision*, 92. See also his observations about Haida 'Aristocrats', 211.

32. Jo-Anne Fiske, 'Carrier Women and the Politics of Mothering', in *Rethinking Canada: The Promise of Women's History,* 4th edn, ed. Veronica Strong-Boag, Mona Gleason, and Adele Perry (Toronto: Oxford University Press, 2002), 359–74.

33. Beverly Hungry Wolf, *Daughters of the Buffalo Women: Maintaining the Tribal Faith* (Skookumchuck, BC: Canadian Caboose Press, 1996).

34. Miller, *Shingwauk's Vision*, 314.

35. See Rita Joe, 'The Honour Song of the Micmac', in *Kelusultiek: Original Women's Voices of Atlantic Canada,* ed. Renate Usmiani et al. (Halifax: Mt St Vincent University Institute for the Study of Women, 1994), 36–42. See the somewhat similar case of Jennie Blackbird at Ontario's Mohawk Institute in Elizabeth Graham, *The Mush Hole,* 318.

36. See Chupick-Hall, '"Good Families Do Not Just Happen"', passim.

37. Ontario, Superintendent of Neglected and Dependent Children, *Annual Report* (1931), 13.

38. BC Superintendent of Neglected Children, *Annual Report* (for the year ending 31 March 1939), 24.

39. Ibid. (for the year ending 31 March 1940), 24.

40. Joan Sangster, *Girl Trouble: Female Delinquency in English Canada* (Toronto: Between the Lines, 2002), 7 and ch. 6.

41. See Hawthorn, *A Survey of the Contemporary Indians of Canada*, 129.

42. BC Superintendent of Child Welfare, *Annual Report* (for the year ending 31 March 1944), 19, in A.G. Singleton, 'Child Welfare Administration under Protection Acts in British Columbia: Its History and Development 1901–1949' (MSW thesis, University of British Columbia, 1950.

43. BC Social Welfare Branch of the Department of Health and Welfare, *Annual Report* (for the year ending 31 March 1949), 42–3.

44. Quoted in Hawthorn, *A Survey of the Contemporary Indians of Canada*, 129.

45. Charlotte Whitton, *Welfare in Alberta: The Report of a Study* (Edmonton: Douglas Printing, 1947), 36.

46. Canada, House of Commons, Debates, 26 June 1954, 6797 (M.J. Coldwell).

47. BC Provincial Advisory Committee on Indian Affairs, *11th Annual Report* (for the year ending 31 March 1961), 19.

48. J.H. Lagasse, *A Study of the Population of Indian Ancestry Living in Manitoba,*

(Winnipeg: Social and Economic Research Office, Manitoba Department of Agriculture and Immigration, 1959), 1: 140. For admission of prejudice, see vol. 2 passim.

49. 'Women Liberals Criticise Attitude toward Indians', *Edmonton Journal*, 22 January 1965, 18.

50. Hawthorn, *A Survey of the Contemporary Indians of Canada*, 316.

51. BC Provincial Advisory Committee on Indian Affairs, *3rd Annual Report* (for the year ending 31 December 1952), 5.

52. Chupik-Hall, '"Good Families Do Not Just Happen"', 38.

53. M.E. Battel, 'Child Welfare in Saskatchewan' (1965), 49 (typescript).

54. R. MacGregor, 'Two Worlds About to Collide in the New Saskatchewan', *Globe and Mail*, 29 December 2004, A4.

55. Saskatchewan, Director of Child Welfare, *Annual Report* (1947–8), 24.

56. BC Provincial Committee on Indian Affairs, *6th Annual Report* (for the year ending 31 March 1955), 12.

57. BC Provincial Committee on Indian Affairs, *7th Annual Report* (for the year ending 31 March 1956), 3.

58. Saskatchewan, Department of Social Welfare and Rehabilitation, Director of the Child Welfare Branch, *Annual Report* (1963–4), 18.

59. Ernie Crey, 'The Perpetual Stranger: Four Generations in my Sto:lo Family', in *Stolen from Our Embrace: The Abduction of First Nations Children and the Restoration of Aboriginal Communities,* ed. Suzanne Fournier and Ernie Crey (Vancouver: Douglas and McIntyre, 1997), 30. His family was broken up in the 1960s.

60. Lawrence, *My People, Myself* , ch. 3.

61. See observations in Child Care Task Force, *A Report on B.C. Indian Child Care* (Program Evaluation Branch, Indian Affairs and Northern Development, May 1982), 4.

62. See Chupik-Hall, '"Good Families Do Not Just Happen"', 73–6.

63. Saskatchewan, Department of Social Welfare and Rehabilitation, Child Welfare Branch, *Report of the Director* (1963–4), 16.

64. Marjory M. Bowker, *Supplementary Report on Adoption in Alberta* (Edmonton, July 1964), 165.

65. Maurice Norbert Coté, 'The Children's Aid Society of the Catholic Archdiocese of Vancouver: Its Origins and Development, 1905 to 1953' (MSW thesis, University of British Columbia, 1953), 58.

66. Alice H. Dales, 'Closing a Children's Institution in Saskatchewan', *Canadian Welfare* 30, no. 6 (1954): 42.

67. Chupik-Hall, '"Good Families Do Not Just Happen"', 85, 88.

68. Ontario, *Report of the Advisory Committee on Child Welfare to the Minister of Public Welfare* (May 1964), C.J. Foster, Chairman, Appendix I, H.B. Treen, 'A Study of Permanent Wards in the Care of Children's Aid Societies in the Province of Ontario' (July 1963), 23.

69. See the case of Alberta reported in Fred R. MacKinnon, 'Foster Home Care and Group Care of Children and Children Pending Adoption: A Study for the Canadian Conference on Children', *Canadian Conference on Children/Conférence Canadienne de l'enfance: Foster Home Care, Group Care for Children and Adopted Children,* Ste Adele, 2

October 1960.

70. Alan Cairns, cited in Hawthorn, *A Survey of the Contemporary Indians of Canada*, 318. See also Cairns, *Citizens Plus: Aboriginal Peoples and the Canadian State* (Vancouver: UBC Press, 2000).

71. Hawthorn, *A Survey of the Contemporary Indians of Canada*, 327–9.

72. Ibid., 329.

73. BC Provincial Advisory Committee on Indian Affairs. *11th Annual Report* (for the year ending 31 March 1961), 7.

74. *Adoption and the Indian Children* (Ottawa: Indian and Northern Affairs Canada in cooperation with the Adoption Desk, Health and Welfare Canada, and Provincial and Territorial Departments of Social Welfare, 1962), 7–8.

75. Chupick-Hall, '"Good Families Do Not Just Happen"', 64. See, too, Andrew Armitage, *Comparing the Policy of Aboriginal Assimilation: Australia, Canada, and New Zealand* (Vancouver: UBC Press, 1995).

76. BC Provincial Advisory Committee on Indian Affairs, *18th Annual Report* (for the year ending 31 March 1967), 17.

77. Alberta, Committee on Adoption in Alberta, *Report* (15 July 1965), 41.

78. BC Provincial Advisory Committee on Indian Affairs, *11th Annual Report* (for the year ending 31 March 1962), 8.

79. Alberta, Committee on Adoption in Alberta, *Report*, 41.

80. Joyce B. Timpson, 'Four Decades of Child Welfare Services to Native Indians in Ontario: A Contemporary Attempt to Understand the "Sixties Scoop" in Historical, Socioeconomic and Political Perspective' (PhD diss., Wilfrid Laurier University, 1993), 63n70.

81. Cited in *Native Education in the Province of Alberta: Report of the Task Force on Intercultural Education*, Submitted to Hon. L.D. Hyndman, Minister of Education, Alberta (June 1972), 117.

82. Editorial, 'Social Work on the Reserve', *Ontario Association of Children's Aid Societies* 22 (February 1979): n.p.

83. See Janet Budgell, *Research Project: Repatriation of Aboriginal Families—Models and a Workplan. Final Report* (Toronto: Native Child and Family Services of Toronto, March 1999), n.p.

84. Case cited in Betty M. Flint, *New Hope for Deprived Children* (Toronto: University of Toronto Press, 1978), 114–16.

85. BC Provincial Advisory Committee on Indian Affairs, *18th Annual Report* (for the year ending 31 March 1967), 19.

86. BC Provincial Advisory Committee on Indian Affairs, *19th Annual Report* (for the year ending 31 March 1968), 18.

87. BC Department of Rehabilitation and Social Improvement, *Annual Report* (for the year ending 31 March 1971), 27.

88. David Fanshel, *Far from the Reservation: The Transracial Adoption of American Indian Children. A Study Conducted under the Auspices of the Child Welfare League of America, New York* (Metuchen, NJ: Scarecrow Press, 1972), 49. See Rita J. Simon and Howard Altstein, *Adoption, Race, and Identity: From Infancy through Adolescence* (New York: Praeger, 1992), 18–29 for a positive assessment.

89. Fanshel, *Far from the Reservation*, 21.

90. Ibid., 59.

91. See Elizabeth M. Armstrong, *Conceiving Risk, Bearing Responsibility: Fetal Alcohol Syndrome and the Diagnosis of Moral Disorder* (Baltimore: Johns Hopkins University Press, 2003).

92. Fanshel, *Far from the Reservation*, 269.

93. Ibid., 49.

94. Saskatchewan, Department of Welfare. Child Welfare Branch, *Annual Report* (1964–5), 17.

95. Chupick-Hall, "'Good Families Do Not Just Happen'", 123.

96. Bowker, *Supplementary Report on Adoption in Alberta*, 102.

97. Gene Elmore, Sharon Clark, and Sharon Dick, *A Survey of Adoption and Child Welfare Services to Indians of B.C.* (Vancouver: Union of BC Indian Chiefs, 18 February 1974), 7.

98. Margaret Ward, *The Adoption of Native Children* (Cobalt, ON: Highway Book Shop, 1984), 9.

99. Johnston, *Native Children and the Child Welfare System*, 89.

100. 'Today's Child', *Toronto Telegram*, 25 November 1965, 51.

101. Ibid., 17 December 1965, 35; 6 January 1966, 62.

102. Ibid., 10 June 1964, 37; 22 June 1964, 35; 7 May 1965, 43.

103. Ibid., 9 November 1964, 25.

104. Ibid., 22 February 1965, 33.

105. Ibid., 8 June 1965, 52.

106. Ibid., 6 January 1965, 43.

107. Ibid., 4 March 1966, 35.

108. Ibid., 5 June 1965, 3.

109. Helen Allen, 'Offers for Orphans Pour In', ibid., 13 June 1964, 3.

110. Dr Hamilton, Alberta, Committee on Adoption, *Report* (Edmonton, 1965), 1: 75–7.

111. Mr Fleming and Dr Hamilton, ibid., 1: 96.

112. 'One of the Family', *Edmonton Journal*, 13 January 1965, 30.

113. 'Eskimo Baby Is Gift', ibid., 29 January 1965, 17.

114. See Deborah Jones, 'Canada's Real Adoption Crisis', *Chatelaine*, May 1998, 44.

115. P.A. Nowlan, 'Big, Happy and Varied: One Sackville Family's Story', *Star Weekly*, 10 March 1973.

116. Canada, House of Commons, *Debates*, 21 February 2000, 3797 (G. Asselin).

117. Mr Carbert, in Alberta, Committee on Adoption, *Report*, 1: 215–18.

118. Bridget Moran, *A Little Rebellion* (Vancouver: Arsenal Pulp Press, 1992), 40–1, 49.

119. BC Department of Rehabilitation and Social Improvement, *Annual Report* (for the year ending 31 March 1972), 33–4.

120. Timpson, 'Four Decades of Child Welfare Services', 9.

121. Richard Thatcher, 'Stop Stealing Our Children', *Canadian Dimension*, October–November 1982, 4.

122. Buffy Sainte-Marie, 'Wants Native Homes', *Perception* 3, no. 2 (1979), 20.

123. See Royal Commission on Aboriginal Peoples, *Public Policy and Aboriginal Peoples, 1965–1992*, vol. 3, *Summaries of Reports by Provincial and Territorial Bodies and Other*

Organizations (Ottawa, 1994).

124.   Richard Wagamese, *Keeper'n Me* (Toronto: Doubleday Canada, 1994), 11–13. The book was acclaimed the best novel of 1995 by the Writers' Guild of Alberta.

125.   S.K. Kawai, 'The Honour Song of the Micmac', in *Kelusultiek,* 129.

126.   Elmore, Clark, and Dick, 'A Survey of Adoption and Child Welfare Services', 22, 8, 22.

127.   BC Department of Human Resources, *Annual Report* (for the year ending 31 March 1974, with fiscal addendum 1 April 1973 to 31 March 1974), 25.

128.   MacDonald, 'The Spallumcheen Indian Band', 84.

129.   On this case, see Douglas Saunders, *Family Law and Native People: Background Paper* (Ottawa: Law Reform Commission of Canada, 1975), and A. McGillivray, 'Transracial Adoption and the Status Indian Child', *CJFL* 4 (1985): 437–67.

130.   Jo-Anne Fiske, 'The Supreme Law and the Grand Law: Changing Significance for Aboriginal Women of British Columbia', *B.C. Studies,* nos. 105/106 (Spring/ Summer 1995): 183.

131.   Marlee Kline, 'Child Welfare Law, "Best Interests of the Child" Ideology, and First Nations', *Osgoode Hall Law Journal* 30, no. 2 (1992): 375–425. See also Susan B. Boyd, *Child Custody, Law, and Women's Work* (Toronto: Oxford University Press, 2003).

132.   For the judgment of the Court of Queen's Bench of Saskatchewan in *In the Matter of the Child and Family Services Act,* see www.lawsociety.sk.ca/judgments/2004/ QB2004/2004skqb503.pdf (accessed 22 December 2005). See also 'Don't Block the Adoption', *Globe and Mail,* 4 January 2005, A12. On cases in general see, *inter alia,* A. McGillivray, 'Transracial Adoption and the Status Indian Child'; M. Lipman, 'Adoption in Canada: Two Decades in Review', in *Adoption in Canada: Current Issues and Trends,* ed. P. Sachdev (Toronto: Butterworths, 1983), 31–41, and D.W. Phillips, R.J. Raphael, D.J. Manning, and J.A. Turnbull, eds., *Adoption Law in Canada: Practice and Procedure* (Toronto: Carswell Thomson Professional Publishing,1995).

133.   Emily F. Carasco, 'Canadian Native Children: Have Child Welfare Laws Broken the Circle?' *CJFL* 5 (1986): 125.

134.   For details, see BC Department of Human Resources, *Annual Report* (with fiscal addendum 1 April 1973 to 31 March 1974), and ibid. (1975), 50.

135.   The same decade also saw somewhat similar conclusions in J.C. Ryant (chairman, Review Group) et al., *A Review of Child Welfare Policies, Programs and Services in Manitoba* (Winnipeg: Human and Social Development, July 1975). It noted that 'the colonial cast of the social service system is reflected by child welfare approaches which insufficiently respect or pay attention to the indigenous culture of repressed minority groups' (21). See also *Native Education in the Province of Alberta.*

136.   MacDonald, 'The Spallumcheen Indian Band By-Law', 86.

137.   Technical Assistance and Planning Associates, ' *Starving Man Doesn't Argue',* Report Prepared for Policy, Research and Evaluation Division, Department of Indian Affairs and Northern Development (1979).

138.   *Community Care: Toward Indian Control of Indian Social Services* (Ontario, 1980), cited in *Child Care Task Force: A Report on B.C. Indian Child Care* (Ottawa: Program Evaluation Branch Indian Affairs and Northern Development, May 1982).

139.   See McGillivray, 'Transracial Adoption and the Status Indian Child', 466.

140. Ralph Garber, *Disclosure of Adoption Information* (Report of the Special Commissioner to the Honourable John Sweeney, Minister of Community and Social Services, Government of Ontario, November 1985), 59, 62. (Emphasis in original.) The same issue has also arisen in the Australian context. See, for example, A. Marshall and M. McDonald, *Many Sided Triangle: Adoption in Australia* (Carlton South, Victoria: Melbourne University Press, 2001), 167.

141. Canada, Royal Commission on Aboriginal Peoples, *Public Policy and Aboriginal Peoples,* 3: 85.

142. Barkwell, Longclaws, and Chartrand, 'Status of Métis Children within the Child Welfare System', 33–53.

143. Peter Hudson and Brad McKenzie, 'Child Welfare and Native People: The Extension of Colonialism', *Social Worker/Le Travailleur social* 49, no. 2 (1981): 63–5, 88.

144. See Frank Tester, 'Still Not Home: The Indian and Native Child and Family Service Provisions of Ontario's Bill 77', ibid. 54, no. 4 (1986): 160–3.

145. Margaret Goodman, in Review Committee on Indian and Métis Adoptions and Placements, *Transcripts and Briefs: Public Hearings, Special Hearings, Briefs,* Associate Chief Judge Edwin C. Kimelman, Chairman (Winnipeg: Manitoba Community Services, 1985), 93, 101, 107.

146. Ibid., 95, 99.

147. Ibid., 107, 114.

148. Betty Schwartz, in ibid., 169.

149. Vladimir Ilnyckyj, in ibid., 197.

150. James L. Dubray, Henry Neufeld, Jean I. Macdonald, 'Children's Aid Society of Central Manitoba', in ibid., 685–6.

151. Ibid., 687.

152. Michael Malazdrewicz, 'Westman Adoptive Parents Group', in ibid., 11–15.

153. Juanita and Calvin Kirby, in ibid., 706. See also the brief from E.H. Ellis, University of Manitoba, Faculty of Medicine, Department of Psychiatry, 749–53, for similar opinions.

154. Brief from 'Parents of Adopted Native Children, Native Ministry Board, United Church of Canada', in ibid., 739–42.

155. Brief from Issac Beaulieu, in ibid., 15–17.

156. Brief from J. Terry, in ibid., 156–9.

157. Russ Rothnay, in ibid., 51–61.

158. J. Young, in ibid., 122–6.

159. H. York, in ibid., 234–40.

160. Gilbert Abraham, in ibid., 420.

161. Harold and Judy Longclaws, in ibid., 635.

162. See Ray Aboud, 'A Death in Kansas', *Saturday Night,* April 1986, 28–39. See also C. Bagley, 'The Institution of Adoption: A Canadian Case Study', in *Adoption in Worldwide Perspective: A Review of Programs, Policies and Legislation in 14 Countries,* ed. R.A.C. Hoksbergen (Berwyn, IL: Swets North America, 1986), which pointed to 'child sex rings in the United States involved in adopting Native youngsters' (222).

163. See the award-winning documentary, *Richard Cardinal: Cry from a Diary of a Métis Child,* dir. Alanis Obomsawin (NFB, 1986)

164. E.C. Kimelman, *No Quiet Place,* Review Committee on Indian and Métis Adoptions and Placements (Winnipeg: Manitoba Department of Community Services, 1985), 275–6.

165. Manitoba, *Report of the Aboriginal Justice Inquiry* (1999), ch. 14. Available at http://www.ajic.mb.ca

166. Brian Thorne, 'Mediating an Adoption the Coast Salish Way', *Legal Perspectives* 13, no. 4 (April 1989): 6.

167. See, for example, 'Child Adopted in Ceremony: Grandmother to Place Native Girl with Métis Mom', *Calgary Herald,* 26 May 2004, B3.

168. BC Ministry of Social Services and Housing, Services for People, *Annual Report* (1988–9), 44.

169. Satzewich and Wotherspoon, *First Nations,* 93.

170. Mignacco, 'Towards Native Control of Child Welfare', 29, 48.

171. R.S. Ratner, 'Child Welfare Services for Urban Native Indians: Report Commissioned by the United Native Nations' (December 1991), 13.

172. Johnston, *Native Children and the Child Welfare System,* 126.

173. Satzewich and Wotherspoon, *First Nations,* 93.

174. See the argument in Timpson, 'Four Decades of Child Welfare Services', 14.

175. See the murder of one little brother and the abuse of another by their aunt and uncle in Duncan on Vancouver Island in 1997. Paul Walton 'Tooshley Appeals May Have Lapsed', *Cowichan Valley Citizen,* 13 October 2002, 12; n.a., 'Aboriginal Heritage Won't Be Considered', *Alberni Valley Times,* 18 October 2001, A2.

176. G.C. Robinson, R.F Conry, and J.L. Conry, *The Canim Lake Survey of Special Needs Children* (Vancouver: University of British Columbia, March 1985), 14, 19. This study, at the request of the Canim Lake Band, identified over 25 per cent of children as handicapped and 6 of 45 resident mothers as accounting for over 60 per cent of youngsters affected by fetal alcohol syndrome.

176. Lavina White and Eva Jacobs, comps., *Liberating Our Children, Liberating Our Nations: Report of the Aboriginal Committee. Community Panel, Family and Children's Services Legislation Review in British Columbia* (Victoria: The Committee, October 1992), 10.

177. Margaret Lord, *Final Report to the Minister of Social Services of the Panel to Review Adoption Legislation* (Victoria: Ministry of Social Services, July 1994), 90.

178. J. Bauman in *D.H. v. H.M.* (26 September 1997) Vancouver, F950814 (B.C. S.C.), affirmed [1999] 1 S.C.R. 328, cited on the website of the Continuing Legal Education Society of British Columbia http://www.cle.bc.ca/Cle/Practice+Desk/Practice+Articles/Collection/02-app-custodysupport (accessed 2 April 2005).

179. Canada, Royal Commission on Aboriginal Peoples, *Report,* vol. 3, *Gathering Strength,* 25–6.

180. *Lethbridge Herald,* 8 April 2005, D1.

181. See E.J. Dickson-Gilmore, '"More Mohawk Than My Blood": Citizenship, Membership and the Struggle over Identity in Kahnawake', *Canadian Issues* 21 (1999): 44–62. See also G.R. Alfred, *Heeding the Voices of Our Ancestors: Kahnawake Mohawk Politics and the Rise of Native Nationalism* (Toronto: Oxford University Press, 1995).

182. D. Jones, 'Canada's Real Adoption Crisis', *Chatelaine,* May 1998.

183. See Pierre Berton, *My Times: Living with History, 1947–1995* (Toronto: Doubleday Canada, 1995), 419, and Marie Adams, *Our Son, a Stranger: Adoption Breakdown* (Montreal and Kingston: McGill-Queen's University, 2002). On the phenomenon more generally, see also Anne-Marie Ambert, *The Effect of Children on Parents* (New York: Haworth Press, 1992), 189.

184. See the editorial, 'A Child's Best Interest v. Political Correctness', *National Post*, 26 July 2003. See also M. Wente, 'The Best Interests of the Child?' *Globe and Mail*, 22 February 2003, A15; R. Skelly, 'The Kid Caught in the Middle', *Alberta Report*, 7 December 1993, 25–7.

185. Ben Wicks, *Yesterday They Took My Baby: True Stories of Adoption* (Toronto: Stoddart, 1993), 76–7.

186. Charles Bennett, 'Lives Lived: Robert Arthur King', *Globe and Mail*, 20 August 1998, A20.

187. Leanne Green, 'Foster Care and After', *Canadian Woman Studies* 10, nos 2/3 (1989): 41–3.

188. See Caroline L. Tait, *Fetal Alcohol Syndrome among Aboriginal People in Canada: Review and Analysis of the Intergenerational Links to Residential Schools* (Winnipeg: Aboriginal Healing Foundation, 2003).

189. Christopher Bagley, with Loretta Young and Anne Scully, *International and Transracial Adoptions: A Mental Health Perspective* (Brookfield, VT: Ashgate Publishing, 1993).

190. See the discussion of these terms in chapter 5.

Chapter 7

1. On the ethnocentrism of this view of childhood, see William Myers, 'Considering Child Labour: Changing Terms, Issues and Actors at the International Level', *Childhood* 6, no. 1 (1999): 13–26, and Jim McKechnie and Sandy Hobbs, 'Child Labour: The View from the North', ibid.: 89–100.

2. Laura Briggs, 'Mother, Child, Race, Nation: The Visual Iconography of Rescue and the Politics of Transnational and Transracial Adoption', *Gender and History* 15, no. 2 (2003): 180.

3. Claudia Castaneda, *Figurations: Child, Bodies, Worlds* (Durham: Duke University Press, 2002), 91–2.

4. Ibid., 107.

5. For the United States, see C. Klein, 'Families and Political Obligation: The Discourse of Adoption and the Cold War Commitment to Asia', in *Cold War Constructions: The Political Culture of United States Imperialism, 1945–1966*, ed. Christian G. Appy (Amherst: University of Massachusetts Press, 2000), 181.

6. Canada, House of Commons, *Debates*, 26 May 1954, 6796–7.

7. Ibid., 18 March 1988, 1390.

8. W.E. Washburn, ed., *The Garland Library of North American Indian Captivities*, 11 vols. (New York: Garland Publishing, 1976–83). See also June Namias, *White Captives: Gender and Ethnicity on the American Frontier* (Chapel Hill: University of North Carolina Press, 1993).

9. Ontario, Superintendent of Neglected and Dependent Children, *7th Annual Report* (for the year ending 15 December 1899), 17.

10. Jean Little, *The Belonging Place* (Toronto:Viking, 1997), 121.

11. Susanna Moodie, *Life in the Clearings versus the Bush* (London: R. Bentley, 1853), 161.

12. *Dominion Churchman,* 16 March 1876, 122.

13. Clara M.S. Lowe, *God's Answers: A Record of Miss Annie Macpherson's Work at the Home of Industry, Spitalfields, London, and in Canada* (London: James Nisbet, 1882), 182.

14. 'Importing Waifs', *Saturday Night,* 11 June 1882, 6.

15. 'Editorial Notes', *Evangelical Churchman,* 31 July 1984, 142.

16. Ontario, *1st Report under the Children's Protection Act* (1893), *Sessional Papers of Ontario* (1894), 33.

17. Ontario, Superintendent of Neglected and Dependent Children, *18th Annual Report, Sessional Papers of Ontario* (1911), 115.

18. See Paul Langan, *Hespeler's Hidden Secret: The Coombe Orphanage, 1905–1947* (n.p.: 2000), and for the views of advocates see 'A Dream Realized: The Story of the Coombe Boys' Home at Hespeler, Ontario', *Canadian Churchman,* 6 March 1913, 133.

19. 'Dr. Barnardo's Homes', *Canadian Churchman,* 3 December 1914, 773.

20. G.B. Smart, 'Giving the Children a Chance: How Canada Looks after Her Juvenile Immigrants—A Beneficent System', *Canada: An Illustrated Weekly Journal,* 4 April 1914, 13.

21. 'Canada and Children', *Canadian Churchman,* 16 September 1915, 583.

22. Rosemary R. Gagan, *Sensitive Independence: Canadian Methodist Women Missionaries in Canada and the Orient, 1881–1925* (Montreal and Kingston: McGill-Queen's University Press, 1992), and Ruth C. Brouwer, *New Women for God: Canadian Presbyterian Women and Indian Missions, 1876–1914* (Toronto: University of Toronto Press, 1990).

23. *Dominion Churchman,* 19 April 1883, 252.

24. Karen Balcom, 'The Traffic in Babies: Cross-Border Adoption, Baby-Selling and the Development of Child Welfare Systems in the United States and Canada' (PhD thesis, Rutgers University, 2002). See also the important biography by Patricia T. Rooke and Rudy L. Schnell, *No Bleeding Heart: Charlotte Whitton, a Feminist on the Right* (Vancouver: UBC Press, 1987).

25. On the evolution of international efforts at regulation, see A. Lepp, 'Interrogating Developments in International Human Right Law on Intercountry Adoptions (Work in Progress)' (paper presented to the Canadian Historical Association, Toronto 2002).

26. *Toronto Star,* 17 December 1926; 'Child Adopted by England's Queen', ibid., 8 January 1929.

27. L.E. Lowman, 'Mail-Order Babies', *Chatelaine,* April 1932, 32, 34.

28. On this seemingly sad story, see Mary Kinnear, *Woman of the World: Mary McGeachy and International Cooperation* (Toronto: University of Toronto Press, 2004), 186–208.

29. 'Minni, Sheila Audrey (nee Walker)', *Vancouver Sun,* 21 June 2003, B8.

30. Case No. 258, *Report of the New Brunswick Child Welfare Survey* (Canadian Council on Child Welfare, 1928–9), 38–9.

31. 'Vancouver Children's Aid Society', *Child Welfare News* 5, no. 2 (1929): 34–5.

32. Canada, House of Commons, *Debates,* 23 May 1922, 2144 (Charles A. Stewart).

33. Ibid., 23 May 1922, 2153 (Agnes Macphail).

34. Ibid., 16 June 1922, 3063 (E.J. Garland).
35. Ibid., 7 June 1922, 2634 (H.E. Spencer).
36. Ibid., 13 March 1923, 1099 (C.A. Stewart).
37. Bogue G. Smart, 'Juvenile Immigration', *4th Annual Canadian Conference on Child Welfare: Proceedings and Papers* (Winnipeg: King's Printer, 1923), 193, 197.
38. Percy Roberts, 'Barnardo's Contribution to Ontario', *5th Annual Canadian Conference on Child Welfare* (Ottawa, 1925), 181.
39. Canada, House of Commons, *Debates,* 6 February 1926, 105 (H.C. Hocken).
40. Patrick Dunae, 'Waifs: The Fairbridge Society in British Columbia, 1931–1951', *Histoire sociale/Social History* 21, no. 42 (1988): 224–50.
41. Mrs Plumptre, *5th Annual Canadian Conference on Child Welfare* (Ottawa, 1925), 185.
42. Tom Moore, ibid., 192.
43. Mrs J. Breckernridge McGregor, *'Several Years After': An Analysis of the Histories of a Selected Group of Juvenile Immigrants brought to Canada in 1910, and in 1920, by British Emigration Societies* (Ottawa: Canadian Council on Child Welfare, 1928).
44. *Report of the New Brunswick Child Welfare Survey,* 144.
45. Patrick A. Dunae, 'Gender, Generations and Social Class: The Fairbridge Society and British Child Migration to Canada, 1930–1960', in *Child Welfare and Social Action in the Nineteenth and Twentieth Centuries: International Perspectives,* ed. Jon Lawrence and Pat Starkey (Liverpool: Liverpool University Press, 2001), 92. See also P. Dunae, 'Waifs: The Fairbridge Society in British Columbia, 1931–1951'; G. Sherington and C. Jeffery, *Fairbridge: Empire and Child Migration* (London: Woburn Press, 1988). For the BC social worker who set out to rescue the Fairbridge youngsters, see Anne Margaret Angus, 'Profiles 3: Winona D. Armitage', *Canadian Welfare* 41, no. 5 (1965): 226–31.
46. The numbers are variously estimated. While Dunae, 'Waifs', 224, cites 80,000 up to the 1920s, Gillian Wagner suggested that between 1870 and 1930 Canadian received more than 100,000 home children. Gillian Wagner, *Children of the Empire* (London: Weidenfeld and Nicolson, 1982), xi.
47. Val Ross, 'George Miles', *Globe and Mail,* 14 October 1996, A12.
48. F. Vye, 'Roy Edward Henley', ibid., 28 April 1998, A24.
49. T. Hawthorn, 'Robert (Steve) Brodie', ibid., 23 January 1998, A16.
50. Rev. Dr. Jamie Gripton, 'John T. Lake', ibid., 24 October 2001, A22.
51. Charlotte Whitton, '"No Man's" Child Seeks Justice from the World', *Child and Family Welfare,* September 1936; reprinted by the Canadian Council on Child and Family Welfare (Ottawa: Council House, 1939).
52. Saskatchewan, Child Welfare Division, *Annual Report* (1951–2), 17. See United Nations, Department of Social Affairs, *Study on Adoption of Children: A Study on the Practice and Procedures Related to the Adoption of Children* (New York: United Nations, 1953).
53. New Brunswick, Chief Welfare Officer, *1st Annual Report* (for the fiscal year ending 31 March 1955), 108.
54. See Stephen O'Connor, *Orphan Trains: The Story of Charles Loring Brace and the Children He Saved and Failed* (Boston: Houghton Mifflin, 2001), and Marilyn I. Holt, *Orphan Trains: Placing out in America* (Lincoln: University of Nebraska Press, 1992).

294   *Notes*

55. Newfoundland Provincial Archives, Secretary of the Commission of Government, Files GN38, S6-1-7, Folder 10, 'Child Welfare Act 1944', Copies of Reports of Division of Child Welfare (report for period 1 July to 30 September 1945), 4.

56. Alberta, Child Welfare Branch, the Royal Commission on Child Welfare, *Report* (Edmonton: n.p., 1948), 34.

57. Newfoundland, Division of Child Welfare, Department of Public Health and Welfare, *Annual Report* (1947), 24.

58. BC Social Welfare Branch of the Department of Health and Welfare, *Annual Report* (for the year ending 1949), 47.

59. BC Department of Health and Welfare, Social Welfare Branch, *Annual Report* (for the year ending 31 March 1956), 56.

60. BC Superintendent of Neglected Children, *Annual Report* (for the year ending 31 March 1941), 3.

61. Nova Scotia, Royal Commission on Provincial Development and Rehabilitation, *Report on Public Welfare Services* (Halifax: n.p., 1944), 4: 151.

62. See Karen Balcom, 'Buying Babies and Purchasing Motherhood: The Canada-to-US Black Market in Babies in the 1950s' (paper presented to the Berkshire Conference on the History of Women, June 2005).

63. Charlotte Whitton, *Welfare in Alberta: The Report of a Study* (Edmonton: Douglas Printing, 1947), i, passim.

64. 'Rising Export Trade in Canadian Babies', *Vancouver Sun,* 29 October 1947.

65. See Canada, House of Commons, *Debates,* 24 May 1948, 4289 (Alexander M. Campbell); 31 May 1948, 4552 (Alexander Maxwell Campbell); 26 February 1953, 2416 (J.W. Noseworthy); 19 February 1954, 2245 (Hon. Stuart S. Garson).

66. 'BC Orphans Exported', *Victoria Colonist,* 31 January 1961, 1.

67. H. Weir, 'Keep BC Babies in Canada', *Vancouver Sun,* 7 February 1961.

68. G. Donaldson, 'US Senators Told: Baby Salesmen Busy in Montreal', *Toronto Telegram,* 16 June 1964, 1.

69. New Brunswick, Chief Welfare Officer, *1st Annual Report* (for the fiscal year ending 31 March 1955), 36.

70. W.I. Fletcher, 'For the Record', *Vancouver Sun,* 7 February 1961, 6.

71. Wesley Black quoted in R. Rush, 'Baby Export Story Unfair', *Vancouver Sun,* 15 February 1961, 11.

72. BC Superintendent of Neglected Children, *Annual Report* (for the year ending 31 March 1938), 3.

73. Marion Splane, 'The International Conference of Social Work', in *Concerning Children* (newsletter published by the Child Welfare Division, Canadian Welfare Council) (September 1954), 5–6 (mimeograph).

74. BC Department of Social Welfare, Division of Child Welfare, *Annual Report* (for the year ending 31 March 1960), 42.

75. Manitoba, Department of Health and Social Services, *Annual Report* (1968), 11.

76. M.E. Battel, 'Child Welfare in Saskatchewan, 1952–64' (1965), 39 (mimeograph).

77. Nova Scotia, Family and Child Welfare Division, *6th Annual Report* (1974), 11.

78. Sister Mary Henry, 'Inter-Country Adoption', *Canadian Welfare* 49, no. 2 (1973): 3.

79. Whitton, *Welfare in Alberta,* 99.

80. Ibid., 111.
81. Alberta, Royal Commission on Child Welfare, *Report* (1948), 34–5.
82. Alberta, Department of Public Welfare, Child Welfare Branch, *19th Annual Report* (1962–3), 23.
83. H.S. Coulter, Alberta, Committee on Adoption, *Report,* (Edmonton, 1965), 3: 621–2.
84. M.M. Bowker, *Supplementary Report on Adoption in Alberta* (July 1965), 31–3.
85. Provincial Archives of Alberta, ACC 73.51, Legislative Assembly Sessional Papers etc. Box 24, Alberta Child Welfare Commission Submission to the 'Adoption Study Committee' (folder 896) (February 1968), 11–12.
86. Council for Social Services of the Church of England in Canada, *9th Annual Report* (1924), 27.
87. 'Open Hearts in Schools', *Globe and Mail,* 22 May 1919.
88. 'The Light Within', *Canadian Churchman,* 9 September 1943, 497.
89. Gerald E. Dirks, *Canada's Refugee Policy: Indifference or Opportunism?* (Montreal and Kingston: McGill-Queen's University Press, 1977), 63–77.
90. 'The Protection of the Child Refugee', *Canadian Child and Family Welfare* (hereafter *CCFW*), January 1940, 55.
91. See Frank Chamberlain, 'Save the Children Now, Before It Is Too Late', *Saturday Night,* 18 December 1943, 5.
92. See generally Geoffrey Bilson, *The Guest Children: The Story of the British Child Evacuees Sent to Canada during WWII* (Saskatoon: Fifth House, 1988), and Michael Henderson, *See You After the Duration: The Story of British Evacuees to North America in World War II* (Washington: PublishBritannica, 2004).
93. See S. McCormick, 'Safe from the War', *Chatelaine,* February 194), 5–7, 18, 35, 38; F.E. Smith, 'Good Britons Don't Cry', ibid., February 1942, 14–15, 35–8, and H.B. Cave, 'Someone to Care For', ibid., July 1942, 10–11, 23–4, 26, 30.
94. 'The School Migration', *Saturday Night,* 24 August 1940, 1.
95. See 'Locum Tenens', 'Our Little Guests', *Saturday Night,* 14 December 1940, 10; L. Doyle, 'British Boys Home at "Fettercairn"', ibid., 14 September 1940, 14; M. Karsh, 'An English Private School Carries on in Ottawa', ibid., 23 November 1940, 4; H. Sutherland, 'St. Hilda's College, Yorkshire, Moves to Canada', ibid., 22 February 1941, 5.
96. W.C. Currey, 'Canada Welcomes Britannia's Children', *Saturday Night,* 20 July 1940, n.p.
97. Canada, House of Commons, *Debates,* 3 July 1940, 1297 (F.D. Shaw).
98. Ibid., 21 April 1943, 2420 (M. Coldwell).
99. See the preference of the Honourable T.A. Crerar, Minister of Mines and Resources, ibid., 27 June 1940, 1182.
100. G.H. Tays, 'Twenty Five British Guest Children under Supervision of the Department of Public Welfare in Nova Scotia' (Diploma in Social Work, Maritime School of Social Work, 1949), 45.
101. Alberta, Royal Commission on Child Welfare, *Report* (1948), 36.
102. See the reference in Manitoba Archives, Knowles Home for Boys/Knowles School for Boys, 1907–ca.1950, at http://www.mbarchives.mb.ca/orphanage/ccinstitution.asp?id=21.

103. BC Social Welfare Branch of the Department of Health and Welfare, *Annual Report* (for the year ending 31 March 1947), 26.
104. Irving Abella and Harold Troper, *None Is Too Many: Canada and the Jews of Europe, 1933–1948* (Toronto: Key Porter, 2000).
105. See, for example, D. Wilensky, 'From Juvenile Immigrant to Canadian Citizen', *Proceedings,* 12th Biennial Meeting of the Canadian Conference on Social Work, Vancouver (June 1950), 79–85.
106. Ben W. Lappin, *The Redeemed Children: The Story of the Rescue of War Orphans by the Jewish Community of Canada* (Toronto: University of Toronto Press, 1963), 53–4.
107. Ibid., 75, 73.
108. BC Social Welfare Branch of the Department of Health and Welfare, 'Immigration of Children', *Annual Report* (for the year ending 31 March 1948), 89.
109. BC Social Welfare Branch of the Department of Health and Welfare, *Annual Report* (for the year ended 1949), 47.
110. Wilensky, 'From Juvenile Immigrant to Canadian Citizen', 83.
111. S. Katz, 'The Redeemed Children', *Maclean's,* 10 February 1962, 44.
112. BC Department of Health and Welfare, Social Welfare Branch, *Annual Report* (for the year ending 31 March 1955), 57.
113. Ibid. (for the year ending 31 March 1950), 57.
114. Canada, House of Commons, *Debates,* 14 December 1948, 3533 (Gladys Strum).
115. 'Has Canada a Place for Us?' *Canadian Churchman,* 18 August 1949, 270.
116. 'The Children of Europe', *Concerning Children* 1, no. 4 (1947): 2.
117. Canada, House of Commons, *Debates,* 28 March 1946, 353 (F.S. Zaplitny).
118. Ibid., 22 February 1954, 2327 (J.A. Byrne).
119. R. Taylor, 'Foster Mother to Millions', *Star Weekly,* 27 April 1954, 4.
120. 'Christmas for Orphans Possible through Fund', *Globe and Mail,* 6 December 1956, 9.
121. 'Clear Way for Adoption of Orphans from Hungary', ibid., 15 November 1956, 5.
122. BC Department of Health and Welfare, Social Welfare Branch, *Annual Report* (for the year ending 31 March 1958), 51.
123. 'Today's Children—Abroad. She's 4, Cute—and Doomed', *Toronto Telegram,* 27 July 1964, 54.
124. *Maclean's,* 2 December 1964, 48.
125. Peggy Jennings, with David MacDonald, 'Must These Children Suffer?' *Star Weekly,* 9 July 1960, 16–17, 30.
126. Henry D. Molumphy, *For Common Decency: The History of Foster Parents Plan, 1937–1983* (Warwick, RI: Foster Parents Plan International, 1984), 313.
127. Kirsten Lovelock, 'Intercountry Adoption as a Migratory Practice: A Comparative Analysis of Intercountry Adoption and Immigration Policy and Practice in the United States, Canada and New Zealand in the Post–W.W.II Period', *International Migration Review* 34, no. 3 (2000): 912.
128. 'A Korean Orphan Arrives Home', *Toronto Star,* 23 March 1968, 1. For the United Church missionaries who adopted three children while in Korea, see Tim Bentley, 'Face of the Family Changing' *United Church Observer,* December 1981, 20–1.
129. Lovelock, 'Intercountry Adoption as a Migratory Practice', 920.

130. 'Those Japanese War Babies?' *United Church Observer,* 1 December 1956, 13–15, 26–7. See also 'Keep Out the Poor', ibid., 15 February 1962, 10, and 'Muriel Tonge and Her Abandoned Babies', ibid., 1 September 1963, 25.

131. 'Canada Throws Open Doors to World Refugee Orphans; Will Allow Adoptions, PM States', *Globe and Mail,* 16 July 1960, 1.

132. 'Only 6 Inquire: No Applicants Appear for Refugee Adoptions', ibid., 6 October 1960.

133. I. McNeill, 'The Problem of Adopting a Hong Kong Orphan', *United Church Observer,* 1 December 1969, 30–2, 40

134. Joyce Ireland, 'By Air from Hong Kong', *Canadian Welfare* 39 (July–August 1963): 156.

135. *New Families for Young Canadians: The History and Current Practice of Adoption in British Columbia* (Victoria: Department of Social Welfare, 1967), 8.

136. See Peter Sypnowich, 'Canada Awakens to the Agony of Viet Nam's Maimed Children', *Star Weekly,* 29 April 1967, 2–6.

137. See '2-Year Old Project to Adopt Foreign Child Still Tied in Red Tape', *Globe and Mail,* 29 December 1965, 9, and 'Adopted Son Makes Their Dream Reality', *Toronto Telegram,* 14 April 1965, 28.

138. Val Ross, 'The Young People No One Wanted', *Maclean's,* 27 October 1980, 59.

139. See 'Few Canadians Offer to Take Nigerian Orphans', *Globe and Mail,* 6 November 1968.

140. 'Adoption as an International Problem', *International Child Welfare Review* 3, no. 6 (1949): 236–7.

141. Lovelock, 'Intercountry Adoption as a Migratory Practice', 918.

142. BC Department of Social Services, *Annual Report* (for the year ending 31 March 1970), 26.

143. Lovelock, 'Intercountry Adoption as a Migratory Practice', 922.

144. Ysabel M. Llerena, 'A Comparative/Analytical Study of Social Policies on Adoptions between Alberta, Canada, and Selected Latin American Countries, and Their Implications on International Adoptions' (MA thesis, University of Calgary, 1986), 155.

145. BC Department of Rehabilitation and Social Improvement, *Annual Report* (for the year ending 31 March 1972) and PEI Department of Health and Social Services, Social Services Branch, *Annual Reports, 1984–5, 1985–6, 1986–7, 1987–8, 1988–9.*

146. Newfoundland, Department of Public Welfare, *Annual Report* (1972), 101–2.

147. Newfoundland, Department of Social Services, *Annual Report* (1983), 35.

148. Susan Becker, in conversation with Phyllis Harrison, 'Inter-Country Adoption: Going to Bat for Safeguards', *Canadian Welfare* 48, no. 4 (1972): 4.

149. Sydney Byma, 'Overseas Adoptions Threaten Development of Local Services', *Canadian Welfare* 50, no. 3 (1974): 7–11.

150. Victoria Leach, 'International Adoptions: Risks and Rewards', *Ontario Association of Children's Aid Societies Journal* 21, no. 1 (1978): 15.

151. Llerena, 'A Comparative/Analytical Study of Social Policies', 30.

152. Ibid., 153.

153. Katherine McDade, 'International Adoption in Canada: Public Policy Issues', discus-

sion paper 91.B.1 *Studies in Social Policy* (Ottawa, April 1991), 38, 34.

154. Ibid., 19–23.

155. Lovelock, 'Intercountry Adoption as a Migratory Practice', 940–2.

156. Lepp, 'Interrogating Developments in International Human Right Law', 16, 25. On Conventions see also Sharon Stephens, 'Introduction: Children and the Politics of Culture in "Late Capitalism"', in *Children and the Politics of Culture,* ed. Sharon Stephens (Princeton, NJ: Princeton University Press, 1995), 3–50.

157. See Canada, House of Commons, *Debates,* 14 July 1993, 20756–7 (Shirley Maheu) and 14 July 1993, 20757 (Hon. G. Weiner).

158. Ibid., 3 February 1999, 11383 (Hon. Lucienne Robillard).

159. See Rosaline Frith, 'Citizenship of Canada Act: Strengthening the Value of Our Citizenship', *Canadian Diversity/é Canadienne* 2, no. 1 (2003): 72–4.

160. McDade, 'International Adoption in Canada', 35–6.

161. Alberta, Social Services and Community Health Library, Canada, *Report of the Committee on International Adoptions / Rapport du Comité sur les adoptions internationales* (Ottawa, October 1974) (typescript), Letter from Margot Carr Ribeiro of "Enfants Du Monde/Children of the World".

162. Ibid., 'Families for Children', Pt. Claire, QC, to Monique Perron, Service de Consultation Psychosociale, Quebec (7 March 1974).

163. Ibid., M.J. Ferrari, MD, JMJ Children's Fund of Canada, Ottawa to Mrs Victoria Leach, Adoption Co-ordinator, Ministry of Community and Social Services, Queen's Park, Toronto (29 March 1974).

164. Ibid., Robert K. Ferrie, MD, Irving Copeland, Barrister/Solicitor, and Helke Ferrie, Kuan-Yin Foundation Inc., Burlington, ON, to Mrs Victoria Leach (21 February 1974).

165. Ibid., David B. Knight to Victoria Leach (22 February 1974).

166. 'Burlington Mother Hopes to Bring in 50 More War Orphans', *Globe and Mail,* 1 September 1972.

167. 'Waiting for Notification from High Commission: 2 Women Conflict over Program to Bring Bengali Orphans to Canada', *Globe and Mail,* 6 October 1972.

168. BC Department of Human Resources, Services for People, *Annual Report* (with fiscal addendum 1 April 1974 to 31 March 1975), 50.

169. '1,000 in Toronto Ask for Orphans', *Globe and Mail,* 8 April 1975.

170. 'The Ultimate Humanity', ibid., 5 April 1975, 6.

171. See Canada, House of Commons, *Debates,* 7 April 1975, 4538 (O. Jellinek) and 4588 (D. Roche).

172. For the continuing coverage see 'Way Cleared to Adopt Orphans from Asia', *Globe and Mail,* 28 August 1973; 'Orphan Flights Called Abductions', ibid., 10 April 1975; 'Airlift Plans Are Scrapped', ibid., 10 April 1975; 'Saigon Orphans: Only Future Will Reveal Who's Right', ibid., 11 April 1975.

173. See 'Canadians, Orphans Are Flown from Vietnam', *Globe and Mail,* 5 April 1975 and 'Crashed Jet Had 34 Heading to Canada', ibid., 5 April 1975, 1.

174. Quoted in Lovelock, 'Intercountry Adoption as a Migratory Practice', 924.

175. See the request for federal assistance for Italian orphans by Conservative Flora MacDonald in Canada, House of Commons, *Debates,* 2 December 1980, 5240.

176. See the reports by Human Rights Watch, *Romania's Orphans: A Legacy of Repression* (New York: Human Rights Watch, 1990) and *Abandoned to the State: Cruelty and Neglect in Russian Orphanages* (New York: Human Rights Watch, December 1998).

177. Christine Ward Gailey, 'Race, Class and Gender in Intercountry Adoption in the USA', in *Intercountry Adoption: Developments, Trends and Perspectives,* ed. Peter Selman (London: British Agencies for Adoption and Fostering, 2000), 302.

178. Lovelock, 'Intercountry Adoption as a Migratory Practice', 932.

179. Sharon Marcovitch and Laura Cesaroni, 'Romanian Adoption: Parents' Dreams, Nightmares, and Realities', *Child Welfare* 74, no. 5 (1995): 993–8.

180. For suggestions of this troubling story see 'Deal Limits Adoptions of Romanian Orphans: Canadians Must Send Applications through Government Authorities', *Globe and Mail,* 28 February 1992; 'New Hope for Ceausescu's Littlest Victims: A New Law Redefines the Abandoned Child and Opens the Door to more International Adoptions', ibid., 31 July 1993; 'Adopted Romanians Lagging: Study Blames Early Deprivation,' ibid., 24 May 1996; 'A Rescue Mission's Troubled Aftermath: For Romania's Orphans, Life in Canada Will Heal the Body. The Mind Is Another Matter', ibid., 5 August 1998; 'Problems Haunt Romanian Babies Eight Years after Adoption Frenzy', ibid., 5 August 1998), A04. See also the influential study by Elinor W. Ames, 'The Development of Romanian Orphanage Children Adopted to Canada' (Surrey, BC: Adoptive Parents Association of British Columbia, January 1997).

181. See letters from Joyce S. Cohen, social work scholar, and Jennifer Smart, editor of the *Post-adoption Helper Magazine,* in the *Globe and Mail,* 12 August 1998, A17.

182. 'Culture's Not the Only Shock: Why It takes Time for a Russian Orphan to Leave the Past Behind', *Globe and Mail,* 16 September 1998, A02.

183. P. Clough, 'Perilous Journey of Adoptive Parents: Many BC Parents Who Want to Adopt Are Forced to Look Abroad', *Vancouver Province,* 10 March 2002.

184. M. Philip, 'And Baby Makes One', *Globe and Mail,* 19 April 2003. For outcomes that similarly left unhappy Canadians, see also Colin Thomas, 'Babies without Borders', *Georgia Straight,* 22–9 January 2004, 17. On corruption see A.M. Owens, 'Canadian Charged in Baby-Selling Scheme: Parents Told Healthy Infants Were Dead', *National Post,* available at http://www.theadoptionguide.com?News/ Canada-babyselling.html 02/12/02 (accessed 2 December 2002).

185. See 'Adoption from Hell: Couple's Ordeal in Adopting Peruvian Twins', *Chatelaine,* March 1994, 83, 85, and S. Ferguson with K. Borel, 'A New Community Comes of Age', *Maclean's,* 24 February 2003, 48. See also Human Rights Watch, *Death by Default: A Policy of Fatal Neglect in China's Orphanages* (New York: Human Rights Watch, 1996).

186. 'Paying the Price to Have a Child' and 'Canadians Adopting Chinese Babies', *Globe and Mail,* 21 March 1991, A1, A17.

187. 'Canadian Bundles of Joy', *Globe and Mail,* 13 April 1999.

188. 'Single Women Who Adopted Children Don't Regret the Decision', *Globe and Mail,* 27 April 1978, T07.

189. Llerena, 'A Comparative/Analytical Study of Social Policies', 163.

190. '2 Orphans Get Names and Home', *Vancouver Sun,* 24 December 1985, X2.

191. Darlene Ryan, *A Mother's Adoption Journey* (Toronto: Second Story Press, 2001), 40, 55, 133. On such discrimination and feminist sympathies see Karin Evans, *The Lost Daughters of China: Abandoned Girls, Their Journey to America, and the Search for a Missing Past* (New York: Jeremy P. Tarcher/Putnam, 2000), and K.J. Hermann and B. Kasper, 'International Adoption: The Exploitation of Women and Children', *Affilia: Journal of Women and Social Work* 7 (1992), 45–58.

192. Steve Whan, 'The Story behind the Stories', *Rice Paper* 8, no. 4 (2003): 36–7.

193. See Thomas, 'Babies without Borders', 17–18, 22.

194. 'Rwandan Factions Agree on Ceasefire', *Globe and Mail*, 15 June 1994, A02.

195. See 'Two Children Are to Be Deported after 3 Year Immigration Battle', *Globe and Mail*, 30 August 1977.

196. Thomas, 'Babies without Borders', 22.

197. 'Kidneys Sold by Poor for Transplants, MD Says', *Globe and Mail*, 22 August 1989, A1, A15.

198. His cause has been taken up the Adoption Council of Canada. See the appeal to the Minister of Citizenship and Immigration, 21 July 2003, and the outline of the case provided in http://www.adoption.ca/news/030721perez.htm (accessed 29 January 2005). See also 'Judge Allows Hearing on Orphan's Bid for Right to See Sister', *Globe and Mail*, 3 January 1998.

199. 'BC Couple Caught in Adoption Limbo: Nepalese Police Stymie Process', *Globe and Mail*, 3 January 1998.

200. The film was shown on CBC-TV and CBC Newsworld on 14 and 16 February 2005. See also Olivia Ward, 'Return to Sender: An Orphan's Tale', *Toronto Star* www.thestar.com (accessed 12 February 2005). Since then, Alexandra Austin has undertaken to sue her adopters.

201. See the musings of the House of Commons Standing Committee on Labour, Employment and Immigration in 1985 in McDade, 'International Adoption in Canada', 1.

202. Tom Kent, '"In the National Interest": A Social Policy Agenda for a New Century— Restore Cooperative Federalism, Modernize Medicare, Put Children First', *Policy Options*, August 2004: 24–9.

203. BC Ministry of Human Resources, Services for People, *Annual Report* (1976), 49.

204. *Re Khan* (1979), 92 D.L.R. 287.

205. *Re Government of Punjab*, India, Birth Registration No. 77 (1978), 9 B.C.L.R. 184 (S.C.) in *Adoption Law in Canada: Practice and Procedure*, ed. W. Douglas Phillips, Ruth J. Raphael, Douglas J. Manning, and Julia A. Turnbull (Toronto: Carswell Thomson Professional Publishing, 1995), 1–8.

206. *Re L. (H.K.)* (1988), 63 Alta. L.R. (2d) 36, [1989] 1 W.W.R. 556 (Q.B.), in ibid., 1–3.

207. A. Westhues and J.C. Cohen, *Intercountry Adoption in Canada* (Ottawa: Human Resources Development Canada, 1994).

208. Thomas, 'Babies without Borders', 22.

209. John Bowen, *A Canadian Guide to International Adoptions: How to Find, Adopt, and Bring Home Your Child* (North Vancouver: Self-Counsel Press, 1992), xvii, 8–9.

210. Margaret Lord, *Final Report to the Minister of Social Services of the Panel to Review Adoption Legislation in British Columbia* (Victoria: Ministry of Social Services, July

1994), 93. On just this point see Ann Anagnost, 'Scenes of Misrecognition: Maternal Citizenship in the Age of Transnational Adoption', *Positions* 8, no. 2 (2000): 401.

211. Zoltan Horvath, 'Re Adoption Is Forever, Barbara Kay', *National Post,* 8 April 2005.

212. Anagnost, 'Scenes of Misrecognition', 389–421.

213. Chantal Saclier, 'In the Best Interests of the Child?' in *Intercountry Adoption: Developments, Trends and Perspectives,* ed. Selman Peter (London: British Agencies for Adoption and Fostering, 2000), 57.

214. Derek Kirton, 'Intercountry Adoption in the UK: Towards an Ethical Foreign Policy?' in ibid., 82, 78.

215. See S. Marcelo, 'The Other Side of Transracial Adoption', *Rice Paper* 8, no. 4 (2003): 34–5.

216. Lovelock, 'Intercountry Adoption as a Migratory Practice', 910.

217. See McDade, 'International Adoption in Canada', 1 for its description of policy papers and reports on immigration that make just this point.

218. Lovelock, 'Intercountry Adoption as a Migratory Practice', 942.

Chapter 8

1. Lucy Maud Montgomery, *Anne of the Island* (London, ON: Gatefold Books, 1982), ch. 21, 'Roses of Yesterday'.

2. Lee Maracle, *Sojourners and Sundogs: First Nations Fiction* (Vancouver: Press Gang Publishers, 1999), 114.

3. Ontario, Department of Neglected and Dependent Children, *Annual Report* (for the year ending 15 December 1899), 20–2.

4. Ibid., 40.

5. Annie Shepherd Swan, *Mrs. Keith Hamilton, M.B.: More Experiences of Elizabeth Glen* (Toronto: W. Briggs; London: Hutchinson & Co., 1897), 258.

6. 'Tighten Up Rules of Adoption, Mrs Smith Urges House', *Victoria Times,* 24 November 1926.

7. Robert E. Mills, 'The Placing of Children in Families', *Canadian Child and Family Welfare* (hereafter *CCFW*) 14, no. 1 (July 1938): 50.

8. Robert E. Mills, 'The Child and the Institution', *CCFW* 14, no. 3 (1939): 45.

9. Public Archives of Alberta (hereafter PAA), Papers of Marjorie Montgomery Bowker, Access 93.45/14, 'Talk to Guidance Clinic Staff . . . adoptions', vol. 2 of Collected Speeches, 16 February 1966, 382.

10. Joy Parr, *Labouring Children: British Immigrant Apprentices to Canada, 1869–1924* (Toronto: University of Toronto Press, 1994), 75.

11. Marjory Harper, 'Cossar's Colonists: Juvenile Migration to New Brunswick in the 1920s', *Acadiensis* 28, no. 1 (1998): 64.

12. Mrs McGregor J. Breckenridge, *Several Years After: An Analysis of the Histories of a Selected Group of Juvenile Immigrants brought to Canada in 1910, and in 1920, by British Emigration Societies* (Ottawa: Canadian Council on Child Welfare, 1928), 21–3.

13. Miss Grace A. Towers, 'Problems in Institutional Care', *CCFW* 8, no. 2 (1932): 55.

14. New Brunswick, Department of Health and Social Services, Social Services Branch, Report of the Case of Westmorland County, *Annual Report* (for the fiscal year ending 31 March 1957), 79.

15. Nova Scotia, Department of Public Welfare, Children's Aid Society of Cape Breton, *Annual Report* (for the fiscal year ending 31 March 1954), 32.
16. Breckenridge, *Several Years After*, 22–3.
17. Quoted in Parr, *Labouring Children*, 75.
18. Dolly Griffin in Gail Helena Corbett, *Barnardo Children in Canada* (Peterborough, ON: Woodland Publishing, 1981), 85.
19. BC Superintendent of Neglected Children, *Annual Report* (for the year ending 31 March 1939), 2.
20. Children's Aid Society of Vancouver, *Staff Bulletin* 4, no. 27 (19 May 1970): 4 (mimeograph).
21. June Rose, *For the Sake of the Children: Inside Dr. Barnardo's. 120 Years of Caring for Children* (London: Hodder & Stoughton, 1987), 96.
22. Parr, *Labouring Children*, 75, and 'Child Migrant Index', in Barnardo's Giving Children back their Future website. Available at http://www.barnardos.org.uk/whatwedo/aftercare/migrant.html (accessed 24 November 2002).
23. Ontario, Superintendent of Neglected Children, *Annual Report* (1906), 21, 49–50.
24. Ibid. (1902), 50.
25. Ibid. (1901), 14.
26. Susan Becker, 'Inter-Country Adoption: Going to Bat for Safeguards' [Interview with Phyllis Harrison] *Canadian Welfare* 48, no. 4 (1972): 4.
27. Ibid. (1906), 53.
28. Helen Colton, 'If a Child Is Adopted', *Star Weekly*, 14 June 1952, 7.
29. Minda M. Posen, *A Study of Adopted Children* (MSW thesis, University of Toronto, 1948), 39.
30. Ibid., 42.
31. Ibid., 56.
32. Ibid., 80.
33. Adrienne MacLeod, 'Telling a Child About His Adoption', *Canadian Welfare* 35, no. 3 (1959): 103.
34. Juanita Chambers, 'The Triumph of Adoption', ibid. 35, no. 3 (1959): 105.
35. Anne Margaret Angus, 'Profiles 3: Winona D. Armitage', ibid. 41, no. 5 (1965): 229.
36. Charlene E. Miall and Karen March, 'Social Support for Adoption in Canada: Preliminary Findings of a Canada-wide Survey' (2000), available at http://www.adoptioninstitute.org/survey_intro.html (accessed 24 December 2005).
37. Anonymous, 'We Found the Key to Happy Adoption', *Star Weekly*, 10 November 1962, 14.
38. Mrs M.J.W. (Nova Scotia) and 'Adopted Mother' (Saskatchewan), letters to the editor, ibid., 2 July 1966, 31.
39. 'I Gave My Baby Away, As Told to Marie LaCoste', ibid., 21 May 1966, 24.
40. Alberta, Committee on Adoption, *Hearings* (Calgary, 1965), 3: 783–6.
41. Ibid., 787.
42. BC Department of Rehabilitation and Social Improvement, *Annual Report* (for the year ending 31 March 1971), 31.
43. BC Department of Human Resources, *Annual Report* (with fiscal addendum 1 April 1974 to 31 March 1975), 53.

44. Clare Marcus, *Adopted? A Canadian Guide for Adopted Adults in Search of Their Origins* (Vancouver: International Self-Counsel Press, 1979), 77.

45. June Callwood, 'Adoption Not All Hearts and Flowers', *Chatelaine,* June 1976, 110.

46. Marvin Bernstein and Mary Allan, 'Submission to the Standing Committee on General Government Regarding Bill 77: Adoption Disclosure Amendment Act, 2001', *Ontario Association of Children's Aid Societies Journal* 4, no. 2 (2001): 12–20.

47. Nico Trocmé, 'Child Welfare Services', in *The State of the Child in Ontario,* ed. Richard Barnhorst and Laura C. Johnson (Toronto: Oxford University Press, 1991), 79.

48. Saskatchewan Department of Social Services, *Annual Report* (1977–8), 28.

49. *Kelly v. Superintendent of Child Welfare* (1980), 23 B.C.L.R. 299 (S.C.), in *Adoption Law in Canada: Practice and Procedure,* ed. Douglas W. Phillips, Ruth J. Raphael, Douglas J. Manning, Julia A. Turnbull (Toronto: Carswell Thomson Professional Publishing, 1995), 9–4.

50. *Re Adoption of A. (B.)* (1980), 17 R.F.L. (2d) 140 (Man. Co. Ct.), in ibid., 9–7. For another case, see *Ferguson v. Director of Child Welfare of Ontario* (1983), 40 O.R. (2d) 294, 142 D.L.R. (3d) 609 (Co. Ct.), ibid. 9–14 and 9–15.

51. *Tyler v. Ontario District Court,* [1986]1 R.F.L. (3d) 139 (Ont. Dist. Ct.), in ibid., 9–15.

52. *Phelps v. Director of Child and Family Services (Manitoba)* (1987), 51 Man. R. (2d) 64 (Q.B.), in ibid., 9–6 and 9–7.

53. *Ross v. Prince Edward Island (Registrar of the Supreme Court, Family Division)* (1985), 56 Nfld. & P.E.I.R. 248 (P.E.I.S.C.), in ibid., 8–58 and 8–59.

54. Ralph Garber, *Disclosure of Adoption Information,* Report of the Special Commissioner to the Honourable John Sweeney, Minister of Community and Social Services, Ontario (November 1985), 4.

55. Penelope A. Lithgow, 'The Adoption Disclosure Registry: The First Year', *Ontario Association of Children's Aid Societies Journal* 23 (September 1980): 2.

56. Newfoundland, Department of Social Services, *Annual Report* (1984–5), 27.

57. Nova Scotia, *Social Services in Nova Scotia* (1 November 1984), 25.

58. PEI, Department of Health and Social Services, Social Services Branch, Child and Family Services Division, *Annual Report* (1989–90), 20.

59. Ibid., (1997–8), 23.

60. Joan Marshall, *How to Search in Canada: Resources for Adoptees, Birth Parents and Relatives When Accessing Information to Reunite Families Separated by Adoption* (Nepean, ON: SearchLine Publication, 1989), 9.

61. Karen March, 'Perception of Adoption as Social Stigma: Motivation for Search and Reunion', *Journal of Marriage and the Family* 57 (August 1995): 654.

62. See Jean M. Paton, *The Adopted Break Silence* (Philadelphia: Life History Study Center, 1954).

63. See Carole Gault, 'Flesh of the Flesh: Adoptees in Search of Their Natural Parents', *Maclean's,* 28 June 1971, 41.

64. Clare Marcus, *Who Is My Mother? Birth Parents, Adoptive Parents and Adoptees Talk about Living with Adoption and the Search for Lost Family* (Toronto: Macmillan, 1981), 2.

65. Ibid., 15. See also Gault, 'Flesh of the Flesh', 41.

66. Clare Marcus, *Adopted?*, 10.
67. See Robert Hartlen, *Butterbox Survivors: Life after the Ideal Maternity Home* (Halifax: Nimbus, 1999) for a good range of positive and negative first-person responses to adoption and relinquishment.
68. See Charlene E. Miall, 'The Stigma of Adoptive Parent Status: Perceptions of Community Attitudes toward Adoption and the Experience of Informal Social Sanction', *Family Relations* 36, no. 1 (1987): 35.
69. Nancy Verrier, *The Primal Wound: Understanding the Adopted Child* (Baltimore: Gateway Press, 1993). For a passionate scholarly discussion by one adoptee of the dangers of biological essentialism, see Katarina Wegar, *Adoption, Identity, and Kinship: The Debate over Sealed Birth Records* (New Haven, CT: Yale University Press, 1997).
70. Audrey Marshall and Margaret McDonald, *Many Sided Triangle: Adoption in Australia* (Carlton South, Victoria: Melbourne University Press, 2001), 217.
71. Michelle McColm, *Adoption Reunions: A Book for Adoptees, Birth Parents and Adoptive Families* (Toronto: Second Story Press, 1993), 11–12.
72. See the discussion of the career of medical researcher Madge Thurlow Macklin in the 1920s and 1930s in Angus McLaren, *Our Own Master Race: Eugenics in Canada, 1885–1945* (Toronto: McClelland and Stewart, 1990), especially ch. 7. At the end of the twentieth century, J. Philippe Rushton, author of *Race, Evolution and Behavior: A Life History Perspective* (New Brunswick, NJ: Transaction Publishers, 1995) and member of University of Western Ontario's psychology department, was a leading exponent of scientific racism.
73. McColm, *Adoption Reunions*, 14. For another adoptee who felt a permanent 'scar', see K. Smithen, 'Adoption Series Reminds Us That Secrecy Is Destructive', Letter to the Editor, *Toronto Star*, 3 October 2001, A23.
74. McColm, *Adoption Reunions*, 69.
75. Ibid., 87.
76. Ibid., 79.
77. Ibid., 248–9.
78. Ibid., 253.
79. Madelene Allen, *Reunion: The Search for My Birth Family* (Toronto: Stoddart, 1992), vii.
80. Ibid., 5, 7–8.
81. Ibid., 13, 15, 17.
82. Ibid., 171, 174–5, 177.
83. Marie Klassen, with director Beverly Shaffer, *To My Birthmother* (National Film Board, 2002).
84. Rick Ouston, *Finding Family: A Journalist's Search for the Mother Who Left Him in an Orphanage at Birth* (Vancouver: New Star, 1994).
85. Ibid., 5, 14, 81.
86. Marcus, *Who Is My Mother?*, 92.
87. Karen March, *The Stranger Who Bore Me* (Toronto: University of Toronto Press, 1995), 43.
88. Ibid., xi.
89. Marcus, *Who Is My Mother?*, 162–3.

90. March, *The Stranger Who Bore Me*, 133.

91. See the memories of the 'first family' described by one man in Adopted Foster Child, 'Looking Back 32 Years', *Ontario Association of Children's Aid Societies Journal* (March 1972), 5–7. Reprinted from the *Cornwall Standard-Freeholder*.

92. B. Hitchcock, 'My Real Mother', *Chatelaine*, May 2002, 110–11, 115.

93. Paul Sachdev, *Unlocking the Adoption Files* (Lexington, MA: Lexington Books, 1989), 3–5, and Karen March, 'The Dilemma of Adoption Reunion: Establishing Open Communication between Adoptees and Their Birth Mothers', *Family Relations* 46 (1997): 100.

94. See March, 'The Dilemma of Adoption Reunion', 1–7.

95. Sachdev, *Unlocking the Adoption Files*, 10.

96. Penelope A. Lithgow, 'The Adoption Disclosure Registry: The First Year,' *Ontario Association of Children's Aid Societies Journal* 23 (September 1980): 2.

97. Mary Smith, pseudonym, 'A Young Pregnant Girl Tells Her Story', *Canadian Nurse*, October 1975, 35.

98. Anne Petrie, *Gone to an Aunt's: Remembering Canada's Homes for Unwed Mothers* (Toronto: McClelland and Stewart, 1995).

99. Quoted in Ben Wicks, *Yesterday They Took My Baby: True Stories of Adoption* (Toronto: Stoddart, 1993), 27.

100. Lacy Westin, 'Putting the Pieces Together: The Natural Mother Experience of Adoption Reunion' (Psychology Honours Thesis, University of Calgary, 2004), 10, 14.

101. Miall, 'The Stigma of Adoptive Parent Status', 35. See also her 'The Social Construction of Adoption: Clinical and Community Perspectives', *Family Relations* 45, no. 3 (1996): 312.

102. Barbara Melosh, *Strangers and Kin: The American Way of Adoption* (Cambridge: Harvard University Press, 2002), 255–7.

103. Hartlen, *Butterbox Survivors*, 14.

104. Wicks, *Yesterday They Took My Baby*, 27, 31, 10.

105. Ibid., 111.

106. Ibid., 102.

107. On the similar situation in Australia see Marshall and McDonald, *Many Sided Triangle*, 14.

108. Richard Sullivan and David Groden, *Report on the Evaluation of the Adoption Reunion Registry* (Vancouver: UBC School of Social Work, June 1995), n.p.

109. Fergus Colm O'Donnell, 'The Four-Sided Triangle: A Comparative Study of the Confidentiality of Adoption Records,' *University of Western Ontario Law Review* 21, no. 1 (1983): 135; David Rodenhiser, 'Knowing One's Origins a Right: Hamm Government Has Failed Nova Scotia's Adoptees', available at http://www.canada.com (accessed 2 December 2002).

110. See http://www.geocities.com/pgpg_ca/ (accessed 19 February 2005).

111. Sachdev, *Unlocking the Adoption Files*, 26.

112. Mary Martin Mason, *Out of the Shadows: Birth Fathers' Stories* (Edina, MN: O.J. Howard Publishing, 1995).

113. See *Z. (J.N.) v. D. (J.)* (1994), 98 B.C.L.R. (2d) 237 (S.C.), in Phillips et al., *Adoption*

Law in Canada, 3–14; *Family & Children's Services of Kings (County) v. C. (T.G.S.)* (1985), 70 N.S.R. (2d) 213, 166 A.P.R. 213 (C.A.), in ibid., 3–74; *Bajric v. Alibegic* (1980), 23 B.C.L.R. 36 (S.C.) in ibid., 4–7 and 4–8; *Hobbs (Buck) v. Coradazzo* (1984), 54 B.C.L. R. 303 (C.A.), in ibid., 4–8; *S. (J.W.) v. M. (N.C.)* (1993), 10 Alta. L.R. (3d) 395 (Q.B.), affirmed (1993), 12 Alta. L.R. (3d) 379 (*sub nom. D. (H.A.) v. M. (N.C.)*, 55 W.A.C. 200 (C.A.), leave to appeal to S.C.C. refused (1994), 1 R.F.L. (4th) 60 (note), 15 Alta. L.R. (3d) lii (note) (S.C.C.), in ibid.: 4-84-85 4-84 and 4-85. On similar developments in Australia see Marshall and McDonald, *Many Sided Triangle*, ch. 4 and p. 87.

114. Lynn Kettler Penrod, 'Adoption in Canada' (Master of Laws thesis, University of Alberta, 1986), 258.

115. Barrie Clark, *My Search for Catherine Anne: One Man's Story of an Adoption Reunion* (Toronto: Lorimer, 1989).

116. R. Shore, 'The First Supper', *Vancouver Sun,* 27 October 2003, C1, C3.

117. Garber, *Disclosure of Adoption Information*, 3.

118. P.S. Stevenson, 'An Evaluation of Adoption Reunions in British Columbia', *Social Worker / Le Travailleur Social* 44 (1976): 9.

119. Ellen T. Libman and Gregory P. Lubimiv, 'Adoption Disclosure', in *Families: Canada,* ed. Benjamin Schlesinger (Toronto: McGraw-Hill Ryerson, 1979), 21.

120. Cited from J. Callwood, 'Adopted People May Never Know', *Globe and Mail,* 3 May 1985, 13, in Penrod, *Adoption in Canada*, 226.

121. Libman and Lubimiv, 'Adoption Disclosure', 20.

122. Sachdev, *Unlocking the Adoption Files*, 56. Lou Stoneman, Jan Thompson, Joan Webber, 'Adoption Reunion: A Perspective', *Ontario Association of Children's Aid Societies Journal* 24 (December 1982), 10. See also Garber, *Disclosure of Adoption Information*, 18.

123. Libman and Lubimiv, 'Adoption Disclosure', 9–25.

124. Sullivan and Groden, *Report on the Evaluation of the Adoption Reunion Registry*, n.p.

125. Miall and March, 'Social Support for Adoption in Canada'.

126. Marshall and McDonald, *Many Sided Triangle*, 9.

127. Melosh, *Strangers and Kin*, 252.

128. Stevenson, 'An Evaluation of Adoption Reunions', 9–10.

129. Joan Webber, 'Adult Adoptees Search for Birth Parents', *Ontario Association of Children's Aid Societies Journal,* January–February 1979, 30–1.

130. Jan Thompson, 'Adoption Today: Viable or Vulnerable?' ibid. , April 1979, 7.

131. March, 'Perception of Adoption as Social Stigma', 659.

132. C. Gladwell, 'An Adoptee's Search', *United Church Observer,* November 1987, 6.

133. Frank Maidman, 'Repatriation: Guidelines for Service' quoted in Aboriginal Healing and Wellness Strategy Research Project: Repatriation of Aboriginal Families— Issues, Models, and a Workplan Issues, *Final Report,* prepared by Native Child and Family Services of Toronto, Stevenato and Associates, Janet Budgell (n.p., March 1999), 8.

134. See Christopher Bagley, with Loretta Young and Anne Scully, *International and Transracial Adoptions: A Mental Health Perspective* (Aldershot, UK, and Brookfield, VT: Avebury, 1993), 421.

135. Melosh, *Strangers and Kin*, 256.

136. D. Jones, 'Canada's Real Adoption Crisis', *Chatelaine*, May 1998, 44.

137. Marie Adams, *Our Son, a Stranger: Adoption Breakdown and Its Effects on Parents* (Montreal and Kingston: McGill-Queen's University Press, 2002), 181.

138. See, for example, the cases of Metis Jonathan Savan and André Chamberlain in Wicks, *Yesterday They Took My Baby*, 76–7, 126.

139. Anne-Marie Ambert, *The Effect of Children on Parents* (New York: Haworth Press, 1992), 189.

140. For a seeming example of religious certainty, see Kim Westad, *The God-Sent Child: The Bitter Adoption of Baby David* (Toronto: Viking, 1994).

141. BC Royal Commission on Family and Children's Law, *5th Report* (March 1975), Part 7, Adoption, 76–9 and passim.

142. Garber, *Disclosure of Adoption Information*, 62.

143. Margaret Lord, *Final Report of the B.C. Panel to Review Adoption Legislation to the Minister of Social Services* (Victoria: BC Ministry of Social Services, July 1994), 10.

144. Ibid., 63, 67–8, 73, 86, 88

145. Ibid., 89–90.

146. See also the case of a teen foster child who resisted efforts by the BC Sto:lo Nation to return her to her birth family and the community. Cori Howard, 'Stealing Home', *Vancouver Magazine,* October 2003, 60–6.

147. Royal Commission on Aboriginal Peoples, *Report*, vol. 3, *Gathering Strength* (Ottawa: Ministry of Supply and Services, 1996), and Rosemary Kuptana, *No More Secrets: Acknowledging the Problem of Child Sexual Abuse in Inuit Communities—The First Step towards Healing* (Ottawa: Pauktuutit, 1991).

148. Westad, *The God-Sent Child*, 466.

149. Anne McGillivray, 'Transracial Adoption and the Status Indian Child', *CJFL* 4 (1985): 437–67.

150. Diane Riggs, 'Manitoba Repatriation Program Connects First Nations Adoptees with Their Heritage', *Adoptalk Sampler* (n.p.: North American Council on Adoptable Children, 2003), 6–7.

151. See R.T. Dumont, 'Repatriation of Children Placed Transracially: A Discussion Paper' (Edmonton, Alberta: Amicus Populi Consulting Ltd. (September 1987), iii–iv.

152. Ibid., 44–5.

153. Aboriginal Healing and Wellness Strategy Research Project, *Final Report*, 51.

154. Ibid., 9.

155. Ibid., 40.

156. A Dr Blue, not further identified, in Dumont, 'Repatriation of Children Placed Transracially', 17–18.

157. Aboriginal Healing and Wellness Strategy Research Project, *Final Report*.

158. Ibid., 76.

159. See ibid., 5–6.

160. On this lack of interest in women's concerns, see ibid., 82.

161. Ibid., 53.

162. Ibid.

163. Diane Riggs, 'Manitoba Repatriation Program Connects First Nations Adoptees',

Adoptalk Sampler, 7.

164. For another case of a Sto:lo girl in the BC interior, see Howard, 'Stealing Home'.

165. Heather Whiteford, 'Special Needs Adoption: Perspectives on Policy and Practice' (MSW thesis, University of British Columbia, 1988), 136.

166. S. McClelland, 'Who's My Birth Father?' *Maclean's,* 20 May 2002, see http.//www.macleans.ca/topstories/article.jsp?content=966662# (accessed 24 December 2005).

167. See Gail Aitken, 'Changing Adoption Policy and Practice to Deal with Children in Limbo', *Child Welfare* 74, no. 3 (1995): 679–94.

168. For this extraordinary story, see anonymous, 'Open Adoption' and 'What's in a Name?' *Ontario Association of Children's Aid Societies Journal* 32, no. 3 (March 1988): 2–8.

169. *From We to Just Me: A Birth Mother's Journey* (Winnipeg: Freedom to Be Me Seminars, 1990).

170. Judith Wine, *The Canadian Adoption Guide: A Family at Last* (Toronto: McGraw-Hill Ryerson, 1995), 14–15.

171. Sandy Bexon, *Family: An Open Adoption Adventure* (Calgary and Edmonton: Adoption Options, 1999), 7.

172. L. Priest, 'Special Delivery', *Globe and Mail,* 31 August 2002, F1, F6.

173. BC Panel to Review Adoption Legislation, *Final Report* (July 1994), 42.

174. Shirley Senoff, 'Open Adoptions in Ontario and the Need for Legislative Reform', *CJFL* 15, no. 1 (1998): 202.

175. *Statutes of Manitoba, 1997,* c. 47, p. 528.

176. Judith S. Modell, *Kinship with Strangers: Adoption and Interpretations of Kinship in American Culture* (Berkeley: University of California Press, 1994), 238.

177. H. David Kirk, *Shared Fate: A Theory and Method of Adoptive Relationships* (Port Angeles, WA; Brentwood Bay, BC: Ben-Simon Publications 1984), 289.

178. Adoption Act, *Statutes of British Columbia,* July 1995, 564.

179. 'Open Adoption Is the Wrong Option', *National Post,* 1 February 2003.

180. Melosh, *Strangers and Kin,* 289

181. See the overall assessment in Anne Marie Ambert, 'The Negative Social Consequences of Adoptions: Its Effects on Children and Parents' (April 2003). Available at http://www.arts.yorku.ca/soci/ambert/writings/pdf/ADOPTION.pdf

182. See Garber, *Disclosure of Adoption Information,* for its recognition that 'safeguards sought now in the use and disclosure of surrogate or artificial reproduction are similar if not identical to the safeguards and secrecy visited upon the birth parents and adoptive parents of the "illegitimate" child of earlier decades' (10).

Conclusion

1. Eva Mackey, *The House of Difference: Cultural Politics and National Identity in Canada* (Toronto: University of Toronto Press, 2002).

2. Himani Bannerji, *The Dark Side of Nation: Essays on Multiculturalism, Nationalism and Gender* (Toronto: Canadian Scholars' Press, 2000).

3. Peter H. Schuck, *Citizens, Strangers, and In-Betweens: Essays on Immigration and Citizenship* (Boulder, CO: Westview Press, 1998), 227–8.

4. See Neil Bissoondath, *Selling Illusions: The Cult of Multiculturalism in Canada* (Toronto: Penguin Books, 1994; rev. 2002).

5. Canada, House of Commons, 'Canadian Citizenship: A Sense of Belonging', *Report of the Standing Committee on Citizenship and Immigration* (June 1994), 15.

6. L.M.G. Clark, 'Life Style and Interracial Adoption: A Personal Perspective', in *Black Presence in Multi-Ethnic Canada,* ed. Vincet D'Oyley (Vancouver: Centre for the Study of Curriculum and Instruction, University of British Columbia, 1982). See the similar aspirations of the president of Ottawa's Open Door Society, David B. Knight, 'Transracial Adoption', *Journal of the Children's Aid Societies of Ontario* (February 1974): 5–8.

7. Matt James, 'Do Campaigns for Historical Redress Help Erode the Canadian Welfare State', in *Is Multiculturalism Bad for the Welfare State?* ed, Keith Banting and Will Kymlicka (Toronto: Oxford University Press, 2006). Many thanks to the author for providing me with a draft of this chapter, which helped me think about this connection.

8. Even as I finished this manuscript, the *Globe and Mail* and the *Vancouver Sun* provided sensationalized accounts of the death of children in 'kith and kin' care. See Miro Cernetig, 'Why Did Sherry Charlie Die?' *Vancouver Sun,* 23 September 2005, A1, A2, and Christie Blatchford, 'Judge Halts Trial until Aid Files Are Found', *Globe and Mail,* 21 September 2005, A14. For other reminders of families as unsafe spaces for children, see Sylvia Fraser, *My Father's House: A Memoir of Incest and of Healing* (Toronto: Doubleday Canada, 1987); Queer Press Collective, eds., *Loving in Fear: An Anthology of Lesbian and Gay Survivors of Childhood Sexual Abuse* (Toronto: Queer Press, 1991); Charlotte Vale Allen, *Daddy's Girl* (Toronto: McClelland and Stewart, 1980), and Rosemary Kuptana, *No More Secrets: Acknowledging the Problem of Child Sexual Abuse in Inuit Communities: The First Step Towards Healing* (Ottawa: Pauktuutit, 1991). See also, for the United States, the powerful reminder that 'ideology easily obscured the fact that family preservation was a risky venture for many children' in LeRoy Ashby, *Endangered Children: Dependency, Neglect, and Abuse in American History* (New York: Prentice Hall International, 1997), 181.

9. Marianne Novy, 'Introduction: Imagining Adoption,' in *Imagining Adoption: Essays on Literature and Culture,* ed. Marianne Novy (Ann Arbor: University of Michigan Press, 2001):, 11.

10. See many of the accounts by survivors of Nova Scotia's Ideal Maternity Home, in Robert Hartlen, *Butterbox Survivors: Life after the Ideal Maternity Home* (Halifax: Nimbus, 1999). See also Karen Balcom, 'Scandal and Social Policy: The Ideal Maternity Home and the Evolution of Social Policy in Nova Scotia, 1940–51', *Acadiensis* 31, no. 2 (2002): 3–37.

11. See Charlene Miall and Karen March, 'Social Support for Adoption in Canada: Preliminary Findings of a Canada-Wide Survey' (2000), available at http://www. adptioninstitute.org/survey_intro.html (accessed 24 December 2005).

12. John Ibbitson, 'The Remarkable New Governor-General Personifies the Free and Open Country Canada Wants to Be', *Globe and Mail,* 28 September 2005, A1.

Index

Aboriginal peoples, xii–xiii; adoption law and, 17, 35–6, 44–5, 162–3; adoption statistics on, 155–9; agencies run by, 169–71, 236–8; band permission and, 163–5; children's status, 44–5, 158–9, 162–4, 235; confidentiality, and, 164–5; consents and, 163–5; custom adoption and, 16–17, 164, 234–5; diversity among, 135–40; elites among, 136–7; family ideology and, 2, 138; foster care and, 68–9; individual and collective rights and, 235; male domination among, 236, 237; repatriation and, 212, 233–8; rights of, 117, 161–73, 212, 233–8; services for, 142–50; war captives and, 176–7; white children and, 139–40; see also schools, residential; women, Aboriginal

Aboriginal Women's Unity Coalitions, 236

Abrams, Lynn, 17–18

abuse, 62–3, 100, 173, 183

Adams, Marie, 96

Adopt Indian Métis (AIM), 40, 152–3

adoptees: ethnicity and, 117–34; gender and, 97–102; preferred, 72, 74–5, 97–102; religion and, 113–17, 123–7; searching and, 211–28, 232–3; see also babies; children

adopters: Aboriginal, 151, 166; African Canadian, 131; class and, 71–9; inter-country, 197, 206–8, 210; investigation of, 56, 75; men as, 105–6; origins of adoptees and, 211–12; preferred, 71–2; qualifications of, 26, 33, 34–5, 38, 39–40, 48; single women as, 92–6; v. fos-

ter parents, 64, 66; veto of, 221, 231; white, 131, 167–8

adoption: custom, 16–18, 164, 234–5; early, 23–4; 'immigration', vii–viii; as injury, 224–5; institutions and, 18–23; inter-faith, 107–9, 113–17; law on, 25–51; numbers of, 51, 77, 122–9, 151, 156–9, 182, 199–202; open, 48–9, 231, 238–41; 'over the counter', 186; private, 9–16, 35, 50, 75, 77–8, 180, 212–13; probationary, 38; subsidized, 11–12, 48, 71; transracial, 46–7, 107–9, 111–13, 152–61; see also intercountry adoption; private arrangements

Adoption Council of Ontario, 133

Adoption Resource Exchange of North America (ARENA), 129–30, 152

adoptive parent: as term, xii

advertisement, 97, 98–9, 101, 118, 130–1; Aboriginal children and, 153–4; fostering and, 66–7

Advisory Committee on Child Welfare (ON), 116

Advisory Committee on Indian Affairs (BC), 144, 151–2

African Canadians, 9, 11, 185, 207; orphanages and, 20, 119–20; transracial adoption and, 128–31

Africa: refugees from, 196, 207

Ahenakew, David, 164, 236

Alberta: Aboriginal peoples in, 144; adoption law in, 27–30, 33, 35–9, 41, 47, 48, 49, 50, 117; cross-border placements in, 188–9

Alberta Child Welfare Commission, 64
Alberta Medical Journal, 85
Alberta Women's Liberal Association, 144
Alexander Orphanage, 20
Allen, Helen, 97, 99, 101, 119, 131, 153–4
Allen, Madelene, 225–6
Alton, Mary Anne, 208
Ambert, Anne-Marie, 234
Ames, Elinor, 205
Anderson, Benedict, ix
Anishinaabe Child and Family Services, 236, 237
Anne of Green Gables, xiii, 5, 58, 91–2, 211
apprenticeships, 11, 18, 59, 64; *see also* labour, child
Armitage, Winona, 218
artificial insemination (AI), 238–9
Asia: refugees from, 195
Assembly of First Nations (AFN), 137, 164, 236, 237
AWARE (Awareness to World Adoption and Responsibility to Everyone), 203
Axworthy, Lloyd, 198

babies: 'blue-ribbon', 8; 'chosen', 218–19; 'crack', 63; 'pink-ribbon', 97–102; 'sale of', 186; 'special needs', 8; *see also* adoptees; children
Bagley, Chris, 173
Bakan, Abigail B., and Daiva Stasiulis, 106
Balcom, Karen, 114, 179
Bangladesh: children from, 204
Bannerji, Himani, 110, 242
Barnardo Aftercare UK, 208
Barnardo Homes, 11, 183, 215, 216; *see also* children, 'home'
Barnardo, Thomas, 177, 178
bastardry, 7; *see also* illegitimacy
Berebitsky, Julie, 90, 95
Berger, Bernard, 130
Berger, Thomas, 53, 162, 164, 234
Berton, Janet and Pierre, 112–13, 130
'best interests of the child', 30, 31, 37, 41, 163
Biggs, Laura, 175

birth parents: control of children and, 15; international adoption and, 209; 'nuisance', 214–15; religious preference and, 117; rights of, 29, 34; searching and, 228–33; term, xii
Birthright, 88
Bisoondath, Neil, 243
black Canadians; *see* African Canadians
Blackthorne, Tom, 139
Bondfield, Margaret, 183
Bowker, Marjorie, 189–90
Boyd, Susan B., 104
boys: as adoptees, 98, 100–2; foster care and, 69; *see also* gender
Bradbury, Bettina, 6, 19–20
'Brisbin, Mrs', 75–6
Britain: adoption in, 17; children from, 11, 59–60, 177, 178–9, 180–5; evacuated children from, 190–2
British Columbia: Aboriginal peoples and, 143, 144, 146, 162–4; Aboriginal repatriation in, 234–5, 236; adoption law in, 28, 29, 32, 37–9, 43 46–50, 117; children in care in, 139; searching in, 221, 231, 232
Brodie, Robert (Steve), 184
Brooks, Mrs Wilson, 130

Cain, Jo, 138
Cairns, Alan, 148–9
Calgary Herald, 100
Callwood, June, 221
Canadadopt, 203
Canadian Association of Welfare Workers, 143
Canadian Churchman, 21, 62, 87
Canadian Council on Child Welfare, 183
Canadian Council of Natural Mothers, 88–9, 228
Canadian Jewish Congress, 100, 192
Canadian National Committee on Refugees (CNCR), 190
Canadian Welfare, 85–6, 113
Canadian Welfare Council, 143, 184, 190, 195
Cardinal, Richard, 169

Casteneda, Claudia, 175
Catholics, 10, 113–17, 118; *see also* religion
Chambers, Juanita, 218
Charlottetown Orphanage, 20
Charter of Rights and Freedoms, 46, 103, 104, 163, 231
Chatelaine, 72–3, 86, 90, 92, 180, 227–8
children: 'guest', 190–2; 'home', 59–60, 208; immigrant, 59–60; 'in service', 6, 7, 11, 18, 23–4; mixed-race, 121–31, 147–8; rights of, 41–2; special category, 2; *see also* adoptees; babies
Children's Service Centre (CSC), 128–9
child-rescue movement, 140
child-study movement, 111
China: children from, 206–7
Chrétien, Aline and Jean, 113
Christian, Wayne, 236–7
Christian Guardian, 20
Christie, Nancy, 12
Chupik-Hall, Jessa, 142, 145
citizens: 'minus/plus', 148
citizenship: foreign adoptees and, 203; mothering and, 81
Clark, Barrie, 104–5, 230
Clarkson, Adrienne, 245
class, 52–79; acknowledgement of, 55–8; adoption and, 71–9; birth parents and, 58–63; fostering and, 64–71; legal and judicial middle, 56, 71–2; working, 64–8
Coldwell, Major James William, 176
Collins, Patricia Hill, vii, 71, 81
Collura, Mary-Ellen L., 161
colour blindness, 109–13
'colour evasiveness', 109
Comacchio, Cynthia, 102
Committee for the Adoption of Coloured Youngsters (CACY), 112, 130
Committee on International Adoptions, 78
confidentiality: adoption and, 30, 31, 33, 164–5; international adoption and, 180; searching and, 212
consents: adoption law and, 26–7, 31, 36–8, 42, 163–5; birth fathers and, 103; finality of, 35–6; religion and, 117

Coombe Orphanage, 19
Co-operative Commonwealth Federation (CCF), 143–4, 176
court cases: Aboriginal adoption and, 17, 162–3; adoption and, 30, 35–6, 37–8, 38–9, 44–5; class and, 56–8; fathers' rights and, 103, 104; religious matching and, 114–15; searching and, 221–2
criminal justice system, 142–3
'cultural genocide', 110, 166, 235
culture: Aboriginal, 151–2, 235–7; inter-country adoption and, 209–10; maintenance of, 132–3

Dakota Ojibway Child and Family Services (DOCFS), 165, 167, 168
Daly, Kerry, and Michael Sobol, 4
Davin, Anna, 17
De Kiriline, Louise, 89–90
de la Roche, Mazo, 92
Department of Immigration and Citizenship, 144–5
Department of Indian Affairs (DIA), 162–3
Department of Indian Affairs and Northern Development (DIAND), 164
Department of Indian and Northern Affairs, 149–50
Department of National Health and Welfare, 4
De Roo, Remi, 73, 111
Diefenbaker, John, 195
Dionne quintuplets, 28, 89–90
'disadvantaged', 54
'disciplinary regimes', 56
Doxtator, Susie, 60
Drea, Frank, 231
Dubinsky, Andrée, 83
Dubinsky, Karen, 46, 128

Edgar, Margaret, 128–9
Edmonton Journal, 155
education: Aboriginal peoples', 136; birth mothers', 61
Eichler, Margrit, 3
employment: adopting mothers and, 76,

91; birth mothers and, 61; foster mothers and, 68
essentialism: racial, 135; searching and, 224–5, 228–9, 230
ethnicity, 107–9, 117–19; African, 119–34; Asian, 119–27; European, 119; French/English, 119; mixed, 121–31
eugenics, 28, 110
Europe: refugees from 193–4

facts: difficulties with, 3–6, 212–13
Fairbridge Farm School, 11, 34, 184, 218
Families for Children, 198, 203
families: fluidity of, 1, 5; ideologies of, 1–3; meaning of, viii; as 'nations', vii–ix; vulnerable, 6–9; *see also* kin
Fanshel, David, 152
fathers: birth, 102–5; economic support and, 102–3; rights of, 43–4, 103, 104–5, 230
federal government: Aboriginal peoples and, 141, 143, 144–5, 162–3, 164; adoption and, 50–1, 198–9
Ferrie, Robert and Helke, 204
fetal alcohol syndrome disorders (FASD), 63, 152, 173
fiction: adoptees' past in, 211; adoption in, 90–2, 97; class and adoption in, 58, 72; families, in 5–6; intercountry adoption in, 177–8; transracial adoption in, 161–2
first parent: as term, xii
Fiske, Jo-Anne, 63, 141, 163
Fiske, Jo-Anne, and Claudien Herlihey, 35–6, 138
Flint, Betty, 111
Foster Parents Plan, 195
fostering, 11–12; Aboriginal peoples and, 68–9, 149; class and, 64–71; early, 23–4; 'free', 64–5; kin and, 12–13, 67; profile of parents in, 66; same-sex couples and, 67; shortage in, 66–9; single people and, 67
Foucault, Michel, 56
Frankenberg, Ruth, 109, 110
fraternal societies, 21
Freedom of Information and Privacy Act, 231

Froebel, Friedrich, 213
Frum, Barbara, 113

Gagan, Rosemary, and Ruth Compton Brouwer, 179
Garber, Ralph, 164, 221, 222, 231, 235
Garland Library of North American Indian Captivities, 177
Gasco, Elyse, 211
gays and lesbians, 67, 96
gender, 80–106; adoptees and, 97–102; residential schools and, 141
Geneva Declaration of the Rights of the Child, 180
Georgia Strait, 208
Gillis, John, 9
girls: as adoptees, 97–100; *see also* gender
Gitksan First Nation, 237, 238
Globe and Mail, 13, 62, 81, 93–4, 195, 206, 210
Gordon Residential School, 141
Gossage, Peter, 15
Gove Commission, 62
Grey, Ernie, 146
Gruchy, Helen E., 147

Hague Convention on Protection of Children (HCIA), 50, 199
Haliburton, Thomas Chandler, 53
Hawthorne, Harry, 145, 148
Henley, Roy Edward, 184
Henry, Frances, et al., 108
Hepworth, H. Philip, 4, 97–8
Herman, Ellen, 115
Hill, Charles B., 65
Hill, Daniel, 130
Holt, Simma, 85, 140
'Honour Song of the Micmac, The', 161–2
Hughes, Adaline Mareau, 110–11
Hungary: refugees from, 194
Hungry Wolf, Beverly, 141

Ideal Maternity Home, 34, 75
illegitimacy, 7, 83; concealment of, 29, 30, 31

immigration: links with international adoption, 208; race and, 106; *see also* intercountry adoption

Imperial Order Daughters of the Empire (IODE), 143, 186

indenture: children and, 6, 7, 11, 26, 27, 178; *see also* labour, child

Independent Order of Foresters, 21

Indian Act, 143, 145

Indian Adoption Project (IAP), 152

Indian Affairs Branch, 143, 144–5, 148

infertility, 10–11, 81, 82

information: access to, 46–9; *see also* confidentiality

inheritance: adoption law and, 26–7, 38

institutions: adoption and, 29; childcare, 18–23, 141; maternity homes, 33–4; mortality rates in, 19; residential, 10; unwed mothers and, 7–8

integration: Aboriginal peoples and, 135, 143–4

intercountry adoption (ICA), 49–51, 56, 77–8, 99, 174–210, 217; activism in, 203–4; monitoring of, 186–7, 197–8; number of, 199–202; policies on, 195, 198–9

International Social Service (ISS), 195, 217

Inuit: adoption among, 16–17; *see also* Aboriginal peoples

James, Matt, 244

Jean, Michaëlle, 243, 245

Jelinek, Otto, 204–5

Jericho School for the Deaf, 19

Jewish Canadians: orphanages and, 20; refugees, 190, 192–3; religious matching and, 115–16

Joe, Rita, 141

Johnson, E. Pauline, 58, 86

Johnson, George Martin, 136

Johnston, Patrick, 155, 170

Johnstone, Catherine, 11

Kelso, J.J., 19, 23–4, 64, 71, 72, 97, 213–14, 216–17

Kennedy, Gilbert D., 38

Kerley, Cameron, 169, 234

Killins, Harriet Ethel (Fry), 13

Kimelman, Edwin, 166, 169, 235

kin: Aboriginal, 139; adoption and, 43–4; fostering and, 12–13, 67; *see also* families

King, Mary, 52

Kirk, H. David, viii, 3, 98, 132, 211, 218, 240, 243

Kirton, Derek, 210

Klassen, Marie, 226

Kline, Marlee, 86, 163

Kuptana, Rosemary, 236

labour, child, 6, 7, 11, 18, 23–4; Aboriginal children and, 177, 178–9, 183–4; class and, 59–60, 64, 65; gender and, 97; law and, 27, 28; race and, 120

Ladies' Benevolent Society (Montreal), 19, 215

Lake, John T., 184

Latin America: children from, 206

Laurence, Margaret, 5

law: adoption, 25–51, 117; 'child-centred', 28; *see also* specific provinces

Lee, Karin, 245

Lejac Residential School, 141

Lepp, Annalee, 199

lesbians and gays, 67, 96

liberalism: Aboriginal peoples and, 150–61; colour-blind, 109–13

Little, Jean, 5, 92, 177–8

Lovelock, Kirsten, 210

Loyal Order of the Moose, 21

McColm, Michelle, 224–5

Mcdonald, Lisey, 6

McGeachy, Mary, 180

Mackey, Eva, viii–ix, 242

McKinnon, F.B., 147

Maclean's, 14–15, 63, 70

MacLeod, Alistair, 5

Macphail, Agnes, 181

Macpherson, Annie, 177

Malarek, Victor, 13

Ma Mawi Wi Chi Itata Centre, 166
Manitoba: Aboriginal peoples in, 144,
  165–9; Aboriginal repatriation in, 234,
  236–8; adoption law in, 27, 28, 29, 32–3,
  35, 39, 41–3, 47–50, 117; searching in,
  221–2
Manitoba Indian Brotherhood, 165
Manitoba Métis Federation, 165
Maracle, Lee, 5, 81
March, Karen, 224, 227, 232–3
Marchant, Bessie, 91
Marcus, Clare, 224
Marshall, Audrey, and Margaret McDonald,
  232
matching: Aboriginal peoples and, 150–3;
  liberalism and, 109–13; race, religion,
  ethnicity, 107–9, 113–17, 121–8; wide-
  ranging efforts to, 121, 129–30
maternity: value of, 80–1
May, Elaine Tyler, 81
MD of Canada, 95
Melosh, Barbara, 104, 229, 232, 241
men: as adopters, 105–6; as birth fathers,
  102–5; *see also* gender
Miall, Charlene, and Karen March, 229,
  232
Mignacco, Charlene, 170
Miles, George, 184
Miller, J.R., 141
Milloy, John, 60–1
Mills, Robert, 65, 95–6
minorities: class and, 53; unwed mothers
  and, 9; *see also* ethnicity; race
Miss Rye's, 11
Modell, Judith S., 240
Mohawk Institute, 60
Montgomery, Lucy Maude, xv, 5
Montreal: orphanages in, 19–20; transracial
  adoption in, 128–9
Moodie, Susanna, 10, 178
Mooseheart, 21
'moral panic': export of children and, 186
morality: birth mothers and, 82–5
Moran, Bridget, 97, 120, 160
Morton, Suzanne, 28

mothers, 80–97; adjectives for, 89; adoptive,
  90–7; birth, 81–90, 117; 'blameless', 82;
  class of, 61–2; as 'donors', 87–8; foster,
  66, 68; as 'keepers', 87–8; preferred, 81;
  single, 61, 88; unwed, 6–9, 14, 61, 83–90
mothers' allowances/pensions, 8, 28, 82
Mount Cashel, 19
Mount Elgin Indian Residential School,
  141
Mount St Mary's Orphanage, 20
Mowat, Farley, 5

Naistaohkomi, Terance 'Duke' Across the
  Mountain/Hairy Bull, 172
National Adoption Desk (NAD), 198–9,
  203
nation-building: families and, vii–x
Neil McNeil Home, 19, 111
Nelson, Claudia, 82
New Brunswick: adoption law in, 25–7,
  32, 34, 35, 41, 42, 49, 50
New Brunswick Child Welfare Survey, 4
Newfoundland: adoption law in, 28, 29,
  32, 33, 36, 37, 39, 41, 47, 49, 50; military
  in, 103, 185; searching in, 222
Newfoundland Child Welfare Association,
  4
Newfoundland Division of Child Welfare,
  7, 15
New Right: single mothers and, 88
non-governmental organizations (NGOs),
  176, 190
No Quiet Place, 166–9, 235
Northwest Territories: adoption law in, 35,
  36, 39, 41, 42, 49, 50
Nova Scotia: adoption law in, 26, 28, 29,
  32, 33, 34, 37, 41, 46, 49, 50; transracial
  adoption in, 131–2; searching in, 222–3,
  230
Nova Scotia Home for Coloured Children
  (NSHCC), 20, 120, 132
Nuu-chah-nulth Tribal Council, 169–70

Ojibway Child Welfare Agency, 236
Ontario: Aboriginal peoples in, 145,

164–5; Aboriginal repatriation in, 235–8; adoption law in, 25, 28, 30, 36–9, 41, 43, 46, 47, 49, 50; searching in, 221, 231

Open Door Society (ODS), 40, 128–9, 134, 153, 204

openness, 48–9, 231, 238–41

Organization to Save the Adopted Family, 231

Origins Canada, 88

origins: search for, 211–41

orphanages, 18–22, 141

Ouston, Rick, 102, 226–7

parents; *see* adopters; birth parents; fathers; mothers; step-parents

Parent Finders, 212, 224

Parlby, Irene, 83

Parr, Joy, 59

Paton, Jean, 224

Patterson, H.S., 220

Paul, Andy, 235

payment: fostering and, 11–12, 24, 64–7

Penrod, Lynn, 37–8

Petrie, Anne, 228

Peyakowak agency, 236

Pitre, Elizabeth, 6

Plaut, Gunther, 115–16

pluralism: adoption and, viii–ix, 242

Pocock, Philip F., 116

'politics of recognition', 132

poor, 'deserving and undeserving', 18–19, 54–5

Poor Law, 18, 59

Porter, John, 79

post-adoption services, 220, 221, 222; *see also* searching

poverty, 6–9; Aboriginal peoples and, 143; class and, 53–5

'power evasiveness', 109

Prince Edward Island: adoption law in, 28, 32, 33, 36, 39, 42, 47, 48; searching in, 222, 223

private arrangements, 9–16, 35, 50; class and, 75, 77–8; costs of, 12–13; inter-

country adoption and, 180; proportion of, 77; searching and, 212–13

professionalization: adoption and, 32

Project Opikihiwawin, 234

property: class and, 55; inheritance of, 26–7, 38

prostitution: international adoption and, 207

Protestants, 10, 113–17; *see also* religion

provinces: Aboriginal peoples and, 142, 145; adoption law in, 25–51; mothers' allowances and, 8; open adoption and, 240; *see also* specific provinces

psychology: adoptive mothers', 95–6; birth mothers', 84–8

Pulkingham, Jane, and Gordon Ternowetsky, 54–5

Purvey, Diane, 20

Quarrier, William, 177

Quarrier Homes, 11

Quebec: religious matching in, 114

race, 107–9, 117–34; Aboriginal peoples and, 140–2; class and, 61; gender and, 97, 99; immigration and, 106; single women adopters and, 93–4

'race cognizance', 110

racism, 108, 109, 110, 132; Aboriginal peoples and, 141, 147–8, 150; 'essential', 109, 135

Raven, Garnet, 161

Real Poverty Report, The, 54

refugees: child, 100, 190–7; Jewish, 190, 192–3

registration, birth, 3–4, 36, 48

registries, reunion, 220–3; passive and active, 47–8

religion, 107–9, 113–17, 123–7; Aboriginal peoples and, 22, 135, 140–2; intercountry adoption and, 179, 190; matching of, 29, 38–9, 75–6; orphanages and, 20–1; race and, 119; residential schools and, 22, 140–2

repatriation, Aboriginal, 212, 233–8

rescue: education and, 140; intercountry adoption and, 174–6, 179–97
Roche, Douglas, 205
Romania: children from, 205
Rooke, Patricia, and Rudy Schnell, 2, 19
Royal Commission on Aboriginal Peoples (RCAP), 2, 40, 51, 171–2, 236
Royal Commission on Family and Children's Law (BC), 53, 104, 162, 163–4, 221, 234–5
Royal Commission on New Reproductive Technologies, 10, 40, 51, 80–1, 82, 171
Russia: children from, 205–6
Rwanda: children from, 207

Sachdev, Paul, 103–4, 228, 230, 231
Saddle Lake Band, 150
Sainte-Marie, Buffy, 153, 161
St Paul's Anglican Residential School, 141
Sangster, Joan, 142
Saskatchewan: Aboriginal peoples in, 146; adoption law in, 28, 30, 32, 33, 36, 38, 39, 42, 46, 48–9, 50, 117; searching in, 221
Saturday Night, 114
Save the Children Fund, 194–5
Schlesinger, Benjamin, 96
schools: industrial, 135, 140–2; residential, 22–3, 60–1, 135, 137, 139, 140–2
Schuck, Peter, 242–3
Scotland: adoption in, 17–18
Scott, Duncan Campbell, 22
searching, 211–41; adoptees and, 224–8; applicants and relationships and, 222–3; birth fathers and, 230–1; birth mothers and, 88–9, 228–30; human right, 231; siblings and, 216
second parent: as term, xii
Segal, Sydney, 111
self-government, Aboriginal, 169–70; *see also* repatriation
Shaffer, Beverly, 226
Shore, Randy, 105, 230–1
Shubenacadie Residential School, 141
Sinclair, Adelaide, 194

Sissons, Jack, 35
Six Nations, 150
'sixties scoop', 44–5, 150
Smart, Carol, 5
Smart, G. Bogue, 179
Smith, Mary Ellen, 214
Solinger, Rickie, xiv, 86
Spallumcheen Band, 137, 165, 236
Squamish Nation, 137
Stackhouse, Reginald, 176
Stanbury, William, 136
Star Weekly, 99, 115–16, 120, 155
step-parents: adoption and, 15, 44
Stevens, Barry, 102, 240
Stirrett, J.T., 58
Strachan, John, 11
Strickland, Isabel, 14
Strum, Gladys, 193
Sullivan, Richard, and David Groden, 230, 232
Survey of the Contemporary Indians of Canada, 148
Sutherland, Neil, 1

Taylor, Charles, 132
teens: foster care and, 69
'telling', 217–19
Timpson, Joyce, 160
'Today's Child', 97, 99, 101, 118, 130–1, 153–4
Tom, Moses, 150
Toronto Boys' Home, 20
Toronto: Children's Aid Society, 74–5, 129, 214; interracial adoption in, 129–30
Toronto Star, 180, 195
Toronto Telegram, 97, 99, 118, 180
Trudeau, Pierre, 196
Tynan, Nora, 58

Union of BC Indian Chiefs (UBCIC), 162, 235
United Church Observer, 93, 101, 195
United Nations Convention on the Civil Aspects of International Child Abduction, 50

United Nations Declaration of the Rights of the Child, 116, 180, 199
United Native Nations, 170, 236–7
United States: export of children to, 185, 186–90; transracial adoption in, 152–3, 168–9
Upper Canada College, 19

Van Krieken, Robert, 67–8
Vancouver: Catholic Children's Aid Society, 147–8; Children's Aid Society, 141
Vancouver Province, 93
Vancouver Sun, 15, 100, 186
Vanstone, Joan, 224
Vaudreuil, Verna, 62
Vernon, P.A., 225
Verrier, Nancy, 224
vertical mosaic, 79
Victoria Colonist, 180
Victoria Times, 93
Vietnam: children from, 204–5

Wagamese, Richard, 161

Walker, Norma Ford, 130
'warphans', 190
welfare state: birth mothers and, 83
Westhues, Anne, and Joyce C. Cohen, 208
Wetherald, Ethelwyn, 10, 92–3
Whiteford, Heather, 238
Whitton, Charlotte, 96, 179, 184, 186
Wicks, Ben, 228
Williams, Carla, 234
Willingdon School for Girls, 142–3
Wilson, Ethel, 12
Winnipeg Urban Indian Coalition, 166
Wisdom, Jane B., 3
women: Aboriginal, 86, 89, 163, 164, 167, 235–6, 237; adopters, 90–7; adoption law and, 28, 29; birth mothers, 81–90; childless, 90–1; mothers, 80–97; networks of, 97; working, 61, 68, 76, 91
Woodward, Reta Ellen, 13–14

Yellowhead Tribal Council, 164, 236
Yukon: adoption law in, 32, 35, 39, 41, 42, 43, 46